10644241

ADAM KARLIN

MIAMI & THE KEYS

C I T Y   G U I D E

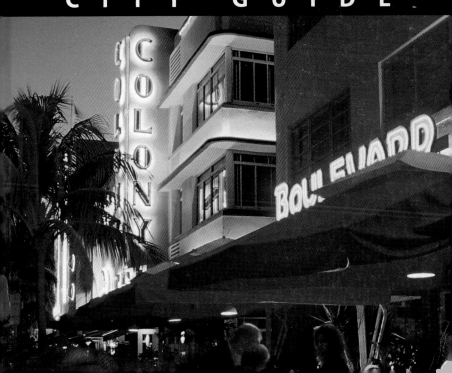

Miami Beach (p57), bound by waters emerald and azure

Little known fact: on the Eighth Day, God shook all the eccentrics of America into the nation's Southeast corner pocket. And They Became South Florida. And It Was Weird.

Here's how it works: cruise down I-95 from the northeast corridor and at some point, near Richmond, you cross the invisible line separating the North from the South. Now go further, all the way to America's tip. Somewhere around Orlando, you crossed another line, separating the rest of Florida from reality. Here in Miami, the Everglades and the Keys, things are a little Alice in Sweaty Wonderland. It's the weather, y'know; all the humidity and hurricanes drive everyone a little crazy. And the alligators. And the mosquitoes, goddamn them. And the people, of course.

What was once a citrus farming town is now a pan-American mosaic, the most Latin city in the world north of Mexico. Throw in enterprising Caribbean immigrants, Jewish Holocaust survivors and their children, a fantabulous gay party scene, mad rednecks, the cast-off spawn of the dinosaur age cruising local waterways, and a South Beach celebrity scene that would make *OK!* magazine wee itself in joy, and, well…Look guys: it's *weird* here. And beautiful. Think of those clean lines slimming down a deco hotel on Miami Beach. The impossibly sexy people lining up at a Fort Lauderdale club. That pale full moon making love to the Everglades on a dank, sweaty night.

Which isn't to say modern Miami lacks problems. This international city has both the cheerful energy and hungry Third World edge of the Caribbean and Latin America. Economic inequality is rampant, and the grandiose spirit of American capitalism has mixed with Miami's Latin/Mediterranean flair, making the gulf between the haves and have-nots here seem particularly vast.

But that shimmering mirage **'The World is Yours'** was the iconic catchphrase of Miami's hyperextravagant 1980s, and the citizens of this town have taken that motto to heart.

West of here is the Everglades, possibly the most unique ecosystem in North America, a flooded wetland that feels like nature's own musty womb. To the north, Fort Lauderdale sips a martini by its yachting fleets. Down south stretch the mangrove islands and sultry sandbars of the Florida Keys, islands of both exile and refuge for those nonconformists who are too out there for even South Florida's misfit mentality.

Sounds good? Come on down. The air feels like a silk kiss and the beach smells like lotion and hormones. Welcome to Miami. The party started five minutes ago. You gonna dance?

CITY LIFE

Today, middle-class Miamians dream of being able to live in Miami. The 'Magic City' has become a murderously expensive one, and buying a good home in Miami proper is often beyond the means of teachers, policemen and other essential workers. Far-off areas like Kendall are now fast-growing residential neighborhoods; the incredibly distant SW 200 blocks are today's outer suburbs.

To re-center the city and compete for tourists with ever-popular Miami Beach, the city of Miami wants to turn ragged Downtown into an urban center that will be the envy of other American cities. In South Beach, deco architecture has become a vehicle of urban rebirth. Downtown Miami is pinning its hopes on cultural venues: the Arsht Center for the Performing Arts, Cisneros Fontanal Arts Foundation and the conversion of blighted Bicentennial Park into Museum Park, which will house new art and science museums. A fresh stadium for the new 'Miami' Marlins will replace the old Orange Bowl and (city officials hope) spruce up Little Havana, but the biggest new arrival could be thousands of Cubans, depending on when, if ever, the Castro brothers' regime comes to a close.

Miami feels like a city on the edge. Political changes in Latin America continue to have repercussions in this most Latin of cities. Economically, it seems Miami will become either a town split between patricians and poverty, or a first-class city that lets its own citizens in on the good life it promises to the rest of the world.

Sunshine, blue skies, palm trees and blades...welcome to Ocean Drive, Miami Beach (p57)

HIGHLIGHTS

INTERNATIONAL MIAMI

'The nice thing about Miami,' folks say, 'is how close it is to America.' More than an immigrant entrepôt, Miami is the crossroads of the Caribbean and Latin America. Actually, this endless diversity makes the city more quintessentially American than the cutest Midwestern Main Street.

❶ Cuban Flavor
Cuban men play dominoes and evoke *Havana Viejo* (Old Havana) in Máximo Gómez Park (p89)

❷ Voodoo Doctors
Make an appointment with a *vodou* (voodoo) doctor in Little Haiti (p85)

❸ Little Havana
Little Havana (p87): home to Nicaraguans, Colombians, Salvadorans, Mexicans…oh, and Cubans

❹ Salsa Lessons
Seriously, if you're gonna salsa, learn from local experts (p244)

1 Fort Lauderdale
Fort Lauderdale's white sands are perfect for sunset-spotting (p230)

2 South Beach
Where models, Euros, yuppies, yokels and yobs unite (p46)

3 The Keys
Florida Bay? Gulf of Mexico? Choices, choices in the Keys (p184)

4 Key Biscayne
Miami's skyline looks lovely when viewed from this family-friendly spot (p91)

BEACH BUMS

If Miami's international population is her heart and soul, her beaches are the face and body she shows off to the world. Makes sense, as said beaches have no shortage of beautiful bods sunning themselves on the sand.

EAT, DRINK & BE MIAMI

Combine tropical weather, immigrant ambience and a 'Just say Yes' attitude towards life and you get a city that loves to eat out and stay out until the sun comes up.

❶ Latino Cuisine
Eat well everywhere, from the finest Nuevo Latino to a sizzling slab of prime grilled beef (p136)

❷ Cuban Classics
Roll up, roll up for a steaming shot of *cortadito* at a Cuban coffee counter (p136)

❸ South Beach Party
Gay? Straight? Miscellaneous? South Beach loves ya (p144)

❹ Clubbing Downtown
Savvy club kids party in north Downtown Miami (p148)

THE MAGIC CITY – FOR ARTISTS & DESIGNERS

Just because she's beautiful doesn't mean she's stupid. Creative energies from across the world, particularly Latin America, are funneled into Miami, which is emerging as a major player on the global arts circuit.

① Where the Art Is
Soak up the artsy vibes and live the gallery good life in Wynwood and the Design District (p81)

② Miami Museums
Get culturally correct at the city's many museums, such as the Wolfsonian-FIU (p50)

③ Hot Hotels
The world's hottest hotel design hits South Beach (p171)

④ Art Basel
Miami hosts the international art world during Art Basel (p15)

NATURAL WONDERS

What's the most beautiful thing about South Florida? South Florida. This unique ecosystem struggles to survive in the shadow of Miami, and shocks visitors with her subtle, sultry appeal: teal waters, red mangroves and the awesome Everglades.

❶ Exploring the Keys
Explore any one of the 45 Florida Keys (p183), such as largely undeveloped Big Pine

❷ Mangrove Forests
Huge mangrove forests form the Florida coast (p226)

❸ Diving
Dive or snorkel the world's third-largest reef at Biscayne National Park (p227)

❹ River of Grass
Experience the otherworldly beauty of the Everglades (p216), among lurking alligators and wading birds

CONTENTS

Continued from previous page.

THE AUTHOR

Adam Karlin

Adam remembers being seven and walking around his grandmother's retirement village in West Palm Beach in a T-shirt in December, thinking, 'Why don't I live in Florida?'

Seventeen years later he made good on that impulse when he moved to Marathon to cover the Middle Keys for *The Key West Citizen*. He lasted about six months. The reporting was good – hurricanes, trailer park evictions, a gay mosquito control officer who introduced larvae-eating guppies into Keys waterways, that sort of thing – but Adam decided he'd rather visit an isolated island than live on one.

On the bright side, he passed Lonely Planet's writing test during this little stint in tropical limbo. Now he visits the Keys, Miami, the Glades and wherever else he's lucky enough to be sent by Lonely Planet and loves every minute of it. This is him having another rough day in the office (a Florida beach).

ADAM'S TOP MIAMI & THE KEYS DAY

Ouch. What did I drink last night? An ashtray, based on the taste of my mouth. Best get some caffeine to stave off the hangover, and fresh Florida orange juice to wash off the tongue, at Puerto Sagua (p128) in South Beach. Then I believe I'll sleep on the beach…

What? Oh, you want a *full* top day. Well, assuming my head is clear, after a swim I might stroll past some deco hotels and visit the Wolfsonian-FIU (p50) to put their design in cultural context. I sip a coffee and browse the shelves in Books and Books (p110) on Lincoln Rd, and then I roll up Collins Ave in my station wagon, listening to '80s music and imagining I'm in *Grand Theft Auto: Vice City*.

I hang a left onto Arthur Godfrey Rd, Miami Beach's Jewish main street, because it's lunch time and I want a chopped liver sandwich, stat. Except that the deli food, while delicious, doesn't help my stomach. So I head over Julia Tuttle Causeway and into Little Haiti to stop at a *botanica* to visit a *vodou* (voodoo) doctor (p85). I don't know if his medicine helps me, but the colors and smells of this neighborhood always lift my spirits.

As evening sets in I have a great meal at Michy's (p132) – foie gras on corncake, mmm – then drive into Downtown to catch live shows at PS 14 (p150) and Transit Lounge (p149). As last call rings out, the sun is rising and I'm craving a Colombian hot dog topped with mayonnaise and God-knows-what-else, plus a *refajo* (beer with red soda) at the great, late-night diner La Moon (p134). Then it's back over A1A, cranking out the '80s again as the sun rises, to sleep the next day off – another perfect itinerary, come to think of it.

Miami is a city made for tourists, staffed by folks who abase themselves before tourists as if they were Greek Gods. As long as you can pay, expect some serious tropical coddling and cuddling. Unfortunately, this town still manages to aggravate. There can be snooty and/or self-absorbed attitude at some hotels and restaurants (although even the most upscale joints have realized that you don't make money by pissing off potential customers). Driving through heavy traffic and around frequent construction sucks almost as much as the state of the city's public transportation. In general, as in many things American, you can expect a very high level of service off the bat, although long-term consideration is sometimes lacking. The Keys are more laid-back, although their small size makes advance booking for lodging and eating advisable.

WHEN TO GO

Learn this word: snowbird. That's Floridian for 'folks who migrate south to escape the northern winter', and we have a feeling you'll be joining the flock. Yes, there'll be crowds, but consider fighting them, as Miami's year-round heat and humidity gets downright hellish come summer. Temperatures regularly top 90°F (32°C) from about June through September, and local mosquitoes have a series of fecund orgies, which is why the tourism industry experiences a lull during this time. It's not unusual, though, for Miami to experience bouts of chilliness (though locals and weather presenters alike keep this info close to their chests). In midwinter, temperatures can often dip into the low 40s at night, and hover in the barely warm 50s during the day – despite unwavering forecasts that claim 'tomorrow will bring highs in the 70s!' If it's between December and February, don't believe that until you feel it, and be sure to pack for a variety of possibilities.

FESTIVALS

No matter when you choose to make your way to Miami, you're bound to find something fun going on – especially in high season, when folks flock here to escape the cold and play in the sun. For information on official holidays, see p246. And see p155 for more extensive information on arts and entertainment festivals.

January

The beginning of the new year also happens to be the height of the tourist season in these parts. Expect fair weather, crowds of visitors, higher prices than usual and a slew of special events. New Year's Eve brings fireworks and festivals to South Beach and Downtown's bay front.

FEDEX ORANGE BOWL FOOTBALL GAME
☎ 305-341-4700; www.orangebowl.org; Pro Player Stadium, 2269 NW 199th St, Opa-Locka
In early January, flocks of football fanatics descend on Pro Player Stadium in Opa-

---

HURRICANE FORECASTING

Though Miami has been lucky in recent years, the threat of a hurricane, during a season that lasts from June through November, is always looming – and memories of past destruction make that a very scary threat indeed. The most devastating hurricane to ever rip through town was back in 1926, when a mighty storm destroyed much of the city (leaving around 300 people dead). Other biggies were on Labor Day in 1935, killing 400 people, and 1992's Hurricane Andrew. While a nasty series of storms wreaked serious havoc on most of South Florida in 2004, Miami got off easy with just minimal damage. But is the worst still to come? If so, the National Hurricane Center (NHC) hopes to minimize the damage, as it's focused on tracking these storms as early as possible and then issuing warnings, allowing folks to prepare. The NHC uses sophisticated tracking methods, including satellite photography and advanced computer systems; as of 2005 these systems became faster than ever, with strong backups and a processing speed that has jumped from 450 billion calculations per second to a whopping 1.3 trillion. It's heady stuff, but comforting, especially to the residents of the vulnerable Miami area. Just ask those folks who were evacuated in time from the disastrous flooding that swamped the Keys during Hurricane Wilma.

Locka for the Orange Bowl, the Superbowl of college football.

ART DECO WEEKEND
☎ 305-672-2014; www.artdecoweekend.com; Ocean Dr between 1st & 23rd Sts
This weekend fair featuring guided tours, concerts, classic-auto shows, sidewalk cafés, and vendors of arts and antiques is held in mid-January.

KEY BISCAYNE ART FESTIVAL
☎ 305-361-0049; Crandon Blvd, Key Biscayne
Held in late January since the early 1960s, this is a showcase of more than 150 local artists, from painters to glass blowers.

MIAMI JEWISH FILM FESTIVAL
☎ 305-573-7304; www.caje-miami.org; 4200 Biscayne Blvd, Key Biscayne
There are few better chances to kvetch with one of the biggest Jewish communities in America.

February
The last hurrah for Northerners needing to escape the harsh winter, February brings arts festivals and street parties, as well as warm days and cool nights. February 14 is Valentine's Day, when lovers celebrate their amour.

MIAMI INTERNATIONAL FILM FESTIVAL
☎ 305-377-3456; www.miamifilmfestival.com
This early-February (sometimes late-January) event, which is sponsored by Miami-Dade College, is a two-week festival showcasing documentaries and features from all over the world.

COCONUT GROVE ARTS FESTIVAL
☎ 305-447-0401; www.coconutgroveartsfest.com; Biscayne Blvd between NE 1st & 5th Sts, Coconut Grove
One of the most prestigious arts festivals in the country, this late-February fair features more than 300 artists.

MIAMI INTERNATIONAL BOAT SHOW & STRICTLY SAIL
☎ 305-531-8410; www.discoverboating.com /miami; Miami Beach Convention Center, South Beach

top picks

UNIQUE EVENTS

- King Mango Strut (p15) Old-school Coconut Grove: wacky and fun.
- South Florida Dragon Boat Festival (p15) Chow on lo mein and watch festive dragon boats race along the waterway.
- Carnaval Miami (p14) Early March brings this festival – 10 days of parades, fashion shows and concerts, ending with an over-the-top fest along Calle Ocho.
- Goombay Festival (p14) Skip the Bahamas and head to Miami in the first week of June for this colorful Caribbean food and arts fest.
- Winter Party Week (p14) Come to town and spend a week among 10,000 hot, shirtless boys cruising dance floors all over town.

With more than 250,000 attendees, this late-February event is a serious water-lovers' extravaganza and one of the largest new-boat shows in the world.

MIAMI BEACH FESTIVAL OF THE ARTS
☎ 305-865-4147; http://gonorthbeach.com; Ocean Tce (east of Collins on 73rd & 75th Sts)
Expect some 30,000 visitors to descend on more than 100 artists at this two-day, family-friendly festival.

SOUTH BEACH WINE & FOOD FESTIVAL
☎ 305-460-6563; www.sobewineandfoodfest.com
In late February, *Food & Wine* magazine and the Food Network presents this fest of fine dining and sipping to promote South Florida's culinary image. Expect star-studded brunches, dinners and barbecues.

March
Spring arrives, bringing warmer weather, world-class golf and tennis tournaments, outdoor festivals and the Irish party holiday of St Patrick's Day, on March 17. Expect some spring breakers to behave badly on the beach.

MIAMI INTERNATIONAL FILM FESTIVAL
☎ 305-237-3456; www.miamifilmfestival.com

Dubbed 'The Cannes of the Americas' by *The New York Times*, this one-week festival (usually held in early March) includes *encuentros*, a showcase of some of the best new cinematic talent in Spain and Latin America.

CARNAVAL MIAMI

☎ 305-644-8888; www.carnavalmiami.com
In early to mid-March, this is a nine-day party of festivals, concerts, a beauty contest, an in-line skating contest, a Latin drag-queen show and a Calle Ocho cooking contest.

MIAMI ORCHID SHOW

☎ 305-255-3656; 2700 S Bayshore Dr, Coconut Grove Exhibition Center, Coconut Grove
Held since the mid-1940s, the flowers in this annual mid-month show come from statewide growers.

MIAMI-DADE COUNTY FAIR

☎ 305-223-7060; www.fairexpo.com
The fair goes off in either late March or early April, and is one of the largest county fairs in America. Pet the livestock, ride the rides, and have a go at the carnies.

NASDAQ 100 TENNIS TOURNAMENT

☎ 305-230-7223; Tennis Center at Crandon Park, 7300 Crandon Blvd, Key Biscayne
In late March, and formerly known as the Lipton and Ericsson Open, top-ranked tennis pros play for hordes of spectators.

WINTER MUSIC CONFERENCE

☎ 954-563-4444; www.wmcon.com
Party promoters, DJs, producers and revelers come from around the globe to hear new artists, catch up on technology and party the nights away.

WINTER PARTY WEEK

☎ 305-572-1841; www.winterparty.com
The gay-circuit party bonanza in mid-March benefits gay-rights organizations, including the National Gay and Lesbian Task Force.

April

Welcome to the shoulder season, bringing quieter days, lower prices, balmier temperatures and a few choice events. The religious holidays of Easter and Passover fall in April, as does the final of the Nasdaq 100 Tennis Tournament.

BILLBOARD LATIN MUSIC AWARDS

☎ 646-654-4660; www.billboardevents.com
This prestigious awards show in late April draws top industry execs, star performers and a slew of Latin music fans.

MIAMI GAY & LESBIAN FILM FESTIVAL

☎ 305-534-9924; www.mglff.com
Held in late April to early May, this annual event features shorts, feature films and docs screened at various South Beach theaters.

May & June

May and June boast increased heat, fewer visitors and several cultural events. Memorial Day is the official start of summer, bringing a beach-oriented three-day weekend.

FASHION WEEK OF THE AMERICAS

☎ 305-604-1000; www.fashionweekamericas.com
This annual May showcase features runway shows from Latin, Caribbean, American and European designers.

GOOMBAY FESTIVAL

☎ 305-567-1399
A massive fest, held on the first week of June, that celebrates Bahaman culture.

FLORIDA DANCE FESTIVAL

☎ 305-674-6575; www.floridadanceassociation .org/dance_festival
In mid-June, this festival brings performances, classes, workshops and seminars on dance to Miami.

July & August

The most beastly, humidity-drenched days are during these months, when locals either vacation elsewhere or spend their days melting on the beach. Official celebrations are few and far between.

INDEPENDENCE DAY CELEBRATION

☎ 305-358-7550; Bayfront Park, Downtown
July 4 features an excellent fireworks and laser show with live music that draws more than 100,000 people to breezy Bayfront Park.

MIAMI SPICE RESTAURANT MONTH

☎ 305-358-7550; www.miamirestaurant month.com

Top restaurants around Miami offer prix-fixe lunches and dinners to try to lure folks out during the heat wave.

September & October

In September the days and nights are still steamy and the start of school brings back college students. There are just a couple of tourist-oriented events in September, but they're followed by a wealth of cultural offerings come October.

HISPANIC HERITAGE FESTIVAL

☎ 305-541-5023; www.hispanicfestival.com
Held in late October, it's one of the largest festivals in the country, commemorating the discovery of the Americas with a range of concerts, food, games and folkloric groups.

SOUTH FLORIDA DRAGON BOAT FESTIVAL

☎ 305-633-0168; www.miamidragonboat.com; Haulover Beach Park, Bal Harbour
This new event in early to mid-October brings thousands for Chinese food, a crafts fair and the main event: festive dragon-boat races along the Florida East Coast Canal, accompanied by dramatic drumming.

MIAMI REGGAE FESTIVAL

☎ 305-891-2944; Bayfront Park, Downtown
It's been one of the largest reggae events in the country since it was established in the 1980s.

November

Tourist season kicks off at the end of the month, bringing more crowds and slightly cooler, more bearable days. Thanksgiving falls on the last Thursday of the month.

RASIN

☎ 305-751-3740
This annual Haitian cultural festival hits in early November with music, food, crafts and more.

MIAMI BOOK FAIR INTERNATIONAL

☎ 305-237-3258; www.miamibookfair.com
Occurring in mid- to late November, this is among the most important and well-attended book fairs in the USA, with hundreds of nationally known writers joining hundreds of publishers and hundreds of thousands of visitors.

WHITE PARTY

☎ 305-667-9296; www.whiteparty.net
If you're gay and not here, there's a problem. This week-long extravaganza draws more than 15,000 gay men and women for nonstop partying at clubs and venues all over town.

December

Tourist season is in full swing, with Northerners escaping south and booking rooms so they can loll about in the sunshine and be here for the Christmas and New Year's Eve festivities.

ART MIAMI

☎ 866-727-7953; www.art-miami.com
Sometimes held in January (sometimes in December) is this massive fair, a display of modern and contemporary works from more than 100 galleries and international artists.

ART BASEL MIAMI BEACH

☎ 305-674-1292; www.artbasel.com/miami _beach
Occurring in early December, this is one of the most important international art shows in the US, with works from more than 150 galleries and a raft of trendy parties and events.

KING MANGO STRUT

☎ 305-401-1171; Main Ave & Grand Ave, Coconut Grove
Held each year just after Christmas, this quirky 24-year-old Coconut Grove parade is a politically charged, fun freak that began as a spoof on current events and the now-defunct Orange Bowl Parade.

COSTS & MONEY

Miami's economy relies heavily on tourism, but its position as gateway to Latin America has given it powerhouse status as an international business city. More than 150 multinational companies have operations in Miami, including Burger King, Carnival Cruise Lines, and Citizen Savings Financial; and at least 100 have their Latin American headquarters here, from Johnson & Johnson to the Gap. The city is also establishing itself as an international banking center – more than 40 international banks call it home. But leading the way today is the business of development, causing investors and builders to jump for joy.

While the growth of the national economy is at its weakest in many years, Miami's economy is booming. And that could mean high prices for the traveler. It's still possible to experience Miami on about $90 a day – $60 for a room in a hostel, $20 on a combo of diner and take-out food with the rest spent on drinks and/or transport – but the reality is that you will be tempted to spend quite a bit more to truly enjoy your time here. Depending on the location and the time of year, a nice hotel room is going to cost you at least $120, with popular South Beach midrange haunts going for closer to $170 to $250. On the high end of the spectrum, expect to pay anywhere from $400 to $1000 a night. Then there's food. The preponderance of ethnic cuisines, delis and diners means that it is possible to find dinner for as little as $10 – but once you throw in ambience and alcohol, you'll find it's $10 just for your glass of wine and at least $25 per person for the food. Other costly activities will seduce you as well: nightclubbing, with entrance fees of about $20 and cocktails that cost about $10 apiece; bicycling, with rentals averaging $20 daily; sky's-the-limit shopping; children's attractions such as the Seaquarium (p93); and live entertainment and sporting events, where ticket prices can cost anywhere from $15 to $100 or more. Expect to spend about $200 a week on a rental car – more if it's peak tourist season.

Bargain seekers, take note: while museums do charge entrance fees, usually around $5, many have free days or hours, including the Bass Museum of Art (p51; 6pm until 9pm second Thursday of the month), the Historical Museum of Southern Florida (p69; Sunday) and the Miami Art Museum (p70; Sunday).

Expect prices to generally be a bit cheaper in the Keys, especially when it comes to lodging and dining (although top-end restaurants, while not as ubiquitous as they are in Miami, charge much the same rates). Unfortunately, because the Keys are islands, certain staples like water and gasoline can cost a dollar or so more than they do on the mainland.

INTERNET RESOURCES

Miami Herald (www.herald.com) The best stop for local and regional news.

Miami Beach 411 (www.miamibeach411.com) A great guide for Miami Beach visitors, covering just about all concerns.

Miami Today News (www.miamitodaynews.com) An excellent online source for business and other daily updates.

City Search (www.miami.citysearch.com) Particularly useful for finding detailed nightlife and dining reviews, often with photos.

Miami New Times (www.newtimes.com) Alternative coverage with an activist bent.

Sun Post (www.miamisunpost.com) This new newspaper gives in-depth coverage of a lot of stories the mainstream media seems to miss.

Cool Junkie (www.cooljunkie.com/miami) A must for trendies, with info on nightclubs, fashion and more.

Mango & Lime (www.mangoandlime.net) The best local food blog is always ahead of the curve on eating events in the Magic City.

Meatless Miami (www.meatlessmiami.com) Vegetarians in need of an eating guide: look no further.

Miami Nights (www.miaminights.com) Get a good, opinionated down low on Miami's ever-shifting after-dark scene.

Art Circuits (www.artcircuits.com) The best insider info on art events; includes excellent neighborhood-by-neighborhood gallery maps.

Three Guys From Miami (www.3guysfrommiami.com) An amusing, insightful visitor's guide to Miami by, you guessed it, three local guys who offer a good Cuban-American perspective on their hometown.

HOW MUCH?

Gallon of gas: $3.40

8oz bottle of water: $2.50

Martini: $11

Bottle of Bud: $3–5

Souvenir T-shirt: $10

Cuban sandwich: $5

Sunscreen: $9

Club admission: $20

Oceanfront hotel room: $300

Car rental: per week $200

ADVANCE PLANNING

- If you're coming during the high season (December to March), it's essential to book lodging ahead of time. Enormous resorts with upwards of hundreds of rooms are regularly booked out in January and February. Try and find online rates, which tend to offer the best deals (p170); 'rack' rates (ie those rates directly quoted by the hotel) are always the most expensive.
- Restaurants aren't quite as bad, but you'd do well to make reservations at high-end places just to be safe. Foreign travelers should remember that unless you're told service charge is included with your bill, it is the height of rudeness not to tip.
- Winter visitors should bring some warm clothes. Really. It can get nippy at night when the ocean breeze is blowing.
- If you're going to be driving a lot, get your hands on an up-to-date road map (or better yet, a GPS). Frequent construction means roads are regularly re-routed and closed off at a moment's notice.

SUSTAINABLE MIAMI & THE KEYS

Environmental issues are many and sundry here, mainly because Miami is simply too big a city built on too small a strip of land. Haphazard planning (often fueled by irresponsible development and ill-advised infrastructure) often results in terrible traffic snarls, which tend to add smog, heat and frustration to an already steamy cityscape. The source of the Everglades, Florida's water table, is threatened by run-off pollution and water diversion (also see p220). The tiny Keys are protected by impossibly complex zoning laws, but affordable housing – especially home ownership – remains a pipe dream for most of the islands' inhabitants.

What's this got to do with you?

Everything, in a way, since servicing visitors remains the engine of South Florida's economic growth. As a tourist, your voice is stronger in Florida than almost anywhere in America. So let your hotel owners, restaurateurs and bar staff know you appreciate any green initiatives they can take (and fortunately, green sensibility seems to be popular in trend-conscious Miami). If you'll be staying in relatively compact Miami Beach and Key West, reduce traffic and your own stress by biking. If you need to rent a car, ask for hybrid vehicles – hybrids often come with discounts

and are sometimes offered special parking places around Miami. Avoid power boating in Miami and the Keys, and swamp buggies and airboats in the Everglades, as these practices invariably disturb fragile ecosystems and wildlife habitats (manatees in particular suffer from power boating). Do not patronize businesses that extend beyond Miami's Urban Development Line, which abuts the Everglades. And whenever you can, patronize city green spaces (parks, public spaces, even some museums) and contribute to them – Florida can be notoriously bad at subsidizing environmental issues, and your private contributions to the good fight are always appreciated.

Some good web resources for sustainable travelers include the following:

www.handsonmiami.org Sponsors green volunteering opportunities.

www.miami.edu/staticfiles/UM/FTP/umgreen/experts .html List of University of Miami experts on green-related issues and initiatives.

http://florida.sierraclub.org Website for the Florida Sierra Club.

www.uel.org Information on the Urban Environmental League of Miami.

www.udbline.com Site for Hold the Line, which seeks to maintain the Urban Development Line, the boundary of Miami's outward expansion.

www.miamidade.gov/derm Miami-Dade County Department of Environmental Resources.

HISTORY

Rest assured: the Miami you visit today will be gone by the time you come back.

This is a city built on boom and bust, by dreamers who took advantage of nice weather and opportunists who took advantage of natural disasters. Every chapter of this town's saga is closed by a hurricane, building boom or riot, and when the dust settles a new Miami is left sizzling on the beach. That's an ironically jerky rate of growth, considering it took about 400 years for Miami to turn into a city (since Ponce de León missed the fountain of youth). But when this town decided to go large, it played catch-up with a vengeance.

In some ways, the story of Greater Miami is a classic American tale of displacement, entrepreneurship, refugee hopes and desperate innovation. But don't forget the footnotes: corruption, neglect, and fraught – and occasionally bloody – community divisions. The end product is hardly perfect. But it's also continuously resurrecting itself, as new immigrants push into low-rise tenements, and the nouveau riche reinvent the glittering Miami skyline.

THE RECENT PAST

Let's be clear: Miamians still don't like Castro, so this isn't the best place to flash your Che T-shirt. In the past, street carnivals in Little Havana have been set off by rumors of Fidel's ill health. When Rafael Del Pino, a former Cuban general and defector, suggested some détente with his motherland in 2008, a caller to Radio Mambi suggested that the highest-ranking Castro official to ever reach American shores be lynched. Del Pino subsequently filed a lawsuit, which was promptly thrown out of a federal court.

In 2008 Castro finally announced his intent to step down from power. Surely a retirement announcement warranted a party, at least a handover-of-power mojito? Nope. The reaction among Cuban exiles never topped cautious optimism. Will Fidel's brother and successor Raul be a reformer? Delfin Gonzalez, uncle of the famous Elian, told us, 'Fidel, Raul – they have the same mother.'

In 2008, the newer wave of Cuban immigrants – the working class who've been

top picks

MIAMI HISTORY BOOKS

- *Miami* (1987, Vintage), by Joan Didion. How Cuban politics shape US policy.
- *The Corpse Had a Familiar Face* (1987, Simon & Schuster), by Edna Buchanan. Written by a former *Miami Herald* reporter, this is an addictive read on real-life Miami murders.
- *Black Miami in the Twentieth Century* (1997, University Press of Florida), by Marvin Dunn. This was the first book devoted to the issue of race in Miami.
- *This Land Is Our Land: Immigrants and Power in Miami* (2003, University of California Press), by Alex Stepick. Stepick and other authors break it down.
- *Miami, USA* (2000, University Press of Florida), by Helen Muir. A recently expanded 1950s title that's full of anecdotes.

TIMELINE

10,000 BC	1513	1565
Tequesta Indians arrive in South Florida. They live as hunter-gatherers in the area that includes modern Miami, the Everglades and the Keys, but leave little trace of their existence for archaeologists.	Juan Ponce de León is the first European to land in Florida, supposedly seeking out the fountain of youth. He misses the fountain, but does find the Gulf Stream current, an extremely important current for navigators.	Pedro Menéndez de Avilés lands in Florida and founds the city of St Augustine, the first permanent (European) settlement in what is now the continental United States.

coming to America since 1980 – defined the public face of the community response. They have little love of Castro, but are more concerned with making a better life for themselves then settling political scores.

One Cuban waitress tersely reacted to the latest chapter of the Fidel chronicles with these words: 'I don't have time for the news.' Then she went back to work.

The issue of legalizing slot machines consistently appears on voters' ballots, but whether or not they'll ever appear at local race tracks remains anyone's guess – for years the fight has been shot down, resurrected and debated again and again, ad nauseum. And as Miamians debate the ins and outs of gambling, their city fathers are pushing for complete incorporation of Miami-Dade county by 2010. This would cause huge swathes of unincorporated county – including the area around Everglades National Park – to fall under city control. At issue: who would do a better job of managing Miami-Dade? County commissioners? City council members? Local governments? The logic behind incorporation runs like so: divide Miami-Dade into dozens of small cities governed by local councils, and those councils will have a better idea of their constituents' needs, particularly in poorer areas. But there are plenty of examples of local councils using local connections to make a cut off real estate development, as opposed to funding infrastructure for the underclass.

Besides, who has time to care about the poor when the *South Florida Sun Sentinel* estimates that one in 10 Floridians in Broward, Miami-Dade and Palm Beach counties is a millionaire (when you include the value of their homes, cars and stocks)? Just drive from the condo coast of A1A, through a valley of poor and middle-income homes, and re-emerge at the eastern edge of the Everglades, where the newly wealthy are carving wetlands into personal palaces of the ego. To top it all off, the region's original inhabitants, the Seminoles (p20), are busily preparing to turn their ancient tribal homeland into a Las Vegas–style casino block. This could be bad news for endangered species like the Florida panther, but *hold on, there are free drinks at the craps tables!*

FROM THE BEGINNING
Tequesta Indians
In 1998, 24 holes, inscribed in bedrock and arranged in the shape of a perfect circle, were found in downtown Miami. The 'Miami Circle,' as it was dubbed, is thought to be the foundations of a permanent structure and, at some 2000 years old, it's the oldest contender for that title on the US East Coast.

Archaeologists think the Circle was built by Miami's earliest known inhabitants, the Tequesta (Tekesta) Indians, who are otherwise a mystery. The usual depressing scenario of European (in this case Spanish) first contact, violence and disease wiped out the tribe, whose survivors likely melted into the local Miccosukee and Seminole nations.

Spain, Britain, & Spain Again
Juan Ponce de León was the first European to get lost here back in 1513, on a fruitless quest for the mythical fountain of youth. But the man widely credited for leading Florida's colonization is the Spanish explorer Pedro Menéndez de Avilés. In 1565 – several decades before the Pilgrims landed on Plymouth Rock and English aristocrats starved in Jamestown,

1783	1821	1835–42
The British grant America independence at the Treaty of Paris. They also vacate Florida and give it back to the Spanish, who now have to contend with American territorial ambitions.	The USA acquires Florida from Spain. Settlers arrive in great numbers, and tensions between mainly white migrants and Native American communities, many of which have taken in runaway black slaves, run high.	Second Seminole War. Seminoles and black allies fight a guerilla war against the US Army, which ends with much of the tribe exiled west, although elements remain in South Florida to this day.

Virginia – Menéndez de Avilés landed in what he soon dubbed St Augustine. From here he headed north and massacred many an encroaching French fleet, and Florida became to North America what Poland is to Europe: the flattest piece of land between battling super-powers. Before Florida was officially ceded to the US by Spain in 1821, the entire northeast section of the state was sacked, looted, burned and occupied by Spanish, then English, and finally US forces.

Although the Spanish could claim to be king of the castle after weathering repeated British attacks in 1586, 1668 and 1702, they screwed up during the French and Indian War by enter-ing late and on the losing side – against the British and their (at the time) American colonial allies. The blunder cost the Spanish Florida, which they traded for Britain's Havana in 1763. Then came the American Revolution, upsetting the whole status quo all over again. When the British granted America independence at the Treaty of Paris, they also handed Florida back to Spain.

So Spain had Florida all to itself again – and a big, land-hungry new nation lying just to the north. Relations chilled when escaped American slaves made for Spanish Florida, where slavery was illegal and freed black slaves were employed as standing militia members. White American Southerners saw all those armed black militia and started sweating the notion of slave revolts in their back plantation yard.

The Unconquered People

Plenty of said slaves passed up the Spanish and ran for the southern swamps – the modern Everglades – where they were taken in by the Seminole Nation, itself a collection of refu-gees and exiles from several Southern American Indian tribes. Black newcomers were also occasionally kept as slaves among the Seminole, although this slavery was more akin to indentured servitude (slaves, for example, had their own homes that they inhabited with their families).

When the huge Creek Indian tribe of Georgia and Alabama was forced west across the Missis-sippi River in 1817, Americans figured everything east of that body of water was now theirs for the settling. But the Seminoles and their black allies had no intention of leaving their homes. As American squatters filtered into Spanish Florida, they found that their imagined open frontier was actually cultivated and grazed by Seminole farmers and ranchers. The presence of black Seminoles (integrated slaves) particularly put off the slave-owning Southerners.

Bad blood and sporadic violence between the Americans and Seminoles eventually gave the US the excuse it needed to make a bid for Florida, which was finally bought from Spain in 1821. Before and after that date, the US military embarked on several campaigns against the Seminoles and their allies, who took to the swamps, fought three guerilla wars, and scored a respectable amount of victories against an enemy several times their size. In fact, the Second Seminole War (1835–42) was the longest in American history between the American Revolu-tion and the Vietnam War.

Indeed, operationally the Seminole wars were a 19th-century version of Vietnam, a never-ending parade of long, pointless patrols into impenetrable swamps, always searching for an ever-invisible enemy. By 1830 Congress came up with a shockingly Nazi-like scheme: the Removal Act, a law that told Native Americans to pack up their things and move across the country to the barren plains that would later become Oklahoma. Some went, enticed by sacks of bribe

1845	1896	1898
Florida becomes the 27th state in the Union. Almost half of the state's popula-tion is slaves, which partially accounts for Florida joining the Confederacy during the Civil War.	Henry Flagler finishes construction of his railroad; Miami is incorporated. Miami, a small city quite literally at the edge of America, is accessible to the rest of the country by overland travel.	Army camps are set up in Miami during the Spanish–American War, beginning a trend of migration; soldiers who are barracked in Miami decide they like the area and move their families there.

money, but chief Osceola and his band (never exceeding more than 100 warriors) refused to sign the treaty and fled into the Everglades. After keeping thousands of soldiers jumping at the barest hint of his presence for years, in 1837 Osceola was finally captured under a false flag of truce. Yet resistance continued, and eventually, while the Seminoles gave up on fighting, the government also gave up on moving them west.

By 1842 the warring had ended, but no peace treaty was ever signed, which is why the Seminoles remain to this day the unconquered people. Those Seminoles who remained in Florida still live in and around the Everglades, and are now organized under a tribal government and run the Ah-Tah-Thi-Ki Museum (p222) and, um, the Hard Rock Café. Not one Hard Rock Café: we mean the entire Hard Rock *chain*, bought for $965 million in 2007 with money made from gambling revenue. The Seminoles were the first Native American tribe to cash in on gambling, starting with a bingo hall in 1979 that has since expanded to a multi-billion-dollar empire. That's not bad for a Seminole population of a little over 3000, but questions remain as to how evenly all that money is spread around by the tribal council.

Freezes, Flagler & Tuttle Too

Sunny Miami? Bet you didn't know it's the baby of an ice storm.

But we're jumping ahead. First, let's address John S Collins, the original beachfront buyer on Miami Beach, who purchased the 5-mile strip between the Atlantic and Biscayne Bay (what is now 14th to 67th Sts). Collins began selling parcels of beachfront property in 1896, but it was Julia Tuttle and Henry Morrison Flagler who really deserve the credit for carving Greater Miami out of the sand.

Tuttle arrived in 1875 with a tubercular husband, and after his death she returned to the land she had inherited as a widow. Proving her worth as a true Floridian, over the next 20 years she proceeded to buy up property like crazy.

In the meantime, Flagler, a business partner of John D Rockefeller, had realized Florida's tourism potential and been busy developing the northern Florida coast in St Augustine and Palm Beach. He also built the Florida East Coast Railroad, which extended down as far as Palm Beach. Tuttle saw a business opportunity and contacted Flagler with a proposition: if he would extend his railroad to Miami, Tuttle would split her property with him.

Miami? Way down at the end of nowhere? Flagler wasn't interested.

Then, in 1895, a record freeze enveloped most of Florida (but not Miami), wiping out citrus crops and sending vacationers scurrying. Legend has it that Tuttle – who is said to have been rather quick both on the uptake and with an 'I told you so' – went into her garden at Fort Dallas on the Miami River, snipped off some orange blossoms and sent them to Flagler, who hightailed it down to Miami to see for himself.

Well, like Will Smith, Gianni Versace and millions of others, Flagler was hooked. He and Tuttle came to terms, and all those Floridians whose lives had been wiped out by the freeze followed Flagler south. Passenger-train service to Miami began on April 22, 1896, the year the city of Miami became incorporated.

Tuttle, a woman, had essentially founded an American city at a time when women's rights were…wha? Women's rights? But that's about the only blow for equal opportunity to be found in this story. Of Miami's 502 original inhabitants, 100 of them were black, conscripted for hard labor and regulated to the northwest neighborhood of Colored Town (no, really).

1914	1915	1926
Miami Beach's first hotel, the WJ Brown Hotel, opens for business. The initial boom of hotel development, often spurred by Jewish investors, starts turning the beach into the 'American Riviera'.	Carl Fischer dredges Biscayne Bay to build Miami. To this day the Bay divides the city of Miami Beach and the island of Key Biscayne from Miami proper.	A hurricane demolishes much of the city. At least 373 people are killed, but Miami rebuilds herself in the hurricane's aftermath. To a much lesser degree, the cycle of storm and rebuild continues to this day.

FIVE WHO SHAPED SOUTH FLORIDA

Henry Morrison Flagler The developer whose Florida East Coast Railroad brought scores of visitors to sunny paradise.

Julia Tuttle The woman behind the Flagler man, who (supposedly) lured the skeptical developer to Miami with a handful of orange blossoms.

Fidel Castro He may be reviled by local Cubans, but then again, said Cubans wouldn't be here if it wasn't for the bushy-bearded Caribbean communist.

Morris Lapidus The Fontainebleau, Eden Roc, Lincoln Road Mall…is there anything this MiMo (Miami Modern) god *didn't* design?

Ian Schrager The hotelier who forever raised the bar on chic inns, starting with the Delano.

The First Big Booms

The USA was getting insecure about its place in the world in the late 19th century, and nothing spells compensation like beating up on a second-rate European power. Cue the 10-week-long Spanish–American War. In 1898, as Cuba struggled for independence from Spanish rule, William Randolph Hearst's New York *Journal* began a campaign for the 'humanitarian annexation' of Cuba, which perhaps not coincidentally would have been a culmination of the USA's manifest destiny and a happy windfall to US businesspeople.

Two and a half months of fighting ended with Spain ceding Cuba (until its independence in 1902), Puerto Rico and Guam to the US. America's presence in the Caribbean was expanding – and vice versa. Islanders were moving to America, and specifically South Florida, to earn a cut of sugar farming, cattle ranching, and the immensely profitable business of wrecking (or salvaging shipwrecked vessels off the Florida coast).

That promise of money and the expansion of Flagler's railway fueled yet another, bigger wave of settlement from up north. The development of Miami and Miami Beach kicked off, and in 1914 the Chicago industrialist James Deering began building the eye-popping Vizcaya mansion (p96). The wave of population growth peaked during WWI, when the US military established an aviation training facility here. Many of the thousands of people who came to work and train figured, 'Hey, the weather's nice,' and Miami's population shot from 1681 people in 1900 to almost 30,000 by 1920. The new Floridians wrote home and got their relatives in on the act, and after the war came the first full-fledged Miami boom (1923–25), when Coconut Grove and Allapattah were annexed into what was dubbed, for the first time, Greater Miami.

Even then, Miami was a town built for good times. People weren't flocking south just for the idyllic beachfront and perfect weather; they wanted to get trashed and gamble, too, because although it was illegal, liquor flowed freely here throughout the entire Prohibition period.

Depression, Deco & Another World War

Last call on this party was announced by two events: the Great Miami Hurricane of 1926, which left perhaps 300 people dead and some 50,000 homeless; and the Great Depression. But it's in Miami's nature to weather every disaster with an even better resurgence, and in

1935	1959	1961–2
Miami Beach population hits 13,350 – doubling from just five years earlier. Art Deco architecture is prevalent and the 'tropical deco' style is in vogue, giving Greater Miami's buildings a distinctive global cachet.	Fidel Castro takes over Cuba and the influx of Cuban exiles begins. The new Cuban-American population will define Miami demographics, culture and politics to the present day.	The failed Bay of Pigs invasion and the Cuban Missile Crisis deepen the already fraught tensions between America – particularly South Florida, home of many Cuban exiles – and Castro's Cuba.

the interwar period Miami's phoenix rose in two stages. First, Franklin Roosevelt's New Deal brought the Civilian Conservation Corps, jobs and a spurt of rise-from-the-ashes building projects. Then, in the early 1930s, a group of mostly Jewish developers began erecting small, stylish hotels along Collins Ave and Ocean Dr, jump-starting a miniboom that resulted in the creation and development of Miami Beach's famous Art Deco district. This, of course, led to a brief rise in anti-Semitism, as the Beach became segregated and 'Gentiles Only' signs began popping up in the north. The election of a Jewish governor of Florida in 1933 led to improvement in this area, as did the rise in airplane travel, which brought plenty of Jewish visitors and settlers from the north.

But ironically, while Jews helped Miami rise from the Depression, it was (indirectly) the Nazis who truly revitalized Miami in the mid-20th century. After a German U-Boat sank a tanker near here during WWII, South Florida was converted into what was, for all intents, a massive military base. The Army's central Anti-U-boat Warfare School was based in Miami, while Miami Beach's hotels were full of soldiers, who marched up and down the beach in full combat gear. More than a few of them decided it was nice enough here and didn't bother to go home when the war ended.

Cuba Comes Over

During the 1950s Miami solidified its star in America's tourism firmament as a great destination in its own right, and stepping stone to the floating Las Vegas that was Batista's Cuba. Progress also seemed inexorable; in 1954 Leroy Collins became the first Southern governor to publicly declare racial segregation 'morally wrong,' while an entire 'Space Coast' was created around Cape Canaveral (between Daytona and Miami on the east coast) to support the development of the National Aeronautics & Space Administration (NASA).

Then, in 1959, Fidel Castro marched onto the 20th-century stage and forever changed the destiny of Cuba and Miami.

As communists swept into Havana, huge portions of the upper and middle classes of Cuba fled north and established a fiercely anti-Castro Cuban community, now 50 years old and, in some ways, as angry as ever about the big hairy dictator to the south. At the time, counterrevolutionary politics were discussed, and a group of exiles formed the 2506th Brigade, sanctioned by the US government, which provided weapons and Central Intelligence Agency (CIA) training for the purpose of launching an attack on Cuba.

The resulting badly executed attack was little more than an ambush, remembered today as the Bay of Pigs fiasco. The first wave of counterrevolutionaries, left on the beach without reinforcements or supplies, were all captured or killed (though all prisoners were released by Cuba about three months later).

Kennedy Versus Khrushchev

Kennedy and the CIA both looked rather silly after the Bay of Pigs fiasco, which is probably why JFK stood his ground so firmly when the world was brought to the brink of nuclear war.

Smelling blood after the Bay of Pigs, the USSR's Nikita Khrushchev began secretly installing missile bases in Cuba, but the CIA managed to take photographs of the unarmed warheads, which were shown to Kennedy in October 1962. The result: the Cuban Missile Crisis, one of the most knuckle-biting, we're-all-gonna-die standoffs of the 20th century. Kennedy went on

1973	1979	1980
The Miami Dolphins win Super Bowl VII, capping off their 17–0 1972 season, which remains, to date, the only perfect season in National Football League history.	The Miami Beach Architectural District gets historic-landmark status with the National Register. Miami Beach begins preserving its deco hotels, which will become the foundation of the tourism boom that later transforms South Beach.	Race riots tear up Miami while the Mariel Boatlift, the largest nonmilitary naval fleet in history brings in 125,000 Cubans. Tensions between blacks, whites and Latinos remain high for some time.

CAPTURING CHE

Can you describe how the operation to capture Che occurred? In 1967 the CIA sent me to Bolivia to help the Bolivian army capture Che. He was down to a few followers by then. He's the only guerilla I know of who couldn't recruit a single farmer. Most people claim we had electronic surveillance and satellites and stuff. Bullshit. We had a man who spoke Quechua who spoke to a farmer who said he heard noises where there should be none. When we finally found (Che), he said, 'Don't shoot! I'm Che Guevara.' And then we confirmed it was 'The Foreigner' (the codename for Che).

What happened then? He didn't know I was Cuban at first. Then he said, 'You're Puerto Rican. Or Cuban. And I would guess Cuban.' And I said, 'I am a Cuban, and I was at the Bay of Pigs.'

How did he die? As far as the US government was concerned we wanted him alive. We wanted to win him over because we knew he had fallen out with Castro. Then an execution order came over the phone (from the Bolivian military). We tried to change their minds. At 12:30 a woman came with a radio and said, 'Why don't you kill him? On the radio they say he's dead of combat wounds.' Then I knew there was no other way. I told (Che) 'I'm sorry.' He turned white and said, 'It's better this way. I should never have been captured alive.' Then he said sarcastically, 'Tell Fidel he can expect a successful revolution in the Americas.' And added, sincerely, 'Tell my wife to be happy and re-marry.' I left and told the executor to shoot him below the neck, because he was supposed to have died of combat wounds.

What do you think of the Cult of Personality that has evolved around Che? I knew a woman (in Cuba) who had a 15-year-old son who wrote some anti-Castro graffiti. This lady went to Che to personally appeal for her son. He said, 'What is your son's name?' And when she told him, he said, 'Execute so-and-so so his mother does not have to wait.' Instead of inspiring respect, Che inspired fear.

An interview with Felix Rodriguez, ex-CIA officer who captured Che Guevara in Bolivia

national TV and said that Soviet missiles located 90 miles south of Florida constituted a direct threat to the safety and security of the country. A naval 'quarantine' of Cuba (a nice euphemism for 'blockade,' which would have been an act of war) was announced, as well as this doozy: any attack on the USA from Cuba would be regarded as an attack by the USSR.

A series of high-school notes were passed between the most powerful men on Earth: 'Well, okay, we *do* have missiles, but they're just a deterrent, cool? C'mon, let's not annihilate civilization.' The Soviets broke the stalemate and on October 26 agreed to remove the missiles in exchange for a promise by the USA not to attack Cuba and to pull up similar American missile sites in Turkey.

In the meantime, if Castro could attract missiles to his country, he couldn't keep his people there, and in 1965 alone some 100,000 Cubans hopped the 'freedom flight' from Havana to Miami.

Racial Tensions

The Cubans were greeted with fear by many black locals, who saw competition in the local cheap employment stakes. In addition, the Ku Klux Klan had been active in Florida since the 1920s, and bombings of black-owned housing were not unknown. Sensing the tension that was building between the black and Cuban populations, Dr Martin Luther King Jr pleaded with the two sides not to let animosity lead to bloodshed.

1984	1985	1992
Miami Vice hits the air, giving Miami and Miami Beach a distinctive brand name associated with convertibles, palm trees and pastel suits. Models, fashion designers and photo shoots soon follow.	First Winter Music Conference (WMC) solidifies Miami's hip reputation. The WMC continues to bring DJs, the gay community and a large crowd of Europeans to Miami every year.	Hurricane Andrew slams nearby Homestead, but leaves Miami relatively unscathed. The devastation forces Homestead and nearby towns to almost completely rebuild themselves from the ground up. Damages are estimated at $20 billion.

Riots and skirmishes broke out anyways, including acts of gang-style violence. But not all were caused by simmering Cuban/black tensions, as white folk got into the fray as well. In 1968 a riot broke out after it was discovered that two white police officers had arrested a 17-year-old black male, stripped him naked and hung him by his ankles from a bridge.

In 1970 the 'rotten meat' riot began when black locals picketed a white-owned shop they had accused of selling spoiled meat. After three days of picketing, white officers attempted to disperse the crowds and fired on them with tear gas. During the 1970s, there were 13 other race-related violent confrontations.

Racial tensions exploded on May 17, 1980, when four white police officers, being tried on charges that they beat a black suspect to death while he was in custody, were acquitted by an all-white jury. When the verdict was announced, race riots broke out all over Miami and lasted for three days. But beyond all these riots was a subtler, more insidious and more far-reaching legacy of Miami's racial tension: a great white flight from inner-city Miami into suburbs, gated communities and gentrified neighborhoods.

The Mariel Boatlift

In the late 1970s, Fidel suddenly declared that anyone who wanted to leave Cuba had open access to the docks at Mariel Harbor. Before the ink was dry on the proclamation, the largest flotilla ever launched for nonmilitary purposes set sail (or paddled) from Cuba in practically anything that would float the 90 miles between Cuba and the USA.

The Mariel Boatlift, as the largest of these would be called, brought 125,000 Cubans to Florida. This included an estimated 25,000 prisoners and mental patients that Fidel decided to foist off on the Cuban-American population, which raised suspicions he had always wanted to make Florida the penitentiary Australia to his Cuban England.

Mariel shattered the stereotype of the wealthy Batista-exiled Cuban. The old Caribbean aristocracy was replaced by thousands of jailed or hungry peasants and their families, often exiled with their prisoner relatives. The resulting strain on the economy, logistics and infrastructure of South Florida added to still-simmering racial tensions and provoked even more white flight; by 1990, it was estimated that 90% of Miami's Caucasian populace was Hispanic.

And the tension carried over from Hispanic-Anglo divisions to rifts between older Cubans and the new *marielitos*. The middle- to upper-class white Cubans of the 1960s immigration waves, who had always vocally longed for 'Old Cuba,' were reintroduced to that nation in the form of thousands of Afro-Cubans and *santeros*, or worshippers of *Santeria*, Cuba's version of *vodou* (voodoo). In a sense, Miami did not truly become a Cuban city until both elements of Cuban culture – white Catholic and black and mixed-race *santero* – found themselves sharing space in Little Havana and Hialeah.

Miami Not So Nice

If *Scarface* is accused of being over the top, the exaggeration only reflects, to an inflated degree, the Roman Empire reality that was 1980s Miami. The decade's soundtrack wasn't just the new wave ambient synth of *Miami Vice*; the big backtrack of the day was 'cha-ching.' Corrupt dollars could be bled from corporations jilting retirees out of their pensions, or cocaine cowboys literally gutting their competition in the street.

1996	1997	1998
The city of Miami turns 100, the same year it is named the fourth-poorest city in the USA. Economic issues continue until Manny Diaz is elected mayor in 2001.	Gianni Versace is murdered on the steps of his Ocean Dr home. Ironically, this murder of a European fashionista in turn encourages more European tourism to South Beach.	Mayor Xavier Suarez is ousted from office for absentee-ballot fraud (dead people voting). Suarez is, to date, the last vestige of Miami's notoriously colorful and corrupt mayors.

Thanks to its proximity to South America, Miami became the major East Coast entry port for drug dealers, their product and unbelievable sums of money. It was during this period the town earned the nickname 'Mi-Yay-Mi', 'yay' being slang for cocaine. As if to keep up with the corruption, many savings and loans (S&Ls) opened in newly built Miami headquarters. While *Newsweek* magazine called Miami 'America's Casablanca,' locals dubbed it the 'City with the S&L Skyline.'

A Latin love of grandiosity (perhaps egged on by the insecurity of traditional *machismo*) and a nouveau riche penchant for showing off equaled a 'Caligula meets the corporate world' era of interior design. CenTrust, a particularly wealthy S&L, used a helicopter to load a marble staircase into its IM Pei–designed Downtown headquarters (today the Bank of America Tower), installed gold-plated faucets in the bathrooms and hung several million dollars' worth of art on the walls. A plethora of businesses – legitimate concerns as well as drug-financed fronts – and buildings sprang up all over Miami. Downtown was completely remodeled. But it was reborn in the grip of drug smugglers: shoot-outs were common, as were gangland slayings by cocaine cowboys. At one stage, up to three people per week were being gunned down (or carved up) in cocaine-related clashes.

The police, Coast Guard, Drug Enforcement Agency (DEA), Border Patrol and Federal Bureau of Investigation (FBI) were in a tizzy trying to keep track of it all. Roadblocks were set up along the Overseas Hwy to Key West (prompting the quirky and headstrong residents down there to call for a secession, which eventually sent the cops on their way). Police on I-95, the main East Coast north–south highway, were given extraordinary powers to stop vehicles that matched a 'drug-runner profile.' According to one public defender, this amounted to, well, anyone.

Then it happened: *Miami Vice.*

Don Johnson, Philip Michael Thomas, long, panning shots of SoBe (South Beach) and a lot of pastel suits gave Miami something the local Chamber of Commerce could never really provide: a brand. *Vice* was single-handedly responsible for Miami Beach rising to international fabulousness in the mid-1980s, its slick soundtrack and music video–style montages glamorizing the rich South Florida lifestyle. Before long, people were coming down to check it out for themselves – especially photographer Bruce Weber, who began using South Beach as a grittily fashionable backdrop for modeling shoots in the early 1980s, leading to imitators and eventually the situation that exists today: model-jam.

Celebrities were wintering in Miami, international photographers were shooting here, and the Art Deco District, having been granted federal protection, was going through renovation and renaissance. Gay men, always on the cutting edge of trends, discovered South Beach's gritty glamour and began holding the annual White Party, an A-list AIDS fund-raiser party, at Vizcaya, and partied along South Beach's oceanfront before and after. The city was fast becoming a showpiece of fashion and trendiness (and party drugs, natch).

The 1990s

A combination of Hurricane Andrew and a crime wave against tourists, particularly carjackings, equaled a drop in visitors, until tourist-oriented community policing and other visible programs reversed the curse. Miami went from being the US city with the most violent crime to one with average crime statistics for a city its size. From 1992 to 1998, tourist-related crimes

1999	2002	2003
Elián Gonzalez is rescued at sea and brought to the USA. A prolonged custody battle ensues between his maternal American family and his father in Cuba, ending with Gonzalez being repatriated to Cuba.	The first Art Basel Miami Beach brings the art world to South Beach, adding the cachets of 'art city' and 'design city' to Miami's global tourism brand and pulling, yet again, more European tourists.	*Nip/Tuck*, a series about Miami plastic surgeons, premieres. The show shifts Miami's depiction in popular culture from a city of crime and hot weather to a city of shallow, beautiful people and hot weather.

NORTHERN CAPITAL OF THE LATIN WORLD

Miami may technically be part of the USA, but it's widely touted as the 'capital of the Americas' and the 'center of the New World.' That's a coup, really, when it comes to marketing Miami to the rest of the world, and especially to the USA, where Latinos are now the largest minority. Miami's pan-Latin mixture makes it more ethnically diverse than any Latin American city. At the turn of the century, the western suburbs of Hialeah and Hialeah Gardens were listed second and first respectively on the register of American cities where Spanish is spoken as a first language.

How did this happen? Many of Miami's Latinos arrived in this geographically convenient city as political refugees – Cubans fleeing Castro starting in 1959, Venezuelans fleeing President Hugo Chavez, Brazilians and Argentines running from economic woes, Mexicans and Guatemalans long arriving to find migrant work. And gringos, long fascinated with Latin American flavors, now visit Miami in part to get a taste of the pan-Latin stew without even having to leave the country.

It's all led to the growth of Latin American business here, which has boosted the local economy. Miami is the US headquarters of many Latin companies, including LanChile, a Chilean airline; Televisa, a Mexican TV conglomerate; and Embraer, a Brazilian aircraft manufacturer. It's home to Telemundo, one of America's biggest Spanish-language broadcasters, as well as MTV Networks Latin America and the Latin branch of the Universal Music Group. It's also the host city of the annual Billboard Latin Music Conference & Awards.

Cubans do still lead the pack of Latinos in Miami, though – and Cubans have a strong influence on local and international politics. Conservative exile groups have often been characterized as extremists; many refuse to visit Cuba while Castro is still in power. A newer generation, however – often referred to as the 'YUCAs' (Young Urban Cuban Americans) – are much more willing to see both sides and not nearly as caught up in ending Cuba's current way of life as their parents are.

While many of the subtleties may escape you as a Miami visitor, one thing is obvious: the Latino influence, which you can experience whether you seek it out or wait for it to fall in your lap. Whether you're dining out, listening to live music, overhearing Spanish conversations, visiting Little Havana or Little Buenos Aires or simply sipping a chilled mojito (a Cuban rum-based cocktail) at the edge of your hotel pool, the Latin American energy is palpable, beautiful and everywhere you go.

decreased a whopping 80%. Probably the most famous murder of this decade was the 1997 slaying of fashion designer Gianni Versace (see p51).

Immigration policy came in for an overhaul under Bill Clinton. The USA stopped instantly accepting Cuban refugees in an effort to keep the hotheads with Fidel rather than on Miami streets. But the US was still open to admitting 20,000 Cubans a year (not counting immediate family members of existing Cuban-Americans). In addition, the Wet-Foot-Dry-Foot policy meant any Cuban who made landfall could expect to stay in America, although those intercepted at sea were sent back south.

The Cuban-American population dominated headlines again during the Elián Gonzalez nightmare, an international custody fight that ended with federal agents storming the Little Havana house where the seven-year-old was staying to have him shipped back to Cuba and, as per normal, anti-Castro Cubans protesting in Miami streets.

In 1998 sweeping trade embargoes were slightly loosened for the first time since commercial transactions ceased in 1963. Medical supplies were allowed, then came agricultural products, as long as Cuba paid in cash. Although Cuba was struck hard by a hurricane, Fidel's pronouncement in 2000 that he'd not take 'one grain of rice' from the USA was tempered by his cash

2005	2006	2008
Hurricane Wilma wrecks the Keys and ex-acerbates the pre-existing affordable housing crisis in those islands. Employees of Keys hotels, bars and restaurants commute for hours from Homestead to their jobs.	The Arsht Center (then called the Carnival Center) opens, the second-biggest performing arts venue in America. The much-delayed, much over-budgeted project is nonetheless warmly embraced, and kicks off a series of Downtown revitalization projects.	Plans are approved for a new Miami Marlins stadium to replace the Orange Bowl. The 37,000 seat, retractable-roof stadium has an estimated $525 million price tag, mainly covered by the City of Miami.

acquisition in 2002 of $17 million worth of US grain. President Bush, with the support of his brother Jeb, didn't waste much time tightening the embargo again.

On the bright side, corruption was slightly cleaned out after the removal of Mayor Xavier Suarez in 1998, whose election was overturned following the discovery of many illegal votes. The successive mayor Manuel Diaz hasn't been universally loved, but he's been relatively scandal free (with the exception of a Coconut Grove real estate conflict of interest), which is more than most of his predecessors can claim. As a mayor he's pushed for cementing ties between Miami and the Latin American world – he's fond of saying, 'When Venezuela or Argentina sneezes, Miami catches a cold.'

The 21st Century

The 2003 Free Trade Area of the Americas talks shone the international spotlight on Miami, and more specifically the thousands of anti-globalization protestors who descended on the summit. And yet another shooting – this one a suicide – put Miami's vice on the map again in 2005 when ex-city commissioner Arthur Teele killed himself in the lobby of the *Miami Herald* following an investigation by the alternative *Miami New Times* into the popular politician's history of drug use, prostitutes and money laundering.

The 2005 Hurricane Season, the worst on modern record, generally spared Miami, although it did flatten a substantial part of the Keys and other parts of South Florida. But what the disaster truly left behind, besides a lot of debris, was the raw issue of a looming affordable housing crisis. With disaster insurance premiums through the roof and the housing boom already catering to the upper class, the backbone of South Florida's communities – firefighters, teachers, policemen and postal workers – are being priced out of home owning. Already, the trailer parks that once housed the middle class of the Keys are fast becoming a kitschy tropical memory.

ARTS

Miami knows it has a pretty face, and it knows a lot of people think it's stupid as a result. The stereotype really isn't fair. Because what makes Miami beautiful, from the bodies on the beach to the structure of the skyline, is diversity. The energies of the Western Hemisphere have been channeled into this Gateway to the Americas, and a lot of that drive is rooted in creativity and a search for self-expression.

This artistic impulse tends to be rooted in the immigrant experience, which this town has in spades. There's the pain of exile. The air of a country where you can't be arrested for public expression. The flush of financial success, and its ability to fund art projects. The frustration of being shut out of the often callous American Dream. Miami's greatest quality – her inborn tolerance for eccentricity – is at the root of such public innovations as the Arab fantasyland architecture of Opa Locka, and the modernistic design of the Art Deco District. Plenty of people dismiss Coral Gables and the Vizcaya as gauche and tacky, and through modern and sensible eyes they may appear as such. But they were revolutionary for their time. Concepts like a Mediterranean revival village that would serve as an aesthetic bulwark against sprawl, or an Italianate villa carved out of the seashore, were not likely to be accepted by conservative northeastern Americans untouched by the risk-inducing Florida sun.

Miami's citizens and their memories, realities and visions have created a burgeoning art scene that truly began to be noticed with the 2002 introduction of Art Basel Miami Beach (p15), the US outpost of an annual erudite gathering that is based in Switzerland. By its second year, the event had created electricity throughout the national art world – and had succeeded in wooing 175 exhibitors, more than 30,000 visitors and plenty of celebs to take over the galleries, clubs and hotels of South Beach and the Design District. It has grown, in both size and strength, each year since, and its impact on the local art scene here cannot be overstated; today, Art Basel Miami is the biggest contemporary arts festival in the Western Hemisphere.

The visual arts only represent a tip of this iceberg; since the 1980s a wave of DJs, pop artists and creatures of the night descend on the Winter Music Conference (p14). Authors have always been attracted to South Florida's good weather and quirky characters, and they and their fans

ARTS REVIVAL

Proof positive that this city takes its art scene seriously is the city fathers' plan to use museums, galleries and the new Adrienne Arsht Center for the Performing Arts (p65) to resurrect the northern, depressed side of Downtown (see the boxed text, p68). Local government hopes a new Miami Arts Museum on Bicentennial Park, combined with the Arsht Center and galleries such as the Cisneros Fontanal Arts Foundation (CIFO; p69), will bring in the intellectual scenesters, their money and some life to this oft-blighted transition area just south of Overtown. Local nightlife has already jumped the gun, and some of the most innovative, interesting clubs in the city can be found around NE 14th St, which lies on the faultline between gentrification and cheap rents – prime breeding ground for artists.

Such was the cachet of Wynwood and the Design District, which represent the city's earlier attempts at carving out a Miami arts neighborhood. Although Wynwood, its warehouses and its cheap studio spaces have always attracted artists, it did not necessarily attract city attention until local government figured out that (a) successful artists attract gentrification (just what ratty, working-class Puerto Rican Wynwood seemed to be in need of), and (b) attaching an arts district to the Miami brand would only increase the town's pull among creative-class tourists. But Miami went above and beyond installing Wynwood neighborhood flags. It carved out a small Design District, which inspired *Wallpaper* magazine to declare Miami 'best city' in its 2004 Design Awards.

For a city looking to increase its creative cred while cashing up its outlying neighborhoods, a Design District is a godsend. It's the most profitable arts colony urban planning can produce, a place for creative types that *just happens* to also be a money-maker — concept furniture doesn't come cheap, after all. 'And all that money will revitalize the 'hood and keep its original residents from moving across the tracks, right?' Stop questioning city wisdom you, and buy a dinette set. Today, Design District showrooms pull in luminaries like Holly Hunt (p118), Knoll, Luminaire, Ann Sacks and Kartell (p118). The area's also central for up-and-coming, cutting-edge art galleries in the region, from the Bernice Steinbaum Gallery (p84) to Adamar Fine Arts. In Wynwood, just south of the Design District, one of many notable spaces is the Rubell Family Art Collection (p83), a modern-art collection displayed in a former Drug Enforcement Agency confiscated-drug warehouse. Small streets such as NW 23rd St have become particularly packed with Miami's hip and well-read.

Of course, there's art outside the designated art neighborhoods. The Museum of Contemporary Art (p62), designed by Charles Gwathmey and opened in 1996, fused urban and cultural planning by placing a civic and cultural center within a residential and commercial area. The wonderful artist-run ArtCenter/South Florida (p51) on Lincoln Rd, which helped to bring around Miami's art renaissance, is just about the only such place to have stayed in South Beach, still supporting artists with space for working and exhibiting. The Bass Museum of Art (p51) in South Beach, the Miami Art Museum (p70) Downtown and the Lowe Art Museum (p102) in Coral Gables deliver the goods when it comes to more Eurocentric works (and excellent world archeology at the Lowe), and the Wolfsonian-FIU (p50) is a wonderful house of design. Even hotels, aware of the city's art draw, are getting in on the action; check out the excellent exhibits at the Sagamore (p146) and the Four Seasons (p180), which has a permanent exhibit of Botero sculptures.

Also, as you can imagine, Cuban and Latin American artists have a major impact on Miami's growing art community. You'll find plenty of galleries in both Coral Gables and Little Havana; pick up the detailed *Miami Visual Arts Guide* (available at galleries), which maps the locations of art galleries in almost every neighborhood in Miami and Miami Beach. A great web guide to the city's art scene can be found at www.artcircuits.com.

have the November Miami Book Fair International (p15) to indulge their literary proclivities. Then there are constant film, dance and classical-music festivals, all high-quality showcases that bring in crowds.

LITERATURE

Writers need to be around good stories to keep their narrative wits sharp, and no place provides this like South Florida, land of angry farmers, radical environmentalists, sly financiers, immigrants from a hundred different countries and, every summer, a hurricane. This proximity to real-life drama means, unsurprisingly, many of Miami's best authors cut their writing teeth in journalism. As a result, there's a certain breed of Miami prose that has the terse punch of the best newspaper writing. Beginning with former *Miami Herald* crime-beat reporters Edna Buchanan and Carl Hiaasen, and leading up to new names like Jeff Lindsay, the Miami crime-writing scene is alive and well. On the other hand, local immigrant communities have lent this town's literature the poetry of exiled tongues, narratives that find a thread through the diaspora alleyways that underline Miami's identity. And finally, the subtle beauty of the South Florida landscape has produced a certain breed of nature writer that is able to capture the nuances of the region's subdued scenery while explaining the complicated science that runs through it all – Marjory Stoneman Douglas and Ted Levin spring to mind.

Books & Books (p110) is an excellent source of local lit, both through its stock and its schedule of readings. What follows is a sampling of what you'll find on the shelves.

The Between (Tananarive Due, 1996) Due's debut novel focused on Hilton, who is haunted by powerfully frightening nightmares when his wife – the only elected African-American judge in Dade County – begins receiving racist hate mail.

Cold Case Squad (Edna Buchanan, 2004) Buchanan's 13th novel, done in her typically mesmerizing style, is all about Sergeant Craig Burch, who leads the Miami Police Department's cold-case squad by trying to track killers whose 'trails vanished long ago like footprints on a sea washed beach.'

Continental Drift (Russell Banks, 1985) It's all here – morals, tragedy, love and sex – in the American classic novel about a blue-collar New Hampshire worker who flees for shallow promises in the south of Florida. Banks explores the Miami story in beautiful, haunting prose.

Darkly Dreaming Dexter: A Novel (Jeff Lindsay, 2004) Dexter Morgan is a lab technician who specializes in blood splatter for the Miami-Dade police department. He's also a serial killer. And he's also the good guy. The odd premise has been turned into a TV series that has since attracted a cultish following.

The Everglades: River of Grass (Marjory Stoneman Douglas, 1947) OK, the subject matter isn't technically Miami. Still, Ms. Douglas surely is one of the greatest writers this city has produced, and she's on top of her game with this richly worded tribute to the Glades, a book that essentially lobbed the issue of wetlands conservation straight into public discourse.

Hoot (Carl Hiaasen, 2002) This time the crime master writes for young readers aged nine to 12, weaving a colorful tale of Roy, the new kid in his Coconut Grove school, whose first 'friend,' unfortunately, is a bully. It's a wonderfully quirky Hiaasen intro.

Labrava (Elmore Leonard, 1983) Learn to love (or at least understand) a variety of lowlifes and sleazy folks in the best of the bunch from Leonard. In this suspenseful novel, Joe Labrava is a former secret-service agent who gets mixed up in a Miami scam revolving around a Cuban hitman, a redneck former cop and a fading movie starlet. It's a fast-paced character-driven tale, both intriguing and wacky.

Miami Blues (Charles Willeford, 1984) The late Miami underworld master Willeford first made it big with this addictive novel about a denture-wearing detective's chase after a cold and quirky criminal. It was the basis for the 1990 film of the same name, starring Alec Baldwin.

Miami Purity (Vicki Hendricks, 1996) Hendricks' debut novel is a noirish tale of a stripper who tries to go straight, written in trashy, crisp language that makes this book impossible to put down.

One Hot Summer (Carolina Garcia-Aguilera, 2003) Margarita Solana, a Cuban-American Miami Beach wife and mother, must re-evaluate her life: her lawyer husband is encouraging her to have another child, but meanwhile, her first love has reappeared on the scene. Conflicts of passion sizzle in Garcia-Aguilera's hands.

PUBLIC ART

This city's always been way ahead of the curve when it comes to public art. Miami and Miami Beach established the Art in Public Places program way back in 1973, when it voted to allocate 1.5% of city construction funds to the fostering of public art; since then more than 700 works – sculptures, mosaics, murals, light-based installations and more – have been created in public spots. Here are just a few examples.

Barbara Neijna's *Foreverglades*, in Concourse J of Miami International Airport, uses mosaic, art-installed text from *River of Grass* and waves representing the movement of water over grass to give new arrivals a

top picks

MIAMI PUBLIC ART

- Holocaust Memorial (p54), by Kenneth Treister, South Beach.
- Words Without Thought Never to Heaven Go (p69), by Edward Ruscha.
- Foreverglades (above), by Barbara Neijna, Miami International Airport Concourse J.
- Reaching for Miami Skies (above), by Connie Lloveras, Metromover.
- Mermaid (p54), by Roy Lichtenstein, Jackie Gleason Theater of Performing Arts.

BRIGHT BRITTO

If the top public artist of a given city determines how said city sees itself, we must conclude Miami is a cartoon-y, cubist, chaotic place of bright-happy-shiny-joy-joy-iness.

That's the aesthetic legacy Romero Britto is leaving this town, anyways. The short and seemingly perpetually grinning Brazilian émigré, clad in jackets leftover from a 1980s MTV video, was the hot face of public art in the 2000s, having designed the mural of the Miami Children's Museum (p106), the 'Welcome' structure at Dadeland North Station and many others. You might need sunglasses to appreciate his work, which appeals to the islander in all of us: Saturday-morning cartoon brights, sharp geometric lines and woopy, loopy curls, inner-child character studies and, underlying everything, a scent of teal oceans on a sunny day.

Gloria Estefan loves the guy, and Jeb Bush gave Tony Blair an original Britto piece when the former British PM visited Miami in 2006. Of course, not everyone feels the Romero love; plenty of critics have dubbed Britto more commercial designer than pop artist (but, like, what *is* art man?). Rather than get mired in the debate, we suggest that you go check out a Britto installation for yourself, or Britto Central (p110) on Lincoln Rd. The man's work is as ubiquitous as palm trees and, hey, if you've got a spare $20,000, you can get yourself an original before you go home.

sense of the flow of Florida's most unique ecosystem. A series of hand prints representing Miami's many immigrant communities link into a single community in *Reaching for Miami Skies*, by Connie Lloveras, which greets Metromover commuters at Brickell Station. In Miami-Dade Library, the floating text of *Words Without Thought Never to Heaven Go* by Edward Ruscha challenges readers to engage in thought processes that are inspired by, but go beyond, the books that surround them. The team of Roberto Behar and Rosario Marquardt, hailing from Argentina, have been among the most prolific public artists in town, to the degree that their work is deliberately meant to warp conceptions of what is or isn't public space; they created the giant red *M* at the Metromover Riverwalk Station for the city's centennial back in 1996. In Miami Beach, you'll see the sculpture *Mermaid*, by Roy Lichtenstein, in front of Jackie Gleason Theater of the Performing Arts; the lovely neon work of Jim Morrison, *A Celebration of Light*, as you enter the Beach via the Julia Tuttle Causeway; and the moving murals of the Electrowave bus fleet, giving colorful character to each of these South Beach buses.

Real estate developers have even used public art to win political battles: Pinnacle Housing Group, a Miami-based developer of affordable-housing projects, commissioned renowned pop artist CJ Latimore to paint *The Playground*, a colorful, 40ft-tall mural of children, on the side of a new housing development to help it win support from the community in 2003. It worked – just as it did earlier that year, when Pinnacle commissioned fiber-optic sculptures of butterflies and the sun to enhance a housing project in Little Havana. See www.miamidade.gov/public art for a comprehensive list of public pieces.

MUSIC

As in all things, it's the mad diversity of Miami that makes her music so appealing. The southbound path of American country and Southern Rock, the northbound rhythms of the Caribbean and Latin America, and the homegrown beats of Miami's African-American community get smashed into a musical crossroads of the Americas. Think about the sounds the above influences produce, and you'll hear a certain thread: bouncy, percussive, with a tune you can always dance to. And by dance, we mean get low.

But the 'Clash of Civilizations' thesis holds a special relevance to Miami's music scene. Because the above sounds, rooted in the New World, are fighting another American Revolution against invaders from a far shore: Europeans and their waves of techno, house and electronica. In the narrative of Miami immigrants, we can't leave out the gay community and the Euro-expats, and the latter have brought a strong club music scene, best evidenced by the annual Winter Music Conference (p14) that is held each March, which brings thousands of DJs and producers to town for a nonstop lineup of workshops and parties. Sometimes, the competing thumpa-thumpa of house and hip-hop get along, but usually the scenes stay distinct.

Miami's heart and soul is Latin, and that goes for her music as well. Producers and artists from across Latin America come here for the high-quality studio facilities, the lure of global distribution and the Billboard Latin Music Conference & Awards, held here each April. The Magic City has been the cradle of stars such as Gloria Estefan, Ricky Martin and Albita, and a quick scan over the local airwaves always yields far more Spanish-language stations than English, playing a mix of salsa, *son* (itself an Afro-Cuban-Spanish mélange of musical styles), conga and reggaeton. A night out in La Covacha (p152) or an hour listening to the tunes of 95.7 FM (El Zol!) makes for a good introduction to the scene; or check out our own Latin Music Primer (opposite).

Miami's hip-hop scene has been through a bit of a circular evolution, from the early '90s Miami bass (dirrrty dance music, exemplified by 2 Live Crew) to a more aggressive, street-style rap, which has blended and morphed into today's club-oriented tracks. These modern sounds draw off the crunk beats, southern drawls and Atlanta overproduction of the Dirty South sound. The hit 2008 single 'Low' by Flo Rida encapsulates the genre, which sounds, in a lot of ways, like the club child of Miami bass and everything that has come along since. Local hip-hop heroes work hard to keep Miami on the map and strongly rep neighborhoods such as Opa Locka, Liberty City and Overtown in a Dirty South that's still dominated by Atlanta and New Orleans; some local artists to listen out for include DJ Smallz, Pitbull, Rick Ross, Flo Rida and Uncle Luke.

There's been a small but strong indie and punk boom over the past decade, and it's mainly centered on Sweat Records (p118) and Churchill's (p150) in Little Haiti. The crop of home-grown bands is still thin compared to many other cities, but it's starting to grow; you can expect to find bands like Sparkydog, Nothing Rhymes With Orange and 10 Sheen rocking out in local live-music venues. Besides Churchill's, a good spot to see the cutting edge of Miami rock is the Transit Lounge (p149).

Last but not least is the stalwart world of classical music, given a huge boost by the opening of the Arsht Center. The Florida Grand Opera (p156) and New World Symphony (p157) are both highly respected, often host celebrity conductors and maintain a fierce following among South Florida's large literati class.

top picks

MIAMI TRACKS (AND WHERE TO PLAY THEM)

- Conga, Gloria Estefan and The Miami Sound Machine – Ocean Dr
- Rakata, Wisin y Yandel – Little Havana
- Moon Over Miami, by Joe Burke and Edgar Leslie – Julia Tuttle Causeway
- Miami, by Will Smith – I-95 past Downtown
- Bitch I'm From Dade County, by DJ Khaled, Trina, C-Money, Trick Daddy, Flo Rida and Rick Ross – Overtown or Opa Locka
- Miami, by U2 – Wynwood or North Miami Beach
- Save Hialeah Park, by Los Primeros – Hialeah
- Swamp Music, by Lynyrd Skynyrd – Tamiami Trail to Everglades City
- Jaspora, by Wyclef Jean – Little Haiti
- Your Love, The Outfield – A1A

WINTER MUSIC CONFERENCE

Anyone who is anyone in the dance-music industry, from DJs to promoters to straight-up fans, can be found in Miami come the end of March. That's when the annual Winter Music Conference (WMC; p14) pops off, bringing an eclectic mix of dance parties, performances, seminars, workshops and the International Dance Music Awards to a crowd of about 40,000 enthusiasts and professionals from all around the globe. Stationed in South Beach, the Winter Music Conference has something for everyone who loves music you can move and groove to. There are networking parties for DJs who want to share tips, showcases for DJs who want to strut their spinning stuff, seminars on new-media technology as well as parties galore for folks who just want to dance it out. Along with the death of Versace, probably no other phenomenon has equally raised Miami's profile with Europeans. Some say the WMC is all about the parties and not much else; others go for some serious learning. Either way, make sure you stay out of Miami if none of this interests you, because the conference is a big deal and an extremely crowded affair – hotel rates will be through the roof.

LATIN & CARIBBEAN MUSIC PRIMER

Here's a quick crib sheet for your Miami nightclub explorations.

Salsa is the most commonly heard word used to reference Latin music and dance, which makes sense as it's actually a generic term developed in the mid '60s and early '70s as a way to pull all Latin sounds under one umbrella name for gringos who couldn't recognize the subtle differences between beats. From the Spanish word for 'sauce,' salsa has its roots in Cuban culture and has a sound that's enhanced by textures of jazz. Music that lends itself to salsa dancing has four beats per bar of music.

One specific type of Cuban salsa is *son* – a sound popularized by the release of 1999's *Buena Vista Social Club*. It has roots in African and Spanish cultures and is quite melodic, usually incorporating instruments including the *tres* (a type of guitar with three sets of closely spaced strings), standard guitars and various hand drums.

Merengue originates from the Dominican Republic and can be characterized by a very fast beat, with just two beats to each bar. It's typically played on the tamboura, guiro (a ridged cylindrical percussion instrument made of metal or dried gourd) and accordion.

Hailing from the Andalusian region of Spain is the folk art of flamenco, which consists of hand clapping, finger snapping, vocals, guitar and the flamboyant dance. Miami's Argentines love to tango, a Buenos Aires invention that draws off European classical dance and the immigrant experience of South America's French, Italian, African and indigenous ethnic enclaves.

The popular reggae sound, originating in Jamaica and having strong Rastafarian roots, is a total movement most popularly associated with Bob Marley. It's characterized by rhythm chops on a backbeat and, at least in its beginnings, a political-activist message. There are various styles within reggae, including roots (Marley's sound), dancehall (ie Yosexygirlwannagetboomshackalacka), raga and dub.

But it's rare to just hear one of the above. Miami is a polyglot kind of town, and it loves to blend techno with *son*, give an electronic backbeat to salsa, and overlay everything with dub, hip-hop and *bomba* (African-influenced Puerto Rican dance music). This mixed marriage produces a lot of musical children, and the most recognizable modern sound derived from the above is reggaeton, a driving mash-up that plays like Spanish rap shoved through a sexy backbeat and thumpin' dancehall speakers. Pioneers of the genre include Daddy Yankee, Don Chezina, Tito El Bambino, Wisin Y Yandel, Calle 13 and producers such as Luny Tunes and Noriega. Although it largely originated in Puerto Rico, reggaeton is one of the few musical styles that can get Latins from across the Americas – from Nicaraguans to Mexicans to Colombians – shaking a tail feather. That universal appeal is rooted in diversity and interethnic interaction, which wouldn't exist without crossroad cities like Miami.

CINEMA & TELEVISION

For being such a fabulous place to live, television's most popular depictions of Miami make the city seem populated by (a) coke dealers and corrupt cops *(Miami Vice)*, (b) serial killers and not-so-corrupt cops *(CSI: Miami)* and (c) beautiful people *(Nip/Tuck* and…well, all of the above). Every show about Miami is at pains to remind you there are a lot of hotties down here.

Crime sells this city – at least cinematically. Sam Katzman chose Miami for B-movies about gang wars, and several (lowbrow) classics – as well as the *Jackie Gleason Show*, shot here for TV – in the 1960s. *Scarface,* Brian DePalma's over-the-top story of the excesses of capitalism, entered Miami into hip-hop's common lexicon; and *Miami Vice,* the 1980s TV series about a couple of pastel-clad vice-squad cops, put Miami on the international map. The images – of murders, rapes and drug-turf wars – were far from positive, and the powers-that-be in the city were not initially happy. But *Vice* was more about Ferraris, speedboats and bootie than gang-banging, and as branding goes, it depicted Miami as more than a high-crime slum where everyone's grandparents retired. As William Cullom, a President of the Greater Miami Chamber of Commerce put it, '*[Miami Vice]* has built an awareness of Miami in young people who had never thought of visiting Miami.' A pretty mediocre Hollywood film version starring Colin Farrell and Jamie Foxx was released in 2006 that capitalized on the '80s nostalgia market. There have been loads of comedies filmed here as well, but for our money, *The Birdcage* best captures the fabulosity and, yes, even community vibe, of South Beach. We're forgetting one other genre: porn. Well, what did you expect with all the silicon? There's a fair amount of homegrown adult industry going on here, not that we'd know anything about it.

Today, Miami and Miami Beach governments love the idea of producers coming to town so much that in early 2005 they instituted the One Stop Permitting system, providing a streamlined, online way for makers of films, TV shows and commercials to apply for permits (at www.filmiami.org).

Finally, Miami is the center of the American Spanish-language television industry. Telemundo, the only US producer of Spanish-language soap operas (*telenovelas*), is headquartered in Hialeah, while Univision keeps its major production facilities in Miami.

top picks

MIAMI MOVIES & TV SHOWS

- Scarface (1983)
- Miami Blues (1990)
- Miami Vice (1984)
- There's Something About Mary (1998)
- The Birdcage (1996)

In South Beach alone you'll be walking by some great movie moments: 728 Ocean Dr (above Johnny Rockets) is the sight of the chainsaw (ie 'blood bath') scene from *Scarface*. The Carlyle Hotel (1250 Ocean Dr) is the site of the Birdcage club in the movie of the same name. Among many other flicks, scenes from *There's Something About Mary* and *Any Given Sunday* were shot in the Cardozo Hotel (p172). But, apparently, *Police Academy 5: Assignment Miami Beach* was never filmed here! Damn, that's disappointing.

The following is a list of various films and TV shows that will give you a taste of Miami, both past and present.

The Bellboy (1960) A baby-faced Jerry Lewis stars in this screwball comedy about, you guessed it, a bellboy at the Fontainebleau (p60). Filmed entirely on location (and employing several real-life bellboys in many of the scenes), the film is completely silly, but an interesting look into Miami's storied resort past.

The Birdcage (1996) The Hollywood version of *La Cage Au Folles* stars Robin Williams and Nathan Lane as a gay couple who run a flamboyant South Beach cabaret but try to play it in-the-closet when their son brings his fiancé's right-wing parents to town. It's funny, poignant and a nice visual image of the area.

CSI: Miami (2002) The Miami incarnation of the popular *CSI* TV series about a Crime Scenes Investigation unit revisits Miami's dicey past, but does so from the safety of its now-glitzy present. It's overly produced and a bit too earnest in its writing, but is an interesting peek into the eccentricities of Miami's underbelly.

Get Shorty (1995) Danny DeVito and John Travolta costar in this translation of the Elmore Leonard novel. The smart and hysterical mobster comedy follows a Miami loan shark to Hollywood and Vegas in search of money he's owed.

Mean Season (1985) Loosely based on the experiences of Edna Buchanan and fellow *Herald* newshounds, this drama stars Kurt Russell as Malcolm Anderson, a burnt-out Miami reporter who gets re-inspired when his life becomes intertwined with that of a serial killer. It's gripping and good until the overboard Hollywood ending.

Miami Blues (1990) Based on Charles Willeford's novel, this black comedy with a cultish following has Frederick (Alec Baldwin), a sicko thief and liar, worm his way into the world of the very naive Susie (Jennifer Jason Leigh). It's clever and oddly compelling, with great shots of Coral Gables and the Miami River.

GRAND THEFT GOODNESS

Get in the car. Any car — we suggest the red convertible. Flip the radio to '(I Just) Died in Your Arms,' by Cutting Crew, and drive past a setting sun, an art deco–facade and a strip club to Little Haiti. Carjack a dumptruck and drive it into a burning trailer park while spraying thousands of rival New York gangsters with a pair of Uzis.

Is there any better way to see Miami?

Well, yes, but the above was the preferred vicarious vacation of the thousands who purchased *Grand Theft Auto: Vice City*, released in 2003 and still one of the most popular video games of all time. The cart put you in the Ray Liotta–voiced shoes of a petty gangster out to climb his way to the top of 'Vice City's' criminal underworld. Of course, 'Vice City' was a stand-in for Miami, and the games heavily referenced *Miami Vice* and *Scarface*, including a game-climaxing, World War III-esque shootout in a pseudo-Fountainebleau.

Sure, the game was a violent, misogynistic tap into the repressed id of thousands of basement-bound gamers. But it was aesthetically and technically a gorgeous piece of work, and for a generation born after the hype of *Miami Vice*, it was another drug-fueled banner ad for the excessive life in South Beach.

Miami Vice (1984) The series that started it all. Don Johnson and Philip Michael Thomas are vice-squad detectives, which, in 1980s South Beach, means they drive a fancy car, wear pink or yellow blazers and shoot up the bad-guy drug dealers. A wonderful nostalgia trip!

Nip/Tuck (2003) The newest TV series to use Miami Beach as its backdrop, this one uses it well, and is a quirky, funny, far-reaching drama about two not-so-scrupulous plastic surgeons and their complicated personal lives.

Scarface (1983) This classic Miami crime tale stars Al Pacino as a Cuban immigrant who fast learns how to be a big shot in the drug-dealing underworld. It's sheer over-the-top craziness, especially the grand finale scene, shot in the Fontainebleau.

There's Something About Mary (1998) The Farrelly Brothers' hysterical comedy about a grown-up geek who tracks down his high-school sweetheart has some great shots of South Beach.

THEATER

Miami has always enjoyed a rich theater history, but it enjoyed a major coup in 2003, when Cuban-born Nilo Cruz won a Pulitzer Prize for his *Anna in the Tropics*, becoming the first non-New York production to win the title. The play premiered at the New Theatre (p159) in Coral Gables, allowing stage fans from all over town to rejoice in Cruz's win. Local-star playwrights such as Teo Castellanos and Marco Ramirez continue to leave big marks on the theater world, while Miami's various theater festivals – the International Hispanic Theater Festival in June, Cultura del Lobo in October and the South Florida Theatre Festival (approximately March to May) – annually bring out heavyweight talents. There are famous venues and theater schools all over town, including the Actors' Playhouse (p159) in Coral Gables; the Coconut Grove Playhouse (p159), known for its historic, though disastrous, American premiere of *Waiting for Godot*); and the University of Miami – Coral Gables' acting program (alma mater of both Sylvester Stallone and Ray Liotta). Then there's the whole new armada of cutting-edge venues and troupes, from the innovative Miami Light Project (p156) to the City Theater and its series of original summer shorts.

DANCE

Dance is a relatively new performance genre in Miami, where the oldest companies – Miami City Ballet and Sosyete Koukouy – were both founded in 1985. The strange pairing of these two troupes, one a classical ballet showcase and the other a Haitian dance and theater company (whose name means 'Firefly Society') could not better represent the diversity of the Miami dance scene. While it's the nationally renowned festivals here, namely the Latin-Caribbean flavored Ifé-Ilé Afro-Cuban Dance & Music Festival (p155) and the Brazilian Fla/Bra, that best showcase the international mix of movements here, year-round opportunities abound. La Rosa Flamenco Theatre (p157), for example, blends flamenco with Indian styles and even tap dancing. Momentum Dance (p158) offers modern works by known choreographers such as Isadora Duncan, while the Maximum Dance Company is Miami's modern star, known for using unexpected musical scores (from U2, for example) for their works. Other troupes blend African, Cuban and Brazilian sounds and styles – a constant on-stage reminder that Miami's culture cannot be narrowed down. Today, the lovely new headquarters of the Miami City Ballet (p157) allows visitors to watch the ballerinas practice through large glass walls, which can be a soothing break from nearby Lincoln Rd's pedestrian bustle.

ARCHITECTURE

The local architecture story is defined by more than deco, although we have included a special chapter on this quintessentially Miami design movement (see p73). As in all cities, Miami's architecture reflects the tastes and attitudes of its inhabitants, who tend to adhere to the aesthetic philosophy espoused by Miami Beach's favorite architect, Morris Lapidus: 'Too much is never enough.' The earliest examples of this homegrown over-embellishment are the Mediterranean revival mansions of Coral Gables and the Fabergé egg fantasy of the Vizcaya (p96). These residential wedding cakes established Miami's identity as a city of fantasies and dreams, outside the boundaries of conventional tastes, where experimentation was smiled upon as long as it was done with flash. They also spoke to a distinct Miami attitude that is enshrined in city tastes to this day: If you've got it, flaunt it, then shove it back in their faces for a second serving.

This penchant for imaginative, decorative flair overlaid the muscular postwar hotels and condos of the 1950s, giving birth to Miami Modernism (or Mimo). Mimo drew off the sleek lines and powerful presence of International Modernism, but led by Lapidus, it also eschewed austerity for grand, theatrical staging. Lapidus himself described his most famous structure, the Fontainebleau (p60), as influenced by the most popular mass media of its time: Hollywood and cinema. The glamour Lapidus captured in his buildings would go on to define Miami's aesthetic outlook; Versace incorporated it into his clothes and Ian Schrager has decked out his hotels with this sense of fairy-tale possibility. Which makes sense: the word 'glamour' originally meant a kind of spell that causes people to see things differently from what they really are, which makes it an appropriate inspiration for the buildings of the 'Magic City.'

ENVIRONMENT & PLANNING

THE LAND

Miamians can claim to live in a truly unique North American ecosystem. Forty-mile-long Biscayne Bay, with its mangrove shorelines and underwater coral reefs, teems with pink shrimp, stone crabs and manatees. The bay forms part of the Atlantic Intercoastal Waterway and is a shallow inlet of the Atlantic Ocean. While many of its mangrove forests have been lost to development, those that remain help stabilize the shoreline and provide shelter for birds and animals. Its lush seagrass beds and coral reefs – many of which have been replaced through Miami's Artificial Reef Program, which sinks structures to make homes for coral polyps – are also important elements of the system. The bay's eastern edge contains the northernmost islands of the Florida Keys, protected from development by the establishment of Biscayne National Park (p227) in 1968.

The bay is not the only setting for water-based life in Miami, of course. There's the coastal strand of beaches and sand dunes; the maritime hammock, made up of dunes old enough to sprout delicate trees; coastal wetlands, consisting of swamps and salt marshes; and freshwater marshes, mostly evident throughout the Everglades. It's a beautiful and compelling ecosystem, and therefore one that is forever luring developers and visitors, and needing protection from these 'admirers.'

GREEN MIAMI

Development-loving though they are, the residents of Miami realized a while ago that the beautiful land that lured or kept them here in the first place was in serious danger. Luckily, voters approved a two-year property tax back in 1990 to fund the Environmentally Endangered Lands (EEL) program, which has since acquired and protected more than 21,000 acres of endangered land. Newly nominated parcels are considered every year; those chosen are often boosted with matching funds from the State of Florida's Preservation 2000 program as well as conservation group Florida Forever.

Other efforts to save the earth include an aggressive motor-oil recycling program, a response to the serious issue of illegally dumped oil – more than 300 cases of which were reported in 2000 alone, costing the city $45,000 to clean up. Miami is also home to one of the largest curbside recycling programs in the nation; it's an extensive plan that recycles items including newspapers, batteries, plastic bottles, glass containers and, in a recent addition, computers, VCRs and televisions. Miami's commercial recycling has been mandatory since 1992.

The Miami area boasts some lovely green spaces and parklands – 9000 miles throughout Miami-Dade County – in addition to the Biscayne National Park (p227) and, of course, the nearby Everglades National Park (p221). Nature and city streets often make strange bedfellows, such as when the occasional manatee gets lost in a city sewer or when, in 2004, a crocodile was discovered living among the wilds of the University of Miami Campus. The voice of local environmentalists is strong, and can get loud when potentially destructive development plans are announced, but more often than not it's the builders who win. Currently, the 'Hold the Line' campaign (www.udbline.com) works to keep the Urban Development Boundary from shifting and opening up more land to developers.

CARL HIAASEN: LOVING THE LUNACY

In Carl Hiaasen's Florida the politicians are corrupt, the rednecks are violent, the tourists are clueless, the women are fast and the ambience is smoky noir, brightened by a few buckets of loony pastel. Give it to the man: he knows his home.

Hiaasen, who has worked at the *Miami Herald* since he was 23, is both a writer gifted with crisp prose and a journalist blessed by a reporter's instinct for the offbeat. His success has rested in his ability to basically take the hyperbolic reality that is Florida and tell it to the world. Although his fiction is just that, in many ways it simply draws off the day-to-day eccentricities of the Sunshine State and novelizes them. So: *Tourist Season*, where Hiaasen turns his pen on eco-zealots with a story about a terrorist group that tries to dissuade tourists from coming to Florida and further wrecking the state – namely, by feeding them to a crocodile named Pavlov. In complete thematic contrast comes *Hoot*, a heart-warming tale (odd for Hiaasen) catering to young adults about a 12-year-old boy's fight against a corporation that threatens to pave over a Coconut Grove colony of burrowing owls. *Stormy Weather* takes on the corruption, bureaucracy and disaster tourism that fills the vacuum of the devastation trail left by a hurricane.

Hiaasen's work tends to career between satire and thriller, and betrays both an unceasingly critical eye and deep affection for all of Florida's quirks. Which ironically makes Hiaasen – enemy of almost every special interest group in the Sunshine State – the state's biggest promoter. He is a man who loves Florida for her warts, not her curves, and that, folks, is true romance.

MEDIA

Miami produces some of America's best journalists – Marjory Stoneman Douglas, Edna Buchanan, Carl Hiaasen and Dave Barry to name a storied few – and newspapers here tend to be on top of their game, although they have suffered, like all major media in this country, from budget cuts.

Most everyone reads the *Miami Herald* in Miami – and throughout the state – as it's the daily newspaper of record. The *Sun-Sentinel*, out of Fort Lauderdale, does some great multipart series that get well under the skin of South Florida's most pressing issues.

Still, most people say the *Herald* is the best provider of local, national and international news coverage; the regular columnists tend to be pretty outstanding. On the downside, it's owned by the media conglomerate Knight-Ridder and is 'partners' with most of Miami's other news sources (a common American problem these days), including the local public radio station, WLRN (an excellent National Public Radio affiliate, by the way); the Spanish-language daily *El Nuevo Herald;* the local TV news of both CBS 4 WFOR-TV and UPN 33 WBFS-TV; and radio's Sports Talk 790 The Ticket. There are some great alternative sources, though – mainly the weekly newspaper the *Miami New Times,* which tends to explore the sides of politics that the mainstream may shy away from. This goes almost double for the new and plucky *Sun Post,* which is building a good name out of eschewing shallow day-to-day coverage and investigating the hell out of big issues. Miami Today (www.miamitoday.com), serving the business community, is also a good source, especially for financial and economic news. For more details on local media sources, see p247.

FASHION

With Miami now a hub of cool food, nightlife and arts, it makes sense that it would gain acclaim as an influencer in the world of fashion. And it has, with the annual Fashion Week of the Americas (p14) playing a large role in putting this region on the most stylish global maps. The showcase of Latin American designers is the biggest fashion event in Miami, drawing designers and fans from around the world each May since it was brought to town from Ecuador by Beth Sobel of Sobel Fashion Productions in 2003.

The event is renowned globally, from Paris to Hong Kong – but it's by no means the only game in town. Miami has gained enormous cred among European designers (ironically ever since one of them, Gianni Versace, was killed here) and draws mavens from all over the Old World who find something inspiring in the combination of a Latin emphasis on appearance versus the American love of comfort and the dare-to-bare styles inspired by the sunny weather.

Today Miami is the base city for Perry Ellis International, while GenArt, a national nonprofit dedicated to film, art and fashion, holds an annual Fresh Faces in Fashion showcase focusing on Miami's burgeoning designer scene.

So what defines the 'Miami look?' 'Go to a supermarket. Any supermarket. Nine out of 10 girls: wearing high heels. That's Miami,' says a local journalist. Yup, if you want to hang here, you gotta come correct. But it's a weird style – part laid-back yet totally glam.

On the one hand, you'll see a desperate desire for brand-name cred, of Louis Vuitton–endowed affirmation. But on the flip side is the understated (yes, Miami can do understatement) sense of cool that comes from all that heat, exemplified by a casual dressiness the best-looking Miamians accomplish without any apparent effort. Note, for example, the older Cuban man in his *guayabera*, an elegant but simple brocaded men's shirt; he's classy because he's looking good without seeming to try.

There is a distinctive South Beach style and there's no better place to buy it than at the source, but be warned: you must be bold, unabashed and bikini-waxed to pull off some of the more risqué outfits on display, which is to say, pretty much all of them. For more information on Miami's fashion world, see Shopping (p108).

NEIGHBORHOODS

top picks

- **A1A** (p47) The quintessential Miami drive, from Downtown's glittering skyline, over baby-blue Biscayne right into the sexy solar plexus of South Beach.
- **Ocean Drive** (p47) Beautiful bodies, deco hotels and the scent of too much sun block.
- **Lincoln Road Mall** (p54) Strut. Or just gawk as the bold, brash and beautiful walk this promenade 24/7.
- **Arthur Godfrey Road** (**41st Street**; p57) Yes Virginia, they do great chopped liver outside New York, especially in this tropical corner of the Jewish diaspora.
- **Adrienne Arsht Center for the Performing Arts** (p65) See the swooping lines of this excellent new venue.
- **Little Haiti** (p84) Pay a *vodou* (voodoo) priest a visit here.
- **Máximo Gómez Park** (p89) Cigar smoke, dominoes and *guayaberas*; *bienvenido a* Little Havana.
- **Venetian Pool** (p99) The coolest public pool in America.
- **Vizcaya Museum** (p96) Miami's best over-the-top digs.
- **Jimbo's** (p93) Smoked fish. Beer. Laz-E-Boys. And a mangrove swamp. Aw yeah.

What's your recommendation? www.lonelyplanet.com/miami

NEIGHBORHOODS

Two things divide Miami: water and income. Canals, lakes, bays and bank accounts are the geographic, spatial and social boundaries of this city, where rivers and roads cut design districts from drug dens, and *botanicas* from investment banks. Of course the great water that divides here is Biscayne Bay, holding apart the city of Miami from its preening sibling, Miami Beach. *Never* forget (like many tourists do) that Miami Beach is not Miami's beach, but its own distinct town.

And though Jose-Average Miamian thinks his home is fundamentally laid-back, the truth is community tension, not torpor, defines this town. Maybe it's the sticky tropical nights that remind immigrants of home, or more likely, locally entrenched economic divisions, but

'This steamy, angry edge pricks at the cool deco pastel, endless stucco and ritzy fabulosity.'

Miami's ethnic enclaves retain their identities due to both an abundance of diaspora pride *and* a lack of integration. As a result, crossing from Little Havana to Little Haiti has both the romance, and occasional hostility, of crossing real international borders.

This steamy, angry edge pricks at the cool deco pastel, endless stucco and ritzy fabulosity. It's the rum of the otherwise refreshing Miami mojito, the thrill – always there, and never to be underestimated – of a city where all of Latin America (and plenty of Asia, Africa and Europe) lives side by side, if not in perfect harmony.

Every neighborhood in Miami has its own stereotypes and its own exceptions to those rules. Yes, South Beach is where the pretty people are, but they're gawked at by seething mobs of tourists. Somehow, the celeb-chic-sters and aw-shucks-sters play off each other in a just-amusing-enough way to give South Beach a pleasant bite (in limited doses). North Miami Beach is where real people live, by which we mean enough Jews to form a Lost Tribe and enough Argentines to count Normandy Isle as the northernmost suburb of Buenos Aires.

Downtown is a shiny mountain of corporate muscle and inferiority complexes, best realized in the glass towers of Brickell, but under the shimmer is a warren of streets and alleys inhabited by new immigrants and the old dispossessed. The Design District and Wynwood are little (some say artificial) islands of artsiness north of Downtown; we haven't yet decided if the galleries are staving off gentrification or a sure sign of its arrival.

Little Haiti proves you don't have to leave America to leave America; this is one of the most evocative neighborhoods in the city, although it's also rough around the edges. Little Havana, on the other hand, is more tourist-friendly and almost as 'authentically' foreign; trust us, the chickens sold in local pet shops aren't kept for their fluffy personalities (see p85).

Visitors are re-introduced to a more traditional USA via malls and shopping, both of which are very much in evidence in Coconut Grove and Coral Gables – along with some of the most beautiful Mediterranean-revival architecture in America. And finally, there's Key Biscayne for cheesy seaside fun, or a drink at Jimbo's (p93), which may just be the happiest place on Earth. Sorry, Disney.

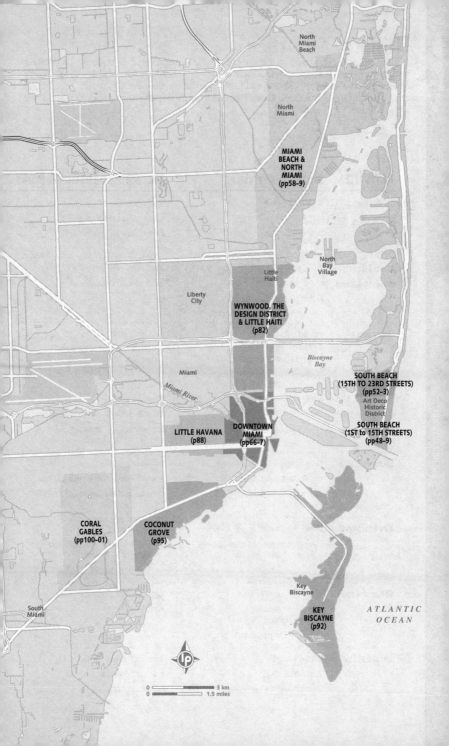

North
Miami Beach

North
Miami

**MIAMI
BEACH &
NORTH
MIAMI**
(pp58–9)

Little
Haiti

North Bay
Village

Liberty
City

**WYNWOOD, THE
DESIGN DISTRICT
& LITTLE HAITI**
(p82)

*Biscayne
Bay*

Miami

Miami River

**SOUTH BEACH
(15TH TO 23RD STREETS)**
(pp52–3)

Art Deco
Historic
District

LITTLE HAVANA
(p88)

**DOWNTOWN
MIAMI**
(pp66–7)

**SOUTH BEACH
(1ST to 15TH STREETS)**
(pp48–9)

**CORAL
GABLES**
(pp100–01)

**COCONUT
GROVE**
(p95)

Key
Biscayne

**KEY
BISCAYNE**
(p92)

*ATLANTIC
OCEAN*

South
Miami

0 _____ 3 km
0 _____ 1.5 miles

ITINERARY BUILDER

It's best to approach Miami by focusing on multiple-neighborhood 'regions.' You'll likely need a day at least for SoBe (South Beach) alone before heading up to Mid-Beach and North Miami Beach. Downtown Miami and Little Havana are close enough to visit together, as are Coconut Grove and Coral Gables, and the north side of Downtown, Wynwood, the Design District and Little Haiti.

AREA	ACTIVITIES	Sights & Activities	Museums, Galleries & Parks
	South Beach	Ocean Drive (p47) Lincoln Road (p54) Delano Lobby (p56)	Wolfsonian-FIU (p50) Bass Museum of Art (p51) World Erotic Art Museum (p51)
	Miami Beach & North Miami	Boardwalk (p57) Fontainebleau Hilton (p60) Arthur Godfrey Road (p57)	Haulover Beach Park (p61) Oleta State Recreation Area (p62)
	Downtown Miami	Adrienne Arsht Center for the Performing Arts (p65) Tobacco Road (p70) Metromover (p70)	Bayfront Park (p68) Historical Museum of Southern Florida (p69) Cisneros Fontanal Arts Foundation (p69)
	Wynwood, the Design District & Little Haiti	Friday night arts walk (p85) City Cemetery (p83)	Moore Space (p84) MoCA at Goldman Warehouse (p83) Haitian Heritage Museum (p84)
	Little Havana	Calle Ocho (p87) Viernes Culturales (Cultural Friday; p89) Cuban Memorial Boulevard (p87)	Máximo Gómez Park (p89) Bay of Pigs Museum & Library (p87) Little Havana Art District (p89)
	Key Biscayne	Miami Seaquarium (p93) Marjory Stoneman Douglas Biscayne Nature Center (p93)	Crandon Park (p93) Bill Baggs Cape Florida State Recreation Area (p91)
	Coconut Grove	Vizcaya Museum (p96) Miami Museum of Science & Planetarium (p96) Plymouth Congregational Church (p96)	Barnacle State Historic Park (p94) Kampong (p96)
	Coral Gables	Biltmore Hotel (p99) Venetian Pool (p99) Drive around the big houses (p98)	Fairchild Tropical Garden (p104) Lowe Art Museum (p102) Coral Gables Museum (p99)

HOW TO USE THIS TABLE

The table below allows you to plan a day's worth of activities in any area of the city. Simply select which area you wish to explore, and then mix and match from the corresponding listings to build your day. The first item in each cell represents a well-known highlight of the area, while the other items are more off-the-beaten-track gems.

Eating	Drinking & Nightlife	Shopping
Osteria Del Teatro (p126) 11th Street Diner (p128) Table 8 (p127)	Room (p144) Skybar (p146) Buck 15 (p147)	Leo (p110) Uncle Sam's Music (p113) Wolfsonian-FIU gift shop (p112)
Wolfie Cohen's Rascal House (p132) Café Prima Pasta (p131) El Rey del Chivito (p132)	Boteca (p148) Circa 39 (p148) Café Nostalgia (p148)	C. Madeleine's (p115) Aventura Mall (p115) Bal Harbour Shops (p115)
Café Sambal (p133) Fresco California (p133) La Moon (p134)	PS 14 (p150) White Room (p150) Transit Lounge (p149)	Historical Museum of South Florida Gift Shop (p116) Wallflower Gallery (p116)
Lost & Found Saloon (p134) Original Restaurant (p135) Michael's Genuine Food & Drink (p134)	Circa 28 (p150) Churchill's (p150)	Moooi (p117) Artisan Antiques Art Deco (p117) Vierge Miracle & St Philippe (p117)
El Cristo (p136) Hy Vong Vietnamese Restaurant (p136) El Rey De Las Fritas (p137)	Casa Panza (p150) Hoy Como Ayer (p150)	Havana-to-go (p119) La Tradición Cubana (p119)
Le Croisic (p137) Oasis (p137)	Jimbo's (p93)	Stefano's (p119) Toy Town (p119)
Last Carrot (p138) Berries Restaurant (p138) Green Street Cafe (p138)	Oxygen Lounge (p151) Sandbar (p151) Miami Improv (p151)	Condom-USA (p120) CocoWalk (p120) Architectural Antiques (p119)
Norman's (p139) Matsuri (p139) Pascal's on Ponce (p139)	Bar (p151) Titanic (p151)	Hip.e (p121) Ma Vie en Lingerie (p120) Books & Books (p120)

GREATER MIAMI

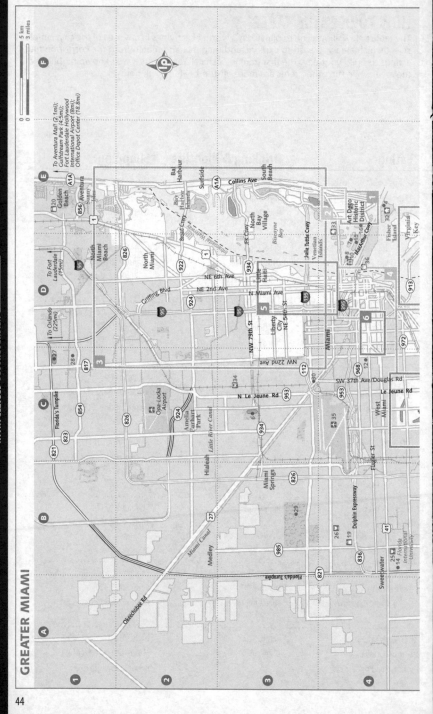

To Aventura Mall (2.1mi);
Gulfstream Park (4.5mi);
Fort Lauderdale Hollywood
International Airport (8mi);
Office Depot Center (18.8mi)

0   5 km
0   3 miles

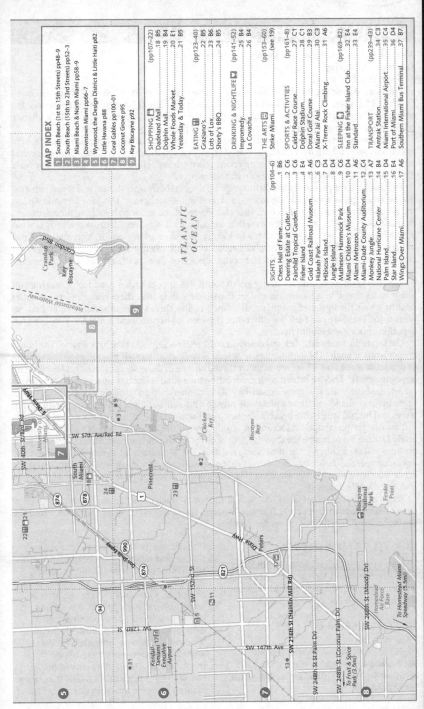

MAP INDEX

1	South Beach (1st to 15th Streets) pp48-9
2	South Beach (15th to 23rd Streets) pp52-3
3	Miami Beach & North Miami pp58-9
4	Downtown Miami pp66-7
5	Wynwood, the Design District & Little Haiti p82
6	Little Havana p88
7	Coral Gables pp100-01
8	Coconut Grove p95
9	Key Biscayne p92

SHOPPING (pp107-22)
Dadeland Mall.................................18 B5
Dolphin Mall...................................19 B4
Whole Foods Market........................20 E1
Yesterday & Today..........................21 B5

EATING (pp123-40)
Graziano's......................................22 B5
Lots of Lox.....................................23 B6
Shorty's BBQ..................................24 B5

DRINKING & NIGHTLIFE (pp141-52)
Impromedy.....................................25 B4
La Covacha.....................................26 B4

THE ARTS (pp153-60)
Strike Miami...............................(see 19)

SPORTS & ACTIVITIES (pp161-8)
Calder Race Course.........................27 C1
Dolphin Stadium.............................28 C1
Doral Golf Course...........................29 B3
Miami Jai Alai.................................30 C3
X-Treme Rock Climbing...................31 A6

SLEEPING (pp169-82)
Inn at the Fisher Island Club..............32 E4
Standard..33 E4

TRANSPORT (pp239-43)
Amtrak Station...............................34 C3
Miami International Airport...............35 C4
Port of Miami.................................36 D4
Southern Miami Bus Terminal............37 B7

SIGHTS (pp104-6)
Chess Hall of Fame...........................1 B6
Deering Estate at Cutler....................2 C6
Fairchild Tropical Garden...................3 C6
Fisher Island....................................4 E4
Gold Coast Railroad Museum..............5 A6
Hialeah Park....................................6 C3
Hibiscus Island.................................7 D4
Jungle Island..................................8 D4
Matheson Hammock Park...................9 C6
Miami Children's Museum.................10 D4
Miami Metrozoo.............................11 A6
Miami-Dade County Auditorium........12 C4
Monkey Jungle..............................13 A7
National Hurricane Center................14 B4
Palm Island...................................15 D4
Star Island....................................16 E4
Wings Over Miami.........................17 A6

ATLANTIC
OCEAN

Crandon Blvd
Crandon
Park
Key
Biscayne

Intracoastal Waterway

SW 40th St/Bird Rd

Kendall Dr

University of
Miami

SW 57th Ave/Red Rd

South
Miami

Chicken
Key

Biscayne
Bay

Pinecrest

Dixie Hwy

Don Shula Expwy

Peters

Pender
Point

Biscayne
National
Park

SW 152nd St

SW 216th St (Hainlin Mill Rd)

SW 248th St (Coconut Palm Dr)

SW 248th St St (Palm Dr)

SW 268th St (Moody Dr)

SW 128th St

SW 147th Ave

Kendall-
Tamiami
Executive
Airport

Homestead
Air Force
Base

To Fruit & Spice
Park (3.5ml)

To Homestead Miami
Speedway (5.5ml)

SOUTH BEACH

Drinking & Nightlife p144; Eating p125; Shopping p109; Sleeping p171

South Beach is *so* hot.

South Beach is *so* over.

You hear *so* much of the above down here you don't know what to believe. Whatever: South Beach is. It *is* where the glut of this town's new hotels are built. It *is* where squatters are evicted from abandoned art deco facades that get renovated into sparkling design icons. It *is* where a celebrity chef such as Govind Armstrong decides to plunk his new restaurant.

When glossy travel magazines and hot travel show hostesses come to Miami, they come here to coo and ooh and aah over this new lounge and its minimalist, Zen yet glam VIP area, or that post-industrial steel-and-stucco dining room serving a reduction of demi-something over a dish that probably has the word 'foie' in it. Somewhere.

This is where rappers party and Britney Spears does embarrassing things, and if you're lucky, maybe you'll get snapped waving to the paparazzi in the background. Which reminds us: has the beach become a victim of its own success? There are more normals looking for celebrities, or more likely playing one for the day, than actual stars down here. Because celebrity is what South Beach sells. So bad news first: when everyone's famous, no-one is. You just gotta pay to play, which makes SoBe's scene oddly egalitarian and totally classist: you can probably get past the red rope if you can afford it, because cash, not class, is the arbiter of cool here. It's quintessentially American, actually.

Now the good news, and it's pretty good: South Beach does such a good job of making you feel famous that if you loosen up and let the silliness slide (was there really a Versace outlet next to where the designer got plugged?), you'll realize there's a lot of spoiling to be had. So what if Joe Frat Boy can't tell the difference between a Michelob and a mojito? You can and, son, they mix a *good* mojito here.

The fact is the food and drink and design in SoBe really is as good as the hype lets on. The hotels are gorgeous enough to be in museums, or at least Scandinavian lifestyle magazines (come to think of it, a lot of them are). There are so many thread counts in those sheets, looms get jealous. The big-name chefs? They've earned their cred; eating their food is like buying a high-class culinary escort. And there are few more evocative walks in America than strolling past the Nighthawk scene of neon-shadowed deco, a pink-and-orange-and-*azul* backlight of sexy laughter, lingering stares and humid smells, the beach's sensory – and sensual – nighttime tapestry.

You can people-watch on Ocean Dr, stroll through the deco canyons of Collins, shop on lovely Lincoln Rd or escape the crowds south of 5th St, also known as SoFi. Streets run east–west; avenues north–south. By the time you read this, the Mondrian (p176) may have turned the once-commercial/residential Bay (west) side of town into an expansion of SoBe glitz, and the scene may have shifted. But wherever it is, rest assured it will pamper the hell out of you, and look good while it does it.

To get here by bus, take C, H, K, M, R, S, or the South Beach Local Circulator (p240). If traveling by car from the mainland, cross at either Venetian Causeway (17th St) or over A1A. From the north, follow Alton Rd or Collins Ave south.

1ST TO 15TH STREETS

This area includes SoFi (South of Fifth Street), a quietly hip 'hood that acts as a counter-weight to the over-the-top carnival of Lincoln Rd, on the north end of South Beach.

JEWISH MUSEUM OF FLORIDA

Map pp48–9

☎ 305-672-5044; www.jewishmuseum.com; 301 Washington Ave; adult/senior & student $6/5, admission Sat free; ☷ 10am-5pm Tue-Sun, closed Jewish holidays

Housed in a 1936 Orthodox synagogue that served Miami's first congregation, this small museum chronicles the rather big contribution Jews have made to the state of Florida, especially this corner. After all, while Cubans made Miami, Jews made Miami Beach (p22), both physically (in a developer's sense) and culturally (in an 'anyone is welcome' attitude). Yet there were times when Jews were barred from the American Riviera they carved out of the sand, and this museum tells that story, along with some amusing anecdotes (such

top picks

SOUTH BEACH

- Ocean Drive at night
- Lincoln Road (p54)
- Wolfsonian-FIU (p50)
- Española Way Promenade (right)
- Bass Museum of Art (p51)

as seashell purim dresses). The mainstay is *Mosaic: Jewish Life in Florida,* a mosaic (imagine that) of photographs and historical bric-a-brac. Also notable is the complete whitewash the museum makes of gangster Meyer Lansky, architect of the modern Mafia, who retired to Miami Beach and comes off here as a nice old guy who always donated to his synagogue.

SOUTH POINTE PARK Map pp48–9
Closed for an overhaul when we visited, this small park at the southern tip of SoBe is getting a $22.3 million facelift into a kid-friendly promenade, with sand dune paths, arcing fountains, turtle-sensitive lighting that won't scare off nesting sea turtles and, ironically, a sculpture of an iceberg.

A1A Map pp48–9
A1A (5th Street)
Beachfront Avenue! Driving this causeway between Miami and Miami Beach, over the glittering turquoise of Biscayne Bay, with a setting sun behind you, enormous cruise ships to the side, the palms swaying in the ocean breeze and, let's just say 'Your Love' by the Outfield on the radio, is basically the essence of Miami. Just try it, and trust us.

ART DECO WELCOME CENTER
Map pp48–9
☎ 305-531-3484; 1001 Ocean Dr; ☼ 9am-7:30pm Mon-Sat, 9am-6:30pm Sun
To be honest, this 'welcome center' is a tatty gift shop. But it's located in the old beach patrol headquarters, one of the best deco buildings out there, and you can book some excellent $20 guided walking tours, which are some of the best introductions to the layout and history of South Beach on offer.

ESPAÑOLA WAY PROMENADE
Map pp48–9
Between 14th & 15th Sts, west of Washington Ave
Española Way is an 'authentic' Spanish promenade, in the Florida theme park spirit of authenticity. Whatever; it's a lovely, terracotta and cobbled arcade of rose pink and Spanish creamy architecture, perfect for art browsing (its original purpose was as an arts colony in the 1920s), window-shopping, people-watching and café sippin'. A craft market operates here on weekend afternoons.

MIAMI BEACH POST OFFICE
Map pp48–9
☎ 305-531-3763; 1300 Washington Ave
If you're going to send the family some corny postcards (of which there is no shortage), do so from this 1937 deco gem, the first South Beach renovation project tackled by preservationists in the '70s. This Depression moderne building in the 'stripped classic' style was constructed thanks to President Franklin D Roosevelt's Works Progress Administration (WPA), which supported unemployed artists during the Great Depression. On the exterior, note the bald eagle; inside, gaze at a beautifully restored painted paper ceiling and a large wall mural of the Seminole Wars.

OCEAN DRIVE Map pp48–9
Ocean Dr, 7th–19th Sts
Yar, here be the belly of the South Beach Beast. It's just a road, right? No, it's America's great cruising strip, an endless parade of classic cars, testosterone-sweating young men, peacock-y young women, street performers, vendors, those guys who yell unintelligible crap at everyone, celebrities pretending to be tourists, tourists who want to play celebrity, beautiful people, ugly people, people people and the best ribbon of deco preservation on the beach. Say 'Miami.' That image in your head? Probably the Drive.

PROMENADE Map pp48–9
Promenade 5th–15th Streets
This beach Promenade, a wavy ribbon sandwiched between the beach and Ocean Dr, extends from 5th to 15th Sts. A popular location for photo shoots, especially during crowd-free early mornings,

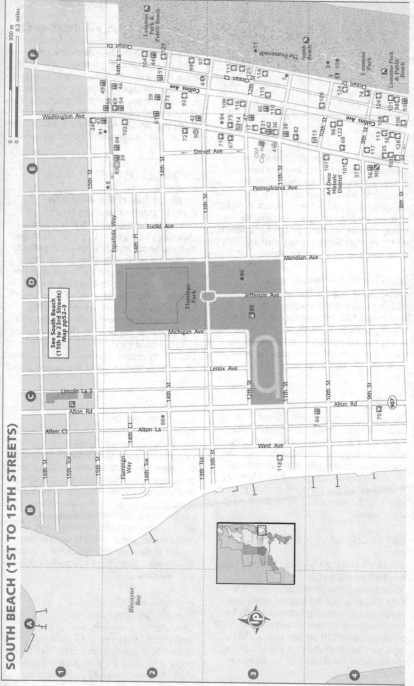

SOUTH BEACH (1ST TO 15TH STREETS)

lonelyplanet.com

NEIGHBORHOODS SOUTH BEACH (1ST TO 15TH STREETS)

48

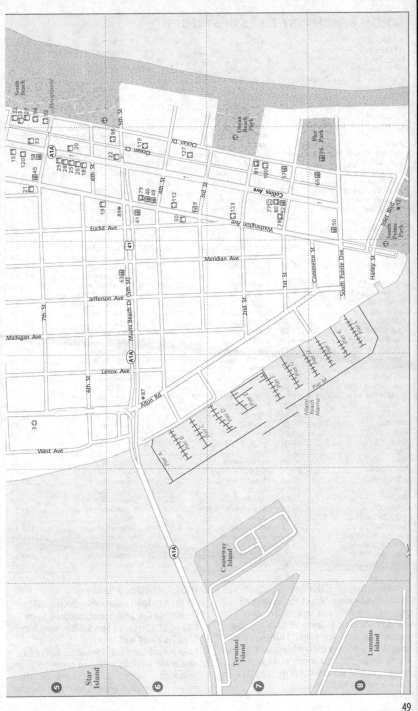

South Beach

Playground

South Beach

Ocean Beach Park

Pier Park

15

120

58

45

21

19

29
28
25
18
26

22

89

41

79
40
48

30

112

9

123

77
80
52
78

81
100

57

65

50

A1A

Euclid Ave

Meridian Ave

Jefferson Ave

Lenox Ave

West Ave

Michigan Ave

7th St

6th St

Alton Rd

87

3

41

A1A

63

Miami Beach Dr (5th St)

5th St

Washington Ave

Collins Ave

1st St

2nd St

Commerce St

South Pointe Dve

Hartley St

South Pointe Park

Pier Blvd

12

76

127

119

95

5th St

Ocean Dr

Ocean Ct

3rd St

4th St

6th St

Pier A

Pier B

Pier C

Pier D

Pier E

Pier F

Pier G

Pier H

Pier I

Pier J

Pier K

Pier M

Miami Beach Marina

Star Island

Causeway Island

Terminal Island

Lummus Island

5

6

7

8

SOUTH BEACH (1ST TO 15TH STREETS)

it's also a breezy, palm tree–lined conduit for in-line skaters, bicyclists, volleyball players (there's a net at 11th St), dog walkers, yahoos, locals and tourists. The beach that it edges, called Lummus Park, sports six floridly colored lifeguard stands. There's a public bathroom at 11th St; heads up, the sinks are a popular place for the homeless to bathe.

WOLFSONIAN-FIU Map pp48–9

☎ 305-531-1001; www.wolfsonian.org; 1001 Washington Ave; adult/senior, student & youth 6-18 yrs $7/5; ☺ noon-6pm Sat-Tue, noon-9pm Thu & Fri, closed Wed

Even folks bored stiff by rooms full of furniture will want to cultivate some aesthetic space after visiting this excellent design museum, which manages to chronicle the

WHEN CELEBRITY SPOTTING GOES GRIM

Casa Casuarina (Map pp48–9; 1116 Ocean Dr) is a bit macabre. Not in and of itself: on its own, the Casa is a gorgeous if gaudy mansion smack on South Beach. But people mainly come here to see where fashion designer Gianni Versace was gunned down (before shopping at, no kidding, a now-closed nearby Versace outlet).

Here's the history: Back in the 1930s the Casa was dubbed the Amsterdam Palace, modeled after the Governor's House in Santo Domingo, where Christopher Columbus' son kicked it. When Versace purchased the property in the 1980s, he locked horns with local preservationists after announcing plans to tear down a neighboring hotel so he could build a pool. The designer eventually won -- but the fight focused attention on loopholes in Miami Beach's Preservation Ordinance that were subsequently closed, an act that would save more than 200 other historic hotels.

None of it seemed important, though, in 1997, when stalker Andrew Cunanan gunned Versace down in front of his beloved mansion. Ironically, just as *Miami Vice*'s fake crime put Miami on the map for American tourists, the Versace shooting gave the Magic City big profile among distraught Euro fashionistas, who came here and decided to stay and tip poorly in cafés. Now the house attracts a steady stream of the morbidly curious, as well as members of some chi-chi members-only club that now occupies the site.

And at the time of research, there was a buzz about a new Versace Murder Walking Tour. Local Diego Caiola had begun offering a two-hour, $25 walking tour that traced Versace's life, and ended right where…well, you can guess. Apparently, it was to run three days a week and start at the News Café (p128).

interior evolution of everyday life architecturally manifested by SoBe's exterior deco. Which reminds us of the Wolfsonian's own facade. Remember the gothic-futurist apartment complex-cum-temple of evil in *Ghostbusters*? Well, this imposing structure, with its grandiose 'frozen fountain' and lion head–studded grand elevator, could serve as a stand-in for that set.

WORLD EROTIC ART MUSEUM
Map pp48–9

☎ 305-532-9336; www.weam.org; 1205 Washington Ave; admission $18, 18 yrs & over only; 11am-midnight

In a neighborhood where no behavior is too shocking, the WEAM screams, 'Hey! We have a giant golden penis!' Unfortunately, that's the problem. We'll sound like nerds as we analyze the historical merits of an old lady's smut collection (WEAM was founded by 70-year old Naomi Wilzig, who turned her 5000-piece erotica collection into a South Beach attraction in 2005), but the exhibits lack the context to be taken seriously. There's titillation (no pun intended) without education. In a way, the WEAM makes erotic art *less* accessible by reinforcing its giggle-provoking aspects and…you still with us? Oh fine, the big golden phallus is towards the exit.

15TH TO 23RD STREETS

The upper end of South Beach includes the pedestrian thoroughfare of Lincoln Rd and its associated shopping, eating and nightlife, plus clusters of 'neo' and renovated deco hotels.

BASS MUSEUM OF ART Map pp52–3

☎ 305-673-7530; www.bassmuseum.org; 2121 Park Ave; adult/senior & student $8/6; 10am-5pm Tue, Wed, Fri & Sat, 10am-9pm Thu, 11am-5pm Sun

The best art museum in Miami Beach has a playfully futurist facade, a crisp interplay of lines and bright white wall-space, like an Orthodox Church on a space-age Greek Isle. All designed, by the way, in 1930 by Russell Pancoast (grandson of John A Collins, who lent his name to Collins Ave). The collection isn't shabby either: permanent highlights range from 16th-century European religious works to Northern European and Renaissance paintings. The Bass forms one point of the Collins Park Cultural Center triangle, which also includes the three-story Miami City Ballet (p157) and the lovingly inviting Miami Beach Regional Library (which is a great place to pick up free wi-fi).

ARTCENTER/SOUTH FLORIDA
Map pp52–3

☎ 305-674-8278; www.artcentersf.org; 800 Lincoln Rd; 11am-10pm Mon-Wed, 11am-11pm Thu-Sun

Established in 1984 by a small but forward-thinking group of artists, this compound is a must, especially if you're looking to buy art on your trip. In addition to 52 artist studios (many of which are open to the public), ArtCenter offers a lineup of classes and lectures, and is home to a gallery where dynamic, inspired shows are the norm.

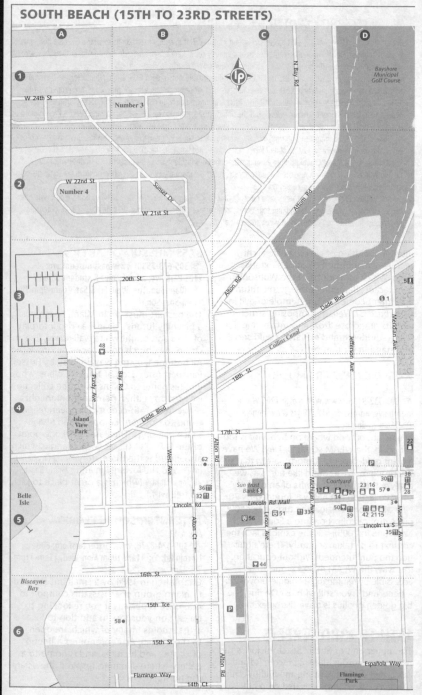

SOUTH BEACH (15TH TO 23RD STREETS)

lonelyplanet.com

NEIGHBORHOODS SOUTH BEACH (15TH TO 23RD STREETS)

Number 3

Number 4

W 24th St

W 22nd St

W 21st St

Sunset Dr

20th St

Alton Rd

Dade Blvd

Collins Canal

18th St

N Bay Rd

Alton Rd

Bayshore Municipal Golf Course

Dade Blvd

Jefferson Ave

Meridian Ave

5

1

48

Purdy Ave

Bay Rd

Island View Park

17th St

West Ave

Alton Rd

62

Sun Trust Bank

Lincoln Rd

36

32

Lincoln Rd Mall

56

51

33

Michigan Ave

Courtyard

13

14

27

23 16

50

39

42 21 15

30

57

3

38

28

22

Meridian Ave

Lincoln La S

35

Belle Isle

Alton Ct

Lenox Ave

Biscayne Bay

16th St

15th Tce

15th St

44

58

Flamingo Way

14th Ct

Alton Rd

Española Way

Flamingo Park

52

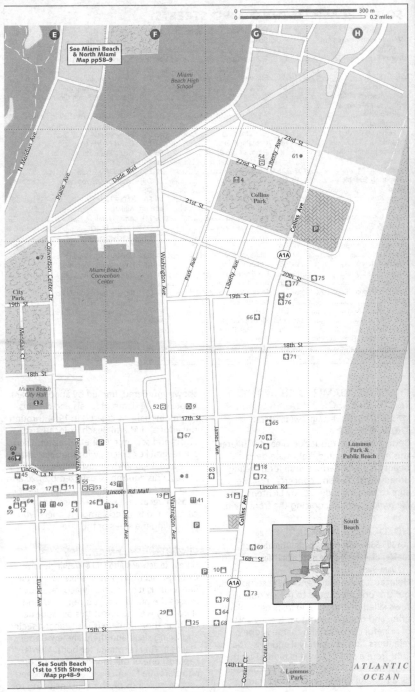

See Miami Beach & North Miami Map pp58–9

Miami Beach High School

23rd St

22nd St

54

61

4

21st St

Collins Park

Collins Ave

P

Convention Center Dr

7

Miami Beach Convention Center

Dade Blvd

Prairie Ave

N Meridian Ave

Washington Ave

Park Ave

Liberty Ave

A1A

20th St

77

75

City Park

19th St

19th St

47

76

Meridian Ct

66

18th St

18th St

Miami Beach City Hall

2

71

52

9

17th St

James Ave

65

67

70

74

Lummus Park & Public Beach

60

46

Lincoln La N

45

Pennsylvania Ave

P

63

8

18

72

49

17

11

55

53

43

Lincoln Rd Mall

19

41

31

Lincoln Rd

20

59

12

6

40

37

24

26

34

Drexel Ave

Washington Ave

Collins Ave

P

69

16th St

P

10

A1A

Euclid Ave

29

15th St

25

78

64

68

73

14th La

Ocean Ct

Ocean Dr

Lummus Park

South Beach

ATLANTIC OCEAN

See South Beach (1st to 15th Streets) Map pp48–9

0 — 300 m
0 — 0.2 miles

SOUTH BEACH (15TH TO 23RD STREETS)

FILLMORE MIAMI BEACH AT THE JACKIE GLEASON THEATER Map pp52–3

☎ 305-673-7300; www.gleasontheater.com;
1700 Washington Ave

Better known as the Jackie Gleason Theater, this newly renovated, light-blue deco beauty is a wonderful venue for traveling Broadway shows and concerts (p154). Be sure to take a gander at Roy Lichtenstein's *Mermaid* sculpture, gracing the front lawn

HOLOCAUST MEMORIAL Map pp52–3

☎ 305-538-1663; www.holocaustmmb.org;
cnr Meridian Ave & Dade Blvd; admission free;
⏱ 9am-9pm

Holocaust memorials tend to be somber, but this one, dedicated to the six million Jews killed during the *shoah*, is particularly grim, and doesn't seem to offer any sort of hopeful end note; the theme is one of relentless sadness, betrayal and loss. The light from a Star of David is blotted by the racist meme of 'Jude'; a family surrounded by a hopeful Anne Frank quote is later shown murdered, framed by another Frank quote on the death of ideals and dreams. The memorial was created in 1984 through the efforts of Miami Beach Holocaust survivors and sculptor Kenneth Treister. There are several key pieces, with the *Sculpture of Love and Anguish* the most visible to passersby. This enormous, oxidized bronze arm bears an Auschwitz tattooed number – chosen because it was never issued at the camp – and terrified camp prisoners who are scaling the sides of the arm.

LINCOLN ROAD MALL Map pp52–3

Lincoln Rd between Alton Rd & Washington Ave
Calling Lincoln Rd a mall is like calling Big Ben a clock; it's technically accurate but misses the point. Yes, you can shop, and shop very well here. But this outdoor pedestrian thoroughfare is really about seeing and being seen, and there are few better places in Greater Miami for both. Morris Lapidus, one of the founders of the loopy, neo-baroque Miami Beach style, designed several buildings on the Mall, including the

Lincoln Theatre (555 Lincoln Rd), Sterling Building (927 Lincoln Rd) and Colony Theater (1040 Lincoln Rd), which looks like the sort of place where gangsters go to watch *Hamlet*. There's an excellent farmers market (9am-7pm Sun) and an Antiques & Collectibles Market (9am-5pm every other Sun Oct-May).

MIAMI BEACH BOTANICAL GARDEN
Map pp52–3

☎ 305-673-7256; www.mbgarden.org; 2000 Convention Center Dr; admission free; 9am-5pm
More of a secret garden, this lush 4.5 acres of plantings flies under most people's radar. That's a shame, as the patch of green, operated by the Miami Beach Garden Conservancy, is an oasis of palm trees, flowering hibiscus plants and glassy ponds.

TEMPLE EMANU EL SYNAGOGUE
Map pp52–3

☎ 305-538-2503; www.tesobe.org; Washington Ave at 17th St
A deco synagogue? Not exactly, but the smooth bubbly dome and sleek, almost aerodynamic profile of this Conservative synagogue, established in 1938, fits right

in on SoBe's deco parade of moderne this and streamline that. Sabbath services are on Fridays at 6:30pm and Saturdays at 8:45am.

HOT HOTELS & NIGHTLIFE
Walking Tour
This walk takes you past (and through) some of the world's best hotel architecture and onto the shops and nightlife along Lincoln Rd. Set out as evening sets in and you'll likely spot a dose of the assorted celebutantes and mad, bad gorgeous types that make South Beach so very special.

1 Shore Club If you're lucky, you slept at the Shore Club (p176), in possibly the best designed rooms on the Beach. If not, walk in anyways

WALK FACTS
Start Shore Club (1901 Collins Ave)
End Buck 15 (707 Lincoln Rd)
Duration 1½ to two hours
Fuel Stop Presto Pizza

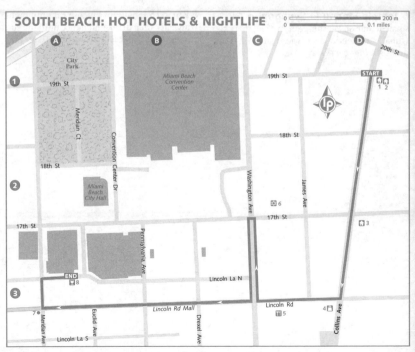

SOUTH BEACH: HOT HOTELS & NIGHTLIFE

and check out the immaculate Skybar (p146), including the oh-so-exclusive Red Room.

2 Surfcomber Proof that corporate chains can be a good thing, the Doubletree-owned Surfcomber (p178) has one of the best deco facades and interiors in America. Note the concrete 'eyebrows' on the exterior and the sleek movement-and-transportation inspired lines that characterize the lobby.

3 Delano Stroll right past the huge double doors of the Delano (p176) with all the attitude you can muster. Then humble yourself in possibly the coolest hotel lobby in the world. Contrast the ultra-modern vibe of the Delano to the old-school style of the Surfcomber and move on.

4 Wings Pop into this kitsch stop, an enormous emporium of tourism crap that is Wings (p110) and buy an obscene T-shirt.

5 Presto Pizza Stroll down the pedestrian Lincoln Road Mall and window shop (or actually buy stuff). If you're hungry, load up on a slice of NYC-style greasy goodness at Presto Pizza (p130).

6 Temple Emanu El Synagogue Take a small detour up Washington Ave and there's – whoa – a pseudo-deco synagogue (p55). You don't see *that* every day.

top picks

IT'S FREE!

- Strolling past the art deco hotels (p55), South Beach
- People-watching and window-shopping at Lincoln Road (p54), South Beach
- Taking A1A (p47) from Miami to Miami Beach
- Enjoying the scene at the Miami Beach Boardwalk (opposite)
- Catching the Metromover (p70)
- Browsing botanicas (p85)
- Wandering around the Wynwood & Design District Gallery Walk (p85) on a Saturday night
- Visiting the Cuban community in Calle Ocho (p87)
- Taking a peek at the grand and gorgeous Biltmore lobby (p99)

7 ArtCenter/South Florida Return to Lincoln Rd. At the southwest corner of the Meridian Ave–Lincoln Rd intersection you'll find ArtCenter/South Florida (p51), a maze of artists' open studios and gallery space that always has something cool on view.

8 Buck 15 Linger on Lincoln Rd until night truly falls, then drink and dance until the sun comes up at the excellent Buck 15 (p147) on Lincoln Lane.

Drinking & Nightlife p148; Eating p130; Shopping p115; Sleeping p179

Some people claim you can't find a good deli outside New York City. Some people think *chivitos* are unique to Uruguay.

Some people have not been north of 23rd St on the Beach.

Mind if we set the scene for you? First, take a wander up Indian Creek Ave, past one of Florida's largest Orthodox Jewish communities. The Jewish diaspora landed heavily here, and you look it in the face when a yarmulke-ed man drives past in a Jeep Cherokee, moving his ringlets out of his ears to chat on a cell phone. Then: 41st St, where kosher culture meets sushi stands and Chinese take-aways and, of course, births its own excellent pastrami on rye.

Jump 30 blocks north, past a Collins Ave canyon of condominiums and high-rise developments. The beach is still there, but you can't see it behind all that MiMo (Miami Modern) architecture, which is as muscle-y and overpowering as deco is sleek and subtle.

Now we're on 71st St, where chopped liver becomes *churrasco* and bagels make way for Buenos Aires. South America seems to have moved to this corner of North Miami Beach, and she's brought plenty of Argentines, Uruguayans, Columbians and all of their associated excellent cuisine and hospitality.

This is Miami Beach: less aggressively sexy than South Beach and much more inviting. People round here will call you 'hun' (or *havrim* or *hermano*, depending on where you are), and they'll mean it. And look – it's not like the quality of the South Beach lifestyle stops at Mid-Beach. Just a lot of the attitude that goes with it. So come up north, have some excellent corned beef or *cortadas* or Colombian hot dogs topped with whipped cream (seriously, see Puerto Sagua, p128). And guess what? You can still hit the sand afterwards (though you might want to wait a good half hour after eating that hot dog before swimming).

To get to Miami Beach by bus, take buses G, H, J, K, L, R, S, or T. To get here by car, Collins passes through all of these neighborhoods; Alton Rd runs north–south to the west of Indian Creek (cross between the two at 41st St).

top picks

MIAMI BEACH & NORTH MIAMI

- Boardwalk (below)
- Fontainebleau Hilton (p60)
- Haulover Beach Park (p61)
- Normandy Isle (p61)
- Arthur Godfrey Road (left)

MID-BEACH

ARTHUR GODFREY ROAD (41ST STREET) Map pp58–9

If the main shopping drag in Miami Beach were a movie, it might be titled *Jews in Paradise*. It's no *shetl*, but Arthur Godfrey Rd is a popular thoroughfare for Miami Beach Jews, and possibly the best place outside Manhattan to enjoy a good Reuben (and the only place outside Tel Aviv with kosher sushi houses). And just as Jews have shaped Miami Beach, so has the beach shaped its Jews: you can eat lox *y arroz con moros* (salmon with rice and beans) and while the Orthodox men don yarmulkes and the women wear headscarves, they've all got nice tans and drive flashy SUVs.

BOARDWALK Map pp58–9

What's trendy in beachwear this season? Seventeenth-century Polish gabardine coats, apparently. There are plenty of skimpy hotties on the mid-Beach boardwalk, which runs from 21st to 46th Sts, but sometimes it feels like there are even more Orthodox Jews going about their business in the midst of gay joggers, strolling tourists and preening sunbathers. Not too much preening though; Mid-Beach is more of a 'real' beach (ie people swim here). Speaking of local Jews, this part of Mid-Beach is within Miami Beach's Eruv (*eh-rev*). The what? Well, during the Sabbath, Orthodox Jews cannot engage in a lot of normal activities (such as carrying anything) outside their homes. The Eruv essentially expands the boundary of home to incorporate one of America's premier

MIAMI BEACH & NORTH MIAMI

INFORMATION	
Mount Sinai Medical Center	1 E8
Ocean View Post Office	2 F8

SIGHTS	(pp57–63)
African Heritage Cultural Arts Center	3 A7
Ancient Spanish Monastery	4 D1
Black Archives History & Research Center of South Florida	5 A7
Boardwalk	6 F8
Haulover Beach Park	7 F2
Liberty City	8 A7
Museum of Contemporary Art	9 C4
Normandy Isle	10 E5
Ocean Terrace	11 F5
Oleta River State Recreation Area	12 E2
Pelican Island	13 D6
Russian & Turkish Baths	14 F7

SHOPPING	(pp107–22)
Bal Harbour Shops	15 F4
Brioni	(see 15)
C Madeleine's	16 D3
Hiho Batik/Sprocket Gift Shop	(see 27)
Lalique	(see 15)
Lambda Passages Bookstore	17 C6
Mini Oxygene	(see 15)
Target	18 D3
Tiffany & Co	(see 15)

EATING	(pp123–40)
Bissaleh Café	19 F1
Café Prima Pasta	20 F5
Canela Café	21 C7
Dogma Grill	22 C6
El Rey Del Chivito	23 F5
Forge	24 F8
Karma Car Wash	25 C6
La Perrada De Edgar	26 F5
Michy's	27 C6
Mister Chopstick	28 F8
Norman's Tavern	29 F6
Sam's Deli & Grill	30 F8

Tamarind	31 E6
Tasti Café	32 F8
Timo's	33 F1
Uva 69	34 C6
Wine 69	35 C6
Wolfie Cohen's Rascal House	36 F1

DRINKING & NIGHTLIFE	(pp141–52)
Boteca	37 D6
Boy Bar	38 F5
Café Nostalgia	39 F8
Club Boi	40 B6

THE ARTS	
Chopin Foundation of the United States	41 E6
Chopin Foundation of the United States	42 E6

SPORTS & ACTIVITIES	(pp161–8)
Aquatic Rental Center and Sailing School	43 D6
Bird's Surf Shop	44 F2
Fantasy Water Sports	45 E1
Haulover Golf Course	46 F3
Haulover Marine Center	47 F2
Kelley Fleet	(see 46)
Urban Trails Kayak Rentals	48 F2

SLEEPING	(pp169–82)
Bay Harbor Inn & Suites	49 F4
Beach House Bal Harbour	50 F8
Circa 39	51 F8
Claridge Hotel	52 F8
Courtyard Hotel	53 F8
Eden Roc Resort	54 F7
Fontainebleau Hilton Hotel & Resort	55 F7
Indian Creek Hotel	56 F8
Palms South Beach	57 F8
Trump International Sonesta Beach Resort	58 F1

TRANSPORTATION	(pp239–43)
North Miami Bus Terminal	59 C2

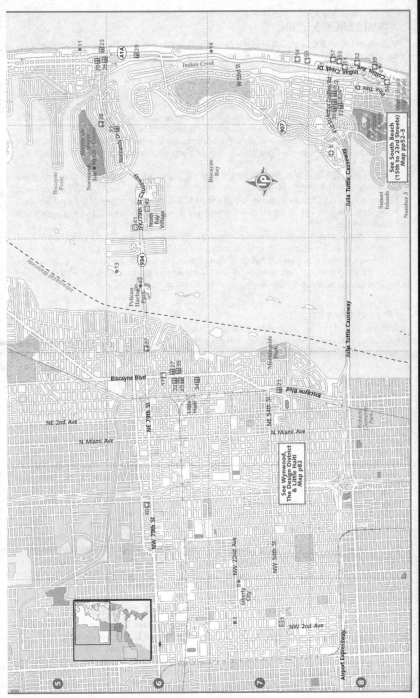

Indian Creek

W 53rd St

Biscayne Bay

Sunset Islands
Number 3

See South Beach
(15th to 23rd Streets)
Map pp52-3

Biscayne Point

Normandy
Shores

Normandy
Isle

Biscayne
Point

North
Bay
Village

NW 79th St

Biscayne Blvd

Little
Haiti

Pelican Harbour
Park

Morningside
Park

Roberto
Clemente
Park

See Wynwood,
The Design District
& Little Haiti
Map p82

NE 2nd Ave

NE 79th St

N Miami Ave

N Miami Ave

NW 79th St

NW 22nd Ave

NW 54th St

Liberty
City

NW 2nd Ave

Airport Expressway

Biscayne Blvd

Julia Tuttle Causeway

Intracoastal Waterway

Julia Tuttle Causeway

5

6

7

8

59

MIAMI BEACHES GUIDE

Miami Beach has perhaps the best city beaches in the country (take that, Honolulu). The water is relatively clear and warm, and the imported sand is relatively white. Beaches are wide, firm and long enough to accommodate the throngs. A whopping 12 miles from South Pointe to 192nd St (William Lehman Causeway), Miami Beach is said to have 35 miles of shoreline when taking into consideration Key Biscayne and the like. That's a lot of sand.

Like a large, accommodating restaurant, Miami's beaches are wordlessly zoned to provide everyone with what they want without offending anyone else. So if you find yourself somewhere where the people around you make you uncomfortable, just move a little further along the coast and you'll be fine. Topless bathing is legal in most places, a happy result of Miami Beach's popularity with Europeans and South Americans. Generally speaking, skimpy swimsuits seem to be the order of the day, which means you'll see plenty of thongs and other minuscule coverings on the bronzed gods and goddesses (though folks with traditional bathing suits will not feel out of place).

The most crowded beaches are from about 5th St to 21st St. You'll see lots of models posing for photo shoots between 6th and 14th Sts, also known as Glitter Beach. Weekends are usually more crowded than weekdays, but except during special events it's usually not too difficult to find a quiet spot, especially in the mid and upper beach. From 21st St to 46th St, the 1½-mile boardwalk is a nice way to see the beach without getting sand between your toes.

Don't forget to check out the funky, Ken Scharf–designed lifeguard tower at 10th St. Other good, locally designed lifeguard towers with a (can you guess?!) deco theme dot 5th to 14th St.

Elsewhere, notwithstanding weekend traffic snarls on the Rickenbacker Causeway, Key Biscayne (Map p92) has some 5 miles of primo sand in a relatively undeveloped, commercial-free zone that offer better views (of the city skyline) than the ocean-fronting experience on Miami Beach.

Family-Fun Beaches

Families go north of 21st St, especially the beach at 53rd St, with a playground and public toilets, as well as the dune-backed one around 73rd St. They also head south to Matheson Hammock Park (Map pp44–5), which has calm artificial lagoons. South Pointe Park (Map pp48–9) is being converted into a very kid-friendly pavilion with good sand access.

Surfing & Windsurfing Beaches

Look, this isn't Hawaii (you win this round, Honolulu!). If you see someone walking around with a board in South Beach, they are probably what some surfers gently deem, 'Big honking posers.' If you need waves, head north to Haulover

beaches; hence, all those Orthodox matrons going about their errands.

EDEN ROC RESORT Map pp58–9
4525 Collins Ave
This enormous place was the second groundbreaking resort from Morris Lapidus – the first was the Fontainebleau (below) – and it's a fine example of the architecture known as MiMo. It was the hangout for the 1960s Rat Pack – Sammy Davis Jr, Dean Martin, Frank Sinatra and crew – and at the time of research, was undergoing a major renovation into a resort-cum–convention center.

FONTAINEBLEAU HILTON HOTEL & RESORT Map pp58–9
4441 Collins Ave
How over the top is the Fontainbleau? Well, when Brian De Palma needed a place

to sign off *Scarface*, he decided this would be a good place for Al Pacino to snort a mountain of coke and slaughter an army of Colombians. Ya gotta be grand to warrant that kind of cinematography, and this iconic 1954 leviathan, another brainchild of Lapidus, is certainly that. Note the spectacular tromp l'oeil mural on the southern exterior, designed by Richard Hass and painted over an eight-week period by Edwin Abreu, the lagoonlike water park out back and the famous 'stairway to nowhere' in the massive lobby.

RUSSIAN & TURKISH BATHS Map pp58–9
☎ 305-867-8316; Castillo del Mar, 5445 Collins Ave; admission $22; ☿ noon-midnight
The Baths were being overhauled when we visited, but they should be open now, and will (hopefully) still be offering the best sort of spa experience: cleanse, cleanse, cleanse,

Beach Park (Map pp58–9) in Sunny Isles or as far south as you can. The breaks between 5th St and South Pointe can actually give pretty good rides (by Florida standards, like 2ft to 4ft). You'll want a longboard. Hobie Beach (also called Windsurfing Beach; Map p92) rules for windsurfing.

Swimming Beaches

What? You wanna swim? Head to 85th St in Surfside (Map pp58–9). It's devoid of high-rise condos and is watched by lifeguards. Or plonk yourself anywhere along the Mid-Beach Boardwalk (p57) or Haulover Beach Park (Map pp58–9).

Nude Beaches

Nude bathing is legal at Haulover Beach Park (Map pp58–9) in Sunny Isles. Head to the north end between the two northernmost parking lots. The area north of the lifeguard tower is predominantly gay; south is straight. Sex is not tolerated on these beaches. You'll get arrested if you're seen heading into the bushes.

Gay Beaches

A lesbian, gay, bisexual and transgender crowd traditionally hits the sand around 12th St, especially after the clubs close on Friday and Saturday. It's not like there's sex going on (there isn't – no big sand dunes); it's just a spot where gay men happen to congregate. Though outnumbered, lesbians gather here, too. Sunday afternoon volleyball at 4pm, after everyone has had a decent night's (morning's) sleep, is popular with fun-loving locals. With that said, there are no spots in Miami Beach where gay people aren't as welcome as everyone else.

Latino Beaches

Latino families, predominantly Cuban, congregate between 5th St and South Pointe (Map pp48–9). Topless bathing is unwise and can be considered offensive here.

Quiet Beaches

Despite the presence of families, it's pretty low-key up around 53rd St (Map pp58–9) and down at Matheson Hammock Park (Map pp44–5). Or try the spot near the municipal parking lot at around 46th St (just north of Eden Roc Resort), which is a sort of no-man's land on most afternoons.

without the glamour. Spend a few hours among soothing saunas, steam rooms and whirlpools and, for an extra fee, indulge in a massage or exfoliating salt scrub. You'll feel like jelly for the rest of the day.

NORTH BEACH TO SUNNY ISLES

HAULOVER BEACH PARK Map pp58–9

☎ 305-944-3040; 10,800 Collins Ave; per car $4; ☼ sunrise-sunset

Where are those tanned men in gold chains and speedos going? That would be the clothing-optional beach, hidden from condos, highway and prying eyes by vegetation at the north end of this 40-acre park. There's more to do here than get in the buff though; most of the beach is 'normal' and constitutes one of the nicer

spots for sand in the area (also note the colorful deco-ish shower 'cones'). Recreational boaters shouldn't miss Urban Trails Kayak Rentals (p164).

NORMANDY ISLE Map pp58–9

71st St west of Collins Ave

A few years ago Normandy Isle was dubbed Little Argentina, and it's still one of the best places outside Mendoza to people-watch with a *cortada* before digging into the sort of pasta and steak dishes the *gauchos* love so well. But today the Argentines compete with their neighbors, the Uruguayans, their rivals, the Brazilians, and even a big crop of Colombians for first place in the Normandy Isle ethnic enclave stakes. Not that there's tension; this is as prosperous and pleasant as Miami gets. On Saturday mornings the small village green hosts a lovely farmers market.

OCEAN TERRACE Map pp58–9
Beach between 73rd & 75th Sts
While this shopping strip along Collins is evocative of an old-Miami main street (note the colorful tile facade of Walgreens, formerly a Woolworths), the short Ocean Tce behind the dunes and along the beach evokes South Beach in miniature. You'll find quaint shops, oceanfront cafés, MiMo apartment buildings and a strong Argentine flavor.

OLETA RIVER STATE RECREATION AREA Map pp58–9
☎ 305-919-1846; 3400 NE 163rd St; per person $2, 2-4 people $4, plus per additional person over 4 yrs $1; ☙ 8am-sunset

Tequesta Indians were boating this rich estuary (our favorite body of water, by the way) as early as 500 BC, so you're just following in a long tradition if you paddle in a canoe or kayak. At almost 1000 acres, this is the largest urban park in the state and one of the best places in Miami to escape the maddening throng. Boat out to the local mangrove island, watch the eagles fly by, or just chill on the pretension-free beach.

NORTH MIAMI
ANCIENT SPANISH MONASTERY
Map pp58–9
☎ 305-945-1461; www.spanishmonastery.com; 16711 W Dixie Hwy; adult/child $5/2; ☙ 9am-5pm Mon-Sat, 2-5pm Sun

Miami is full of Spanish-style churches, but none with the soft cupolas and Moorish arches of the Episcopal Church of St Bernard de Clairvaux, which was actually built in 1141(!) in Segovia, Spain. In the 19th century the church was converted to a granary and eventually bought by newspaper tycoon William Randolph Hearst. He dismantled it and shipped it to the USA intending to reconstruct it, but construction was never approved and the church sat in boxes until a group of Miami developers purchased and reassembled it here. Now it's a popular oasis (especially for weddings, so call ahead), allegedly the oldest building in the Americas. The rare lambskin parchment books and telescopic stained-glass windows practically sweat

top picks

FOR KIDS

- Venetian Pool (p99)
- Miami Museum of Science & Planetarium (p96)
- Monkey Jungle (p106)
- Jungle Island (p105)
- Miami Children's Museum (p106)
- Miami Metrozoo (p106)
- Miami Seaquarium (p93)
- Historical Museum of Southern Florida (p69)
- Botanicas (p85) – be respectful!

history. Church services are held Sunday at 8am, 10:30am and noon, and a healing service on Wednesday at 10am.

LIBERTY CITY Map pp58–9
Liberty City, northwest of Downtown, is a misnomer. Made infamous by the Liberty City Riots in 1980 (p24), the area is poor and crime is higher than in other parts of the city (see Safety, p248). And, while plans exist to renovate the area by creating a village of cultural and tourist attractions, the prospects of that happening in the near future look doubtful. Whites, fearing 'black encroachment' on their neighborhoods, actually went so far as to build a wall at the then-border of Liberty City – NW 12th Ave from NW 62nd to NW 67th Sts – to separate their neighborhoods. Part of the wall still stands, at NW 12th Ave between NW 63rd and 64th Sts.

For information on Liberty City, Overtown and other areas significant to black history, contact the very helpful Black Archives History & Research Center of South Florida (Map pp58–9; ☎ 305-636-2390; 5400 NW 22nd Ave; ☙ 9am-5pm Mon-Fri, specific research projects 1-5pm) in the Caleb Center.

MUSEUM OF CONTEMPORARY ART
Map pp58–9
MoCA; ☎ 305-893-6211; www.mocanomi.org; 770 NE 125th St; adult/senior & student $5/3; ☙ 11am-5pm Tue-Sat, noon-5pm Sun, 11am-5pm & 7-10pm last Fri every month

Even though it's opened a satellite gallery in Wynwood (p83), you should still hike waaay up to North Miami to see the excellent collection at the main MoCA building. The sharp, geometric grounds are pleasurable enough, but even better are exhibitions from artists such as Jorge Pardo and Robert Moss and pieces on loan from institutions such as the Tate Modern in London.

PELICAN ISLAND Map pp58–9

On weekends you can take a short tootle over to itsy-bitsy Pelican Island on a free ferry from the JFK Causeway west of North Bay Village, about 2 miles west of 71st St in Miami Beach. It's a pleasant little beach spot to unpack a picnic and peer at dozens of congregating pelicans.

ETHNIC ENCLAVE DRIVE
Walking & Driving Tour

Miami Beach consists of several walkable ethnic enclaves separated by longish driving distances. You'll be strolling and hitting the wheel on this tour, which takes you through the heart of the Beach's main Jewish and South American neighborhoods.

1 Circa 39 Park in the metered lot across the street and take a look at the modish, Patrick Kennedy–designed lobby of Circa 39 (p148), one of the coolest spaces in Miami (north, south or mid) Beach.

2 Indian Creek Take a quick walk up Indian Creek Dr to 41st St. To your left is the pretty creek itself. On your right are condos inhabited by older Orthodox Jews, many of whom converse in Yiddish.

3 Boardwalk Head back to your car, but not before checking out the odd juxtaposition of Orthodox matrons and skinny model types sharing space on the Mid-Beach Boardwalk (p57).

WALK FACTS

Start Circa 39 (3900 Collins Ave)
End Café Prima Pasta (414 71st St)
Duration 1½ to two hours
Fuel Stop El Rey del Chivito

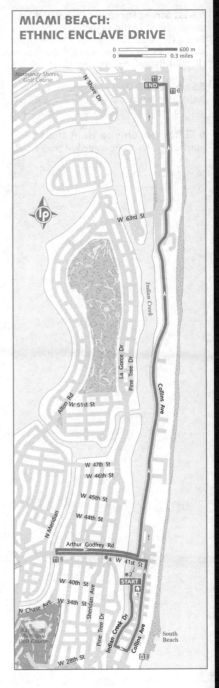

MIAMI BEACH: ETHNIC ENCLAVE DRIVE

4 41st Street Put pedal to metal and head up to 41st St (Arthur Godfrey Rd), Miami Beach's Jewish main street. Park in the garage on Sheridan Ave and check out all the Judaica shops, delis and, yes, kosher sushi spots.

5 Sam's Deli & Grill Pick up some delicious bagels for breakfast at bustling Sam's Deli & Grill (p131), one of the best delis in Greater Miami.

6 El Rey del Chivito Heart attack time. Forget that feast you nailed at Sam's Deli & Grill and drive up to El Rey del Chivito (p132), eat the signature Uruguayan *chivito* sandwich (steak, ham, fried egg, French fries) and die.

7 Café Prima Pasta More food? Not really. Just walk across Collins Ave, sit down at Café Prima Pasta (p131) and grab an espresso. In three quick drives you've interacted with Jews, Argentines and Uruguayans. Now digest that *chivito* and head to Mt Sinai Medical Center.

Drinking & Nightlife p148; Eating p133; Shopping p116; Sleeping p180

Miami's urban core is bright and shiny, crack-laced and dangerous, a Performing Arts Center like no other on one end, a great library on the other, and a city center fighting urban blight throughout. It's worth a visit, anyways.

This is where Miami, the city, goes to work and runs itself. To be frank, it could do a better job of it (and it's trying). The urban dichotomies are many and stark; office workers and the homeless, glass skyscrapers and gunked-out alleyways. But behind this yin-yang surface is a city center that lends itself – and rewards – thorough exploration.

The Miami River still smells a bit like mangrove mud and seediness, while Brickell Key glitters like a fist of steely style and exclusivity. Bayfront Park beckons you (and lots of office workers) to take a siesta, and in between the hot dog stalls and ratty motels west of Biscayne are gut-busting Latin buffets. Best of all is the Miami Cultural Center (p70), an oasis of, well, culture in the heart of Downtown.

The north edge of Downtown shifts into Overtown, one of the oldest, poorest and blackest neighborhoods in the city. In its day, Overtown was the pulse of Miami's black community, but when desegregation opened up housing opportunities for successful blacks in other parts of the city, a long rot set in. A never-ending series of government proposals aimed at improving this broken part of town has barely begun to scrub the dirt off the edges, and even the relentless tide of gentrification seems frozen by Overtown's poverty, as if the condos had bumped into an invisible wall. The thin silver lining to this very dark cloud: thanks to cheap rents, some of Miami's best clubs and nightspots have opened in the median area between Overtown and Downtown, centered near North Miami Ave and NE 14th St.

Downtown is laid out in an easy to navigate grid. Flagler St is one of the main east–west drags and NE 2nd Ave is a major north–south conduit. Brickell Ave runs south to Coconut Grove along the water, while the Miami River divides Downtown into north and south and is crossed by the Brickell Ave Bridge. In the east, Biscayne Blvd runs north from the river, and Brickell Ave runs south from it.

To get to Downtown Miami by train, get the Metromover, Metrorail to Brickell Memorial or Government Center. Take buses 2, 3, 8, 6, 7, 9, 77, 95, K, or T. To get here by car from South Beach, the MacArthur Causeway leads you right into Downtown. From further away, I-95 has several downtown exits. From southern Miami, follow Brickell Ave, and from northern Miami, follow NE 2nd Ave or Biscayne Blvd.

top picks

DOWNTOWN MIAMI

- Adrienne Arsht Center for the Performing Arts (left)
- Historical Museum of Southern Florida (p69)
- Miami Riverfront (p70)
- Metromover (p70)
- Brickell Key (p69)

BAYFRONT & AROUND

ADRIENNE ARSHT CENTER FOR THE PERFORMING ARTS Map pp66–7

☎ 305-949-6722, 786-468-2000; www.arshtcenter .org; 1300 Biscayne Blvd; Metromover Omni

The second-largest performing arts center in America is Miami's beautiful, beloved baby, and a major component of Downtown's urban equivalent of a facelift and several regimens of botox. Designed by Cesar Pelli (the man who brought you Kuala Lumpur's Pertonas Towers), the center has two main components, the Ziff Ballet Opera House and Knight Concert Hall, which span both sides of Biscayne Blvd. The venues are connected by a thin, elegant pedestrian bridge, while inside the theaters there's a sense of ocean and land sculpted by wind; the rounded balconies rise up in spirals that resemble a sliced open seashell. It took five years and a *lot* of money to get the Arsht Center open and running, but now (most) everyone loves it, including big name performers from around the world, particularly Latin America.

DOWNTOWN MIAMI

INFORMATION	
British Consulate	1 E7
Canadian Consulate	2 E5
Downtown Miami Welcome Center	(see 46)
Greater Miami & the Beaches Convention & Visitors Bureau	3 E6
Miami Police Department	4 E4

SIGHTS	(pp65–70)
American Airlines Arena	5 E3
Bayfront Park	6 E4
Bayfront Park Amphitheater	7 E4
Brickell Ave Bridge	8 E5
Brickell Key	9 F6
Challenger Memorial	10 E5
Dade County Courthouse	11 D4
Federal Courthouse	12 D4
Freedom Tower	13 E3
Historical Museum of Southern Florida	14 C4
JFK Torch of Friendship	15 E4
Miami Art Museum	(see 14)
Miami Sky Lift	16 E4
Miami-Dade Community College	17 D3
Old US Post Office	18 D4
South End Amphitheater	19 E5

SHOPPING	(pp123–22)
Bayside Marketplace	20 E3
Historical Museum of Southern Florida Gift Shop	(see 14)
Macy's	21 D4
Seybold Building	22 D4
Wallflower Gallery	(see 49)

EATING	(pp123–40)
Azul	(see 54)
Big Fish	23 D6
Café Sambal	24 E5
Capital Grille	25 E4
Emily's Restaurante	26 C7
Fresco California	27 B4

Granny Feelgoods	28 D4
Jamaica International Café	29 D4
La Moon	30 D6
Mini Healthy Deli	31 D4
Pasha's	32 D7
Porção	33 E6

DRINKING & NIGHTLIFE	(pp141–52)
Bahia	(see 53)
Casino Princesa	34 E4
Karu & Y	35 D1
Level 25	(see 52)
M Bar	36 F6
Pawn Shop	37 E4
PS 14	38 D2
Space	39 D2
Studio A	40 D2
Tobacco Road	41 D6
Transit Lounge	42 D6
White Room	43 D2

See Wynwood, the Design District & Little Haiti Map p82

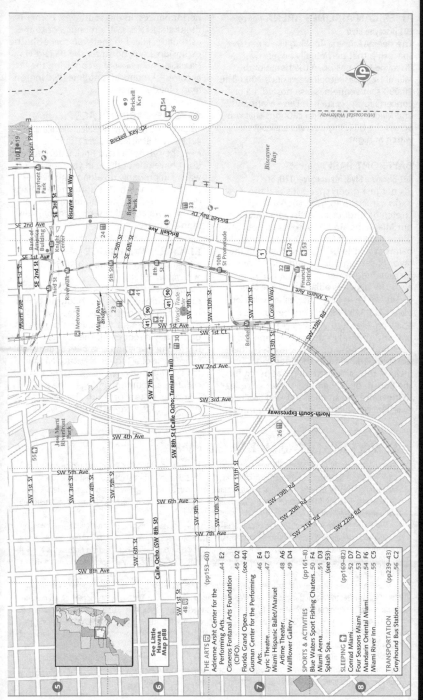

See Little
Havana
Map p88

THE ARTS 🎭	(pp153–60)
Adrienne Arsht Center for the	
Performing Arts........................	44 E2
Cisneros Fontanal Arts Foundation	
(CIFO)..	45 D2
Florida Grand Opera.................	(see 44)
Gusman Center for the Performing	
Arts..	46 E4
Lyric Theatre..............................	47 C3
Miami Hispanic Ballet/Manuel	
Artime Theater........................	48 A6
Wallflower Gallery.....................	49 D4

SPORTS & ACTIVITIES	(pp161–8)
Blue Waters Sport Fishing Charters..	50 F4
Miami Arena...............................	51 D3
Splash Spa..................................	(see 53)

SLEEPING 🛏	(pp169–82)
Conrad Miami.............................	52 D7
Four Seasons Miami....................	53 D7
Mandarin Oriental Miami...........	54 F6
Miami River Inn..........................	55 C5

TRANSPORTATION	(pp239–43)
Greyhound Bus Station...............	56 C2

AMERICAN AIRLINES ARENA Map pp66–7
601 Biscayne Blvd
The sleek AA Arena, looking like a massive spaceship that perpetually hovers over Biscayne Bay, has been the home of the Miami Heat basketball team since 2000. The 20,000-seat venue has also hosted major concerts for folks such as Dave Matthews and Madonna. The neon captions that run across the building's curves are cool to watch at night.

BAYFRONT PARK Map pp66–7
301 Biscayne Blvd; Metromover 11th St
It's not just green space: it's teal too. Few parks can claim to front such a lovely stretch of turquoise (ie Biscayne Bay), but Miamians are lucky like that. Lots of office workers catch quick naps under the palms at a little beach that does you the favor of setting out 'sit and chill' chairs for watching water and not a hell of a lot else. The beach is adjacent to the Miami Sky Lift (☎ 305-444-0422; http://miamiskylift.com; adult/child $15.89/8.88; 🕑 11am-7pm, to 10pm Fri & Sat), an 'elevated viewing platform (ie balloon) that takes up to 30 people on a 15-minute photo op over the city. Other notable park features (besides vagrants) include the Amphitheater, a great perch for the Fourth of July and New Year's Eve festivities, and the smaller 200-seat South End Amphitheater, which hosts free springtime

performances. In the southwest corner is the Challenger Memorial, a monument to the astronauts killed in the 1986 space-shuttle explosion. Look north for the JFK Torch of Friendship and a fountain recognizing the accomplishments of longtime US congressman Claude Pepper.

BAYSIDE MARKETPLACE Map pp66–7
☎ 305-577-3344; www.baysidemarketplace.com; 401 Biscayne Blvd; Metromover 11th St
Hey, they've got a Hard Rock Café. Bet you don't have one of those in your town…no, wait, you probably do along with everything else in this mall. But the marketplace does face the bay, making this at least one of the more attractive semi-outdoor malls in the country.

BRICKELL AVE BRIDGE Map pp66–7
Brickell Ave between SW 4th & SE 5th Sts; Metromover 5th St
Miami Vice wasn't all exaggeration; drug-runners zipped under this bridge in power boats during a high speed chase with DEA (Drug Enforcement Administration) agents on the day it reopened. The bridge crosses the Miami River, and cars pass under a 17ft bronze statue of a Tequesta warrior and his family, which sits perched atop the Pillar of History, a column that details the pre-European history of South Florida. Note that due to the aggressive traffic you'll

---

WE BUILT THIS CITY! (ON MUSEUMS & PARKS)

Miami's downtown has always been the ugly stepsister to the tourist-magnet beaches. Critics (with some justification) attack the sharp dichotomies between high office buildings and dead blocks of shuttered shopfronts, and say the downtown grid lacks a cohesive pedestrian-friendly center. At the same time, designers (with perhaps less justification) say the elevated Miami-Dade Cultural Center's Spanish-style compound is publicly inaccessible because of its perch on high concrete foundations.

To reverse these twin perceptions, the city of Miami has decided to hedge its bets on the grand re-imagining, re-building and re-opening of two of its main museums: the Miami Art Museum (p70) and Miami Museum of Science (p96). The two institutions will occupy what is currently abandoned Bicentennial Park, turning this swathe of dried out green space into (everyone hopes) a showcase for two world-class yet distinctly Miami museums in a distinctly Miami setting.

It's an ambitious idea, but it seems worthy too; rather than using unchecked condo lots to resurrect Downtown, Miami wants to let the arts and sciences take a crack at performing the facelift. And blueprints for the new art museum look incredible: a series of 'floating' exhibits, seemingly unconnected to the ground, will rise out of a tropical hammock (forest), supported by 'living pillars' – columns enveloped in local plantlife. These green supports and their shade, plus the wind off Biscayne Bay, will provide a natural cooling mechanism for museum goers. In addition, the relocation of the museum will allow it to redefine (and expand) on its permanent collection.

The whole plan sounds like it will involve a lot of money and more hope. But the Arsht Center faced the same odds. We hope, in 2010, when the new art museum is set to open (the science museum will open in 2011), we can say Miami took the right step towards revitalization when it put its money on the museums.

inevitably be driving in, it can be tough to appreciate the bridge from your car; you may want to walk here to get a sense of the sculptures.

BRICKELL KEY Map pp66–7
At SW 8th St
This island looks like a floating porcupine with condos for quills, and is worth visiting to get a scary glimpse of a world where real estate barons rule unopposed. To live the life of Miami glitterati, come here, pretend you belong, and head into a patrician hangout such as the Mandarin Oriental Hotel (p180), whose lobby and intimate M Bar (p149) afford sweeping views of Biscayne Bay.

WEST OF BRICKELL

CISNEROS FONTANAL ARTS FOUNDATION (CIFO) Map pp66–7
☎ 305-455-3380; www.cifo.org; 1018 N Miami Ave; Metromover 11 St
CIFO is one of the best spots in Miami to catch the work of contemporary Latin American artists, and has a pretty impressive showroom to boot. Even the exterior blends post-industrial rawness with a lurking, natural ambience, offset by the extensive use of Bisazza tiles to create an overarching tropical motif. Similar to the Arsht Center, CIFO was built near the rattier edge of Downtown with the intention of revitalizing this semi-blighted area via fresh arts spaces.

DADE COUNTY COURTHOUSE
Map pp66–7
73 W Flagler St; Metromover Government Center
If you end up on trial here, at least you'll get a free tour of one of the most imposing courthouses in America. When Miami outgrew its first courthouse (see Old US Post Office, p70), it moved legal proceedings to this neoclassical icon, built between 1925 and 1929 for $4 million. It's a very…appropriate building; if structures were people, the courthouse would *definitely* be a judge. Some useless trivia: back in the day, the top nine floors served as a 'secure' prison, from which more than 70 prisoners escaped.

FREEDOM TOWER Map pp66–7
600 Biscayne Blvd; Metromover Freedom Tower
The 'Ellis Island of the South' served as an immigration processing center for almost

half a million Cuban refugees in the 1960s. Placed on the National Register of Historic Places in 1979, it was also home to the *Miami Daily News* for 32 years. The top facade is one of two surviving area towers modeled after the Giralda bell tower in Spain's Cathedral of Seville – the second is at the Biltmore Hotel (p99) in Coral Gables.

GUSMAN CENTER FOR THE PERFORMING ARTS/OLYMPIA THEATER Map pp66–7
☎ 305-577-3344; www.gusmancenter.org; 174 E Flagler St; Metromover Knight Center
The Arsht Center is modernly pretty, but the Olympia is a one-of-a-kind classic. You know how the kids in Hogwarts can see the sky through their dining hall roof? Well the Olympia recreates the whole effect sans Dumbledore, using 246 twinkling stars and clouds cast over an indigo-deep, sensual shade of a ceiling. The theater first opened in 1925; today the lobby serves as the Downtown Miami Welcome Center, doling out helpful visitor information and organizing tours of the historic district; at night you can still catch a range of theater and music performances (also see p156).

HISTORICAL MUSEUM OF SOUTHERN FLORIDA Map pp66–7
☎ 305-375-1492; www.hmsf.org; 101 W Flagler St; adult/child 6-12 yrs/senior $8/5/7, admission free Sun; ☽ 10am-5pm Mon-Sat, noon-5pm Sun, 10am-9pm 3rd Thu of every month; Metromover Government Center
It takes a special kind of history to create the idiosyncratic character of a place such as South Florida, and it takes a special kind of museum to capture that narrative. This place, located in the Miami-Dade Cultural Center, does just that, weaving together the stories of the region's successive waves of population, from Native Americans to Nicaraguans. It's particularly interesting for kids. The next door Miami-Dade Public Library is a lovely escape from Downtown's bustle. And if you've got the time, book a tour with Dr Paul George, Florida native, author and eccentric history buff, for a historical peek under the ultra-modern skin of this city. See Al Capone's house, cruise the rum runner routes or go back further to Tequesta times; call

☎ 305-375-1621 or email historictours@hmsf.org for more info. Tours generally run between $25 and $42.

LYRIC THEATRE Map pp66–7

☎ 305-358-1146; 819 NW 2nd Ave

Hallowed names such as Duke Ellington and Ella Fitzgerald once walked across the Lyric stage when it was major stop on the 'Chitlin' Circuit,' the black live entertainment trail of pre-integration America. But as years passed both the theater and the neighborhood it served, Overtown, fell into dysfunctional disuse. Then the Black Archives History & Research Center of South Florida (Map pp58–9; ☎ 305-636-2390; www.theblackarchives.org; 5400 NW 22nd Ave) kicked in $1.5 million for renovations and overhauled everything. The phoenix reopened its doors in 1999 to appreciative neighbors, civic leaders and entertainers alike. A 2003 expansion feels a little too modern when juxtaposed with the Lyric's elegant early-20th century exterior, but it's shiny, we guess.

METROMOVER Map pp66–7

This elevated, electric monorail is hardly big enough to serve the mass transit needs of the city, and has become something of a tourist attraction and occasional commuting tool. Because it's free, Metromover has also become a hangout for the homeless, making the monorail an interesting place to gain insights into both the exterior and interior (and grittier) character of the city.

MIAMI ART MUSEUM Map pp66–7

MAM; ☎ 305-375-3000; www.miamiartmuseum.org; 101 W Flagler St; adult/child under 12 yrs/senior & student $5/free/2.50, admission free Sun; ☺ 10am-5pm Tue-Fri, noon-5pm Sat & Sun, noon-9pm 3rd Thu of every month; Metromover Government Center

Also within the Miami-Dade Cultural Center, this museum is ensconced in spectacular Philip Johnson–designed digs. Without a permanent collection, its fine rotating exhibits concentrate on post-WWII international art. In 2010 MAM will be moving to a new waterfront location at Bicentennial Park (p68); the future of the current location is up in the air, but both the library and historical society have expressed interest in moving into the space.

MIAMI-DADE COMMUNITY COLLEGE Map pp66–7

☎ 305-237-3696; 300 NE 2nd Ave; admission free; ☺ 10am-6pm Mon-Fri; Metromover College/Bayside

Though the college itself isn't very exciting, there are two art galleries with rotating exhibitions at the Wolfson Campus of the Miami-Dade Community College. Both the 3rd-floor Centre Gallery and 5th-floor Frances Wolfson Gallery often have photography shows.

MIAMI RIVER Map pp66–7

For a taste of a seedy old Florida that reeks of Humphrey Bogart in shirt sleeves and a fedora, come to the lazy, sultry and still kinda spicy Miami River. Just don't be reckless; the aura of seediness isn't artificial, and there are some areas where you don't want to be alone and on foot. Much of the shore feels abandoned, and is lined with makeshift warehouses, where you-can-only-imagine-what is loaded and unloaded onto small tugboats bound for you-can-only-imagine-where.

OLD US POST OFFICE Map pp66–7

100 NE 1st St; ☺ 9am-5pm Mon-Fri; Metromover College North

Constructed in 1912, this post office and county courthouse served as the first federal building in Miami. The building, with its elaborate doors and carved entryways, was purchased in 1937 to serve as the country's first savings and loan (and ergo, the core of the industry that would fund Miami's skyline). Government prosecutors moved into the adjacent Federal Courthouse and Federal Justice Building. Today you can visit the old courthouse to check out Denman Fink's 1940 mural Law Guides Florida Progress in the main courtroom on the 2nd floor.

TOBACCO ROAD Map pp66–7

☎ 305-374-1198; 626 S Miami Ave; ☺ 11:30am-5am Mon-Sat, 1pm-5am Sun; Metromover 8th St

Just south of the Miami River Bridge, Tobacco Road proudly reminds you its liquor license was the first one issued in a city that loves its mojitos. The Road has been here since the 1920s when it was a Prohibition-era speakeasy; today it's a decent (if slightly touristy) place to order a drink or listen to live music. Film buffs may recognize it as the place where Kurt Russell has a drink in The Mean Season (1985).

METROMOVER RIDE
Public Transportation Tour

Downtown Miami's driverless Metromover – a one-car train that glides over the city – is a strange creature. But using it to sightsee feels safer than pounding the occasionally crumbling pavement. Plus, it's free! Which is why the monorail tends to attract an odd crowd of businessmen, vagrants – and you.

1 College/Bayside Station Start your trip at the College/Bayside Station, which is a short walk from the metered parking along Biscayne Blvd. Board the northbound Brickell Outer Loop. Settle next to that friendly crack addict or corporate lawyer and notice how every other building seems to be under construction – cranes are everywhere, and there are plenty of half-toppled edifices.

2 Freedom Tower There's plenty of buildings intact along the way, including the spectacularly ornate yellow Freedom Tower (p69), a 1924 Mediterranean Revival structure that housed the *Miami Daily News* for 32 years and became a processing station for Cuban exiles in the 1960s.

3 American Airlines Arena Just beyond, perched on the edge of the bay, sits the sprawling American Airlines Arena (p68), home of the Miami Heat basketball team.

4 Arsht Center To your left from Omni Station is the newest apple of Miami's eye, the stunning Arsht Center (p65), the second-biggest performing arts center in the nation. Note the massive double theaters, like giant seashells washed on Downtown's shore.

5 Miami-Dade Cultural Center When you get to Government Center station, get off and have a walk around the Miami-Dade Cultural Center, home to the Miami Art Museum (opposite), excellent city library and Historical Museum of Southern Florida (p69). From here you can also see the 1928 Dade County Courthouse (p69), which looks like it inspired George Orwell's *1984* government ministries.

6 Coppertone Sign Keep your eyes peeled for a dog pulling the pants off a little girl. Er, not the real thing, an advertisement: the Concord Building and its famed neon Coppertone sign, which was preserved and brought here by the Dade Heritage Trust.

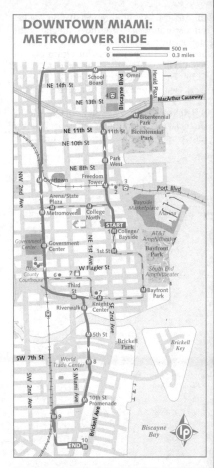

DOWNTOWN MIAMI: METROMOVER RIDE

RIDE FACTS

Start College/Bayside Metromover station
End Financial District
Time About 50 minutes

7 Macy's & Bank of America Building Next, in quick succession, is the site of the original Burdines, now a Macy's (p116) department store (remodeled into its current streamline look in 1936); and the ultramodern Bank of America Building, whose spherical tower adds a beautiful blue glow to the night skyline.

8 Eighth Street Station At Eighth Street Station, have a peek out the door. The city's 'Art en Route' public arts initiative is to thank for a two-fold sculpture installation – a ceramic royal palm tree at the south end of the station and the *Portón de Sentimientos* (Gate of Sentiments) at the north, which features door handles of red tile to mark the gateway to Calle Ocho. The artist, local ceramicist Carlos Alves, works with found objects and broken tiles.

9 Brickell Station As you head towards the financial district, the glass jungle gets thicker and wilder and the corporate types more ubiquitous. There's still art about, though; at Brickell Station, artist Connie Lloveras has created *Reaching for Miami Skies,* a concave ceiling mural of colorful, hand-formed ceramic tiles.

10 Financial District The ride ends among the sky-high towers of the Financial District. If you don't want to stick around here, just board the next Metromover car and ride back to Bayside Station and the start of the tour.

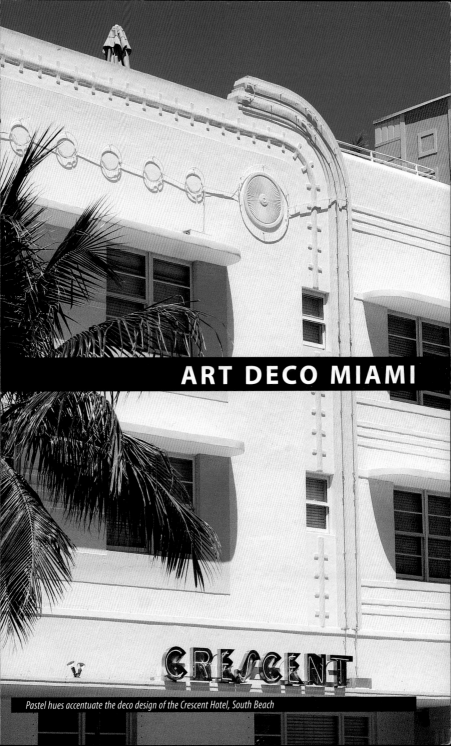

ART DECO MIAMI

Pastel hues accentuate the deco design of the Crescent Hotel, South Beach

For years now, south Miami Beach – also known as 'South Beach' for those of you who've been living with the Yanomamo – has been 'hot,' in the shrieking, Paris Hilton-induced, awe-of-celebrity sense of the word, and it owes this cachet to two words: Art Deco. The early-20th-century school of design was the aesthetic backbone of old South Beach, and the driving force of its 1980s resurrection. A sustained campaign to preserve the wonderful deco hotels of Miami Beach provided what tons of tourism brochures could never create: brand. Sun, sand, surf: a lot of cities can lay claim to them. But it was deco that first made Miami Beach distinctive, and when the celebs find a new spot to act sexy, it will (hopefully) be deco that remains: the signature, sleek face of the American Riviera.

The end of WWI in 1918 ushered in an era of increased interest in the romance and glamour of travel, which lasted well into the 1930s. There was a giddy fascination with speed and cars, ocean liners, trains and planes. Not coincidentally, the US post-industrial revolution, concerned

top picks

CLASSICAL DECO SOUTH BEACH STRUCTURES

- **Cardozo Hotel** (p172) Owned by Gloria Estefan, this lovely building and the Carlyle were the first hotels rescued by the original Miami Design Preservation League.
- **Essex House Hotel** (p175) Porthole windows lend the feel of a grand cruise ship, while its spire is rocket ship all the way.
- **Century Hotel** (p172) A standout of the tropical deco genre, the Greek-island white Century captures both the futurism-meets-cubism vibe of the style with the coziness of boutique lodging.
- **Carlyle Hotel** (1250 Ocean Dr) Comes with futuristic styling, triple parapets, a *Jetsons* sort of vibe and some cinematic cachet: *The Birdcage* was filmed here.
- **Jerry's Famous Deli** (p128) Housed in the Hoffman Cafeteria Building, this spacious 1939 Henry Hohauser gem has a front that looks like the prow of a Buck Rogers–inspired sea ship breaking through the waves of Collins Ave. The carved owls on the roof are meant to scare off pigeons (and their poo).

Jerry's Famous Deli (p128) lights up South Beach with its classical art deco lines

with mass production, kicked into high gear. New materials such as aluminum, polished bronze and stainless steel were utilized in new and exciting ways. Americans began looking to the future, and they wanted to be on the cutting edge.

Meanwhile, in Europe, at a 1925 Paris design fair officially called the Exposition Internationale des Arts Décoratifs et Industriels Modernes (and eventually abbreviated to Arts Deco), decorative arts were highlighted, but the US had nothing to contribute. Europeans were experimenting with repeating patterns in cubism and were influenced by ancient cultures (King Tut's tomb was discovered in 1921), and Americans had to play catch-up.

Back in the States, a mere year later, a devastating hurricane blew through Miami Beach, leaving few buildings standing. The wealthy folks who were living here before the hurricane chose to decamp. The second blow of a one-two punch for Miami's economy was delivered by the Great Depression. But in this dark time, opportunity soon came knocking. In Miami real estate, everything was up for grabs. The clean slate of the South Florida coastline was practically begging for experimentation.

Hotel rebuilding began in Miami Beach at the rate of about 100 per year during the 1930s. Many architects had 40 to 50 buildings in production at any one time until the inception of WWII. This overlapped with a surge in middle-class tourism between 1936 and 1941, when visitors started coming for a month at a time.

The post-Depression era was an optimistic time, with hopes and dreams pinned on scientific and technological revolutions. Reverence for machines took on almost spiritual dimensions, and found its aesthetic expression in both symbolic and functional ways.

What does all this have to do with architecture? Everything. The principles of efficiency and streamlining translated into mass-produced, modest buildings without superfluous ornamentation – at least in the northeast USA.

Miami Beach, a more romantic and glamorous resort, developed what came to be known

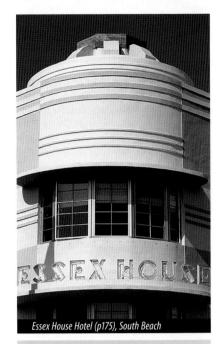

Essex House Hotel (p175), South Beach

CLASSIC TROPICAL DECO

There are some unifying themes to classical deco structures that are easy enough to spot with a discerning eye. Perhaps most noticeable is a sense of streamlined movement, exemplified by rounded walls, racing-stripe details and 'eyebrows,' rounded buttresses that provided shade and visual eye candy to passersby. Porthole windows evoke cruise liners, while lamps and other daily homewares represent long-past idealizations of a space-age future. Call it 'ray-gun chic.' An intimate (some say cramped) sense of space is offset by terrazzo flooring, often imprinted with the fossils of sea animals, and open verandahs, which would naturally cool building inhabitants in pre-air-conditioning days. The idea was to venerate technology while seizing on the natural features of the landscape (sea breezes and golden sunlight), adding a dash of organic aesthetic to the overall structure.

as tropical deco architecture. It organically reflected the natural world around it. For example, glass architectural blocks let bright Florida light in but kept sweltering heat out. They also served a geometric or cubist aesthetic. Floral reliefs, popular during the art nouveau period, appeared here, too. Friezes on facades or etched into glass reflected native flora and fauna such as palm trees, pelicans and flamingos. Friezes also took their cues from the uniquely American jazz movement, harmonious and lyrical. Surrounded by water, Miami Beach deco also developed a rhythmic language, with scalloped waves and fountains.

Whereas northeast deco buildings had socialist overtones, the clean lines of Miami Beach architecture still made room for joyful, playful, hopeful characteristics. Forward thinking and dreaming about the future took hold. Space travel was explored through design: buildings began to loosely resemble rockets, and rooflines embodied fantasies about traveling the universe. Geometric and abstract zigzag (or ziggurat) patterns not only reflected Aztec and Egyptian cultures, they also symbolized lightning bolts of electricity. Sun rays, more imagery borrowed from an ancient culture, were employed as life-affirming elements to counter the dark days of the Depression.

Since all hotels were built on the same size lots, South Beach architects began distinguishing themselves from their next-door neighbors through decorative finials and parapets. Neon signage also helped individualize buildings. Miami Beach deco relied on 'stepped-back' facades that disrupted the harsh, flat light and contributed to the rhythmical feel. Cantilevered 'eyebrows' jutted out above windows to protect interiors from unrelenting sun. Canopy porches gave hotel patrons a cool place to sit. To reflect the heat, buildings were originally painted white, with animated accent colors highlighting smaller elements. (It was only later, during the 1980s, that interior designer Leonard Horowitz decreed the pastel palette that became the standard. We're kinda happy he did.)

With the effects of the Depression lingering, ornamentation was limited to the facades; interiors were stripped down. Labor was cheap and readily available. Italians were hired to create terrazzo floors. They'd lay out a patterned grid and pour various colors of terrazzo – crushed

stones, shells, marble chips or granite, mixed with concrete – into the grid and then polish it. It's a remarkable marriage of form and function, since terrazzo also cools the feet.

Miami Beach needed a large number of rooms, most of which ended up being built small. With no expectation that they remain standing this long, most hotels were built with inexpensive concrete and mortar that had too much sand in it. Stucco exteriors prevailed, but locally quarried native keystone (an indigenous limestone) was also used. Except for the keystone, none of this would withstand the test of time with grace, which is one reason the district fell into such a state of disrepair and neglect. It's also why the district remains under a constant state of renovation.

The fanciful contoured facade of South Beach's Berkeley Shore Hotel

DISTINCT DECO DETAILS

A fun way to conduct an art deco walking tour is to seek out certain design trends, such as Mesoamerican temple flourishes, cruise liner modeled buildings, specific space-age structures and the like. There's not really any one hotel in Miami Beach that combines all of the above characteristics (a good thing too, as the aesthetic impression would be a little too overwhelming), but there are certain buildings that are exemplars of one or more themes.

top picks

DECO ELEMENTS & EMBELLISHMENTS

- **Waldorf Towers Hotel** (p173) Deco guru L Murray Dixon designed the tower of this hotel to resemble a lighthouse, surely meant to shine the way home for drunken Ocean Drive revelers.
- **Colony Hotel** (736 Ocean Dr) The Colony is the oldest deco hotel in Miami Beach. It was the first hotel in Miami, and perhaps America, to incorporate its sign (a zigzaggy neon wonder) as part of its overall design. Inside the lobby are excellent examples of space-age interiors, including Saturn-shaped lamps and Flash Gordon elevators.
- **Cavalier Hotel** (p178) The step-pyramid sides and geometric carvings that grace the front of this classic are some of the best examples of the 'Aztec/Maya temple-as-hotel' school of design.
- **Wolfsonian-FIU** (p50) The lobby of this hotel contains a phenomenally theatrical example of a 'frozen fountain.' The gold-leaf fountain, formerly gracing a movie theater lobby (you can bet it wasn't a multiplex!), shoots vertically up and flows symmetrically downward.
- **Crescent Hotel** (1420 Ocean Dr) Besides having one of the most recognizable neon facades in Miami Beach, the Crescent's signage is novel in that it attracts the eye down, rather than up. Straight on down, in fact: right into the lobby, which was kinda the point.

Bold neon signage is a key design element of the Colony Hotel

RESTORING THE DECO DISTRICT

Royal Palm

Ocean Drive – at the heart of South Beach's Art Deco Historic District

South Beach's heart is its Art Deco Historic District, one of the largest in the USA on the National Register of Historic Places. In fact, the area's rejuvenation and rebirth as a major tourist destination results directly from its protection as a historic place in 1979. The National Register designation prevents developers from wholeheartedly razing significant portions of what was, in the 1980s, a crime-ridden collection of crumbling eyesores populated primarily by drug-crazed lunatics, Cuban refugees and elderly residents. It's a far cry from that now. Today, hotel and apartment facades are decidedly colorful, with pastel architectural details. Depending on your perspective, the bright buildings catapult you back to the Roaring Twenties or on a wacky tour of American kitsch.

The National Register listing was fought for and pushed through by the Miami Design Preservation League (MDPL), founded by Barbara Baer Capitman in 1976. She was appalled when she heard of plans by the city of Miami to bulldoze several historic buildings in what is now the Omni Center. And she acted, forcefully.

MDPL cofounder Leonard Horowitz played a pivotal role in putting South Beach back on the map, painting the then-drab deco buildings in shocking pink, lavender and turquoise. When his restoration of Friedman's Pharmacy made the cover of Progressive Architecture in 1982, the would-be Hollywood producers of *Miami Vice* saw something they liked, and the rest is history.

THE FUTURE OF DECO

There are excellent deco renovations all along Miami Beach which manage to combine modern aesthetic tastes with classical deco details. But in a sense, the modern South Beach school of design is just the natural evolution of principles laid down by deco in the early 20th century. Hoteliers such as Ian Schrager combine a faith in technology – in this case flat-screen TVs, Lucite 'ghost chairs' and computer-controlled lobby displays – with a general air of fantastical glamour. Conceptions of the future (a fantasy of the best the future can be), plus a deep bow to the best of historical decorative arts, still drives the design on Miami Beach.

The Deco District is bounded by Dade Blvd to the north, 6th St to the south, the Atlantic Ocean to the east and Lenox Ave to the west. One of the best things about these 1000 or so buildings is their scale: most are no taller than the palm trees that surround them. And while the architecture is by no means uniform – you'll see Streamline Moderne, Mediterranean revival and tropical art deco designs – it's all quite harmonious. The 1-sq-mile district feels like a small village, albeit a village inhabited by freaks, geeks and the gorgeous. Which is pretty cool in and of itself.

Interestingly, the value of these Miami Beach deco buildings is based more on the sheer number of structures that have been designated protected status from the National Register of Historic Places. Individually, the inexpensively constructed houses would be worth far less.

With more than 400 registered historic landmarks, it's hard not to have an interesting walk through the District. And if you know a bit about the architecture (and you should by now!), you can follow the Beach boom phases: beginning in the 1930s when 5th St through Mid-Beach was developed; moving from the late '30s to early '40s up toward 27th St; and heading north of that into the '50s, when resorts and luxury hotels were interspersed with condominiums.

top picks

'NEW' DECO HOTELS

- **Delano Hotel** (p176) The top tower evokes old-school deco rocket-ship fantasies, but the theater-set-on-acid interior is a flight of pure modern fancy.
- **Hotel Victor** (p171) The Hyatt has done an excellent job of turning this L Murray Dixon original into an undersea wonderland of jellyfish lamps and sea-green terrazzo floors.
- **Tides** (p171) The biggest deco structure of its day; today, the lobby of the Tides feels like Poseidon's audience chamber.
- **Royal Palm Hotel** (p177) There's no better place to feel a sense of sea-borne movement than the Titanic-esque, ocean-liner back lobby of this massive, beautifully restored hotel.
- **Surfcomber** (p178) One of the best deco renovations on the beach is offset by sleek, transit lounge lines in the lobby and a lovely series of rounded eyebrows.

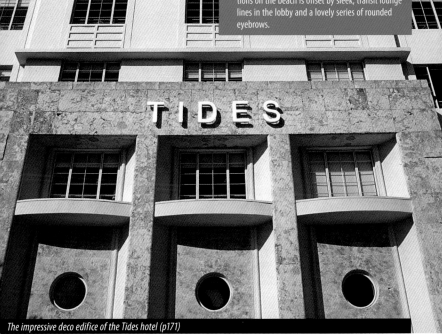

The impressive deco edifice of the Tides hotel (p171)

The streamline style of the Avalon Hotel (p174), South Beach

So what, you may ask, is the big deal about art deco? God knows, the term gets thrown around enough in Miami. Given the way this architectural style is whispered about by hotel marketing types, you'd be forgiven for thinking art deco was the Second Coming. 'Well, the so-and-so resort has a lovely deco facade.' 'Our boutique properties incorporate deco porches.' 'Did you notice the deco columns in our lounge?' And so on.

But to be fair, deco *has* been a sort of Second Coming for Miami Beach. It was art deco that made these buildings unique, that spurred their salvation, that caught the eye of Hollywood, which saw something romantically American in the optimism and innovation of a style that blends cubism, futurism, modernism and, most of all, a sense of movement. Beyond that was a nod to, and sometimes even reverence for, the elaborate embellishment of Old World decor. In art deco, we see the link between the lavish design aesthetic of the 19th century and the stripped-down efficiency of the 20th. Unlike a skyscraper, a deco hotel is modern yet accessible, even friendly, with its frescoed walls and shady window eyebrows.

There's always been plenty of innovative energy in American architecture. What makes Miami deco so special is the way this exuberance is constantly underlined by a sense of Jazz Age dignity. The best art deco speaks to a bygone era in a way that is simultaneously dated yet forward-looking. It is the past's conception of the future, in building form. One of life's little ironies is this: deco was supposed to make its contemporary viewers contemplate tomorrow. Today, it puts modern viewers in mind of yesterday.

But what's truly great about Deco Miami is the example it sets. The Art Deco District of South Beach, one of the hottest tourist destinations in the world, reminds city fathers that preserving historic neighborhoods is both morally and practically the right thing to do. In a city built on fast real estate, it's a bit delicious that the heart of the sexiest neighborhood in the city is the child of blocked development.

WYNWOOD, THE DESIGN DISTRICT & LITTLE HAITI

Drinking & Nightlife p150; Eating p134; Shopping p117

There's something odd about Wynwood and the Design District, Miami's official arts neighborhoods. Come in from I-95 and you land in the heart of the studio spaces. 'Oh honey, look at the galleries.' But come north on US Hwy 1, or from the side, and you'll see the jagged edges of the working class Puerto Rican neighborhood Wynwood once was.

By the early 2000s industrial jobs were leaving Wynwood just as creative types came seeking warehouses for studio spaces and apartments. The city of Miami, blushing in the then-early Art Basel afterglow, saw the opportunity to add 'Arts City' to its brand. The trick was to rapidly evolve a neighborhood primarily known for its blight (unless you called it home). Locals say rent went from $10 per square foot to $25 in a year, as Little San Juan gave way to Soho South, from a place where artists lived to an officially designated Arts District.

Look, we like Wynwood (where the art is) and the Design District (where the expensive furniture is). People are creative, the art is (generally) interesting, and the knob on 'shallow posturing,' turned up to '11' on the Beach, is only set at a mildly pretentious '7' here. But it does seem all those contemporary art spaces were bought at the price of a community, however depressed.

Several blocks north of this created creativity is a borough that fairly screams 'authenticity': Little Haiti (La Petite Haïti). If you haven't been to Port-au-Prince, this is the next best thing. Young men in tank tops listen to Francophone rap, while broad-necked women in bright wraps gossip in front of the *botanicas* – which, by the way, are not selling plants. A *botanica* here is a *vodou* (voodoo) shop; for more on this oft-stereotyped and misunderstood belief system, see p85.

With one-third of the population below the poverty line, Little Haiti may not be the easiest neighborhood to walk around, but try to; listening to the local *patois* of Spanish, French and Creole (one of the prettiest languages we've ever heard) is uniquely Miami. In a very real way, the energy of displacement and multiculturalism exemplified by Little Haiti lends itself to a creative impulse that is refined into the chic galleries of Wynwood, and even glossy South Beach, a few miles and several worlds away.

NEIGHBORHOODS WYNWOOD, THE DESIGN DISTRICT & LITTLE HAITI

top picks

WYNWOOD, THE DESIGN DISTRICT & LITTLE HAITI

- Friday night arts walks (p84)
- Browsing the botanicas(p85)
- Moore Space (p84)
- Purvis Young Studio Gallery (p83)
- Concept furniture shopping near N Miami Ave and/or NE 40th St

Little Haiti is roughly bounded by Biscayne Blvd to the east, I-95 to the west, 84th St to the north and 34th St to the south, but the heart and soul of the 'hood centers on 54th St. While Wynwood is loosely defined as being west of Biscayne Blvd and east of I-95, between NE 17th and 35th Sts, the Design District is a small, neat grid: between 38th and 41st Sts and NE 2nd Ave and North Miami Ave. Today the city is trying to turn eastern Overtown, southern Wynwood and north of Downtown into a new region dubbed Midtown Miami; it still feels cobbled together, but it's likely here to stay. In time, it should take on its own character and not feel like such a forced entity.

To get to Wynwood, the Design District and Little Haiti you can take buses 2, 3, 9, 10, 36, 54, 202, J, T, as well as the 62 bus. Little Haiti is served by all of the previous buses except the 36 and 62. If you are traveling from South Beach by car, the Julia Tuttle Causeway leads you right into the Design District, as does exit 2C from I-95. Follow Biscayne Blvd or NE 2nd Ave south into Wynwood and north into Little Haiti.

WYNWOOD

Note that many galleries are open on an appointment-only basis; try to call ahead before making a visit. To see a list of galleries, go to www.artcircuits.com/c_ww.

BACARDI BUILDING Map p82

☎ 305-573-8511; 2100 Biscayne Blvd; admission free; ☻ 9am-3:30pm Mon-Fri

You don't need to down 151 to appreciate the striking Miami headquarters of

the world's largest family-owned spirits company. The main event is a beautifully decorated tower that looks like the mosaic pattern of a tropical bathhouse on steroids; inside is a small art gallery and museum dedicated to the famously anti-Castro Bacardis (think about what 'Cuba Libre' actually means the next time you order one).

LOCUST PROJECTS
Map p82

☎ 305-576-8570; www.locustprojects.org; 105 NW 23rd St; ☷ noon-5pm Thu-Sat
Look for the squat black building emblazoned with the slogan 'I [Heart] New Art' and you'll have found Locust, widely regarded as one of the edgier art spaces in the district (which can be a compliment or insult depending on your tastes).

MOCA AT GOLDMAN WAREHOUSE
Map p82

MoCA; ☎ 305-573-5411; www.mocanomi.org /warehouse; 404 NW 26th St; ☷ noon-5pm Wed-Sat, to 7pm 2nd Sat of every month
Thank God the Museum of Contemporary Art (MoCA) expanded into this Wynwood satellite; the main exhibit, while worth the drive, is a ways away (see p62). In the meantime, the MoCA at Goldman has dibs on this space through 2009; pay a visit, as it's a good, Downtown-adjacent spot to see some of the highlights of the MoCA's excellent collection.

PURVIS YOUNG GALLERY
Map p82

☎ 305-785-8833; 1753 NE 2nd Ave
Vagrant, convict and creator, Purvis Young (1943–) is Overtown's favorite native son.

Although his artwork is often dubbed 'outsider' or 'folk' art (ie he didn't go to art school), we'd just classify it as good. His paintings, often done on pieces of wood and samples of carpet, portray ink-blotty mothers, horses, angels, African idols and people striving for freedom from an ambiguous captivity, a poignant and well-realized message in studio spaces that abut Miami's poorest neighborhoods.

RUBELL FAMILY ART COLLECTION
Map p82

☎ 305-573-6090; www.rubellfamilycollection .com; 95 NW 29th St; adult/senior & student $10/5; ☷ 10am-5pm Wed-Sat Dec-May
The Rubell family – specifically, the niece and nephew of the late Steve, better known as Ian Schrager's Studio 54 partner – operates some top-end hotels in Miami Beach, but it has also amassed an impressive contemporary art compilation that has works that span the last 30 years. The most admirable quality of this collection is its commitment to not just display one or two of its artists' pieces; rather, the aim is to focus on a contributor's entire career.

MIAMI CITY CEMETERY: DEADLY COOL

Fast fact: the first person that was buried in Miami was black. Depressing addendum: the first *recorded* burial in Miami was of a white guy. The long narrative of this troubled, diverse city is in its bones, and 'dem bones are concentrated in this eerie, quiet graveyard (Map p82; ☎ 305-579-6938; 1800 NE 2nd Ave; admission free; ☷ 7am-3:30pm Mon-Fri, 8am-4:30pm Sat & Sun). The dichotomy of history and modernity gets a nice visual representation in the form of looming condos shadowing the last abode of the Magic City's late, great ones. More than 9000 graves are divided into separate white, black and Jewish sections, including mayors, veterans (including about 90 Confederate soldiers) and the Godmother of South Florida, Julia Tuttle herself. Note the grave of Mrs Carrie Miller, who died in 1926; her husband, William, wrapped her body in a sheet and encased it in a concrete block 6ft high. 'After the body has gone to dust, her sleeping form will remain,' reads the epitaph. William apparently wanted to join his wife eventually, but died broke after the Great Depression. He's buried in an unmarked plot nearby.

THE DESIGN DISTRICT

BERNICE STEINBAUM GALLERY
Map p82

☎ 305-573-2700; www.bernicesteinbaum gallery.com; 3550 N Miami Ave; ⏰ 10am-6pm Mon-Sat

After two decades in NYC, the Steinbaum has moved south, where it's received a grand welcome for its mid-career contemporary artists such as Hung Liu, Kate Moran and Peter Walters.

BUICK BUILDING Map p82

☎ 305-573-8116; 3841 NE 2nd Ave; ⏰ by appointment

This gallery exhibits some pretty outstanding installation shows, but it's best known as the gateway of the Design District because of its striking mural facade. Done on canvas in bright yellow and black, the images of Latin mythological figures were completed in 2000 by the married artist team of Roberto Behar and Rosario Marquardt (see the Living Room, below).

HAITIAN HERITAGE MUSEUM Map p82

☎ 305-371-5988; 3940 N Miami Ave; ⏰ by appointment

Miami has the largest community of *Ayisens* in the world outside Haiti; come here to learn their story. The museum aims to be a comprehensive mosaic of Miami's Haitian community and draws off the collection of the Diaspora Vibe Gallery, which hosts the works of consistently excellent Caribbean and Latin American artists. At the time of our research, you really needed to call ahead to get inside, so make sure you make an appointment before you visit.

LIVING ROOM Map p82

Cnr NW 40th St & N Miami Ave

Just to remind you you're entering the Design District is a big honking sculpture of, yep, a living room, just the sort of thing you're supposed to shop for while you're here. Well, actually this Living Room is an 'urban intervention' meant to be a criticism of the disappearance of public space, but hey, we all add our own interpretations.

MELIN BUILDING Map p82

☎ 3930 NE 2nd Ave; ⏰ hrs vary

This small art and design 'mall,' for lack of a better word, houses Imelda Marcos' most lurid fantasy: a shoe the size of a small house. Created by Antoni Miralda, *Gondola Shoe* is one story high and crafted to fit the Statue of Liberty's feet.

MOORE SPACE Map p82

☎ 305-438-1163; www.themoorespace.org; 4040 NE 2nd Ave; ⏰ 10am-5pm Wed-Sat

The 2nd floor of this huge space consistently shows some of the most cutting-edge exhibitions around. Conceived in response to the first Art Basel Miami Beach, you should definitely check out what's going on here when you're in town; it's usually interesting but can be hit or miss – when we stopped in, one of the pieces was a looped video of a French guy crushing a coke can with his foot. Deep, man.

LITTLE HAITI

AFRICAN HERITAGE CULTURAL ARTS CENTER Map pp58–9

☎ 305-638-6771; 6161 NW 22nd Ave

This huge multipurpose area includes a 300-seat concert hall, dance studio and the

---

ART WALKS: THE NEW CLUBBING?

It's hipsters gone wild! Hmm, that doesn't actually sound like much fun, so we'll put it another way: it's free wine! And artsy types, and galleries open 'til late, and the eye candy of a club, and the drunken momentum of a pub crawl, and best of all, no red ropes. The Wynwood and Design District Arts Walk is, for our money (ie none, because it's free) one of the best nightlife experiences in Miami. And we're not (just) being cheapskates. The experience of strolling from gallery to gallery (That piece is *gorgeous*. Pour me another), perusing the paintings (No, I don't think there's a bathroom behind the performance artist), delving into the nuances of aesthetic styles (The wine's run out? Let's bounce) and, erm, getting tanked is as genuinely innovative as…well, the best contemporary art. Just be careful, as a lot of galleries in Wynwood are separated by short drives (the Design District is more walkable). Arts walks go down on the second Saturday of each month, from 7pm to 10pm (some galleries stretch 'til 11); when it's all over, lots of folks repair to Circa 28 (p150). Visit www.artcircuits.com for more-detailed information on participating galleries.

VOUDOU VOICES

Who do vodou worshipers pray to? One God. Only one God. Priests talk to God, and the *loa*.

Who are the loa? There are many *loa*. Dambala is one, Papa Legba. They go between. You talk to God first. The *loa* is second. First to God and then to the spirit.

What's your role in the community? If you go to the doctor and the doctor can say nothing, I can. *Houngan* (priests) and *mambos* (priestesses) are here to make you feel good. I learned (to be a priest) from my godmother and I've taught my children.

How do you communicate with God? You pray to God. You address God, and take a few minutes to take His power.

Does anyone ask you to hurt people? No. If you want to help yourself, I'm here for you. I don't hurt people. (Pauses) But I can refer you.

An interview with Papa Leider Andre, vodou priest, Little Haiti, who runs 3x3 Santa Barbara Botanica
(☎ 786-262-7895; 5700 NE 2nd Ave)

Amladozi Gallery, which regularly features the work of African-American, Afro-Caribbean and plain African artists. Call ahead and plan a visit during the frequent concerts and dance recitals held throughout the year.

BOTANICAS Map p82
All along NE 54th St
The *botanica* storefronts promise to help in matters of love, work and sometimes 'immigration services,' but trust us, there are no marriage counselors or INS guys in these shops. Welcome to the wide old world of *vodou*. As you enter you will probably get a funny look, but just remember to be courteous, curious and respectful and you should be welcomed. Before you browse, forget your stereotypes about pins and dolls, because *vodou* is no scarier than wine turning into blood on Communion. Like many traditional religions, *vodou* recognizes supernatural forces in everyday objects, powers that are both distinct and part of a single overarching deity. Ergo, you'll see shrines to Jesus next to altars to traditional deities. Notice the large statues of what look like people; these actually represent *loa* (pronounced 'lwa'), intermediary spirits that form a pantheon below God in the *vodou* religious hierarchy. Drop a coin into one of the *loa's* offering bowls before you leave, especially to Papa Legba, spirit of crossroads and, by our reckoning, travelers. Two good *botanicas* are Vierge Miracle & St Phillipe (p117) and 3x3 Santa Barbara Botanica (☎ 786-262-7895; 5700 NE 2nd Ave). Also see the boxed text (above).

LIBRERI MAPOU Map p82
☎ 305-757-9922; 5919 NE 2nd Ave
For another taste of Haitian culture, peruse the shelves at this bookstore, bursting with 3000 titles (including periodicals) in English, French and Creole, as well as crafts and recorded music.

ART WALK: DESIGN DISTRICT DETOUR
Walking Tour
If you're on foot, Wynwood can feel like a bunch of warehouses surrounded by gas stations. On the other hand, the Design District forms a nicely walkable (if oddly placed) island of expensive homewares and good art. Just don't visit on Sunday, when everything's closed.

1 Haitian Heritage Museum Call ahead to arrange a tour at this museum (opposite), where there's both excellent art and valuable cultural context on Miami's Haitian diaspora.

2 Living Room Get introduced to the Design District via (what else) a giant public art-y representation of a Living Room (opposite). In the midst of what looks like an abandoned lowrise, the installation is a nice metaphor for the Design District as a whole: plop contemporary interiors into the middle of urban decay.

3 Art Fusion Gallery Head down NE 40th St, which is pretty much the main strip in these parts, and pop into the Art Fusion Gallery (p117) right on the corner.

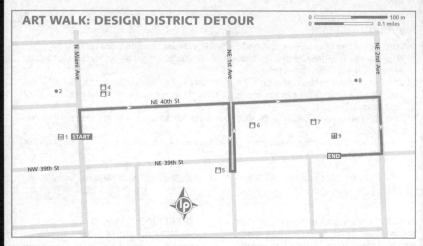

ART WALK: DESIGN DISTRICT DETOUR

WALK FACTS

Start Haitian Heritage Museum (3940 N Miami Ave)
Finish Michael's Genuine Food & Drink (NE 2nd Ave at NE 38th St)
Duration 45 minutes
Fuel Stop Coma's

4 Luxe I love lamp. Really? You'll love walking down NE 40th St, where the lamps (and other homewares) are pretty and cost about $4000. Our favorite coffee table conversation piece: one store's $750 'fertility symbol' (read: stone penis). Check out the lighting in Luxe (p118).

5 Lurie Gallery Take a small detour down NE 1st Ave and have a look in the excellent Lurie Gallery (p117), which tends to slice along on the cutting edge of contemporary art.

6 Artisan Antiques Art Deco Back on 40th St, Artisan Antiques Art Deco (p117) is a gorgeous showroom of art-deco lighting and furniture. Despite Miami being the heart of American deco, the pieces are from the French school.

7 Kuma Central There are all kinds of custom furniture galleries on 40th St. Take your pick and have the couch of your dreams shipped home, or go to Kuma Central (p117), a 'children's' store that sells 'unique urban art toys.' Hey – it's never too early to become a scene-obsessed prat!

8 Moore Space Head to the end of the road and up to the 2nd floor of the Moore Space (p84), which consistently displays excellent, challenging exhibitions.

9 Michael's Genuine Food & Drink Can we eat, already? Hey, we've saved the best for last. Backtrack into Atlas Plaza and take a seat (you'll want to have made reservations) at Michael's Genuine Food & Drink (p134), an acclaimed eatery that specializes in locally sourced organic American cuisine.

Drinking & Nightlife p150; Eating p136; Shopping p118

Bienvenido a Little Havana. Espanol es la lengua primera aqui, y – que? No entiendas? Ah, we're only messin'; you don't have to speak Spanish to get by here. In fact, that's sort of the point; while it helps to drop some *palabras* in the mother tongue, Little Havana is probably the best place in the city to engage with Miami's Spanish-speaking world without speaking Spanish. But that doesn't mean this neighborhood is the heart and soul of Miami's Latin community, because everywhere in Miami is Latin. Technically, Little Havana ends around SW 37th Ave; in reality it encompasses all of South Florida.

The official Little Havana is the accessible introduction to this greater Latin soul. Calle Ocho is where tourists are expected to gawk at the *cortaditos*, salsa clubs and dead chickens (*Santeria*, not bird flu) most Miamians take for granted. That said, we have to stress: Little Havana isn't just for tourists. It's a real neighborhood with day-to-day problems and day-to-day joys. And remember, although it bears the name of Cuba's capital, there are not just Cubans here. Even in Little Havana there's a Little Managua for the Nicaraguans – who have a much bigger Little Managua in Sweetwater.

One of the nicest things about Little Havana

top picks

LITTLE HAVANA

- Strolling down Calle Ocho (left)
- Máximo Gómez Park (p89)
- Outdoor *cortaditos* (espresso) at El Cristo (p136)
- Little Havana Art District (p89)
- Soaking up Viernes Culturales (Cultural Fridays; p89)

is how close it is to America. Even in the midst of all those Cuban cafés, *Santeria* shops (again, *botanicas*) and Latin American art galleries, you can still find a McDonalds if you want one.

The main thoroughfare here is Calle Ocho (SW 8th St), and the area we'd deem the *corazon* of Little Havana clings to Calle Ocho between NW 22nd Ave and SW 10th Ave. For the purposes of our exploration, the neighborhood extends roughly from W Flagler St to SW 13th St and from SW 3rd Ave to SW 37th Ave. The Miami River separates Little Havana from Downtown on the northeast border.

To get to Little Havana by train, take a Metromover to 8th St station, or buses 6, 8, 12, 17, or 207. If you are getting here by car follow I-95 to NW 7th St; Calle Ocho only goes one way, east, here, so you'll have to head west on NW 7th St and then circle back around.

BAY OF PIGS MUSEUM & LIBRARY
Map p88

☎ 305-649-4719; 1821 SW 9th St; admission free;
🕒 10am-5pm Mon-Fri

This small museum is more of a memorial to the 2506 Brigade, otherwise known as the crew of the ill-fated Bay of Pigs invasion. Whatever your thoughts on Fidel Castro and Cuban-Americans, pay a visit here to flesh out one side of this contentious story. You'll likely chat with survivors of the Bay of Pigs, who like to hang out here surrounded by pictures of those white, Afro- and Chinese Cuban comrades who never made it back to America. And for God's sake, leave the Che T-shirt at home (see p24).

CALLE OCHO Map p88

Little Havana's main thoroughfare is SW 8th St, better known by its Spanish name of Calle Ocho. In a lot of ways, it's like every immi-

grant enclave in America, full of foreign restaurants, mom-and-pop convenience shops and cheap phonecard sales. But it's also the public face that Miami's Cuban community – many of whom have made their fortune and left this neighborhood – presents to the world. Thus, the Cubaness of Calle Ocho is slightly exaggerated for visitors. On the other hand, this is a real street serving real people, and past the embellishment is a real community going on about their lives.

CUBAN MEMORIAL BOULEVARD
Map p88

The two blocks of SW 13th Ave south of Calle Ocho contain a series of monuments to Cuban patriots and freedom fighters, which here includes the dead of the Cuban Independence struggle and anti-Castro fighters. The memorials include the Eternal Torch in Honor of the 2506th Brigade (the exiles who died dur-

LITTLE HAVANA

SIGHTS	(pp87-9)
Bay of Pigs Museum & Library....	.1 C4
Casa Elián...............................	.2 A1
Ceiba Tree............................	(see 7)
Cuba Brass Map......................	.3 E4
Eternal Torch in Honor of the 2506th	
Brigade.............................	.4 E4
José Martí Memorial.................	.5 E4
La Plaza De la Cubanidad.........	.6 D2
Madonna Statue.....................	.7 E4
Máximo Gómez Park (Domino Park)..8 D4	

SHOPPING	(pp107-22)
Do Re Mi Music Center..............	.9 C4
El Aguila Vidente....................	.10 F4
El Crédito Cigars.....................	.11 F4
La Casa de Los Trucos.............	.12 E4
La Tradición Cubana................	.13 C4
Little-Havana-to-Go................	.14 E4
Los Pinarenos.......................	.15 E4

EATING	(pp123-40)
Casa Juancho........................	.16 A4
El Cristo..............................	.17 D4
El Rey De Las Fritas...............	.18 C4
Guayacan............................	.19 E4
I Love Calle Ocho..................	.20 D4
Mi Rinconcito Mexicano..........	.21 C4

DRINKING & NIGHTLIFE	(pp141-52)
Casa Panza..........................	.22 D4
Hoy Como Ayer.....................	.23 B4

THE ARTS	(pp153-60)
Tower Theater.......................	.24 D4

See Downtown
Miami
Map pp66-7

Orange
Bowl Stadium

Little Havana
Art District

Cuban
Memorial
Blvd

0   500 m
0   0.3 miles

To Islas
Canarias (4mi)

To Teatro de Bellas
Artes (0.3 mi); Miami-Dade County
Auditorium (3.5mi)

To Versailles (1mi);
Hy Vong Vietnamese
Restaurant (1mi)

CASA ELIÁN

The surreal house of Elián Gonzalez (Map p88; 2319 NW 2nd St; donations requested; ⏰ 10am-6pm), subject of one of the most bitter international custody battles of the 1990s, is a shrine, a time capsule and an exercise in the creation of public iconography. Since 2001 the house has become a temple to the symbology of the most anti-Castro Cuban exile politics. The little property is scattered with homages to Jesus, American flags and images of Elian himself, who is all but explicitly labeled a little saint of his people. Elián's great-uncle Delfin bought the house in late 2000 and then froze time inside: Elian's clothes hang in the closet, the inner tube that saved his life at sea hangs on the wall and his Spiderman pajamas are laid out on the bed. And then there's the life-sized enlargement of the Pulitzer prize—winning photograph of Elián hiding in the closet and being seized by federal border-patrol agents at gunpoint. When we came, Delfin seemed surprised to see us, and we assume visitors have slacked off as memory of the Elián affair has faded. Today, Elian is a teenager in Cardenas, Cuba, where the Museo a la Batalla de Ideas (Museum of the Battle of Ideas) has its own, pro-Elian's return exhibit on the affair, the Communist yin to Delfin's anti-Castro yang.

ing the botched Bay of Pigs invasion); a huge brass map of Cuba, dedicated to the 'ideals of people who will never forget the pledge of making their Fatherland free'; a bust of José Martí; and a Madonna Statue, which is supposedly illuminated by a shaft of holy light every afternoon. Bursting out of the island in the center of the boulevard is a massive ceiba tree, revered by followers of *Santeria* and an unofficial reminder of the poorer *Marielitos* and successive waves of desperate-for-work Cubans (many of whom are *santeros*) who have come to Miami since the 1980s.

LA PLAZA DE LA CUBANIDAD Map p88
W Flagler St at NW 17th Ave
This fountain and monument is a tribute both to the Cuban provinces and the people drowned by Castro's forces while trying to escape from Cuba in 1994 on a ship, *13 de Mayo*, which was sunk just off the coast.

LITTLE HAVANA ART DISTRICT Map p88
Calle Ocho, between SW 15th & 17th Aves
OK, it's not Wynwood. In fact, it's more 'Art Block' than district. But this little strip of

galleries and studios does house one of the best concentrations of Latin American art (particularly from Cuba) in Miami. Any one of the studios is worth a stop and a browse.

MÁXIMO GÓMEZ PARK Map p88
Domino Park; Calle Ocho at SW 15th Ave;
⏰ **9am-6pm**
Little Havana's most evocative reminder of Old Cuba is 'Domino Park,' where the sound of elderly men trash-talking over games of chess is harmonized by the quick clak-clak of slapping dominoes. The jarring backtrack, plus the heavy smell of cigars and a sunrise bright mural of the 1993 Summit of the Americas, combine to make Máximo Gómez one of the most sensory sites in Miami.

TOWER THEATER Map p88
☎ **305-649-2960; 1508 Calle Ocho**
This renovated 1926 landmark theater has a proud deco facade. Plenty of Spanish-language films are shown here, and Latin American art exhibits are often displayed in the lobby. Note the nearby Walk of Fame of Cuban-American celebrities as you stroll by.

LATIN WALK
Walking Tour
A walk down Calle Ocho emphasizes the fact Miami is and always will be one of the great Pan-Latin cities of the world. It'll also put you face to face with some evocative images of pre-Revolution Cuba.

1 Bay of Pigs Museum & Library Begin at the Bay of Pigs Museum & Library (p87), on SW 9th St at SW 18th Ave, which will provide

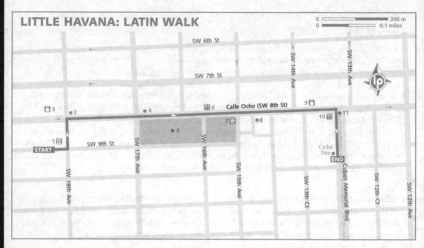

LITTLE HAVANA: LATIN WALK

WALK FACTS

Start Bay of Pigs Museum & Library (SW 9th St at SW 18th Ave)
End Cuban Memorial Blvd (SW 13th Ave)
Duration 45 minutes
Fuel Stop Los Pinareños Fruteria

insights into what drove so many families here to begin with. Though the collection of photos and mementos isn't too organized, talkative curators will gladly walk you through the place.

2 Calle Ocho Turn left onto SW 18th Ave and right onto Calle Ocho (p87), which bustles with eateries, shops and traffic.

3 Do Re Mi Music Center This music store (p119) has one of the best collections of Latin music in Miami; salsa connoisseurs, in particular, will be in heaven.

4 Walk of Fame Head east on the Ocho. As you walk, occasionally look down at the sidewalk to appreciate a local, Latin version of the Walk of Fame, with 23 stars honoring heroes from Celia Cruz to Gloria Estefan.

5 Art District Some of the best art of Latin America is on display in any one of the many galleries in Little Havana's Art District (p89).

6 El Cristo *Oye*: time for some oxtail and yucca at the excellent El Cristo (p136). Have a coffee at one of the outdoor tables while

you're here; it's a good spot for people-watching.

7 Tower Theater You'll next notice the renovated Tower Theater (p89), which shows Spanish-language films, has a small art gallery and hosts occasional theater performances and concerts.

8 Máximo Gómez Park It's so 'Old Cuba' you'd think it was Real Havana, but no, just the goodfellas in Máximo Gómez Park (p89) wiling away the day playing dominoes and cursing each other out (good-naturedly, of course) in Spanish.

9 La Casa de los Trucos We know: you're supposed to get cigars in Little Havana. But for truly unique neighborhood shopping, enter this odd, enormous costume shop (p119), or at least marvel at the monsters lined up out front.

10 Los Pinareños Frutería Then, because it's been a full 20 minutes since you imbibed something, grab a stool at Los Pinareños Frutería (1334 SW 8th St), where you can slurp on refreshing shakes or juices from watermelon to sugarcane.

11 Cuban Memorial Boulevard Head down Cuban Memorial Boulevard (p87), or SW 13th Ave, past its monuments and statues dedicated to independence and anti-Castro casualties. End your tour of Little Havana at the boulevard's massive ceiba tree, sacred to followers of *Santeria*.

Eating p137; Shopping p119; Sleeping p180

If Miamians, with their perfect weather, coastal vistas and sandy beaches, are luc... then Biscayne residents, who inhabit a tiny paradise swathed in green parkland floating off the coast of the big city, are leprechauns. Somehow, Biscayne has so far managed to escape the merciless grasp of condo developers. Drive out here on the 4-mile Rickenbacker Causeway, with the city skyline glittering on one side and the ocean on the other, and try not to be too jealous.

To be fair, it's not all great views and sea breezes. Biscayne's the first neighborhood to be evacuated during a hurricane, and the nightlife is more like nightdead. That downside is offset by outdoor opportunities that are arguably better than anything you'll find on the mainland. Crandon Park (p93) is well worth an afternoon of exploration among the spidery mangroves, while Hobie Beach offers some closer encounters of the sun and surf kind. Or just take a trip out to Virginia Key's city park, say hello to the Nicaraguan family having a picnic, crack a beer, grill yourself a burger and watch the sun set behind downtown's glass mountain range. This sun-beaten, salt-battered Old Florida lifestyle was the main pull of the state before the deco and supermodels – go to Jimbo's (p93) for a sense of the above. One beer and smoked fish platter enjoyed here does a better job of explaining this allure than we can muster.

The Rickenbacker Causeway, the eastern extension of 26th Rd, links the mainland with Key Biscayne via small Virginia Key, which is where you'll find the legendary Miami Seaquarium (p93). Key Biscayne itself is only 7 miles long. Crandon Blvd is the island's only real main road, and runs to the southernmost tip and Cape Florida Lighthouse (below).

To get here by bus, take bus B from Brickell Ave. To get here from the mainland by car, take the Rickenbacker Causeway, accessible from US Hwy 1 and I-95.

BISCAYNE COMMUNITY CENTER & VILLAGE GREEN PARK

Map p92

☎ 305-365-8900; http://keybiscayne.fl.gov/pr; Village Green Way, off Crandon Blvd; ⏲ Community Center 6am-10pm Mon-Fri, 6am-8pm Sat & Sun

A fantastic spot for the kids, there's a swimming pool, a park full of jungle gyms, an activity room with a playset out of a child's happiest fantasies and an African Balboa tree that's over a century old and teeming with tropical birdlife. Did we mention it's free? The unmissable park and community center are on the right side of Crandon Blvd as you drive south.

top picks

OUTDOORS

- Bill Baggs Cape Florida Recreation Area (right)
- Boardwalk (p57)
- Oleta State Recreation Area (p62)
- Marjory Stoneman Douglas Biscayne Nature Center (p93)
- Fairchild Tropical Garden (p104)

BILL BAGGS CAPE FLORIDA STATE RECREATION AREA

Map p92

☎ 305-361-5811; www.floridastateparks.org/cape florida/; 1200 S Crandon Blvd; admission per person $2-4, on foot $1; ⏲ 8am-sundown

If you don't make it to the Florida Keys, come here for a taste of their unique island ecosystem. The 494-acre park is a tangled clot of tropical fauna and dark mangroves – look for the 'snorkel' roots that provide air for the often half-submerged mangrove trees – all interconnected by sandy trails and wooden boardwalks and surrounded by miles of pale ocean.

CAPE FLORIDA LIGHTHOUSE

Map p92

☎ 305-361-8779; Bill Baggs Cape Florida State Recreation Area

At the park's southernmost tip, the 1845 Cape Florida Lighthouse, the oldest structure in Florida, replaced one that was severely damaged in 1836 by attacking Seminole Indians. You can tour at 10am and 1pm (free); tours are limited to about 12 people, so put your name on a sign-up list at least 30 minutes beforehand.

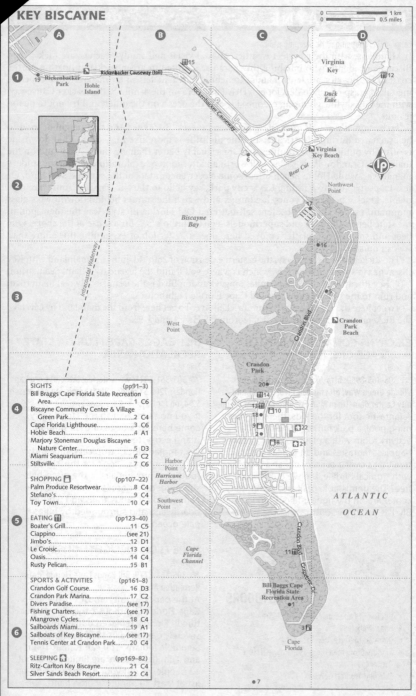

CRANDON PARK Map p92

☎ 305-361-5421; 4000 Crandon Blvd;
☾ 8am-sunset

The 2-mile beach here is one of the city's best, all sand and seagrass beds concealing shrimp, crabs and a coastal marine ecosystem. Within the 1200-acre park you'll find the Marjory Stoneman Douglas Biscayne Nature Center (below) and Bear Cut Preserve. The latter is a nature study area with a mangrove boardwalk that leads to a fossilized reef overlook. Guided tram tours are available, as are daily cabana rentals with showers on a first-come, first-serve basis ($37.50); no overnight stays allowed.

MARJORY STONEMAN DOUGLAS BISCAYNE NATURE CENTER Map p92

☎ 305-361-6767; www.biscaynenaturecenter.org; Crandon Park, 6767 Crandon Blvd; admission free, activities $10; ☾ 10am-4pm

This excellent nature center, the namesake of a beloved environmental crusader (p221), is a perfect little introduction and exploration of the continental USA's own little subtropical ecosystem: South Florida. There are weekend hikes and nature lessons (including programs for tots) that let kids wade into the water with nets and catch sea horses, sponges and other marine life (released after a short lesson).

MIAMI SEAQUARIUM Map p92

☎ 305-361-5705, 305-365-2501 for Dolphin Harbor; www.miamiseaquarium.com; 4400 Rickenbacker Causeway; adult/child $31.95/25.95; ☾ 9:30am-6pm, last entry 4:30pm

The Seaquarium is a 38-acre marine park that excels in preserving, protecting and educating us about aquatic creatures, and was one of the country's first places dedicated to sea life. There are dozens of shows and exhibits including a tropical reef; the Shark Channel, with feeding presentations; and Discovery Bay, a natural mangrove habitat that serves as a refuge for rehabilitating rescued sea turtles. Check out the Pacific white-sided dolphins or injured West Indian manatees being nursed back to health; some are released. Frequent shows put some particularly gorgeous animals on display for the audience's amusement, including a massive killer whale and some precious dolphins and sea lions. Newly opened, Dolphin Harbor is an especially fun venue for watching marine mammals play and show off; it also offers swim-with-the-cetacean fun via its Encounter (adult & child over 9 yrs/child 5-9 yrs $139/$99) and Odyssey ($189) options. We ask that you please read up on the debate on swimming with dolphins (p192) before committing to either of these programs.

STILTSVILLE Map p92

www.stiltsville.org, www.nps.gov/bisc/history culture/stiltsville

This collection of seven houses that stand on pilings out in Biscayne Bay has been around since the early '30s, when 'Crawfish' Eddie Walker sold chowder from his shack, out on the mudflats, and soon gained neighbors who liked the idea of off-shore living. By the end of the '50s there were 27 houses on stilts. Most were wiped away by hurricanes, but the rest are visible, way off in the distance, from the southern shore of Bill Baggs park (p91). In 2003 the nonprofit Stiltsville Trust was set up by the National Parks Service to rehabilitate the buildings into as-yet-unknown facilities; proposals include an NPS Visitor Center, artist-in-residence colony or community center. For updates, call the Stiltsville Trust (☎ 305-443-2266) or take a boat tour (☎ 305-375-1621) out here with the illustrious historian Dr Paul George.

JIMBO'S: THE HAPPIEST PLACE ON EARTH

It's the simple things that make life worth living, and sometimes their simplicity is even more elegant in the face of life's complexity. To wit: come to Jimbo's (Map p92; ☎ 305-361-7026; www.jimbosplace.com; Duck Lake Rd) at the end of Arthur Lamb Jr Rd in Virginia Key. In a city of unfettered development is this bar…no, shrimp shack…no, smoked fish house…no, 24-hour trailer park bonfire…well, whatever. A series of dilapidated river shacks (and a bocce ball court) has been, for decades, its own version of everything that once was right in Florida. Of course, even here the vibe is a little artificial; all those rotting fish houses were set pieces for the 1980 horror movie *Island Claws*. Other flicks filmed here include *Ace Ventura*, *True Lies* and the cinema verite of *Porky's 2*. But today the shacks have been reclaimed into the set pieces of the Jimbo show. The point is this place is unique, and artificial, and authentic or all of the above; you just gotta drop in.

COCONUT GROVE

Drinking & Nightlife p151; Eating p137; Shopping p119; Sleeping p181

In Miami, everything tends towards extremes. But then Coconut Grove comes along, mellow and chilled out, making a big deal about how it isn't a big deal. There's a wealth of museums, historic homes and woodsy parkland here, little reminders that the Grove is *pleasant*, a beautiful word other neighborhoods should aspire to.

Seemingly Middle America gone south, the Grove is as diverse as the rest of Miami, but it's comfortably affluent in a way that blurs (some say blands) its distinctive ethnicities. Everyone from everywhere lives here, but they're too busy shopping to notice their differences, which on a certain level makes this neighborhood quintessentially American.

Back in the day the Grove did have a distinguishing identity: funky-tropi Haight Asbury. There are still vestiges of those pre-gentrification days around: The Last Carrot (p138) is poignantly named, and really feels like a final hippie holdout against American consumerism in all its well-manicured, pre-packaged, focus-group–tested ferocity. The suburbanization of the Grove has even subdued Miami's Latin penchant for partying; in January 2008 the Miami City Commission cut off liquor sales in the Grove at 3am, two hours before last call in the rest of town.

top picks

COCONUT GROVE

- Vizcaya Museum (p96)
- Miami Museum of Science & Planetarium (p96)
- Barnacle State Historic Park (left)

Then again, malls such as CocoWalk and Streets of Mayfair brought economic growth and landscaped the surrounding village into an absolutely agreeable place for a sunny stroll. And to be honest, we lied about the whole lack of immoderation here. The Grove's most impressive site is Miami's original monument to excess: the gorgeous Vizcaya (p96), one of the most beautiful historic houses in America.

The Grove unfolds along S Bayshore Dr, which hugs the shoreline. South Bayshore Dr turns into the central village where it becomes McFarlane Rd and then Main Hwy, which eventually leads to Douglas Rd (SW 37th Ave), Ingraham Hwy, Old Cutler Rd and attractions in South Dade. US Hwy 1 (S Dixie Hwy) acts as the northern boundary for the Grove.

To get to Coconut Grove by train take the Metrorail to Coconut Grove or Vizcaya stations. Buses 6, 22, 27, 37, 42, 48 or 249 will also get you here. If you are traveling by car follow S Dixie Hwy or 27th Ave into the heart of town. You can also get here by rickshaw: Coconut Grove Rickshaw (☎ 305-669-9509) operates 10-minute rides ($5) through the village and 20-minute moonlight rides ($10) from 8pm to 2am.

BARNACLE STATE HISTORIC PARK
Map p95

☎ 305-448-9445; 3485 Main Hwy; admission $1; ☺ park 9am-4pm Fri-Mon, house tours 10am, 11:30am, 1pm & 2:30pm

In the center of the village is the 1891, 5-acre pioneer residence of Ralph Monroe, Miami's first honorable snowbird (a nickname for Northerners who fly south for the winter). The house is open for guided tours, led by folks who are quite knowledgeable and enthusiastic about the park – which is, by the way, a lovely, shady oasis for strolling, especially if you're seeking refuge from the buy-buy-buy madness across Main Hwy. The park hosts frequent moonlight concerts, from jazz to classical.

COCOWALK & STREETS OF MAYFAIR
Map p95

☎ 305-444-0777, 305-448-1700; 3015 Grand Ave, 2911 Grand Ave

Credited for reviving Coconut Grove in the 1990s, this pair of alfresco malls of ubiquitous chain stores is perhaps (and inexplicably) the Grove's biggest tourist draw. See them for yourself if you must, but it's just the usual suspects.

COCONUT GROVE PLAYHOUSE
Map p95

www.cpgplayhouse.org; 3500 Main Hwy

Miami's oldest playhouse premiered Samuel Beckett's *Waiting for Godot* in 1956, but was shut down during its 50th

COCONUT GROVE

anniversary season due to major debt issues. Now the board of the theater is trying to resurrect this grande dame in conjunction with Miami-Dade's Department of Cultural Affairs; check the theater website for the latest updates.

ERMITA DE LA CARIDAD Map p95

☎ 305-854-2404; 3609 S Miami Ave

The Catholic Diocese purchased some bayfront land from Deering's Vizcaya (right) estate and built a shrine here for its displaced Cuban parishioners. Symbolizing a beacon, it faces the homeland, exactly 290 miles due south; note the Cuban history mural. After visiting the villa or the Miami Museum of Science & Planetarium (below), consider picnicking on the water's edge or at nearby Kennedy Park (S Bayshore Dr).

KAMPONG Map p95

4013 Douglas Rd; ☼ tours Mon-Fri by appointment only

If you speak Malay or Indonesian, yes, the Kampong is named for the Bahasa word for village. David Fairchild, Indiana Jones of the botanical world and founder of Fairchild Tropical Gardens (p104), came up with the title, undoubtedly after a long Javanese jaunt. This was where the adventurer would rest in between journeys in search of beautiful and economically viable plant life. Today it's listed on the National Register of Historic Places and the lovely grounds serve as a classroom for the National Tropical Botanical Garden, but tours are available by appointment.

MIAMI MUSEUM OF SCIENCE & PLANETARIUM Map p95

☎ 305-646-4200; www.miamisci.org; 3280 S Miami Ave; adult/child/senior & student $10/6/8; ☼ 10am-6pm

Kids bouncing off the walls? This Smithsonian-affiliated museum has hands-on, creative exhibits, from creepy-crawlies to coral-reef displays. The planetarium hosts space lessons and telescope-viewing sessions, as well as old-school laser shows, with trippy flashes set to classic-rock of the Pink Floyd kind.

PLYMOUTH CONGREGATIONAL CHURCH Map p95

☎ 305-444-6521; 3400 Devon Rd; ☼ 8:30am-4:30pm Mon-Fri

It looks like Antonio Banderas should emerge from this 1917 coral mission–style church with a guitar case full of explosives and Salma Hayek on his arm. The 11-acre grounds are a popular spot for wedding photos and home to Dade County's first schoolhouse, a one-room wooden building that dates to 1887.

VIZCAYA MUSEUM & GARDENS Map p95

☎ 305-250-9133; www.vizcayamuseum.com; 3251 S Miami Ave; adult/child 6-12 yrs $12/5; ☼ museum 9:30am-5pm, last admission 4:30pm, gardens 9:30am-5:30pm

They call Miami the Magic City, and if it is, this Italian villa, the housing equivalent of a Faberge egg, is its most fairy-tale residence. In 1916 industrialist James Deering started a long and storied Miami tradition by making a ton of money and building some ridiculously grandiose digs. Deering employed 1000 people (then 10% of the local population) for four years to fulfill his desire for a pad that looked centuries old. He was so obsessed with creating an atmosphere of old-world old money he had the house stuffed with 15th- to 19th-century furniture, tapestries, paintings and decorative arts, had a monogram fashioned for himself and even had paintings of fake ancestors commissioned. The poetic 30-acre grounds are full of splendid gardens (including a secret garden) and Florentine gazebos, and both the house and gardens are used for the display of rotating contemporary art exhibits. Be sure to take a tour (45 minutes) while you're here, as they are included with the admission price.

GENTRIFICATION JAUNT
Walking Tour

There are chains galore here, but the open-air set-up of the main malls creates a pedestrian-friendly neighborhood core – a rarity in many American cities.

1 Coconut Grove Playhouse The American premier of *Waiting for Godot* in 1956 was apparently as star-studded and fabulous as those things get. Unfortunately, the venue (p94) has since closed its doors, although sources say the theater may be re-opened by the time you read this.

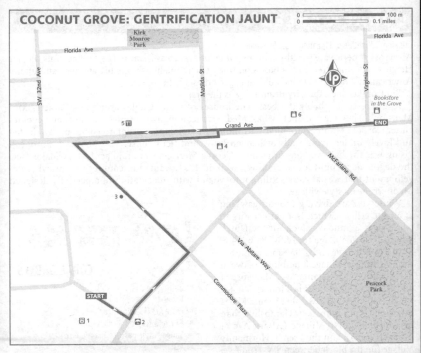

COCONUT GROVE: GENTRIFICATION JAUNT

0 ——— 100 m
0 ——— 0.1 miles

WALK FACTS

Start Coconut Grove Playhouse (3500 Main Hwy)
End CocoWalk and Streets of Mayfair
Duration 45 minutes
Fuel Stop Last Carrot

2 Barnacle State Historic Park Just next to the playhouse is the heart of MTV Spring Break debauchery: Senor Frog's. Run, now, across the street to the excellent Barnacle State Historic Park (p94).

3 Commodore Plaza Having had your dose of nature, walk up Commodore Plaza and note that for all the yuppie-ness of the scene, there are lots of indie galleries and shops along this stretch, in part courtesy of the economic shot provided by all those chain stores.

4 Condom-USA For example, Condom-USA (p120), where you can have your pick of plentiful prophylactics, is hardly family-friendly chain store blah. 'The cherry-flavored ones, please.'

5 Last Carrot One of the last holdouts of the Grove's old hippie character is the Last Carrot (p138), an achingly cute juice bar and sandwich shop that's always bustling – even the corporate types love it. All jokes aside, the juice is to die for.

6 CocoWalk & Streets of Mayfair Now sell your soul. Kidding! Gentrification is a double-edged sword; it can sap the spirit, but it's also buoyed the economy of the Grove and made it a nice place for walking. And even among the malls like CocoWalk (p94), you can find nice indie shops such as Bookstore in the Grove (p119).

CORAL GABLES

All across America are wealthy suburbs with names such as Jasmine Tce, Spruce Walk, Poplar Heights and other tree-and-subdivision titles, where the houses are big and new and utterly American and designed to look old and aged and semi-European.

But Coral Gables, the City Beautiful, was the first.

And it's still probably the best. The houses of Coral Gables aren't no-character Mc-Mansions. They are Italianate villas, Mediterranean manses, mini-Alhambras and cookie-cutter Cordobas (and cynics might say miniature Colombian druglord compounds), shaded and lovely under living walls of Banyan grove and ficus copse. This Southern European vision was the baby of New Englander George Merrick, son of an art history major (see, the degree *does* count for something), who, in 1921, wanted to counter the sprawl of development that was already settling into Miami with the creation of a perfectly designed Mediterranean-style village.

While you are driving around gawking at all the cribs – which is a perfect way to while away a Sunday – look for the Dutch South African Village (6612, 6700, 6704 & 6710 SW 42nd Ave and 6705 San Vicente St); a tiny Chinese Village (one block between San Sovino Ave, Castania Ave, Maggiore St and Riviera Dr); a Florida Pioneer Village (4320, 4409, 4515, 1520 & 4620 Santa Maria St), which looks more New Hampshire than Miami; the Italian Village (Altara Ave at Monserrate St); and the French Normandy Village (on the block between SW 42nd Ave, Viscaya Court, Viscaya Ave and Alesio Ave).

top picks

CORAL GABLES

- Biltmore Hotel (opposite)
- Venetian Pool (opposite)
- Lowe Art Museum (p102)
- Fairchild Tropical Garden (p104)
- Sunday drive past the mansions (p102)

Merrick probably never guessed that his Mediterranean fantasy would one day attract wealthy Latinos who loved the idea of having their own Spanish villa, perhaps one of the happiest planning accidents in Florida history.

Poor George eventually died penniless and neglected, but his city remains a lovely model community, intersected by Miracle Mile, one of the best (well, yuppie-est) shopping strips in Miami. To the south is the University of Miami, where the grounds and student body – and bodies – are jaw-droppingly gorgeous. The university injects a nice dose of punky youth into this aristocratic neighborhood; tune into 90.5 FM to listen to student DJs who sound like the clerks from *High Fidelity*.

Coral Gables is essentially bordered by Calle Ocho to the north, Sunset Dr (SW 72nd St/Hwy 986) to the south, Le Jeune Rd (SW 42nd Ave/Hwy 953) to the east and Red Rd (SW 57th Ave/Hwy 959) to the west. US Hwy 1 slashes through at a 45° angle from northeast to southwest. The main campus of the University of Miami is located just south of the enormous Coral Gables Biltmore Golf Course, north of US Hwy 1 (S Dixie Hwy). Avenues here run east–west, while streets run north–south, the opposite to the rest of Miami. The first Friday night of every month is another fun and free gallery walk night (see www.artcircuits.com/c_cg for more info).

To get to Coral Gables by train, jump onboard the Metrorail to Douglas Rd or University stations. Once you are here, travel along Ponce de León Blvd or Miracle Mile on electric-hybrid trolleys – for free! And there's an accompanying barber shop quartet…meh. The trolley service runs every 10 to 15 minutes from 6:30am to 8pm Monday to Thursday, and to 10pm on Friday. You can also take buses 6, 27, 42, or 224. To get here by car, US Hwy 1 takes you through the edge of town. Head north on Red Rd (SW 57th Ave), Le Jeune Rd (SW 42nd Ave), Granada Blvd, or Douglas Rd (SW 37th Ave), to enter the heart of the Gables, or come from the west on Coral Way (SW 24th St) or Bird Rd (SW 40th St).

BILTMORE HOTEL Map pp100–1

☎ 305-445-1926, 800-727-1926; www.biltmore
hotel.com; 1200 Anastasia Ave

In the most opulent neighborhood of one of the showiest cities in the world, the Biltmore peers down her nose and says, 'Hrmph.' It's one of the greatest of the grand hotels of the American Jazz Age; if this joint was a fictional character from a novel, it'd be, without question, Jay Gatsby.

The history of this landmark establishment reads like an Agatha Christie novel on speed. Al Capone had a speakeasy here, and the Capone Suite is still haunted by the spirit of Fats Walsh, who was murdered here (for more ghost details, join in the weekly storytelling in the lobby, 7pm Thursday). Back in the day, imported gondolas transported celebrity guests such as Judy Garland and the Vanderbilts around. Because, of course, the Biltmore had its own canal system out the back. That's all gone, but the Biltmore now has the largest hotel pool in the continental USA, which resembles a Sultan's water garden from *One Thousand & One Nights*. The hotel's lobby is the real kicker: grand, gorgeous, yet surprisingly ungaudy, it's like a child's fantasy of an Arab castle crossed with a Medici villa. Outside, the palatial grounds are popular spots for *quincenera* shoots, when 15-year old Latino girls get to play princess for a day. For a wonderful overview, whether you are staying here or not, call Dade Heritage Trust (☎ 305-445-1926; tours free; ☉ tours 1:30pm, 2:30pm & 3:30pm Sun).

CORAL GABLES CITY HALL Map pp100–1
405 Biltmore Way

This muscular yet elegant building has been housing tedious city commission meetings since 1928. Check out Denman Fink's *Four Seasons* ceiling painting in the tower, as well as his framed, untitled painting of the underwater world on the 2nd-floor landing. A farmers market is held on the grounds from 8am to 1pm Saturday, January to March.

CORAL GABLES CONGREGATIONAL CHURCH Map pp100–1

☎ 305-448-7421; www.coralgablescongregational
.org; 3010 DeSoto Blvd

George Merrick's father was a New England Congregational minister, which perhaps accounts for him donating land for the city's first church. Built in 1924 as a replica of a church in Costa Rica, the yellow-walled, red-roofed exterior is as far removed from New England as…well, Miami. The interior is graced with beautiful sanctuary and the grounds are landscaped with stately palms.

CORAL GABLES MUSEUM Map pp100–1

☎ 305-460-5090; www.coralgables.com/cgweb
/museum.org; 285 Aragon Ave

Set to open in late 2009, this museum, based on its sample exhibition, should be an excellent, well-plotted introduction to the oddball narrative of the founding and growth of the City Beautiful. The collection will include historical artifacts and mementos of succeeding generations of this tight-knit, eccentric little village.

MERRICK HOUSE Map pp100–1

☎ 305-460-5361; 907 Coral Way; adult/child $5/3;
☉ tours 1pm, 2pm & 3pm Sun & Wed

It's fun to imagine this simple homestead, with its little hints of Med-style, as the core of what would eventually become the gaudy Gables. When George Merrick's father purchased this plot, site unseen, for $1100, it was all dirt, rock and guavas. The property is now used for meetings and receptions, and you can tour both the house and its pretty organic garden.

MIRACLE THEATER Map pp100–1

☎ 305-444-9293; www.actorsplayhouse.org;
280 Miracle Mile

This gorgeous, 80-year old theater is one of the best bits of deco anywhere off the Beach. Today, the Actors' Playhouse company puts on productions in one of three performance spaces – the 600-seat main-stage auditorium, a smaller children's theater and a black box for cutting-edge works – although the theater is nice to visit whether you've got tickets or not.

VENETIAN POOL Map pp100–1

☎ 305-460-5306; 2701 DeSoto Blvd; adult/child
Nov-Mar $6.75/5.50, Apr-Oct $10/6.75;
☉ generally 11am-5pm, call for details

The prettiest public pool in America is this incredible grotto, which happens to

CORAL GABLES

500 m
0.3 miles

To Xixon
(2.2mi)

To Brazatte
Dance Company
(0.3mi)

Alhambra
Entrance
Monuments

SW 37th Ave/Douglas Rd

Alhambra Plaza

Merrick Way

SW 22nd St (Miracle Mile)

Galiano St

Ponce de León Blvd

Navarre Ave
Minorca Ave
Alcazar Ave
Alhambra Cir
Giralda Ave

Salzedo St

Hernando St

La Jeune Rd

Biltmore Way

Valencia Ave
Almeria Ave
Sevilla Ave
Catalonia Ave
Palermo Ave
Malaga Ave
Santander Ave
Anastasia Ave

Prince
Circle
Park

San Sebastian Ave
Romano Ave
Sarto Ave
Camilo Ave
Aledo Ave
Cadima Ave
Alesio Ave
Viscaya Ave
Fluvia Ave
Canda Ave
Velarde Ave

Monegro St
SW 37th Ct
SW 38th Ave
SW 38th Ct
SW 39th Ave
SW 40th (Bird) Rd

SW 22nd Tce
SW 23rd St
SW 23rd Tce
SW 24th St
SW 25th Tce
SW 25th St
SW 25th Tce
SW 26th St

SW 28th St
SW 29th St
SW 37th Ct
SW 40th (Bird) Rd

Douglas
Park

To El Carajo
(2.1mi)

Laguna St

Cardena St

Anderson Rd

Segovia Cir

Greenway Dr

SW 24th St/Coral Way

Andalusia Ave

Granada Blvd

Cordova St

Columbus Blvd

San Domingo St

N Greenway Dr

Ferdinand St

Alhambra Cir

Country Club Prado

Riviera Dr

De Soto Blvd

Anastasia Ave

Salvadore
Park

Granada Golf
Course

S Greenway Dr

Asturia Ave
Castile Ave

Greenway

Coral Way
Entrance
Monuments

Valencia Ave
Sevilla Ave

SW 57th Ave/Red Rd

SW 40th St/Bird Rd

Biltmore Donald Ross
Golf Course

Coral Gables Canal

SW 24th St/Coral Way

Granada Entrance
Monuments

976

972

See Coconut Grove Map p95

be an excellent, rare example of public planning gone very…*right*. Just imagine: it's 1923. Tons of rock have been quarried for one of the most beautiful neighborhoods in Miami, but now an ugly gash sits in the middle of the village. What to do? How about pump the irregular hole full of water, mosaic-and-tile up the whole affair, and make it look like a Roman emperor's aquatic playground? Result: one of the few pools listed on the National Register of Historic Places, a spring-fed wonderland of coral rock caves, cascading waterfalls, a palm-fringed island and Venetian-style moorings. You can get romantic under the big waterfall, drop the tykes in the kiddie area (toddlers must be over 38in tall or a parent must have proof they're at least three years old), do laps or take in the view, which is highly recommended for those who don't swim. Those who do get wet are following in the tradition of stars such as Esther Williams and Johnny 'Tarzan' Weissmuller. You can't bring in your own food, but there is an overpriced snack bar.

UNIVERSITY OF MIAMI

CASA BACARDI Map pp100–1

☎ 305-284-2822; http://casabacardi.iccas.miami
.edu; 1531 Brescia Ave; donation $5; ◯ 10am-5pm
Mon-Fri
This site is of one of the best Cuban and Cuban-American studies programs in America, but there's no reason to drop in unannounced unless you're *really* into the Spanish–American war. Call ahead if you'd like to attend the Casa's open informative lectures and seminars (check the website for a calendar). Movie presentations about Cuba are screened at 2:30pm Monday to Friday, and there's an underwhelming Cuban music pavilion that true *son* buffs will appreciate.

LOWE ART MUSEUM Map pp100–1

☎ 305-284-3535; www.lowemuseum.org; 1301
Stanford Dr; adult/student $7/5; ◯ 10am-5pm Tue,
Wed, Fri & Sat, noon-7pm Thu, noon-5pm Sun
Your love of the Lowe depends on your taste in art. If you're into modern and contemporary works, it's good. If you're into the art and archaeology of cultures from Asia, Africa and the South Pacific, it's great. And if you're into pre-Columbian and Mesoamerican art, it's simply fantastic;

the artifacts are stunning and thoughtfully strung out along an easy-to-follow narrative thread. That isn't to discount the lovely permanent collection of Renaissance and Baroque art, Western sculpture from the 18th to 20th centuries and paintings by Gauguin, Picasso and Monet; they're also gorgeous.

OSTENTATIOUS OPULENCE
Walking & Driving Tour

This tour's main purpose is to take you past some palatial residences and demonstrate that compared to most of the inhabitants of Coral Gables, your life sucks. Just kidding – but you will see some pretty amazing abodes on this trip.

1 Matsuri Konichiwa! We're going to start with the fuel stop on this tour: the excellent bento lunch box (or anything, really) at Matsuri (p139), the best Japanese restaurant in the city (located in a tatty shopping block). When you're done, drive down Bird Rd and gawk at the lovely Gables houses sitting in the Banyan shade.

2 Biltmore Hotel Head up Granada Blvd and turn left onto Anastasia Ave. Park along the road and walk around the grounds of this magnificent hotel (p99) to marvel at the palatial architecture. As crazy as it is, back in the day, that golf course was a private series of Venetian canals used by the likes of Al Capone and Judy Garland (when she was foxy! Rawr).

3 Coral Gables Congregational Church Walk just across the road to the Coral Gables Congregational Church (p99) and admire the fine Mediterranean-revival architecture, a bit of an aesthetic theme in this neighborhood.

4 Venetian Pool Zip up the diagonal of DeSoto Blvd, past the gurgling stone fountain of DeSoto Plaza and into the small, metered parking area for the Venetian Pool (p99). The perfectly sculpted landscaping, waterfalls, palm

DRIVE FACTS

Start Matsuri (5759 Bird Rd)
End Books & Books (296 Aragon Ave)
Duration 1½ to two hours
Fuel Stop Matsuri

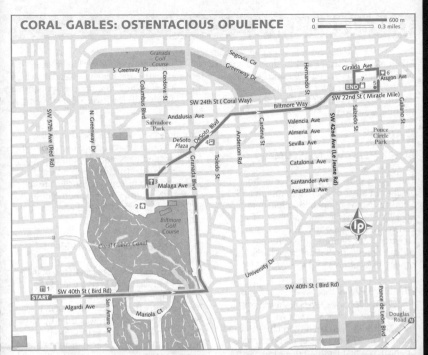

CORAL GABLES: OSTENTACIOUS OPULENCE

groves and shaded pavilions offer a taste, at least, of the Coral Gables' good life.

5 Miracle Mile Head east, past wedding-cake houses and under an organic pavilion of banyan branches, and eventually up and to the east again onto Miracle Mile, a sparkling stretch of the Gables' finest shopping outlets.

6 Bar Take the edge off and chat with some 'Gruppies' (Gables yuppies) at the excellent, the one, the only, the Bar (p151).

7 Books & Books Now go enjoy the lovely outdoor café (because nothing follows a beer like a coffee) and browse the excellent aisles of Books & Books (p120), Miami's best indie bookstore.

GREATER MIAMI

Drinking & Nightlife p151; Eating p140; Shopping p121; Sleeping p182

Miami spreads further and further, particularly south and west, every day. The soaring cost of real estate has priced thousands of Miamians into residential areas such as Kendall, which will become their own hip neighborhoods in coming years. While some of the spots listed are either way north or south of the epicenters, some simply fall in-between the city's many winding waterways.

NORTH

BLACK HERITAGE MUSEUM
☎ 305-252-3535
This roving museum presents rotating exhibits in areas of Miami, Chapman and Deering. It's the brainchild of teachers Priscilla S Kruize, Dr Paul Cadby and Dr Earl Wells, who set out in 1987 to establish a center that celebrates the cultures of African Americans, Bahamians, Haitians and other black cultures in Dade County.

HIALEAH PARK Map pp44–5
☎ 305-885-8000; www.savehialeahpark.com; 2200 E 4th Ave; ☿ 9am-5pm Mon-Fri
Hialeah is more Havanan than Little Havana (more than 90% of the population speaks Spanish as a first language), and the symbol and center of this working-class Cuban community is this grand but endangered former racetrack. Although Seabiscuit and Seattle Slew once raced here, the last race was held in 2001, and since then a fight's been raging to keep this gem from being paved over. The track was even the subject of pop culture protest in the form of the song 'Save Hialeah Park' by Los Primeros, a Hialeah-based Latin boy band in 2008. A walk through the grounds is recommended, if just to gaze at the grand staircases, pastel-painted concourse and listen for the long-stopped thunder of racing hooves. Look for the caps, boots and saddle carved into the window below the administration building and the oft-photographed central fountain.

SOUTH

CHESS HALL OF FAME Map pp44–5
☎ 786-242-4255; www.chessmuseum.org; 13755 SW 119th Ave; suggested donation adult/child $5/3; ☿ 10:30am-5pm
You would think that chess fanatics would have orderly minds and be good at scheduling, but this museum was closed both times we visited, despite coming during regular hours. So we can only tell you that the Chess HoF is located in a big white rook-like structure with a sword-in-the-stone out front (seriously), and is apparently filled with paraphernalia such as Bobby Fischer's table and ancient chess accoutrement.

DEERING ESTATE AT CUTLER
Map pp44–5
☎ 305-235-1668; www.deeringestate.org; 16701 SW 72nd Ave; adult/child 14 yrs & under $7/5; ☿ 10am-5pm, last tickets sold 4pm
The Deering estate is sort of Vizcaya lite, which makes sense as it was built by Charles, brother of James Deering (of Vizcaya fame). The 150-acre grounds are awash in tropical growth, an animal-fossil pit of bones dating back 50,000 years and the prehistoric remains of Native Americans who lived here 2000 years ago. Much of what is appropriate for display can be found in places such as the Historical Museum of Southern Florida (p69), but some artifacts are on display here. You can also take a three-hour guided canoe tour (per person $21; ☎ 10am Sat & Sun) out to the mangrove and marsh habitats of offshore Chicken Key. There's a free tour of the grounds included in admission, and the estate often hosts jazz evenings under the stars.

FAIRCHILD TROPICAL GARDEN
Map pp44–5
☎ 305-667-1651; www.fairchildgarden.org; 10901 Old Cutler Rd; adult/child 3-12 yrs $20/10; ☿ 9:30am-4:30pm
If you need to escape Miami drivers, consider a green day in the country's largest tropical botanical garden. A butterfly grove, jungle biospheres and gentle vistas of marsh and Keys habitat, plus frequent art installations from folks such as Roy Lichtenstein, are all relaxingly stunning. But Fairchild has a serious purpose: the

study of tropical flora by the garden's more than 6000 members. In addition to easy-to-follow self-guided walking tours, a (kinda overlong) free 40-minute tram tours the entire park, on the hour from 10am to 3pm.

FISHER ISLAND Map pp44–5

One day Carl Fisher purchased this little island and planned on dying here. But as is wont to happen, the millionaire got bored. When William K Vanderbilt II fell in love with the place, Fisher traded the island for Vanderbilt's 250ft yacht and its crew. Things were like that in those days. Vanderbilt proceeded to build a splendiferous Spanish-Mediterranean-style mansion, with guest houses, studios, tennis courts and a golf course.

Today, this exclusive resort is accessible only by air and private ferry. The condominiums that line the mile-long private beach range from $1-million hovels to a $7-million-plus pad President Bill Clinton once borrowed. It's said the sun shines over the island even when it's raining on Miami Beach; maybe when you play with nature by importing boatloads of sugary white sand from the Bahamas you have sway over the weather, too. Moneyed readers can overnight on Fisher Island at the Inn at the Fisher Island Club (p182). The island is usually open only to paying guests and residents, but you can arrange a tour with hotel staff if you're especially persistent. Ferries leave from Fisher Island Ferry Terminal off the MacArthur Causeway. The air-conditioned ferries depart every 15 minutes around the clock and the trip takes 10 minutes.

FRUIT & SPICE PARK off map pp44–5

☎ 305-247-5727; www.fruitandspicepark.org; 24801 SW 187th Ave; adult/child $6/1.50; ☾ 10am-5pm

Been Lonely Planet-ing around Australia, Africa or Southeast Asia? Welcome back. Set just on the edge of the Everglades, this 35-acre tropical public park grows all those great tropical fruits you usually have to contract dysentery to enjoy. The park is divided into 'continents' (Africa, Asia, etc) and admission to the pretty grounds includes a free tour; you can't pick the fruit, but you can eat anything that falls to the ground.

GOLD COAST RAILROAD MUSEUM Map pp44–5

☎ 305-253-0063; www.goldcoast-railroad.org; 12450 SW 152nd St; adult/child 3-11 yrs $5/3; ☾ 11am-4pm Mon-Fri, 10am-4pm Sat & Sun

Trainspotters will undoubtedly choo-choo-choose to put this attraction near the top of their itinerary. Sorry. Ralph Wiggumisms aside, over 30 antique railway cars await here, including the Ferdinand Magellan presidential car, which Harry Truman stood on when he held the newspaper with the erroneous headline 'Dewey Defeats Truman.' Train rides and model train building sessions are also available.

HIBISCUS, PALM & STAR ISLANDS Map pp44–5

Somewhere in the midrange of Miami island exclusivity, these little floating Primrose Hills are at least accessible by car. There aren't many famous people living here – just rich ones – although Star Island is home to Gloria Estefan, and for a short time Al Capone lived (and died) on Palm Island. The islands' circular drives are guarded by a security booth, but the roads are public, so if you ask politely and don't look sketchy, you can get in. Star Island is little more than one elliptical road lined with royal palms, sculpted ficus hedges and fancy gates guarding houses you can't see.

JUNGLE ISLAND Map pp44–5

☎ 305-666-7834; www.parrotjungle.com; 1111 Parrot Jungle Trail, off I-395/MacArthur Causeway, Watson Island; adult/child $27.95/22.95, plus parking $6; ☾ 10am-6pm

They call it Jungle Island now, but it'll always be Parrot Jungle to us, a glorious homage to tourism kitsch. Anyways, this is one of those places kids beg to go to, so just give up and prepare for some bright-feathered, bird-poopie-scented fun. Actually, the 18-acre waterfront facility, lushly landscaped and using a minimum of pesticides, is pretty impressive, thanks in part to the parrots, macaws, flamingos and cockatoos flying about in outdoor aviaries. The Cape Penguin colony is especially cute. Other critters include snakes, crocodiles, gibbons and orangutans, and don't worry, the walkways are covered against both rain and bird turds.

MATHESON HAMMOCK PARK Map pp44–5

☎ 305-665-5475; 9610 Old Cutler Rd; admission per car $4; ☼ 6am-sunset

This 100-acre county park is the city's oldest and one of its most scenic. It offers good swimming for children in a closed tidal pool, lots of hungry raccoons, dense mangrove swamps, and (pretty rare) crocodile spotting. There are leafy walking and biking trails, a nice picnic area and a peaceful path edging Biscayne Bay.

MIAMI CHILDREN'S MUSEUM Map pp44–5

☎ 305-373-5437; www.miamichildrensmuseum .org; 980 MacArthur Causeway, Watson Island; admission $8; ☼ 10am-6pm

It's not so much a museum as a glorified playhouse, with areas for kids to practice all sorts of adult activities like banking and food shopping (at models of Bank of America and Publix, which probably paid good money to have their brands imprinted on the brains of the naifs), caring for pets, playing TV news anchor in a studio and acting as a local cop or firefighter. There are also educational displays about subjects ranging from Miami architecture to Brazilian culture. Be forewarned: this place is a zoo on rainy days.

MIAMI METROZOO Map pp44–5

☎ 305-251-0400; www.miamimetrozoo.com; 12400 SW 152nd St; adult/child $11.50/6.75; ☼ 9:30am-5:30pm, last admission 4pm

Miami boasts an excellent zoo, thanks in part to a subtropical climate that allows for large swathes of natural habitat. More than 200 species rep themselves, from elephants to koalas, colobus monkeys, black rhinoceroses, a pair of Komodo dragons and Bengal tigers (including a gorgeous white tiger) prowling an evocative Hindu temple. For a quick overview (because the zoo is so big), hop on the Zoofari Monorail. There's a glut of grounds tours available, and kids will love feeding the Samburu giraffes ($2).

MONKEY JUNGLE Map pp44–5

☎ 305-235-1611; www.monkeyjungle.com; 14805 SW 216th St; adult/child 4-12 yrs $25.95/19.95; ☼ 9:30am-5pm, last admission 4pm

Monkey Jungle brochures have a tag line: 'Where humans are caged and monkeys run free.' And, indeed, you'll be walking through screened-in trails, with primates swinging freely, screeching and chattering all around you. It's actually incredibly fun, and just a bit odorous, especially on warm days (well, most days).

In 1933 animal behaviorist Joseph du Mond released six monkeys into the wild. Today, their descendants live here with orangutans, chimpanzees and the lowland gorilla. The tropical hardwood hammock contains plants collected in South America and feels like the Amazonian ecosystem. The big show of the day takes place at feeding time, when crab-eating monkeys and Southeast Asian macaques dive into the pool for fruit and other treats.

NATIONAL HURRICANE CENTER

Map pp44–5

☎ 305-229-4404; www.nhc.noaa.gov; 11691 SW 17th St; ☼ Hurricane off-season, generally late Jan-May (check website)

Florida and hurricanes go together like peanut butter and destructive jelly, and this fascinating center is the first line of defense against these devastating storms. Free 40-minute tours are available by appointment only, and document both the drama of hurricanes and the intricacies of storm-tracking, one of the main responsibilities of this facility, located on the campus of Florida International University (FIU).

WINGS OVER MIAMI Map pp44–5

☎ 305-233-5197; www.wingsovermiami.com; Kendall-Tamiami Executive Airport, 14710 SW 128th St; adult/senior & child under 13 yrs $9.95/5.95; ☼ 10am-5:30pm Thu-Sun

Plane-spotters will love this Tamiami Airport museum. Highlights include a propeller collection, J47 jet engine and a Soviet bomber from Smolensk. An impressive exhibit on the Tuskegee Airmen features videos of the black pilots telling their own stories. Historic bombers and other craft drop in for occasional visits, so you can never be sure what you'll see.

SHOPPING

top picks

- **Hip.e** (p121)
- **Books & Books** (p120)
- **Delicias de Espana** (p121)
- **Moooi** (p117)
- **Hiho Batik/Sprocket Gift Shop** (p118)
- **Do Re Mi Music Center** (p119)
- **Vierge Miracle & St Philippe Botanica** (p117)
- **La Casa de los Trucos** (p119)
- **Artisan Antiques Art Deco** (p117)
- **C. Madeleine's** (p115)

What's your recommendation? www.lonelyplanet.com/miami

SHOPPING

Did you know the average American consumes as much energy as 31 Indians? A good chunk of that statistic could be probably attributed to the shopping habits of Miamians.

The ingredients are all there. Warm weather. Beaches. Tourists – folks on vacation always splurge. Latin culture, which, to be frank, puts a bit of emphasis on appearance. All those immigrants, who have turned South Florida into a sunny international bazaar, who came to America to consume and buy things they simply couldn't access at home. You don't flee communist Cuba to totally reject consumer capitalism.

And most importantly, there's a *lot* of money floating around. This might blow your mind: a 2008 report by the *South Florida Sun Sentinel* estimated that if you included people's property and possessions, one in 10 residents of Broward, Palm Beach and Miami-Dade counties are millionaires. And maybe millionaires up north act with understatement, but folks here like to live the good life and show off while they're doing it. This is Miami, folks; that sun makes you wanna strut.

So there's a big shopping scene here, as overstated and in your face as a South Beach ensemble of rhinestone-studded jeans, silk muscle shirt, shiny belt buckle and diamante-encrusted shades. It's also as occasionally innovative as a Design District showroom of funny furniture that challenges your conception of 'chair' and laughs while it does it.

There are malls here – lots of 'em – although thanks to the weather, many are open to the elements and feel a little more organic than your average consumo-plex. And despite the genius Americans possess for Starbucking the shopping experience, there's some distinct browsing within Miami's neighborhoods.

Always be aware the Miami shopping scene reflects the tastes of the city's inhabitants. Miami is a creative city, but it's a very commercial one as well, so those tastes can either be startlingly original, or startlingly amateurish attempts at recreating the original. For example: South Beach clothing stores. At their best, they're glamorous and sexy – of course, this is South Beach – but to use the *Zoolander* analogy, they're Magnum. No-one else can replicate the look they sell. To continue with the *Zoolander* theme, the worst stores sell Blue Steel: superficially, the aesthetic looks the same, but it's somehow tackier, less well put together, and trashier. Learn to differentiate between store A (hot) and store B (ho) and you're on your way to becoming a Miami shopping maven.

NOSING AROUND BY NEIGHBORHOOD

South Beach is, of course, high end. Among the chains are some beautiful boutiques, to say nothing of the pleasures of taking a window-shopping stroll down Collins Ave, Washington Ave or Lincoln Rd. Art galleries are scattered throughout the city, but there's obviously a glut in Wynwood and the Design District, which also rule the roost for concept furniture and design stuff (duh). In North Miami Beach, the Bal Harbour shops are an incredibly upscale parade of high-end brand names; look, there are live models twirling around in Saks Fifth Ave!

Downtown has some tame malls, particularly Bayside Marketplace, and dodgy looking (but deal-making) electronic places in the otherwise empty streets near Government Center. Little Havana sells plenty of Latin tat, from Jesus statues to anti-Fidel anything to excellent salsa CDs, and here and in Little Haiti you can explore a new side of the American consumer experience: *botanicas* that sell *vodou* (voodoo) and *Santeria* ingredients. Can you get *sangre de dragon* (dragon's blood) in the Gap? Right on the other end of the scale is Coconut

top picks

SHOPPING STRIPS

- Collins Ave south of 9th St, South Beach
- Grand Ave, Coconut Grove
- Lincoln Road Mall, South Beach
- NE 40th St, Design District
- Miracle Mile, Coral Gables

CLOTHING SIZES

Women's clothing

Aus/UK	8	10	12	14	16	18
Europe	36	38	40	42	44	46
Japan	5	7	9	11	13	15
USA	6	8	10	12	14	16

Women's shoes

Aus/USA	5	6	7	8	9	10
Europe	35	36	37	38	39	40
France only	35	36	38	39	40	42
Japan	22	23	24	25	26	27
UK	3½	4½	5½	6½	7½	8½

Men's clothing

Aus	92	96	100	104	108	112
Europe	46	48	50	52	54	56
Japan	S		M	M		L
UK/USA	35	36	37	38	39	40

Men's shirts (collar sizes)

Aus/Japan	38	39	40	41	42	43
Europe	38	39	40	41	42	43
UK/USA	15	15½	16	16½	17	17½

Men's shoes

Aus/UK	7	8	9	10	11	12
Europe	41	42	43	44½	46	47
Japan	26	27	27½	28	29	30
USA	7½	8½	9½	10½	11½	12½

Measurements approximate only, try before you buy

Grove and American consumer culture at its tacky, comforting best. With that said, Streets of Mayfair and CocoWalk are two of the nicest malls you'll find anywhere. You'd think Coral Gables would be packed with brand bland (and to a degree, it is), but it's also surprisingly awash with indie stores and local businesses that sell everything from lovely lingerie to continental gourmet goodness.

OPENING HOURS & SEASONAL SALES

In South Beach, expect the majority of stores open by 10am and staying open till 9pm or 10pm. More standard hours of operation, such as in malls and in more staid parts of town, are typically 9am or 10am until 7pm or 8pm. Note that almost all Design District businesses are closed Sundays and Mondays; Little Havana shops often close on Sundays as well.

Typically, fashion retailers around Miami have sales in between seasons – but those seasons are shorter than nonfashionistas would think. Just when you're getting used to it being winter, for example in January, winter merchandise will start to get marked down – with savings as high as 60% off – to make way for spring duds. Look for summer sales starting in July. If you're lucky and have a keen eye, you can often come across special sale events as well. In the Design District, for example, major sample sales – showcasing floor samples, surplus stock or brand-new introductions from designers – happen a few times a year. Check www.designmiami.com/events for updates.

TAXES & COSTS

Sales tax in Miami-Dade county is 7%. Where you shop determines how much you pay; there are four-digit jackets for sale on South Beach and dollar stores a-plenty in Little Havana and Haiti. As for bargaining: this is Miami, not India. Unless you're shopping for a used car or real estate, be prepared to pay what's on the price tag.

SOUTH BEACH

You're beautiful, you know it, and the shops on South Beach are here to confirm it. Actually, 'confirm' is an understatement, because South Beach doesn't just offer retail therapy. No, the glut of tack, flash, glitz, and occasional independent innovation here all equals retail empowerment (and ego stroking).

BASS MUSEUM SHOP Map pp52–3 Art & Gifts
☎ 305-673-7530; 2121 Park Ave
The small, well-curated shop inside this excellent art museum has art, photography and architecture books, unique gift items, postcards, educational toys, and affordable original works of art and jewelry made by local artisans.

ARTCENTER/SOUTH FLORIDA
Map pp52–3   Art Gallery
☎ 305-538-7887; 800 Lincoln Rd
If you're in the market for painting, sculpture and any other medium by young, up-and-coming artists, this dynamic space, featuring open studios and gallery exhibits, is a good place to start.

BRITTO CENTRAL Map pp52–3 Art Gallery

☎ 305-531-8821; 818 Lincoln Rd

Should you have several thousand dollars and the desire to purchase one of Romero Britto's (p31) pieces – either iconic Miami or glaringly commercial installation art, depending on your tastes – this is the place to do so.

ESPAÑOLA WAY ART CENTER

Map pp48–9 Art Gallery

☎ 305-673-0946; 405 Española Way

There are three levels of studios here, plus excellent original work and prints for sale, all by local artists.

WINGS Map pp52–3 Beachwear, Kitsch & Gifts

☎ 305-538-3160; www.wingsbeachwear.com; 216 Lincoln Rd

Rather than run through a dozen souvenir/terrible T-shirt shops, just come to this ginormous beach emporium with the surfboard neon sign and load up on all the tatty tourism crap you'll ever need.

BOOKS & BOOKS Map pp52–3 Books

☎ 305-532-3222; 933 Lincoln Rd

Like its branch in Coral Gables (p120), this beautiful indie bookstore has an excellent array of titles, especially when it comes to Floridian and Miamian history, photography, coffee-table tomes, and literature by local authors from Edna Buchanan to Carl Hiaasen. You can also catch poetry readings and author book signings.

KAFKA KAFE Map pp48–9 Books

☎ 305-673-9669; www.kafkascafe.com; 1464 Washington Ave

Like a library run by a bunch of awesome hipsters, Kafka is one-stop shopping for word lovers: you'll find thousands of used books, a terrific magazine and newspaper selection, internet access on 24 computer terminals and a café.

CRIMSON CARBON Map pp48–9 Boutique

☎ 305-538-8262; Ste 101, 524 Washington Ave

Not only will you be hot after emerging from CC, you'll feel better about your place in the Circle of Life. The bubble shorts, California-style dresses and other chic standards this store sells are often organic, chemical-free and eco-friendly. CC carries Carilyn Vaile's green label, made

from raw bamboo, and Mad Imports, which sources its accessories from a Madagascar co-op.

LEO Map pp48–9 Boutique

☎ 305-531-6550; www.leomiami.com; 640 Collins Ave

A welcome break from SoBe's usual glam, Leo caters to the more indie-chic (or at least those who appreciate a decently witty T-shirt). The beautiful come to browse labels such as Diab'less, American Retro and Alexander Wang under a ceiling strewn with 500 light bulbs.

SOHO CLOTHING Map pp48–9 Boutique

☎ 305-531-3036; www.soho-clothing.com; 815 Washington Ave

Chunky, studded T-shirts, artfully ripped hoodies, daring halter dresses and cute kimono tops cinched by beaded belts rule the roost at this thumpin' store. It's a little euro-trashy, but in a 'just euro-trashy enough to be sexy' way. There's another location at 645 Lincoln Rd.

STAR IMAGE Map pp48–9 Boutique

☎ 305-673-0851; http://myspace.com/star_image_sobe; 851 Washington Ave

The clothes here blend hip-hop bagginess with SoBe fabulousness, set off with Miami Ink tattoo accents, at this glitzy and ghetto (as in ghetto fabulous) shop.

ALEXA & JACK

Map pp52–3 Children's Clothing & Toys

☎ 305-534-9300; 635 Lincoln Rd

Can't they just stay little till their Moschinos wear out? This popular Lincoln Rd stop hawks minifashions from the Italian designer, plus D&G Junior and Juicy Couture. Also find quality toys, gifts and accessories.

KIDROBOT INC.

Map pp48–9 Children's Clothing & Toys

☎ 305-673-5807; 638 Collins Ave

If your kid happens to be the hippest thing since sex, then by all means bring them here Brangelina, where they can shop for Ugly Dolls, limited edition 'art toys' (because kids care it's limited edition) and originally designed $200 sneakers that look like they snuck off a 1980s MTV promotional teaser.

DECO DRIVE CIGARS Map pp52–3   Cigars
☎ 305-531-8388; 414 Lincoln Rd
Should you need to risk mouth cancer with a 'vacation cigar', why not do so imitating all the local skinny-minnie models who love a fine Churchill with their martini-and-salad.

DECO DENIM Map pp48–9   Clothing
☎ 305-532-6986; 645 Collins Ave
For basic casualwear, this is your place, especially if you're looking to pick up some classic American Levi's in any form – from 501 button fly and super-low 518s to boot cuts and cargo pants.

EN AVANCE Map pp52–3   Clothing
☎ 305-534-0337; 734 Lincoln Rd
Want your shopping to be as chic as your nightclubbing? Then head here, where you'll be greeted by a velvet rope and a hot collection of high fashion once inside. The friendly staff will help you negotiate through the Rebecca Taylor, Juicy Couture, Tse and more. You'll also find Defile makeup and even designer styles for infants. Don't be surprised if you rub elbows with a celeb or two.

SCOOP Map pp52–3   Clothing
☎ 305-532-5929; www.scoopnyc.com; Shore Club, 1901 Collins Ave
If yours was the real-life story *Zoolander* was based on, you'd probably like to shop in Scoop, located in the Shore Club (p176) and full of hot-ticket fashion for models (male and female) from both its own label and others, including Juicy Couture, Paul Smith and Theory.

BASE Map pp52–3   Clubwear, Accessories & Music
☎ 305-531-4982; www.baseworld.com; 939 Lincoln Rd
This groovy hip-hop outlet has everything you need to be a good clubber – the latest Pumas, edgy streetwear, designer baseball caps, men's shaving and skincare products from gourmet labels, and a whole range of thumpa-thumpa and bom-chika-bom-chika CDs available for sampling at storefront listening stations.

ART DECO WELCOME CENTER
Map pp48–9   Collectibles & Gifts
☎ 305-531-3484; 1001 Ocean Dr
You could get lost in this quirky gift shop – despite the fact that it's teeny. The retail outlet of this information center has shelves stocked with all the books, jewelry, vintage postcards, posters, souvenir T-shirts and cool little knickknacks a deco-obsessive could ever want. If not: dude, you are *really* into deco.

APPLE STORE
Map pp52–3   Computers & Gadgets
☎ 305-538-7348; 738 Lincoln Rd
Macbook junkies and ipod-lovers, get your fix of Apple technology in a showroom that's as stripped down as an ipod nano, and just as preciously cute.

MAC Map pp48–9   Cosmetics
☎ 305-604-9040; 650 Collins Ave
Join the fabulous folks who have, at one point or another, been spokesmodels for this *trés* hip makeup shop: RuPaul, KD Lang, Linda Evangelista and Diana Ross. You'll be ready to do a testimonial, too, once you fall in love with the cosmetics' sleek packaging, fab hues, subtle fragrance and great staying power – as well as the shop's policy to donate all sales profits from its Viva Glam lipstick to the Mac AIDS Fund.

SEPHORA Map pp48–9   Cosmetics & Fragrances
☎ 305-532-0904; 721 Collins Ave
This massive makeup chain emporium has every conceivable line of cosmetics and skin products – Clinique, Hamadi, Clarins, Toni & Tina, Hard Candy, Nars, Estée Lauder, Paula Dorf, Korres and much, much more.

BEATNIX Map pp48–9   Costumes & Kitsch
☎ 305-532-8733; 1149 Washington Ave;
🕑 noon-midnight
Basically, this is where you come to get dressed up in some nightmarish outfit of your better-forgotten past. They've got vinyl dresses, '70s tracksuits and platform heels, plus coasters, postcards, glasses and wacky wigs.

MACY'S Map pp52–3   Department Store
☎ 305-674-6311; 1675 Meridian Ave
A grand Southern department store, this one-stop-shopping spot, hovering at the edge of Lincoln Rd, is an old-school sort of experience where you'll join retired snowbirds (Northerners who fly south during

winter) and hipsters alike, all looking for some sort of dress-lipstick-towel-pillow-sham collection of goods.

A/X ARMANI EXCHANGE
Map pp48–9   Designer Clothing
☎ 305-531-5900; 760 Collins Ave
The 'affordable' (hah!) retail branch of Armani, A/X is well stocked with all manner of sporty-chic pants, sweaters, jackets, button-downs and dresses.

BARNEY'S NEW YORK CO-OP
Map pp48–9   Designer Clothing
☎ 305-421-2010; 832 Collins Ave
The Miami outpost of New York City's den of style, this always-bustling shop has a little of everything to satiate label whores – Seven Jeans, Marc by Marc Jacobs trousers and Carrie-worthy Manolo Blahniks.

CLUB MONACO
Map pp48–9   Designer Clothing
☎ 305-674-7446; 624 Collins Ave
The chain boutique has slick and affordable streetwear with an understated European vibe for both men and women.

COMPASS MARKET Map pp48–9   Essentials
☎ 305-673-2906; Waldorf Towers Hotel, 860 Ocean Dr
Think useful things: this basement market is packed with anything you'd ever need while on a relaxing beach vacation. Cheap sandals, umbrellas, deli items, cigars, wine and newspapers – if you forgot to pack it, they have it here.

SEE Map pp52–3   Eyewear
☎ 305-672-6622; 921 Lincoln Rd

Find high-style eyeglass frames from clunky electroclash-DJ to wireframe bookish-babe, straight from manufacturers used by big-name labels, all at reasonable prices.

WOLFSONIAN-FIU GIFT SHOP
Map pp48–9   Giftwares
☎ 305-531-1001; Wolfsonian-FIU, 1001 Washington Ave
The small gift shop housed in this wonderful quirky museum has one of the most unique collections of eclectic items around. You'll find sleek business-card holders, oddly shaped water pitchers and glassware, technofied bags and notebooks, art and design books, cool wallets and basically any kind of iconic design, or at least great imitations of such, you could ever desire.

EPICURE MARKET
Map pp52–3   Gourmet Food & Wine
☎ 305-672-1861; 1656 Alton Rd
Whether you have cooking facilities in your inn or just want a fancy beach picnic, this is the place. You'll find an outstanding array of fresh produce, sinful baked goods, fresh flowers, premade meals (including matzoball soup, lasagna and salads), imported treats such as jams and tapenades, and an excellent selection of fine, global wines.

BROWNES & CO APOTHECARY
Map pp52–3   Grooming Products
☎ 305-532-8703; 841 Lincoln Rd
This casually chic shop has the best selection of soaps, cosmetics and beauty and skin products from around the world, from labels including Acca Kappa, Agent Provocateur, Bliss, Bumble & Bumble and Dr Hauschka. There are enough lotions and ointments around to make a dead cat smell pretty.

ETHICAL BUYS

You know, your shopping habit can actually help the world. Well, it can at least be more easily justified to yourself. All profits from Viva Glam lipstick sold at Mac (p111) benefit the Mac AIDS Fund, while Crimson Carbon (p110) markets an entire green line of organic textile clothing. Speaking of organic, farmers markets (p125) support local growers and sell the best produce in town besides, while the Whole Foods Market (opposite) sells lots of organic, non-pesticide-y products, plus fair-trade coffee. Karma Car Wash (p132) is an organic wash 'n' wax that happens to sell gourmet tapas and, again, fair-trade coffee, while Condom-USA (p120) supports sex education and sexual health programs every time a rubber changes hands (so to speak). Please peruse indies such as Books & Books (p120), which are cornerstones of neighborhood identity and promote readings from local authors. Sweat Records (p118) has a full-service organic coffee counter, vegan cupcakes and, more importantly, does a good job of pushing the local, loyal rock scene. Finally, in the Lowe Art Museum Gift Shop (p120), you can buy beautiful Claude Monet cards, printed on 100% recycled paper and assembled by disabled US veterans.

KIEHL'S Map pp52–3 — Grooming Products

☎ 305-531-0404; www.kiehls.com; 832 Lincoln Rd

Since 1851, when this old-fashioned apothecary got its start in NYC's East Village, this simple-label, simple-formula line of products has had many ardent fans. This sleek South Beach emporium hawks high-quality lip balms, skin moisturizers, shampoos, soaps, hair-styling lotions and shaving products.

WHOLE FOODS MARKET

Map pp48–9 — Health Food & Groceries

☎ 305-532-1707; 1020 Alton Rd

The latest outpost of this natural-foods chain has a great array of organic produce, packaged products from cereals to soaps, bulk items, prepared meals and an OK salad bar. You'll also find a good range of wines, beers, cheeses and fresh elixirs squeezed at the juice bar. There are good fresh meats and fish for the carnivores, too.

SENZATEMPO Map pp52–3 — Homewares & Gifts

☎ 305-534-5588; 1655 Meridian Ave

Amid all the deco, you'd think there'd be more design shops lying around. Well, come to this retro gallery, with its decorative pieces and 20th-century designer furniture, plus plenty of clocks and watches, to feed that fix.

ME & RO Map pp52–3 — Jewelry

☎ 305-672-3566; Shore Club, 1901 Collins Ave

If it's in the Shore Club, it's got to be good. Right? Join in-the-know bauble mavens (including Julia Roberts) who shop for these bracelets, rings and earrings in silver and gold, crafted with Asian accents by celebrity jewelers Robin Renzi and Michele Quan.

CLAUDIA N Map pp52–3 — Jewelry/Watches

☎ 305-534-5986; 639 Lincoln Rd

This is the spot to deck yourself out in Miami-style jewelry: blingy, *Scarface*-showy pieces that let everyone know you've got it, and by God you will flaunt it. Think iced-out Hello Kitty watches (seriously).

JEWISH MUSEUM OF FLORIDA GIFT SHOP Map pp48–9 — Judaica

☎ 305-672-5044; www.jewishmuseum.com; 301 Washington Ave

The gift shop in the front lobby of this museum is tiny, but it has a lovely little selection of Judaica, including menorahs, Sabbath candle holders, mezuzahs and prayer books.

POP Map pp48–9 — Kitsch

☎ 305-604-9604; 1151 Washington Ave

Find the collectible kitsch of your dreams at this pop-culture purveyor. From George Jetson and his nuclear family to Ken and Barbie, the traditional household unit is covered.

HAVANA SHIRT STORE

Map pp48–9 — Men's Clothing

☎ 786-276-9240; 760 Ocean Dr

Caters a bit to the Carnival Cruise crowd (look, the store's on Ocean Dr), but it's got a decent selection of cool linen *guayaberas* (brocaded men's shirts) here.

WHITTALL & SHON

Map pp48–9 — Men's Clothing

☎ 305-538-2606; 900 Washington Ave

The disco beat here gets your adrenaline going while you flip through racks of way-gay muscle tees, tank tops and sundry other clingy tops, some sporting cruise-y phrases like 'caliente!,' '69' or 'coach.' Teensy, bubble-butt-squeezing swim trunks are also here: hot stuff.

FYE MUSIC Map pp48–9 — Music

☎ 305-534-3667; 501 Collins Ave

FYE is sort of the Virgin Records of Miami: loud, ubiquitous and enormous. This two-story location has a café, listening booths and a so-so selection of CDs, DVDs and videos that leans toward the mainstream.

UNCLE SAM'S MUSIC Map pp48–9 — Music

☎ 305-532-0973; www.unclesamsmusic.com; 1141 Washington Ave

Join hipper-than-thou skate rats, club kids and all the others you sometimes just want to punch as they dig through piles of the coolest new (and used) trance, hip-hop and trip-hop, as well as stickers, clubwear, incense and the like.

PURE PERFUME/THE FRAGRANCE SHOP Map pp52–3 — Perfume

☎ 305-535-0037; 612 Lincoln Rd

There are racks and racks of smells and soaps here, but the most innovative bit: they let you mix up your own scents if you so desire.

SHOPPING SOUTH BEACH

NEWS CAFÉ STORE Map pp48–9 Periodicals
☎ 305-538-6397; 800 Ocean Dr
Look for the separate 24-hour newsstand between the News Café (p128) bar and restaurant. It has a good selection of international and domestic papers.

RICKY'S NYC Map pp52–3 Sexy Costumes & Gifts
☎ 305-674-8511; www.rickys-nyc.com; 536a Lincoln Rd
Ricky's is a nice little example of the 'where the hell did that come from?' school of retail display. There's all kinds of souvenir kitsch downstairs plus everyday useful things you'd find in a convenience store. And then, upstairs, you enter rack upon rack of naughty nurse uniforms, sexy schoolgirl outfits and the like. It's packed here come Halloween.

PLEASURE PLACE
Map pp48–9 Sexy Gifts, Costumes & Lingerie
☎ 305-604-8771; www.pleasureplace.com; 425 Washington Ave
You should focus on buying sex toys and other adult accoutrements here, because the actual clothing is about as risqué as the rest of the clubwear on South Beach. OK, just kidding about the last bit. But only just.

LONDON SOLE Map pp48–9 Shoes
☎ 305-674-8688; www.londonsole.com; 760 Ocean Dr
American girls have not rediscovered the ballerina flat the way their European counterparts have, but London Sole is working to change that, providing colorful, sexy shoes you can wear down the beach and out to the club, all in the course of one long, fashionable day.

STEVEN BY STEVE MADDEN
Map pp52–3 Shoes & Bags
☎ 305-673-9992; www.stevemadden.com; 817 Lincoln Rd
All the glam-y girls from Diablo Cody to Alicia Keys flock to Steven stores around the country for open-toes, flats, heels, boots and all the leather-bound accoutrements a foot and bag freak could ever want.

ABSOLUTELY SUITABLE
Map pp52–3 Swimwear
☎ 305-604-5281; 1560 Collins Ave
For looking your best on the beach and by the pool, peruse these fine racks for bikinis and swimsuits, in all sizes and shapes, plus swim trunks, flip-flops and sun hats.

DESIREE NERCESSIAN
Map pp48–9 Swimwear
☎ 305-604-0521; 710 Washington Ave
We're still not sure how to pronounce the name of this place, but we do know it sells lovely beachwear that gets you noticed without sacrificing your dignity, and for that matter, your wallet.

RITCHIE SWIMWEAR Map pp48–9 Swimwear
☎ 305-538-0201; 106 8th St
Mix-n-match bikini tops and bottoms make a big-busted, tiny-hinied (or flat-chested, big-bootied) gal feel at home. This place is heavy on string-comprised, minimum-coverage styles.

SOFI SWIMWEAR Map pp52–3 Swimwear
www.sofiswimwear.com; 1522 Washington Ave
Goodness gracious glamorous. Founded by Brazilian designer Surya Oliveira, Sofi sells more zen, elegantly subdued swimsuits than the average thong-tha-thong-thong-thong bikinis on display in these parts.

RECYCLED BLUES Map pp52–3 Used Clothing
☎ 305-538-0656; www.recycledbluesinc.com; 1507 Washington Ave
Got budgetary blues? It's wall-to-wall funk-defied used clothing here, although the focus is more discarded modern style than vintage chic. Think of Recycled as a very cool Salvation Army. Find Levi's for $15, shorts for $10 and jackets for $20.

DASZIGN NEW YORK
Map pp52–3 Women's Clothing
☎ 305-531-5531; www.daszign.com; Ritz-Carlton South Beach, 1663 Collins Ave
This boutique is hot, bursting with labels including Rebecca Taylor, Juicy Couture, 2 B Free, and denim from Seven, Paper Denim & Cloth, Joe's, Hudson and more. Unique accessories and footwear from New York designers are also on display.

MISS SIXTY Map pp52–3 Women's Clothing
☎ 305-538-3547; 845 Lincoln Rd
This is one seriously hot Italian label, boasting an array of jeans, dresses, jackets and sweaters for the cool, skinny, model-beautiful gals among us.

NICOLE MILLER Map pp48–9 Women's Clothing
☎ 305-535-2200; www.nicolemiller.com;
656 Collins Ave
Think Hamptons-chic at this boutique:
home to perfect little halter tops, skirts,
cocktail dresses and blouses.

MIAMI BEACH & NORTH MIAMI

This is mall country. To be more precise,
it's high-end mall country; Aventura (right)
is a little upscale, while the Bal Harbour
Shops (right) feel more like a Medici palace
from renaissance Florence than a brand-
name open-air parade (for the record, it is
definitely the latter). Both are stuffed with
pretty outstanding shops of every genre
(despite being airless, Muzak-spewing, fake
environment…well…*malls*). Various little
independent shops pop up around here, especially along North Biscayne Blvd, so keep
your eyes open for fun stops en route to the
megamall of your choice.

MINI OXYGENE Map pp58–9 Children's Clothing
☎ 305-868-4499; Bal Harbour Shops,
9700 Collins Ave
Clothe your baby or toddler in fine French
fashions. Isn't the mini-you worth it?

NORDSTROM'S
off Map pp44-5 Department Store
☎ 305-356-6900; Aventura Mall, 19501
Biscayne Blvd
The granddaddy of American department
stores has staked out an entire new wing of
Aventura, where they hock brand fashion,
watches, perfumes and everything else
under the consumer-crazy sun.

TARGET Map pp58–9 Discount Superstore
☎ 305-944-5341; 14075 Biscayne Blvd, N Miami
Beach
It's the discount store of the moment in US
cities, with good reason. Where else can
you find Isaac Mizrahi fashions, high-thread-
count sheets, a new set of flatware, a digital
camera, shoes, Michael Graves–designed
homewares, toys and a bag of potato chips
all under one roof? Prices are incredibly
cheap, too. There are plenty of locations
around town, including 8350 S Dixie Hwy,
21265 Biscayne Blvd and 15005 SW 8th St.

LALIQUE Map pp58–9 Gifts
☎ 305-861-5211; Bal Harbour Shops,
9700 Collins Ave
The French makers of fine gifts present
their awe-inspiring collection of crystal
vases, fine stemware, leather bags, silk
scarves, porcelain dishes and high-end
watches and jewelry. It's the perfect place
to shop for a high-class bride.

TIFFANY & CO Map pp58–9 Jewelry
☎ 305-864-1801; Bal Harbour Shops,
9700 Collins Ave
If you're gonna go bling, you might as well
come here and do so in immaculate style.

AVENTURA MALL off Map pp44–5 Mall
☎ 305-935-1110; www.shopaventuramall.com;
19501 Biscayne Blvd
This mainstream granddaddy of a mall
attracts families with its enormous indoor
playground, and shoppers with Macy's,
Lord & Taylor and Bloomingdale's department stores, plus smaller boutiques of
every genre. There is also a scarily massive
24-screen movie theater with stadium
seating, as well as hotel shuttles that make
it a cinch for South Beach visitors to haul
themselves up here.

BAL HARBOUR SHOPS Map pp58–9 Mall
☎ 305-866-0311; www.balharbourshops.com;
9700 Collins Ave
The Shops are a mall. OK. But they're also
kind of the ultimate perfection of mall, the
mall all the other malls want to be when
they graduate from Mall School. Perfectly
landscaped, decked in paintings, and exclusively high end, the only places to shop
here are stores such as Chanel and Jimmy
Choo, Prada and Agent Provocateur.
   Then again, end of the day: it's just a
freakin' mall.

KOKO & PALENKI SHOES
off Map pp44–5 Shoes
☎ 305-792-9299; Aventura Mall, 19501
Biscayne Blvd
Get excited over the addiction-inspiring
collection here, with styles from D&G,
Guess, Charles Jourdan and more.

C. MADELEINE'S Map pp58–9 Vintage Clothing
☎ 305-945-7770; http://shop.cmadeleines.com;
13702 Biscayne Blvd

The undisputed queen of vintage Miami, C. Madeleine is more than your standard used-clothes write off. This place is a serious temple to classical style, selling Yves Saint Laurent couture and classic Chanel suits. Come here to pick up the sort of timeless looks that are as beautiful now as they were when they first appeared on the rack.

BETSEY JOHNSON

off Map pp44–5   Women's Wear

☎ 305-673-0023; Aventura Mall, 19501 Biscayne Blvd

The bright, quirky and thoroughly eclectic line from the bright-eyed Betsey specializes in fun and sexy skirts and dresses, with funkified frilly blouses and hose thrown in for good measure.

BRIONI Map pp58–9   Women's Wear

☎ 305-868-9399; Bal Harbour Shops, 9700 Collins Ave

Power suits of the Samantha (of *Sex and the City*) school of design compete for rack space with elegant night wear and perfect-by-day dresses.

LILLY PULITZER

off Map pp44–5   Women's Wear & Accessories

☎ 305-705-1473; Aventura Mall, 19501 Biscayne Blvd

Palm-Beached Lilly Pulitzer sells flowy Florida styles and tropi-bright, pastel pastiche bags and accessories to go with your sunny stylin'.

LULULEMON ATHLETICA

off Map pp44–5   Yoga & Athletic Wear

☎ 305-705-1473; Aventura Mall, 19501 Biscayne Blvd

Rejoice, yoga yuppies: lululemon is a store actually dedicated to athletic wear for yoga practitioners, further proof that America can market anything to anyone.

DOWNTOWN MIAMI

The heart of Downtown, especially along Flagler St, is crammed with dozens upon dozens of shops selling export-ready electronics, primarily to Latin American visitors. You'll also see countless storefronts hawking cheap luggage, watches, cameras (without warranties) and leather items, mainly to the folks who pile off cruise ships day after day at the nearby port. Then, of course, there's the Mall of America-ish Bayside Marketplace (below), with enough mainstream chain stores to make your head spin.

SEYBOLD BUILDING

Map pp66–7   Accessories & Jewelry

☎ 305-374-7922; 36 NE 1st St; ☷ 9am-5:30pm Mon-Sat

This is Miami's gem and jewelry bazaar: some 300 independent stores in this (sort of) mini-mall sell glittery diamonds, gold pendants, rings and other trinkets.

WALLFLOWER GALLERY Map pp66–7   Art

☎ 305-579-0069; 10 NE 3rd St

Put this funky, cool gallery on your short list of places to check out. Between performance pieces, live music and 'regular' art shows featuring local talent, this cultural oasis boasts plenty of artwork worth splurging on.

HISTORICAL MUSEUM OF SOUTHERN FLORIDA GIFT SHOP

Map pp66–7   Collectibles & Gifts

☎ 305-375-1492; 101 W Flagler St

Sort of the classiest place to buy Sunshine State tat, this excellent gift shop in the Historical Museum of Southern Florida (p69) thrives on Florida, Florida and more Florida: think faux alligators and tacky postcards, plus a fine array of Seminole arts, eclectic souvenirs and Miami books.

MACY'S Map pp66–7   Department Store

☎ 305-577-1500; 22 E Flagler St

This enormous department store offers clothing for women, men and children; homewares for the bath and bedroom; jewelry and watches; shoes and a whole lot more.

BAYSIDE MARKETPLACE

Map pp66–7   Outdoor Mall

☎ 305-577-3344; www.baysidemarketplace.com; 401 Biscayne Blvd

This touristy bayfront mall offers browsers entertainment, restaurants, bars, tour-boat docks, push-cart vendors and name-brand shops. A sampling of usual suspects includes the Disney Store, Victoria's Secret, Sunglass Hut, Bath & Body Works, the Gap, Express, Skechers and, of course, Starbucks. There are no surprises, except for the nice views.

WYNWOOD, THE DESIGN DISTRICT & LITTLE HAITI

If you can forget how odd it is for all these high-end, super-sexy homeware stores to be sticking out like a Scandinavian thumb in the middle of North Miami, you will be pleased as punch to commission a five-digit dinette set. And while it can be a tad tricky to pack a sofa in your suitcase, you can always ship it. The Mid-Town mall, with its budget Ross superstore, has obviously been built to attract the poorer residents who live just over the artsy border. In Little Haiti, you can pick up some Francophone and Creole cassettes and cure whatever ails you at one of several *vodou botanicas*. Note that most furniture stores are open from 10am to 5pm Monday to Friday.

LURIE GALLERY Map p82   Art Gallery
☎ 305-759-9155; 3814 NE Miami Ct
From unknown local painters to Rauschenberg and Warhol, to a tried-and-true collection of black-and-white jazz photography by Herman Leonard, this gallery has the lot. It also has staying power and plenty of art-collecting fans.

ART FUSION GALLERY
Map p82   Art Gallery
☎ 305-573-5619; 1st NE 40th St #3
Here you'll find the Design District's largest selection of French art-deco lighting, furniture and accessories, including unique pieces by Lalique Sabino and De Gue.

KUMA CENTRAL Map p82   Art Toys
☎ 305-573-4486; 130 NE 40th St
Another limited-edition toy shop that sells the sort of urban toys and playthings you can only find in Japan. The gidgets and gadgets and toys are all very neato, and the kids will no doubt love them (although they'd arguably be as happy with a fire truck) but it's glaringly obvious parents are here for their own sense of cool.

LAMBDA PASSAGE Map pp58–9   Books & DVDs
☎ 305-754-6900; 7545 Biscayne Blvd
Since the mid-1980s, this bookstore has been a fixture and meeting place for gays and lesbians, and a seller of coming-out books, gay literature, rainbow paraphernalia, magazines and films. There's queer porn in the back, natch.

LIBRERI MAPOU
Map p82   Books & Music
☎ 305-757-9922; 5919 NE 2nd Ave
You don't have to read Creole or French to shop here, but it certainly helps. Otherwise, there's as good a range of English-language titles on Haitian history and culture as you'll find anywhere stateside, as well as crafts, recorded music and Haitian periodicals.

VIERGE MIRACLE & ST PHILIPPE
Map p82   Botanica (Vodou Stores)
☎ 305-759-9100; 5910 NE 2nd Ave
Enter with an attitude full of respect, eyes wide open and some tactful questions, and you'll be treated to a unique experience: the wares, spells and goods of Haitian *vodou*. Be reverent to the large statues of *loa* (akin to angels) who guard the premises, and if you've got some problems with love or work, need dream interpretation or require a cleansing bath, the local *houngan* and *mambos* (respectively, male and female high priests) may be able to help you. Another excellent *botanica* is Halouba (www.haloubatemple.com; 101 NE 54th St).

MOOOI Map p82   Furniture
☎ 305-574-4045; www.moooimiami.com; 3438 N Miami Ave
They've got a great motto here: 'For design addicts, but more for design virgins.' If you've always wanted your house to look conceptual but haven't the slightest idea where to begin (or if you know exactly what you require out of a room), the friendly folks at this Marcel Wanders boutique will get you on the road to a really fine interior.

ARTISAN ANTIQUES ART DECO
Map p82   Furniture & Home Design
☎ 305-573-5619; 110 NE 40th St
This wonderful shop houses one of the world's largest collections of French art-deco lighting, furniture and accessories, including unique pieces by Lalique Sabino and De Gue.

HOLLY HUNT

Map p82   Furniture & Home Design

☎ 305-571-2012; www.hollyhunt.com; 3833 NE 2nd Ave

This spectacular 22,000-sq-ft showroom has a massive selection of furniture, textiles, lighting, art and decorative accessories. Featured designers include Holly Hunt, Christian Liaigre, Rose Tarlow and Kevin Kiley.

JALAN JALAN

Map p82   Furniture & International Antiquities

☎ 305-572-9998; www.jalanmiami.com; 3921 NE 2nd Ave

The name of this place is Indonesian/Malay for 'just walking' (or 'walking around'), but of course you knew that, you intrepid Lonely Planet reader you. More to the point, the owner has clearly been 'jalan'-ing a bit, bringing in incredible furniture, artifacts and antiquities from around the world and selling them in this lovely warehouse space.

HIHO BATIK/SPROCKET GIFT SHOP

Map pp58–9   Gifts & Batiks

☎ 305-754-8890; www.hihobatik.com; 6925 Biscayne Blvd

Hiho's a neat little shop where you can design your own batik (wax-and-dyed artwork; here they usually put it on T-shirts) with a friendly staff of artsy types, or look for an out-there urban gift among the shelves of the attached Spocket's – think mature pop-up books, weird home decor and the like.

KARTELL Map p82   Home Design

☎ 305-573-4010; 170 NE 40th St

This large storefront is filled with a pretty panoply of plastics – all finely sculpted into bona fide works of art (in the form of chairs, shelving units and tables) by designers including Philippe Starck, Giulio Polvara and Anna Castelli Ferrieri.

LUXE Map p82   Lighting

☎ 305-576-6639; 1 NE 40th St

Light up your life – and your home, wherever it may be – with some of the classiest, trendiest designer lighting accessories ever. Choose among chandeliers, wall sconces, table lamps, floor lamps, halogen lighting and lighting controls.

top picks

MIAMI ACCESSORIES

- Dolce & Gabbana sunglasses
- Havaiana flip-flops
- A tattoo (ankle, lower back, upper-arm)
- Big belt buckles, preferably blinged
- Swarovski crystals

SHOPS AT MIDTOWN MIAMI

Map p82   Mall

3200 N Miami Ave

The anchor of the city's plan to revitalize this rough-and-tumble neighborhood is a 600,000-sq-ft mall, which has all kinds of brand-name blah, including stores such as West Elm (a homeware/furniture outlet for those who can't afford the Design District), Target (for those who can't afford West Elm) and Ross (for those who can't afford Target).

SWEAT RECORDS Map p82   Music

☎ 305-758-5862; http://sweatrecordsmiami .blogspot.com; 5505 NE 2nd Ave

Sweat's almost a stereotype of the indie record store: it serves organic coffee, it's got big purple couches, it sells weird Japanese toys and there are skinny guys with thick glasses arguing over LPs you've never heard of. It feels a little out of place in hip-hop-y Latin Miami, but we're glad someone's waving the indie flag in this town.

LITTLE HAVANA

Little Havana has sort of become Miami's official Latin souvenir stand, albeit with a distinct anti-Castro theme (we couldn't help noticing 'Burn in Hell, Fidel' hot sauce as we browsed). There's also great Latin music, Spanish language bookstores and, *si*, plenty of cigars.

EL AGUILA VIDENTE Map p88   Botanica

☎ 305-854-4086; 1122 SW 8th St

Hey, *botanicas* can have variety. El Aguila doesn't do *vodou*, but it does cater to local *Santeria* worshipers with a nice assortment of Afro-Cuban magic recipes, tarot cards and religious icons for the discerning *santero*.

EL CRÉDITO CIGARS Map p88   Cigars
☎ 305-858-4162; 1106 SW 8th St
In one of the most popular cigar stores in Miami, and one of the oldest in Florida, you'll be treated as an old member of the stogie-chomping boy's club.

LA TRADICIÓN CUBANA
Map p88   Cigars
☎ 305-643-4005; 1894 SW 8th St
Watch workers roll your cigars before you buy them at this little factory.

LA CASA DE LOS TRUCOS
Map p88   Costumes
☎ 305-858-5029; 1343 SW 8th St; ⊗ 10am-6pm Mon-Sat
In the middle of Little Havana is a surreal outdoor monster menagerie of vampires and mummies guarding a cavernous yet claustrophobic 'House of Costumes.' Because nothing completes the Little Havana experience like a *cubano* (Cuban sandwich), a cigar and a Bo Peep outfit.

LOS PINARENOS FRUITERIA
Map p88   Farmers Market
☎ 305-285-1135; 1334 SW 8th St
Los Pinarenos is both a farmer's market and *botanica* in the gringo sense of the word: (ie a place that sells plants and flowers, as opposed to spell components). The main goods to pick up here are fresh produce and popular (and very refreshing) juices and smoothies from the attached countertop.

DO RE MI MUSIC CENTER
Map p88   Music
☎ 305-541-3374; 1829 SW 8th St
It's Latin music in all forms – CDs, vinyl, cassettes and even a range of instruments for you to bust out on. Staff are very helpful with those tourists who don't know their samba from their salsa.

LITTLE-HAVANA-TO-GO
Map p88   Souvenirs
☎ 305-857-9720; www.littlehavanatogo.com; 1442 SW 8th St
This is Little Havana's official souvenir store, and it has some pretty cool items, from Cuban-pride T-shirts to posters, flags, paintings, photo books, cigar-box purses and authentic clothing.

KEY BISCAYNE
It's certainly not a shopping destination, but if you find yourself on this fantasy island and need something (well, shorts, toys or gourmet food), you'll be pleasantly surprised with the few worthy options.

PALM PRODUCE RESORTWEAR
Map p92   Beachwear
☎ 305-361-6999; 328 Crandon Blvd
Buy all your swimsuits, flip-flops, sun hats and flowered, draw-string, loungey resort-getups, especially from that classic Jams label, at this mellow beach boutique.

STEFANO'S Map p92   Italian Grocery
☎ 305-361-7007; 24 Crandon Blvd
If you find yourself in need of olive oil, biscotti, ground coffee or canned tomatoes, the small Italian grocery attached to the popular surf-n-turf restaurant is there for you.

TOY TOWN Map p92   Toys
☎ 305-361-5501; 260 Crandon Blvd
This adorable kids' shop has all the distractions you'll need, from Beanie Babies and Barbies to sand toys, model cars, stuffed animals, tricycles and dress-up costumes.

COCONUT GROVE
You're pretty much stuck with CocoWalk and Streets of Mayfair, the two enormous malls (but they're *nice* malls) that form the Grove's backbone. However, should you need old homewares culled from around the world or prophylactics, you are definitely in the right 'hood.

ARCHITECTURAL ANTIQUES
Map p95   Antiques
☎ 305-285-1330; http://miamiantique.com; 2500 SW 28th Lane
The old AA is worth a stop just to look at the amazing range of items, from the beautiful (crystal sculptures, classic globes, old-school posters) to the banal (too much to list), which are stacked like popcorn in this incredible warehouse of found stuff.

BOOKSTORE IN THE GROVE
Map p95   Books
☎ 305-443-2855; 3399 Virginia St
Just what the doctor ordered: a cute little indie bookstore, casual café, community

oriented activity center and cool escape from the gentrified junk so ubiquitous on Grand Ave.

CONDOM-USA
Map p95   Condoms & Sex Stuff
☎ 305-445-7729; www.condom-usa.com; 3066 Grand Ave
It's easy to laugh at this place, but Condom-USA does a great job of promoting sexual-health initiatives, education and frank discussion of some of the major health issues of our time. Plus, they've got Motion Lotion.

COCOWALK Map p95   Mall
☎ 305-444-0777; www.galleryatcocowalk.com; 3015 Grand Ave
In the heart of a formerly charming neighborhood, this open-air mall has a Gap, Victoria's Secret, Banana Republic and all the other usual suspects – plus a 16-screen AMC movie theater.

STREETS OF MAYFAIR
Map p95   Mall
☎ 305-448-1700; www.streetsofmayfair.com; 2911 Grand Ave
Sitting adjacent to CocoWalk, the Streets of Mayfair shopping mall offers a whole other range of chain stores – Borders bookstore, Banana Republic, Bath & Body Works – plus some cute boutiques and a few restaurants and galleries.

CORAL GABLES
You'd think that Miracle Mile would be a straight list of brand-name boringness, but in fact there is some great indie flavor to be found on this lovely pedestrian parade. Those seeking safety in chains such as Ann Taylor, Coach and Victoria's Secret need look no further than the **Village of Merrick Park** (Map pp100–1; ☎ 305-529-0200; www.villageofmerrickpark .com; 358 San Lorenzo Ave) and the **Shops at Sunset Place** (Map pp100–1; ☎ 305-663-0873; www.simon .com/mall; 5701 Sunset Dr), which are – what else? – a pair of malls.

BOOKS & BOOKS
Map pp100–1   Books
☎ 305-442-4408; 296 Aragon Ave
Long live the independents! The best locally owned bookstore, Books & Books

top pic

- Sofi Swimweat (p114)
- Leo (p110)
- C. Madeleine's (p115)
- Hip.e (opposite)
- Crimson Carbon (p110)

hosts visiting authors, disc etry readings and has an e of materials, much like its South Beach (p110).

MA VIE EN LINGERIE
☎ 305-444-1454; 325 Miracle
The gorgeous lingerie at tremely hot. Hot in a 'you either be very uncomfort psyched to be in here wi Designs run the gamut f provocative to Wow.

LOWE ART MUSEUM
Map pp100–1
☎ 305-284-3535; www.lo 1301 Stanford Dr
On the University of M Lowe has one of Dade permanent collections little gift shop filled w excellent art books to jewelry.

DOG BAR Map pp100–
☎ 305-441-8979; 259 M
If you feel the need a walking, farting fa look no further, Ms It' and 'I (Heart) Bit are either a sign of fido or the immine civilization.

CAPRICHO SHO
Map pp100–1
☎ 305-774-0110; 26
Rafe. Marc Jacobs. names mean anyt ably be in access you can go back ing your girlfrien

EATING

top picks

What's your recommendation? www.lonelyplanet.com/miami

EATING

Miami is a major immigrant entrepôt, and the great thing about immigrants – besides being the backbone of the country – is (a) their delicious old-country cuisines and (b) their preference for American-ly excessive portions. Ever tried Cuban cuisine in Cuba? Screw those skimpy commie rations – there's no such moderation in Miami. Break a $10 bill here and the payoff is a steaming surfeit of *ropa vieja* (shredded beef), rice and beans and the sweetest fried plantains ever to kiss your lips.

On top of that, South Florida has always loved showing off. Locals put a lot of emphasis on style and name dropping, and for all the occasional silliness of the four-star scene, a lot of substance breaks through style's excess at the high end of the Miami dining scale.

Thus, there are three sides to the Miami eating scene. First: boring Americana chain sameness – bland, blah, blech. If you eat at TGI Friday's here, frankly, you deserve food poisoning.

Next comes the ethnic eateries: Jewish delis, Japanese sushi stands, Florida stone crab shacks and more Cuban sandwich stalls than you can shake an anti-Castro mural at. We'd say the budget and mid-market dining scene here is reminiscent of the United Nations, but really, it feels more like Organization of the Americas. You won't find a better city in America for Brazilian, Argentine, Venezuelan, Dominican or any other variation of Latin and Caribbean cuisine than here.

Finally comes the haute dining, as fine as the hostess seating you at your *nuevo*-fusioned-pan-Americo-Asian-Caribbean shrine to pretension. Expect some clientele more interested in the name of a celebrity chef (p13) than the food said chef prepares. Also expect, more often than not, an eating experience that will pretty much blow your mind to new levels of gastronomic enlightenment.

MIAMI CUISINE

Let's start with what Miami lacks: Asian food. With some notable exceptions – Matsuri (p139) and Hy Vong (p136) – Miamians seem to think good Asian eats involve ill-advised fusions of Thai and Japanese. No Miami! Bad bastardization of beautiful cuisines! On the other hand, vegetarians are no longer in the lurch here; almost every midrange to high-end restaurant has veggie options and there are more and more dedicated veg choices sprouting up, especially in the Design District. Vegans may admittedly struggle; check www.meatlessmiami.com for up-to-date listings. Otherwise, everyone is catered for, particularly those who love Latin, Italian, French and Spanish cuisine. Delis and diners are also ubiquitous, and the latter often challenges the genre by adding Cuban and Latin twists to the menu. Rather than sludgy diner coffee, you get *cortaditos* (small shots of espresso); along with burgers comes *pan con lechon* (roast pork and onion sandwiches). High-end Miami cuisine loves to fuse – usually Latin and something else. It's a trend known as 'Nuevo Latino.' The other home-grown cuisine is 'Floribbean,' which mixes American Southern influences, tropical produce and an island flair for spice and color.

SELF-CATERING

Epicure Market (Map pp52–3; ☎ 305-672-1861; 1656 Alton Rd; dishes $7-10; ☾ 10am-8pm Mon-Fri, 10am-7pm Sat, 10am-6pm Sun), a gourmet food shop just off Lincoln Rd in South Beach, has a beautiful selection of international cheeses and wines, fresh produce, baked goods and prepared dishes. Many of the more than 25 Publix supermarkets throughout Miami are quite upscale, and the Whole Foods Market (Map pp48–9; ☎ 305-532-1707; 1020 Alton Rd; ☾ 7am-11pm) is the biggest health-food store around, with an

top picks

EAT STREETS

- Española Way Promenade (p47)
- Giralda Ave (p139)
- Ponce De León Blvd (p139)
- North Biscayne Boulevard (p132)
- Arthur Godfrey Road/41st Street (p57)

PRICE GUIDE

The categories used in this chapter indicate the cost of a dinner main dish; lunch is cheaper.

$$$	$25 and over
$$	$13 to $24
$	$12 or less

excellent produce department, pretty good deli and so-so salad bar; its biggest draw is for vegetarians (not so well catered for in these parts) who are seeking a particular brand of soy milk or wheat-free pasta.

For the freshest picnic items around, hit one of several farmers markets (☎ 305-531-0038), which are held in various areas on different days. The one on Lincoln Rd on Sundays is perhaps best known, but you'll find others on Española Way (Sunday), Normandy Village Fountain at 71st St (Saturday), the Aventura Mall (Saturday and Sunday), Downtown on Flagler St at Miami Ave (8am until 2pm Saturday), Coconut Grove on Grand Ave at Margaret St (Saturday) and Coral Gables City Hall (Saturday).

PRACTICALITIES
Opening Hours

Breakfast is generally available from 6:30am to 11am, weekend brunch from 11am to 4pm, lunch from noon to 3pm and dinner from 6pm to 11pm.

At restaurants doubling as nightclubs and lounges, dinner could be churned out until midnight, with special late-night menus available into the wee hours. In the low season, many restaurants close on Mondays.

Tipping

Ask if a tip is included with your bill, as this tends to be the case in Miami (especially South Beach). Many waitstaff now automatically include a tip if they hear an accent, as foreigners have gained a reputation for skipping on tips. Don't do this; serving staff in America are not paid a living wage. The standard formula is to leave 18% of the total check, 15% if service wasn't great, 20% or more if it was excellent. The best way to calculate is to figure out roughly 10% of the total and double it; this is your tip amount (for example, if the check is $150, you would double $15 and leave $30).

SOUTH BEACH

Restaurants open and close on South Beach with the frequency of celebrity spottings (speaking of the latter, during our research Enrique Iglesias, Anna Kournikova, Alonzo Mourning, LL Cool J, Mike Piazza and the King of Jordan were all in Prime 112 – *on the same night*). As eating goes, there is no shortage of variety, price options and presentation, which tends towards ostentatious. Even the stripped-back places are ostentatiously underdone, if you know what we mean. All those restaurants with loud hostesses fronting Ocean Dr get mixed traveler reviews, so be warned that the price of pedestrian-watching might be an expensive, mediocre meal.

1ST TO 15TH STREETS

CHINA GRILL Map pp48–9   Chinese $$$

☎ 305-534-2211; www.chinagrillmgt.com; 404 Washington Ave; mains $28-79; ☽ lunch & dinner

Unsa-unsa I'm so hot. And I eat at the Miami satellite of Manhattan's almost-as-hot-as-me *unsa-unsa* China Grill. I order the also hot (like, spicy) grilled Szechuan beef or Korean barbecue with truffled potato hash *boom-boom*. And I love to listen to club music while I eat. *Weeoooooo.*

ESCOPAZZO Map pp48–9   Italian $$$

☎ 305-674-9450; 1311 Washington Ave; mains $27-62; ☽ dinner Tue-Sun

There's a lot of mediocre Italian in Miami, and you won't find it here. The rustic-and-organic menu gets points for raw, vegan dishes such as nut cheese caprese, and safer but still brilliant fare such as spaghetti with red mullet roe, prosciutto-wrapped veal chops and excellent tasting menus, which all make reservations imperative.

JOE'S STONE CRAB RESTAURANT
Map pp48–9   American $$$

☎ 305-673-0365; www.joesstonecrab.com; 11 Washington Ave; mains $20-60; ☽ dinner daily & lunch Tue-Sat mid-Oct–mid-May

Joe's is overrated. There, we said it. And yet it remains, inexplicably, Miami Beach's most famous restaurant. Look, the surf-n-turf–style menu is good. But it's not great, and at this price, with so many options in Miami, you shouldn't settle for anything less than exceptional. Plus the line is a mile long and no reservations are accepted, so getting in can

MIAMI FOR FOODIES

What's the geography of the Miami eating scene? What's blowing up? First, a lot of chefs from outside Miami have moved here, especially in 2007. And local chefs are moving out of South Beach and into the neighborhoods. You could say those areas are hip, not South Beach. There's a guy opening a restaurant on Biscayne Blvd in a shady area next to a strip club, and everyone's excited. People want good food outside South Beach.

Do Miamians have distinct tastes? Do they like to go out? They like to go out. I don't know about a distinct taste. Some people are afraid to try new things.

So are chefs shaping the industry, or consumers? Oh, consumers. But it's still in between. I think Miami wants to be a foodie city, but it's still in the learning phases.

OK: hypothetically, you're going to be executed tomorrow and you get one last Miami meal, unlimited budget. Where do you eat, lunch and dinner? I'd want to try Palme D'Or (p139) at the Biltmore and splurge on dinner. And for lunch, I'd go to La Moon (p134) for some homey, cheap, greasy Colombian fare; I'd like to feel the comfort of home in my belly on my last day.

An interview with Colombian-American Paula Nino, founder and editor of Miami food blog http://mangoandlime.net.

be a hassle. To top it off (we're really burning bridges here), compared to Dungeness, Alaskan King and Maryland Blue, the stone crabs are pretty bland. There it is. Sorry Joe.

PRIME 112 Map pp48–9 *Steakhouse $$$*
☎ 305-532-8112; www.prime112.com; 112 Ocean Dr; dishes $29-54; ☺ dinner
Sometimes, you need a steak: well-aged, juicy, marbled with the right bit of fat, served in a spot where the walls sweat testosterone, the bar serves Manhattans and the hostesses are models. Chuck the above into Miami Beach's oldest inn, the beautiful 1915 Browns Hotel, and there's Prime 112.

WISH Map pp48–9 *American $$$*
☎ 305-531-2222; Hotel, 801 Collins Ave; mains $31-44; ☺ breakfast & lunch daily, dinner Tue-Sun
Words like 'aioli' and 'foam' get thrown around at Wish, which takes run-of-the-mill classics and evolves them beyond all expectations. Aged-cheddar spaetzle mac 'n' cheese and a 'PB Jay' of Dark Chocolate, Raspberry Jam and Peanut Butter Gelato make this a great place for the unadventurous to try innovative, delicious haute cuisine.

NEMO Map pp48–9 *New American Fusion $$$*
☎ 305-532-4550; www.nemorestaurant.com; 100 Collins Ave; mains $29-44; ☺ lunch & dinner Mon-Fri, dinner Sat & Sun, brunch Sun
Raw bars and warm copper sconces are a good sign. That nudge into greatness comes when Asian elegance graces Latin-American exuberance: grouper with chimichurri sauce and kiss-the-grill nori-dusted tuna are a few jewels plucked from this fusion gem mine.

MARK'S SOUTH BEACH
Map pp48–9 *American Creative $$$*
☎ 305-604-9050; Nash Hotel, 1120 Collins Ave; mains $26-41; ☺ lunch & dinner
Rejoice: Mark's is excellent New American cuisine, and It is Good. Better than good, actually. The menu changes daily based on whatever excellent ingredients the kitchen can procure, the subterranean dining room is cozy and elegant, staff helpful and assured, and appreciative foodies outnumber posing status-seekers – a nice touch.

OSTERIA DEL TEATRO
Map pp48–9 *Italian $$$*
☎ 305-538-7850; 1443 Washington Ave; mains $16-42; ☺ dinner Mon-Sat
There are few things to swear by, and the specials board of Osteria, one of the oldest and best Italian restaurants in Greater Miami, ought to be one. Actually, when you get here, let the gracious Italian waiters seat you, coddle you, and then basically order for you off the board. They never pick wrong.

JASON'S AT THE HARRISON
Map pp48–9 *Fusion $$$*
☎ 305-672-4600; www.jasonattheharrison.com; 411 Washington Ave; mains $21-38; ☺ dinner, late night Fri
The monochrome of zebra patterned chairs and black-and-white dusted walls are offset by a colorful menu of semi-American, Southern-cum-Floribbean-cum-Asian cuisine that's as well traveled as a…Lonely Planet reader: think oxtail and yucca chips and sea bass with mushroom kimchi.

LA MAREA Map pp48-9   Mediterranean $$$
☎ 305-604-5130; Tides Hotel, 1220 Ocean Dr; mains $25-35; ☺ lunch & dinner
What makes Italo-Spanish, sea-kissed cuisine like rigatoni and pork cheek even better? Enjoying it in the deco-does-Poseidon's palace lobby of the Tides hotel, amidst a backdrop of endless off-white and sea turtle shells (actually, that last detail could be done without).

GRAZIE Map pp48-9   Northern Italian $$$
☎ 305-673-1312; 702 Washington Ave; mains $18-34; ☺ 6-11pm Sun-Thu, 6pm-midnight Fri & Sat
Thanks indeed: Grazie is top class and comfortably old-school Northern Italian. There is a distinct lack of gorgeous, clueless waitstaff and unwise menu experimentation. Instead you'll find attentive service, solid and delicious mains and extremely decent prices given the quality of the dining and the high-end nature of the location.

TABLE 8 Map pp48-9   New American $$$
☎ 305-695-4114; www.table8la.com; 1458 Ocean Dr; mains $24-30; ☺ breakfast, lunch & dinner
You know what? Forget that Table 8 has *Oprah* cachet. Forget that celebrity chef Govind Armstrong is a celebrity chef. If all that wasn't so, Table 8 would *still* be one of the best high-end restaurants on South Beach, partly because it never feels too high end. That is to say, it delivers comforting innovation – duck breast with green beans and frisée (endive), mahimahi blue crab chowder and Kobe beef burgers – in an understated, accessible fashion. In a way, Table 8 is the opposite of the mystique that has grown around it. This isn't a spot for silly airs: it offers excellent food that anyone can appreciate. The lunch menu is fantastic value.

CJ'S CRAB SHACK
Map pp48-9   Casual Seafood $$
☎ 305-534-3996; Cavalier Hotel, 1320 Ocean Dr; mains $18-30; ☺ lunch & dinner
This casual spot seems a cut above the rest of its Ocean Dr resto-siblings. As the name promises, there are lots of crustaceans served by a sassy waitstaff with complimentary dry attitude (it's endearing). Happy hour is a happy steal: $5 for a half-dozen oysters, $6 for two stone crab claws.

CAFÉ MAURICE Map pp48-9   French Bistro $$
☎ 305-674-1277; 419 Washington Ave; mains $14-28; ☺ dinner & late night
Post-war Paris meets American theme restaurant at this dark red, playfully fun French bistro. The menu focuses on favorites *à la francaise: magret du canard* (duck breast), goat cheese salad and duck shepherd's pie. Stick around for late-night gypsy dancing after you've gorged.

SUSHI SAIGON
Map pp48-9   Vietnamese & Japanese $$
☎ 305-604-0599; www.sushisaigon.com; 1131 Washington Ave; mains $13-29; ☺ lunch & dinner
The stark simplicity of Japanese cuisine and the colorful (and delicious) energy of Vietnamese are an odd marriage, but the Sushi Saigon menu basically splits rather than combines the flavors, which is probably a good idea. Black and white photos from the two parent cuisine countries cram the walls and create a nice, Old-Asia dining atmosphere.

SPIGA Map pp48-9   Italian $$
☎ 305-534-0079; Impala Hotel, 1228 Collins Ave; mains $15-26; ☺ dinner
This romantic nook is a perfect place to bring your partner and gaze longingly over candlelight, before you both snap out of it and start digging into excellent traditional Italian such as lamb in olive oil and rosemary and baby clams over linguine.

TAPAS Y TINTOS Map pp48-9   Spanish $$
☎ 305-538-8272; www.tapasytintos.com; 448 Española Way; tapas $6-25; ☺ lunch Wed-Sun, dinner daily
This dark, Nuevo-Spanish tapas bar is popular with the sort of good-looking young professionals who like their food and restaurants as pretty as they are. Try the octopus, or fried chickpeas with Spanish ham.

GURU Map pp48-9   Indian $$
☎ 305-534-3996; www.gurufood.com; 232 12th St; mains $15-23; ☺ dinner
A sexy, soft-lit interior of blood reds and black wood sets the stage of this not-so-average Indian eatery, where local ingredients like lobster swim into the korma. Goan fish curry goes down a treat, too.

GRILLFISH Map pp48–9 Seafood $$
☎ 305-538-9908; www.grillfish.com; 1444 Collins Ave; mains $13-22; ☽ dinner

Sometimes it's all in a name. They grill here. They grill fish. They could call it 'Grillfish Awesome' because that's what this simple yet elegant restaurant, with its cutely mismatched plates and church pew benches, serves: fresh seafood, done artfully and simply and joyfully.

TAVERNA OPA Map pp48–9 Greek $$
☎ 305-673-6730; www.tavernaoparestaurant.com; 36 Ocean Dr; mains $11-23; ☽ dinner & late night

Cross Coyote Ugly with a big fat Greek wedding and you get this tourist-oriented restaurant and ouzo fest, where the meze are decent and the vibe resembles something like a Hellenic frat party. By the end of the night, table dancing is pretty much mandatory.

SUM YUNG GAI Map pp48–9 Chinese $$
☎ 305-604-8889; 1403 Washington Ave; mains $11.25-21; ☽ lunch & dinner

Now what could 'Sum Yung Gai' mean in Cantonese – oh, we get it. We dig the 1930s Shanghai opium den interior, which makes us want to carry a tommy gun on one arm and Zhang Ziyi on the other. And they make homemade bird's nest – impressive! – plus more standard black bean sauce–drenched Chinese-American favorites.

TAP TAP Map pp48–9 Haitian $$
☎ 305-672-2898; 819 5th St; dishes $9-20; ☽ dinner

In Haiti, tap-taps are brightly colored pickup trucks–turned–public taxis, and their tropi-psychedelic paint scheme inspires the decor at this excellent Haitian eatery. 'Um, what do Haitians eat?' Meals are a happy marriage of West Africa, France and the Caribbean: spicy pumpkin soup, grilled snapper with lime sauce and Oh-God-yes curried goat. If you need some liquid courage, shoot some Barbancourt rum, available in several grades (all strong).

FRONT PORCH CAFÉ Map pp48–9 Café $$
☎ 305-531-8300; 1418 Ocean Dr; mains $10-18; ☽ breakfast, lunch & dinner

A blue-and-white escape from the madness of the cruising scene, the Porch has been serving excellent salads, sandwiches and the like since 1990 (eons by South Beach standards). Weekend brunch is justifiably mobbed; the big omelettes are delicious, as are the fat pancakes, strong coffee and handsome servers.

JERRY'S FAMOUS DELI Map pp48–9 Deli $$
☎ 305-532-8030; www.jerrysfamousdeli.com; 1450 Collins Ave; mains $10-17; ☽ 24hr

Important: Jerry's delivers. Why? Because when you've gorged out on the pastrami on rye, turkey clubs and other mile-high sandwiches at this enormous Jewish deli (housed in what used to be the Warsaw nightclub), you'll be craving for more of the above 24/7.

PUERTO SAGUA Map pp48–9 Cuban Diner $$
☎ 305-673-1115; 700 Collins Ave; dishes $6-25; ☽ breakfast, lunch, dinner & late night

There's a secret colony of older working-class Cubans and construction workers hidden among South Beach's sex-and-flash, and evidently, they eat here (next to a Benetton, natch). Puerto Sagua challenges the American diner with this reminder: Cubans can greasy-spoon with the best of them. Portions of favorites such as *picadillo* (spiced ground beef with rice, beans and plantains) are stupidly enormous.

NEWS CAFÉ Map pp48–9 American $
☎ 305-538-6397; 800 Ocean Dr; dishes $8-17; ☽ 24hr

Some kind of lodestone attracts every tourist in South Beach to this Ocean Dr landmark. Frankly, we don't get it, but thousands of travelers do and you may as well. So take a perch, eat some above-average but not-too-special food and enjoy the anthropological study that is South Beach as she rollerblades, salsas and otherwise shambles by.

11TH STREET DINER Map pp48–9 Diner $
☎ 305-534-6373; 1065 Washington Ave; dishes $8-15; ☽ 24hr

You've seen the art deco landmarks. Now eat in one: a Pullman car diner trucked down from Wilkes-Barre, Pennsylvania, as sure a slice of Americana as a *Leave it to Beaver* marathon. If you've been drinking all night, we'll split a three-egg omelette with you and the other drunkies at 6am. Dude. The bathroom's in the back. *Not on my leg!*

A LA FOLIE Map pp48–9 Café $

☎ 305-538-4484; www.alafoliecafe.com; 516 Española Way; mains $5-15; ⏱ lunch & dinner

There's a distinct shortage of coffeehouses in Miami (we don't count *cortadito* counters because you can't sit there and read), but this *très* French café bucks the trend. Plus, the waiters have great accents. Why yes, we would like 'zee moka.'

SAN LOCO Map pp48–9 Burritos $

☎ 305-538-3009; 235 14th St; mains $5-10; ⏱ 11am-5am

You'd think laid-back, Latino-influenced South Beach would have more burrito places, because let's face it, nothing goes down better after a cold swim (or beer) than guac, sour cream and beans. But there was a serious shortage of this genre – and then San Loco arrived. The industrially cool interior is fun, but the burritos are better – they kick your hunger in the ass, but in an oh-so-delicious way.

LE SANDWICHERIE Map pp48–9 Sandwiches $

☎ 305-532-8934; 229 14th St; mains $5.50-8; ⏱ 8:30am-5am

French for 'The Sandwicherie' (heh). The bustle-and-flow never stops as an endless stream of customers sidle up to the counter for some of the best baguettes (and other eats of a things-between-bread-nature) on the Beach.

PIZZA RUSTICA Map pp48–9 Pizza $

☎ 305-538-6009; 1447 Washington Ave; slices $4-8; ⏱ lunch

South Beach's favorite pizza has three locations to satisfy the demand for Roman-style crusty/chewy slices topped with exotic offerings. A slice is a meal unto itself. Mosey down to 863 Washington Ave (Map pp48–9; ☎ 305-674-8244) or over to 667 Lincoln Rd (Map pp52–3) to sample similar fare at the other Pizza Rustica branches.

FLAMINGO RESTAURANT

Map pp48–9 Nicaraguan $

☎ 305-673-4302; 1454 Washington Ave; dishes $2.50-7; ⏱ breakfast, lunch & dinner Mon-Sat

This tiny Nicaraguan storefront/café serves the behind-the-scenes laborers who make South Beach function. Workers devour hen soup, pepper chicken and cheap breakfasts prepared by a meticulous husband-and-wife team who like to get details (and portions) just right.

15TH TO 23RD STREETS

BLUE DOOR Map pp52–3 French Fusion $$$

☎ 305-674-6400; Delano Hotel, 1685 Collins Ave; mains $30-46; ⏱ lunch & dinner

'Owned by Madonna' plus 'Delano' plus 'designed by Philippe Starck' equals 'this ain't McDonald's'. They've let Asia and Latin America rub a bit of French shoulder with dishes such as cold chayote soup with pan-seared scallops and ragout of lobster in coconut-milk broth. Enjoy, and realize you live better than most.

YUCA Map pp52–3 Nuevo Latino $$$

☎ 305-532-9822; 501 Lincoln Rd; dishes $22-40; ⏱ 11am-6am

This was one of the first Nuevo Latino hotspots in Miami, and it's still going strong, even if locals say it's lost a little luster over the years. Maybe, but the Yuca Rellena, a mild chili stuffed with truffle-laced mushroom picadillo, and the tender guava ribs, still make our mouth water.

RALEIGH RESTAURANT pp52–3 American $$$

☎ 305-534-6300; Raleigh Hotel, 1775 Collins Ave; mains $18-35; ⏱ breakfast & lunch Mon-Thu, breakfast, lunch & dinner Fri-Sun

You are 1920s class, dammit. Get in your pinstripes (or flapper dress) and kick back on a wicker chair under the seagrape trees on the terrace, or in the wood-paneled dining room – and have some suckling pig with sour orange while you're at it.

ALTAMAR Map pp52–3 Seafood $$

☎ 305-532-3061; 1223 Lincoln Rd; mains $16-25; ⏱ dinner

Located on the west side of Alton Rd – the stretch most pedestrians miss – Altamar rules the fresh fish stakes. Or just about any seafood lists. The jumbo crabcake and mustard sauce, soft-shell crab marinated in lemon and herbs and, yes, any fish on the menu are all good bets.

MISS YIP Map pp52–3 Chinese $$

☎ 305-534-5488; www.misyipchinesecafe.com; 1661 Meridian Ave; dishes $14-25; ⏱ lunch & dinner

If you remember when Cantonese was the only Chinese cuisine you could find stateside and prefer it that way, say hello to Jenny Yip. She's got a bright-red booth and medicine jars full of God-knows-what waiting for you in this seemingly classic Chinese teahouse. Have some Peking duck, *ma-po* tofu (a Szechuan dish of marinated pork, black beans and bean curd), and discover that no matter what you choose, it's prepared flawlessly.

BALANS Map pp52–3   Mediterranean-Asian Fusion $$
☎ 305-534-9191; 1022 Lincoln Rd; mains $10-25; ☺ breakfast, lunch & dinner
Kensington, Chiswick…South Beach? Oi, give this Brit-owned fusion favorite a go. Where else does veal saltimbocca and lamb jalfrezi share a menu? After you down the signature lobster club, you'll agree tired stereotypes about English cooking need to be reconsidered.

CAFÉ PAPILLON Map pp52–3   French $$
☎ 305-673-1139; 530 Lincoln Rd; dishes $8-25; ☺ 8:30am-11pm
In a perfect world, the waitstaff here would wear stripy shirts, berets and have twirly moustaches. Alas, *non*, but there's quiche, *tartines* (filled with marinated artichokes or peppers in pesto), crepes and wrought-iron sidewalk tables. Pass zee Gauloise, Pierre.

VAN DYKE CAFÉ Map pp52–3   American $$
☎ 305-534-3600; www.thevandykecafe.com; 846 Lincoln Rd; dishes $10.50-20.50; ☺ 8am-2am
One of Lincoln Rd's most touristed spots, the Van Dyke is an institution akin to the News Café (p128), serving adequate food in a primo spot for people-watching. It's usually packed and takes over half the sidewalk. Service is friendly and efficient, and you get free preening models with your burgers and eggplant parmigiana. There's also nightly jazz upstairs.

PASHA'S Map pp52–3   Middle Eastern $
☎ 305-673-3919; 900 Lincoln Rd; meals $4-12; ☺ lunch & dinner
Pasha is a serious self-promoter judging by this place, a sleek, two-level, healthy fast-food emporium that has his name everywhere you look. No matter: the food at Pasha's rocks. Have some delicious *labneh* (thick yogurt), a plate of hummus and grilled chicken served over rice. It's all good, and the interior feels as hip as a club. Other Pasha's locations are Downtown (Map

top picks
KIDS
- Jerry's Famous Deli (p128)
- Tap Tap (p128)
- Grillfish (p128)
- Andiamo! (p135)
- Shorty's BBQ (p140)

pp66–7; 1414 Brickell Ave) and in the Design District (Map p82; 3801 N Miami Ave).

DAVID'S CAFE II Map pp52–3   Cuban $
☎ 305-672-8707; 1654 Meridian Ave; dishes $4-11; ☺ 7am-11pm
Come here for a shot of Cuban coffee, cheap breakfasts on a bar stool and a bountiful lunch buffet, served in the dining room. Both you and your wallet should be full when you leave.

PRESTO PIZZA Map pp52–3   Pizza $
☎ 305-531-5454; www.prestopizzasobe.com; 332 Lincoln Rd; pizza slices from $2.25, mains $3-11; ☺ lunch & dinner
Presto goes NYC style on the pie, and is beloved by northeasterners longing for a thin-crust slice of home. It's a good, greasy alternative to all that healthy stuff in Pizza Rustica (p129).

GELATERIA PARMALAT Map pp52–3   Ice Cream $
☎ 786-276-9475; 670 Lincoln Rd; dishes $3.85-6; ☺ 9am-midnight, till 1:30am Fri & Sat
It's hot. You've been walking all day. You need ice cream, stat. Why hello tamarind-and-passionfruit homemade gelato! This is an excellent spot for creamy, pillowy waves of European-style frozen goodness, and based on the crowds, it's the acknowledged favorite ice cream on South Beach.

MIAMI BEACH
There are three good clusters of eats here: Mid-Beach, particularly 41st St, with its Jewish delis, steakhouses and sushi bars; Normandy Isle, with its expat South Americans and their penchant for coronary-inducing cuisine; and far North Beach, around Sunny Isles, home to some eclectic little gems.

MID-BEACH

This area includes 41st St/Arthur Godfrey Rd, which is packed with sushi stands, delis and upscale eateries.

FORGE Map pp58–9   Steakhouse $$$
☎ 305-538-8533; 432 41st St; mains $26-60; ⏲ dinner till late Mon-Sat, brunch & dinner Sun
We've always wanted to eat next to Paris Hilton, but when we visited Forge all we got was Hillary Clinton's press spokesperson. That should give you an idea of the folks who eat at this baroque temple to excess: important ones. Incidentally, the food is good, but you're at this A-list steakhouse to either spot celebrities or feel like one.

NORMAN'S TAVERN
Map pp58–9   Steakhouse $$
☎ 305-868-9248; 6770 Collins Ave; mains $15-25; ⏲ lunch & dinner
Think Diet Forge: same great taste, but fewer calories! Er, celebrities. Norman's Tavern eschews bling and attitude for a sort of high-end sports bar atmosphere; the food is fancy pub fare and everyone here is either shooting pool or watching the game.

TAMARIND Map pp58–9   Thai $$
☎ 305-861-6222; www.tamarindthai.us; 946 Normandy Dr; mains $12-21; ⏲ lunch & dinner
No surprises here (unless you've never eaten Thai food); there's the standard palette of Thai curry (red, green, yellow) and *pad*-everything. And it's excellent: food, service and setting. Sometimes, as the cooks at Tamarind happily know, you stick with the classics.

SAM'S DELI & GRILL
Map pp58–9   Deli $$
☎ 305-538-1616; 740 41st St; dishes $10-20; ⏲ breakfast, lunch & dinner Sun-Thu, breakfast & lunch Fri
'It's good,' says the Israeli, with typical sabra understatement, walking out of what looks like a rabbi convention. Sam's holds the title for most popular deli on the Beach, evidenced by round-the-clock crowds noshing matzo ball soup, brisket and the excellent New Yorker: turkey and corned beef piled on rye and dripping with Russian dressing.

MISTER CHOPSTICK
Map pp58–9   Kosher Chinese $
☎ 305-604-0555; 4020 Royal Palm Ave; mains $9-15; ⏲ lunch Sun-Fri, dinner Sun-Thu & Sat, closed Mon
You read it right: kosher Chinese. That means the menu is short on pork but does serve lots of Chinese-American favorites – General Tso's chicken and Hawaiian duck – in what seems like a never-ending chaotic Jewish wedding.

TASTI CAFÉ Map pp58–9   Israeli Café $
☎ 305-673-5483; 4041 Royal Palm Ave; mains $4-9; ⏲ breakfast, lunch & dinner Mon-Thu, breakfast & lunch Fri & Sun, closed Sat
The bagels at this Israeli-run, kosher café, which could have been plucked off the streets of Tel Aviv, are flown in from New York – now that's commitment to quality. If good bagels aren't your thing, pick from light, veggie entrées to hearty pastas and sandwiches.

NORTH BEACH TO SUNNY ISLES

TIMO'S Map pp58–9   American $$$
☎ 305-936-1008; 17,624 Collins Ave; mains $15-34; ⏲ lunch & dinner
When chef Tim Andriola left Mark's South Beach in 2003, he opened this classy bistro and brought SoBe style into a NoBe setting. His legend grows through dishes such as porcini-dusted veal and cheese platters topped with shaved black truffles.

CAFÉ PRIMA PASTA
Map pp58–9   Argentine Italian $$
☎ 305-867-0106; www.primapasta.com; 414 71st St; dishes $13-24; ⏲ lunch & dinner Mon-Sat, dinner Sun
We're not sure what's better at this Argentine-Italian place: the much-touted pasta, which deserves every one of the accolades heaped on it (try the gnocchi), or the atmosphere, which captures the dignified sexiness of Buenos Aires. Actually, it's no contest: you're the winner, as long as you eat here.

BISSALEH CAFE Map pp58–9   Israeli Café $$
☎ 305-682-2224; www.bissaleh.com; 17,608 Collins Ave; mains $12-24; ⏲ lunch & dinner Sun-Thu, dinner Sat, closed Fri

Another Israeli café, Bissaleh has an extensive menu of fish and pasta, but the real draw is the signature dish, puff pastry stuffed with cheese or olives, potatoes and spinach, plus similar Middle Eastern turnovers like *boreka* and *malawach*.

WOLFIE COHEN'S RASCAL HOUSE

Map pp58–9   American $

☎ 305-947-4581; 17,190 Collins Ave; dishes $7-15; ☯ breakfast, lunch & dinner

Wolfie's is more than a deli: it's also an icon. A serious battering from Hurricane Wilma in 2005 tore away one of the best roadside marquees in America, but the '50s-era red-vinyl booths, warm and sassy service and ginormous deli menu remains, encapsulating a bygone era of American highway culture. And the corned beef on rye is da bomb.

EL REY DEL CHIVITO

Map pp58–9   Uruguayan $

☎ 305-864-5566; www.elreydelchivito.com; 6987 Collins Ave; dishes under $10; ☯ lunch & dinner, till late Fri & Sat

Heart, meet the 'King of Chivitos' and his signature dish: a sandwich of steak, ham, cheese, fried eggs and mayonnaise (there may have been lettuce, peppers and tomatoes too, but the other ingredients just laughed at them). Now run, heart, run away! That's just the basic, by the way, and it comes with fries. We've never heard of Uruguayan restaurants in America, and now we know why: anyone who could spread the word died of a coronary long ago. El Rey also serves Uruguayan pizza; try it topped with *faina*, long strips of bread mixed with cheese and peppers.

LA PERRADA DE EDGAR

Map pp58–9   Colombian Hot Dogs $

☎ 305-866-4546; 6976 Collins Ave; hotdogs $3-5; ☯ 10am-2am

Back in the day, Colombia's most (in)famous export to Miami was cocaine. But seriously, what's powder got on La Perrada and its kookily delicious hot dogs, devised by some Dr Evil of the frankfurter world. Don't believe us? Try an *especial*, topped with plums, pineapple and whipped cream. How about shrimp and potato sticks? Apparently, these are normal hot dog toppings in Colombia.

NORTH BISCAYNE BOULEVARD

An incongruous glut of excellent restaurants is sprouting up along the otherwise unremarkable strip of North Biscayne Blvd. Here are some winners from this unexpected foodie find:

Michy's (Map pp58–9; ☎ 305-759-2001; 6927 Biscayne Blvd; meals $24-43; ☯ lunch & dinner Tue-Fri, dinner Sat & Sun) Blue and white pop-decor. Organic, locally sourced ingredients. A stylish, fantastical bar where Alice could drink before painting Wonderland red. Welcome to Michelle 'Michy' Bernstein's culinary love child, one of the brightest stars in Miami's culinary constellation. The emphasis is good food and fun. The 'half plates' concept lets you halve an order and mix up such delicious fare as foie gras on corn cakes, chicken pot pie with wild mushrooms, white almond gazpacho and blue cheese croquettes.

Wine 69 (Map pp58–9; ☎ 305-759-0122; www.wine69miami.com; 6909 Biscayne Blvd; meals $13-23; ☯ 8am-8pm) Enter this low-slung, sexy wine bar, pick from a dozen categories of the grape, and pair up with – oh, let's see – baked brie and caramelized onions? Or a Miami-inspired charcuterie with chorizo and Spanish ham? Tough decisions, but the helpful owners here love two things: good wine, and telling you what goes with it.

Uva 69 (Map pp58–9; ☎ 305-754-9022; 6900 Biscayne Blvd; mains $8-17; ☯ breakfast, lunch & dinner Mon-Fri, lunch & dinner Sat) Woah – it's like a club. And a restaurant. And an Ikea showroom, all mashed up. The flavors are mixed but consistently rich, running from traditional Miami *cubanos* to flaky, buttery croissants, but damn if it isn't all satisfying and served under immaculately hip conditions.

Karma Car Wash (Map pp58–9; ☎ 305-759-1392; www.karmacarwash.com; 7010 Biscayne Blvd; sandwiches & tapas $4.25-8; ☯ 8am-8pm) This eco-friendly car wash also serves soy chai lattes, organic tapas and good micro-brews. The idea could be precocious in execution, but ends up being fun – more fun than your average wash 'n' wait, anyways. Of course, hybrid drivers get a 25% discount, and the bar becomes a lounge at 8pm, with DJs spinning as you wonder 'Should I have gotten the wax finish?'

Dogma Grill (Map pp58–9; ☎ 305-759-3433; 7030 Biscayne Blvd; dogs $3.15-6.25; ☯ lunch & dinner) Don't worry; we're sparing you more reality-defying Colombian hot dogs (no whipped cream-and-baby-iguanas-on-your-dog here). Just good ol' American toppings – chili, mustard, 'kraut and relish – at this most popular of Miami cheap eat chains.

DOWNTOWN MIAMI

Downtown's eating options run, like Downtown itself, between extremes: from high-end corporate power lunches to down-home Latin hole-in-the-walls. In fact, you could argue the best cheap eats in Miami are concentrated here, and 'cheap' in this case, is often synonymous with 'excellent.'

AZUL Map pp66–7   Fusion $$$
☎ 305-913-8288; Mandarin Oriental, 500 Brickell Key Dr; mains $30-68; ☾ dinner daily, lunch Sun-Fri
Falling water windows, clean metallic spaces and curving copper facades compliment one of the nicest views of the city. The Scandi-tastic decor works in harmony with a menu that marries the Mediterranean to the Asian; try the oysters wrapped in beef and hamachi carpaccio, or some yogurt-marinated swordfish.

PORÇAO Map pp66–7   Brazilian $$$
☎ 305-373-2777; 801 Brickell Bay Dr; per person $44.90; ☾ noon-midnight
What is it with South Americans and meat? We like beef, but this is a butcher with a grill, an all-you-can-eat Brazilian *churrascaria* (steakhouse) where the waiters wander around with swords – swords! – of skewered, juicy, fat-dribbling…actually, come over here with that skirt steak, Sergio.

CAPITAL GRILLE Map pp66–7   Steakhouse $$$
☎ 305-374-4500; www.thecapitalgrille.com; 444 Brickell Ave; mains $37-42; ☾ lunch & dinner Mon-Fri, dinner Sat & Sun
This posh carnivore's paradise boasts steak, steak and more steak, catering to the suited expense-accounters who appreciate chandeliers, marble floors and dark wood paneling.

CAFÉ SAMBAL Map pp66–7   Pan-Asian $$
☎ 305-913-8358; Mandarin Oriental, 500 Brickell Key Dr; mains $20-40; ☾ 6:30am-11pm
Sambal sports what we can only describe as 'nouveau-rice-farmer-conical-hat-chic' and serves intriguing pan-Asian fare in a more laid-back setting than upstairs Azul (both located in the Mandarin Oriental Miami, p180). The just-out-of-the-ocean fresh sushi and rice crab cakes are worth a try, as is the critically acclaimed small plates menu.

BIG FISH Map pp66–7   Seafood $$
☎ 305-373-1770; www.thebigfishmiami.com; 55 SW Miami Ave; mains $15.50-32.50; ☾ lunch & dinner
Big Fish has a catch-the-sun color scheme, open deck and blue-water breezes – could you come closer to Mediterranean island ambience in Miami? OK, the Miami River isn't the Aegean (you're almost under the Metromover), but the seafood is fresh; try anything off the fish menu, sip some wine and love life. Film buffs: Alec Baldwin shot a thief on the back patio here in the '80s cult flick *Miami Blues*.

FRESCO CALIFORNIA
Map pp66–7   Mediterranean $$
☎ 305-858-0608; 1744 SW 3rd Ave; mains $9-15; ☾ lunch & dinner Mon-Sat
Fresco serves all kinds of West Coast takes on the Mediterranean palette. Relax in the candlelit backyard dining room, which feels like an Italian porch in summer when the weather's right. Pear and walnut salad and portobello sandwiches are lovely, while the pumpkin-stuffed ravioli is heavenly.

GARCIA'S Map pp66–7   Seafood $$
☎ 305-375-0765; 398 NW River Dr; dishes $8-15; ☾ lunch
Crowds of Cuban office workers lunch at Garcia's, which feels closer to a smugglers' seafood shack than the financial district. Expect occasionally spotty service (a bad thing), freshly caught-and-cooked fish (a good thing) and pleasantly seedy views of the Miami River (sweet).

GRANNY FEELGOODS
Map pp66–7   Vegetarian $
☎ 305-377-9600; 25 W Flagler St; mains $9-12; ☾ breakfast & lunch Mon-Fri
If you need karmic balance after eating at Porçao (left), pop into this neighborhood health-food staple. Located next to the courthouse, Granny's must have the highest lawyer-to-bean-sprouts ratio in America; try simple vegetarian dishes such as tofu sandwiches and spinach lasagna. Carnivores are catered for too – there's turkey burger.

JAMAICA INTERNATIONAL CAFÉ
Map pp66–7   International $
☎ 305-400-6694; 119 SE 1st Ave; dishes $5.50-11; ☾ breakfast, lunch & dinner

HOWL AT LA MOON

Nothing – and we're not necessarily saying this in a good way – soaks up the beer like a Colombian hot dog topped with eggs and potato sticks. Or fried pork belly and pudding. These delicacies (further proof that South Americans are either totally on to something or have completely different culinary DNA from the rest of us) are the preferred food and drink of Miami's 24-hour party people, and the best place to find this wicked fare is 24-hour La Moon (Map pp66–7; ☎ 305-860-602; 144 SW 8th St), in stumbling distance of the Transit Lounge (p149). To really fit in, order a *refajo*: Colombian beer (Aguila) with Colombiano soda (preferably the red one). Hey, that's the price of street cred.

The menu at this excellent lunch spot has been around the world – you can go Mexican, Italian, etc – but note the title and order something Jamaican: stewed oxtail with butter beans and, yes, jerk pork *please*.

MINI HEALTHY DELI Map pp66–7   Latin Café $
☎ 305-523-2244; Station Mall, 48 E Flagler St; dishes $6-10; ☼ lunch
This surreally excellent café, tucked into a half-vacant mini-mall, is where chef Carlos Bedoya works solo and churns out remarkably fresh and delicious specials, such as grilled tilapia, fresh salad and rice and beans. There are only two little tables, but it's worth waiting – or standing while you eat.

EMILY'S RESTAURANTE Map pp66–7   Latin $
☎ 305-375-0013; 204 NE 1st St; dishes $2-5.50; ☼ 7am-4:30pm
Two bucks gets you two eggs, toast and coffee here; $5 gets you on one of the best buffet deals in town. There are daily specials of Colombian, Cuban and Spanish cuisine: chicken soup, oxtail and *lengua en salsa* (marinated tongue).

WYNWOOD, THE DESIGN DISTRICT & LITTLE HAITI

'You want to eat on South Beach? Dude, you sound like a *tourist*!' The Design District and its little buffers of art are where the foodies flock these days, as well as North Biscayne Blvd, an incongruous strip of highways, cute cafés and excellent fine dining. Past the buzz, there's great Caribbean fare to be had in Little Haiti, and still some vestiges of the Puerto Rican diner scene that used to define Wynwood.

WYNWOOD

LOST & FOUND SALOON
Map p82   Restopub $
☎ 305-576-1008; www.thelostandfoundsaloon-miami.com; 185 NW 36th St; dishes $5.25-11.25; ☼ breakfast, lunch & dinner
The service is as friendly as the omelettes and burritos are awesome at this cute little Wynwood spot, the sort of saloon where microbrews are on tap and the wine list reads like a year abroad. Our only request: more burrito, gentlemen; portions were a little small and we weren't quite filled up last time.

FIVE GUYS Map p82   Burgers $
☎ 305-571-8345; Shops at Midtown Miami, 3401 N Miami Ave; burgers $5.50-8 ☼ lunch & dinner
Yes, it's a chain, but if you live on the East Coast it's the best burger chain in America. A double burger with onions, mushrooms, peppers and hot sauce is as close to heaven as we've been for $5.

ENRIQUETA'S Map p82   Latin Diner $
☎ 305-573-4681; 186 NE 29th St; dishes $5-8; ☼ breakfast & lunch Mon-Sat
Back in the day, Puerto Ricans, not installation artists, ruled Wynwood. Have a taste of those times in this perpetually packed roadhouse, where the Latin diner ambience is as strong as the steaming shots of *cortadito*. Balance the local gallery fluff with a steak-and-potato-stick sandwich.

THE DESIGN DISTRICT & LITTLE HAITI

MICHAEL'S GENUINE FOOD & DRINK
Map p82   New American $$$
☎ 305-573-5550; www.michaelsgenuine.com; Atlas Plaza, 130 NE 40th St; dishes $16-36; ☼ dinner Mon-Sat
The 'genuine' in Michael Schwartz's restaurant is a sincere tribute to locally sourced

ingredients and a healthy dose of innovation moderated by respect for things that work. Hence, pork shoulder in parsley sauce and cheese grits that taste like your grandma just became a cordon bleu chef. The chocolate-and-red interior feels cheerful and welcoming rather than snobbish and intimidating, and that goes for the attentive waitstaff as well.

GRASS RESTAURANT & LOUNGE
Map p82   Asian Fusion $$$
☎ 305-573-3355; www.grasslounge.com; 28 NE 40th St; dishes $22-34; ⏱ dinner Mon-Sat
With models in the courtyard and mudras on the walls, plus double doors that should front a castle and bouncers working the rope, you gotta be sexy (or know someone who is) to get in. If so, dine under thatch roofs or the stars on fusioned meals such as cumin-encrusted beef tenderloin and strut, daahling.

SOYKA Map p82   American Creative $$
☎ 305-759-3117; www.soykacafe.com; 5556 NE 4th Ct; mains $9-29; ⏱ lunch & dinner Mon-Sun, brunch Sun
Mark Soyka, the man behind News Café (p128) and Van Dyke Café (p130), has got the magic touch when it comes to restaurants in Miami, and this gem is his best effort yet. It's housed in a bouncy rococo space, and the eclectic menu jumps across several horizons of flavor, from sautéed chicken livers to sesame-seared salmon, with consistently tasty results.

ANDIAMO! Map p82   Pizza $
☎ 305-762-5751; 5600 Biscayne Blvd; pizzas $8.50-17; ⏱ lunch & dinner
It looks like a '50s drive-through (it's actually an old car wash), but Andiamo! isn't old-fashioned. This airy eatery breaks ground with award-winning pizza and toppings that range from goat cheese to white tuna, so you can get creative or settle for excellent interpretations of classics such as the Vesuvius: salami, hot peppers and olives, mmm.

SHEBA Map p82   Ethiopian $
☎ 305-573-1819; 4029 N Miami Ave; www.sheba miami.com; dishes $7-15; ⏱ dinner daily, lunch Mon-Sat
The only Ethiopian place in Miami is a godsend for vegetarians, especially vegans (although there's meat here too). If you

eat here, eat right; communally, off a big plate of *injera* (spongy bread), which serves as plate, utensil and starch, and scoop up spicy mounds of the many delicious varieties of *wat* (Ethiopian stew).

ORIGINAL RESTAURANT
Map p82   Haitian $
☎ 305-758-9400; 5650 NE 2nd Ave; mains $5-11; ⏱ breakfast, lunch & dinner
Friendly, family-run, clean and bright, this Little Haiti standout serves excellent island standards such as *ragout* (cow's feet), *queu boeuf* (oxtail), *foie* (liver) and *griot* (fried spicy pork); the last is one of our favorite only-in-Miami dishes (well, if you're in America). This is a neighborhood spot, and staff might be surprised to see you, but that doesn't mean they'll be any less courteous to their newfound customer.

SECRET SANDWICH CO Map p82   Deli $
☎ 305-571-9990; www.secretsandwich.com; 3918 N Miami Ave; meals $6-11.50; ⏱ lunch Mon-Fri
Spy-themed gourmet sandwiches? Hey, we can dig it, especially when the goods include the Bay of Pig (thin-sliced pork with onion and mojo marinade). That cute covert ops gimmick runs through the menu, all the way to half-pound burgers and very fresh salads.

CANELA CAFE Map p82   Latin-Vegetarian $
☎ 305-756-3930; canelamiami.com; 5132 Biscayne Blvd; mains $6.25-9.25; ⏱ lunch & dinner Mon-Sat
Miami loves its fusion cuisine but rarely mixes Latin diner with vegetarian fare. Canela challenges this convention; there's meat on the menu (touted as 'Latin soul food'), as well as roasted pepper and goat cheese sandwiches, vegetarian tapas and the trippy art you'd expect at the post-punk cousin to Miami's many Latin greasy-spoons.

KAFA'S CAFE Map p82   Café $
☎ 305-438-0114; 3535 NE 2nd Ave; mains $5-8; ⏱ breakfast & lunch Mon-Sat
New when we visited, Kafa's was a bare-bones café, pretty in that understated way bare-bones cafés can be. There's a pleasing menu of soup, salad and sandwiches that attracts artsy types. Pity the latter; it must be hard to act grim and pathos-driven when you can enjoy a tuna melt under perfect Miami conditions in the sunny outdoor seating area.

EATING WYNWOOD, THE DESIGN DISTRICT & LITTLE HAITI

LITTLE HAVANA

Cuban cuisine is only a small slice of Little Havana's pan-Latin palette; there are menus from all over *el Sud*, from Ecuador to El Salvador and Mexico to Mendoza, Argentina. And while locals say you have to go a bit further afield than Calle Ocho for the best *comida latino*, you'll rarely go wrong when you stroll into ethnic eateries in this part of town.

CASA JUANCHO Map p88   Spanish $$$
☎ 305-446-4914; www.casajuancho.com; 2436 SW 8th St; mains $19-42; ☽ lunch, dinner & late night
A massive, upscale Spanish tavern throbs to a festive mover-and-shaker crowd eating duck with pine nuts and figs, salted cod and sherry-cured rabbit. There's no shortage of tapas, Spanish wine or entertainment, as balladeers stroll and serenade as you dine.

CASA PANZA Map p88   Spanish $$
☎ 305-643-5343; 1620 SW 8th St; mains around $20; ☽ lunch, dinner & late night
They might as well hang out flashing 'Ole!' signs at this kitschy cavern of Spanish stereotypes, where the nightly flamenco entertainment is as good as the food, which includes *caldo gallego* (white-bean soup with pork sausage) and *gambas al ajillo* (shrimp in garlic sauce).

VERSAILLES off Map p88   Cuban $$
☎ 305-444-0240; 3555 SW 8th St; mains $5-20; ☽ breakfast, lunch, dinner & late night
Versailles (pronounced ver-*sigh*-yay) is an institution, and a lot of younger Cubans will tell you it's an overrated one. But older Cubans and Miami's Latin political elite still love coming here, so much so that folks say CNN has reserved a parking space for the day Fidel Castro dies. The Cuban cuisine is decent and unsurprising (there's no French food to be found, incidentally) but the real draw is coming as close as most outsiders can to the city's Cuban aristocracy.

EL CRISTO Map p88   Latin Diner $
☎ 305-261-2947; 1543 SW 8th St; mains $5-15; ☽ breakfast, lunch & dinner
Lots of locals say El Cristo is as good as Calle Ocho gets. The menu has daily specials from all over the Spanish-speaking world, but the stand out is fish: try it fried for a local version of fish 'n' chips, or take

away some excellent fish *empanadas* and *croquetas* (deep-fried in breadcrumbs). The outdoor area is an excellent perch for enjoying 8th St eye candy.

ISLAS CANARIAS off Map p88   Cuban $
☎ 305-649-0440; 285 NW 27th Ave; dishes $8-19; ☽ breakfast, lunch & dinner
Islas may not look like much, sitting in a strip mall, but it serves some of the best Cuban in Miami. The *ropa vieja* is delicious, and there are nice Spanish touches on the menu (the owner's father is from the Canary Islands, hence the restaurant's name). Don't pass up the signature homemade chips, especially the ones cut from plantains.

HY VONG VIETNAMESE RESTAURANT Map p88   Vietnamese $
☎ 305-446-3674; 3458 SW 8th; dishes $7-19; ☽ dinner Tue-Sun
In a neighborhood full of communist regime exiles, it makes sense to find a Vietnamese restaurant. And it's telling that despite all the great Latin food around, Little Havanans still wait hours for a seat here. Why? Because great Vietnamese food – which this absolutely is (with little touches of Florida, like mango marinade) – combines quality produce with Southeast Asian spice and a colonially inherited French penchant for rich flavors. Just be prepared to wait an hour or more for your culinary reward.

GUAYACAN Map p88   Nicaraguan $
☎ 305-649-2015; 1933 SW 8th St; dishes $7-15; ☽ lunch & dinner
Apparently Nicaraguans do diner too, judging by the friendly service and gut-busting satisfaction of Guayacan. *Antojitos*

BUILDING A CUBAN SANDWICH

The traditional Cuban sandwich, also known as a *sandwich mixto*, is not some slapdash creation. It's a craft best left to the experts – but here's some insight on how they do it. Correct bread is crucial. It should be Cuban white bread: fresh, soft and easy to press. The insides, both sides, should be buttered, then layered, in this order, with sliced pickles, slices of roast Cuban pork, ham (preferably sweet-cured) and baby Swiss cheese. Then it all gets pressed in a hot *plancha* (sandwich press) until the cheese melts. Mmmm.

(snacks) like tamales make a meal or settle for specials (we love the roast pork) loaded with sides: salad, rice and beans, plantains, french fries, corn tortillas and bread.

I LOVE CALLE OCHO Map p88   Café $
☎ 305-643-3737; 1547 SW 8th St; dishes $5-12; ☽ breakfast & lunch

And we love you. This eclectic café, with its bagels and chicken-salad wraps, is a good resting spot between rice and beans, although there are apparently two grand-mas in the kitchen who whip up excellent Cuban fare upon request. A rainbow sticker on the door indicates gay-friendly, a bit of a rare pronouncement in these parts.

MI RINCONCITO MEXICANO
Map p88   Mexican $
☎ 305-644-4015; 1961 SW 8th St; dishes $5.50-15; ☽ 10am-9:30pm

The Mexican clientele here is the surest sign of quality, but if you need more evidence, try the *tampinquena* (steak with enchiladas and green sauce) or *pollo mole* (chicken in mole), authentic but cheap Mexican that beats the hell out of your run-of-the-mill burrito.

EL REY DE LAS FRITAS Map p88   Cuban $
☎ 305-644-6054; 1821 SW 8th St; snacks $3 & under; ☽ 8am-10:30pm Mon-Sat

If you've never had a *frita*, or Cuban burger, make your peace with McDonalds and come down to El Rey with the lawyers, developers, construction workers and every other slice of Miami's Latin life. These *fritas* are big, juicy and served under a mountain of shoestring fries. Plus, the *batidos* (milkshakes) definitely bring the boys to the yard.

KEY BISCAYNE

For an eensy island, Biscayne's got good options that'll keep you from trekking all the way over the causeway back into the city.

RUSTY PELICAN Map p92   American $$$
☎ 305-361-3818; 3201 Rickenbacker Causeway; mains $23-50; ☽ lunch & dinner

More than the fare, it's the panoramic views that draw the faithful and romantic to this airy, tropical restaurant. If you do come for a drink, the fresh air could seduce you into sampling the surf-n-turf menu, which is good enough considering the setting and lack of options.

CIAPPINO Map p92   Italian $$$
☎ 305-365-4500; Ritz-Carlton, 455 Grand Bay Dr; mains $18-46; ☽ lunch & dinner

This Ritz Carlton restaurant sells a 'Sinatra in his heyday' vibe, couched in an enormous half deco/half baroque dining room of grand ball proportions. The menu matches the opulence of the setting, offering such over-the-top fare as wild mushroom and truffles stuffed into sea bass.

BOATER'S GRILL Map p92   Seafood $$$
☎ 305-361-0080; 1200 S Crandon Blvd; mains $14-30; ☽ 9am-9pm

In Crandon Park (p93), this waterfront restaurant (actually, water below and all around) feels like a Chesapeake Bay seahouse from up north, except the menu's packed with South Florida maritime goodness: stone crabs, mahimahi and lobster paella.

LE CROISIC Map p92   French Bistro $$
☎ 305-361-5888; 180 Crandon Blvd; dishes $15-25; ☽ dinner

If this artsy Parisian bistro were any cuter it would rub your leg and go 'meow.' As it is, Croisic entertains with the sort of old-school menu even the French appreciate for nostalgia's sake: entrecote with béarnaise sauce, *boeuf bourguignon* and *bouillabaisse* – ooh la la.

OASIS Map p92   Cuban $
☎ 305-361-5709; 19 Harbor Dr; dishes $5-12; ☽ breakfast, lunch & dinner

This excellent Cuban café has a customer base that ranges from the working poor to city players. Between the super-strong coffee and *masas de puerco* – marinated pork chunks, which go great with hot sauce – we're in corner spot heaven.

COCONUT GROVE

The Grove may look chain heavy, but it's actually a strong spot for healthy eats, while the pedestrian-friendly nature of the neighborhood makes for pleasant culinary strolling.

ANOKHA Map p95   Indian $$
☎ 786-552-1030; 3195 Commodore Plaza; mains $12-40; ☽ lunch & dinner

The general consensus is this family-run phenom is as good as Indian gets in Miami, which is either high praise or small potatoes depending on your point of view. We think the curries are pretty praiseworthy, as is anything wrapped in banana leaf.

JAGUAR'S Map p95 — Pan-Latin $$

☎ 305-444-0216; www.jaguarspot.com; 3067 Grand Ave; mains $17-23, ceviche 'spoon' $1.95; ☽ lunch & dinner

The menu spans the Latin world, but really, everyone's here for the ceviche 'spoon bar'. The idea: pick from six styles of ceviche (seafood salad), ranging from swordfish with cilantro to corvina in lime juice, and pull a culinary version of DIY. It's novel and fun, and the ceviche varieties are pretty damn delicious.

BERRIES RESTAURANT

Map p95 — American Creative $$

☎ 305-448-2111; www.berriesinthegrove.com; 2884 SW 27th Ave; dishes $10-25; ☽ lunch & dinner

Plenty of places have jumped on the seasonal produce and fresh ingredient bandwagon, and Berries, with its all-in-black ninja-clan waitstaff, makes the genre accessible and attitude-free. The enormous portions served up here could feed two, but who could bear to share skirt steak with melted blue cheese or three-mushroom risotto, which reminds us: veggies get it good here.

EL CARAJO Map p95 — Spanish $$

☎ 305-856-2424; 2465 SW 17th Ave; tapas $3.50-15; ☽ dinner

Pass the Penzoil…literally. We know it's cool to tuck restaurants into unassuming spots, but the Citgo station on SW 17th Ave? Really? Really: walk past the motor oil into a Granadan wine cellar, and try not to act too phased. And now, the food, *which is absolutely incredible*. Chorizo in cider blends burn, smoke and juice, frittatas are comfortably filling and *sardinas* and *boquerones*…oh God. These anchovies and sardines cooked with just a bit of salt and olive oil are dizzyingly delicious. It's tempting to keep El Carajo a secret, but not singing its praises would be lying, and we're not gonna lie: if there's one restaurant you shouldn't miss in Miami, it's this one.

GREEN STREET CAFE Map p95 — American $

☎ 305-567-0662; www.greenstreet.net; 3110 Commodore Plaza; mains $5-17; ☽ breakfast, lunch & dinner

As sidewalk spots go, it doesn't get more popular (and many say delicious) than Green Street, which is now contending with a next-door Senor Frogs. But the excellent menu of lamb burgers with goat cheese and salmon salads, occasional art shows and general indie-defiance of the gentrifying Grove is definitely up to the challenge.

FLANIGAN'S Map p95 — American $

☎ 305-446-1114; www.flanigans.net; 2721 Bird Ave; mains $8-16; ☽ lunch, dinner & late night

Flanigan's says it has the best ribs in Miami, and they *are* good, but we're not giving much more credit than that. Still, this is a pleasantly rowdy, all-American kind of joint tucked into a liquor store (bonus), and a great spot to drink beer, eat decent grub and yell at TV sports.

XIXON Map p95 — Spanish $

☎ 305-854-9350; 1801 SW 22nd St Ave; tapas $8-15; ☽ 10am-8pm Mon-Wed, till 10pm Thu-Sat, closed Sun

It takes a lot to stand out in Miami's crowded tapas stakes. Having a Basque-country-butcher's-and-baker's-gone-hip interior is a good start. Bread with crackling crust and a soft center that fluffs your tongue, and delicate explosions of *bacalao* (codfish) fritters, secures your spot as a top tapas contender. The *bocadillo* (sandwiches), with their blood-red Serrano ham and salty manchego, are great picnic fare.

FOCCACIA RUSTICA

Map p95 — Bakery & Sandwiches $

☎ 305-476-8292; 3111 Grand Ave; mains $4.75-8; ☽ 7am-6pm Mon, breakfast, lunch & dinner Tue-Sat, breakfast & lunch Sun

If you've been powering through a grease trap of *cubanos* and need a break, rejoice at the curry chicken salads, croissants, lattes, and assorted yuppie goodness at this inviting, continental-European-style spot.

LAST CARROT Map p95 — Health Food $

☎ 305-445-0805; www.thelastcarrot.com; 3133 Grand Ave; mains around $6; ☽ 7am-6pm Mon, breakfast, lunch & dinner Tue-Sat, breakfast & lunch Sun

Folks of all walks, corporate suits included, come here for fresh juice, delicious wraps (veggie options are great but the tuna melt is divine) and old-Grove neighborliness. The Carrot's endurance next to massive CocoWalk is testament to the quality of its good-for-your-body food served in a good-for-your-soul setting, so come here and do something good for the world, or at least your mouth.

CORAL GABLES

The Gables is a goldmine for foodies, with an ample supply of international, eclectic and high-end dining options. Many restaurants are clustered on or near 'Restaurant Row,' on Giralda Ave between Ponce de León Blvd and Le Jeune Rd).

LA PALME D'OR Map pp100–1   French $$$

☎ 305-913-3201; Biltmore Hotel, 1200 Anastasia Ave; meals $42–66; ☽ dinner Tue-Sat

One of the most acclaimed French restaurants in America, Phillipe Ruiz's Palme is the culinary match of the Jazz Age opulence that ensconces it. With its white-gloved, old-world class and American attention to service, unmuddled by pretensions at hipness, the Palme captures, in one elegant stroke, all the exclusivity a dozen South Beach restaurants could never grasp. The menu shifts seasonally but remains consistently magnificent at one of Miami's best splurges.

NORMAN'S Map pp100–1   International $$$

☎ 305-446-6767; www.normans.com; 21 Almeria Ave; mains $28-46; ☽ dinner Mon-Sat

What, Coral Gables? You've already got some of the best tapas, sushi and French food in the city; now you get Norman Van Aiken, touted by critics as possibly the best chef in the southeastern USA? The menu is a culinary mirror of the state of Florida, fusing the Caribbean to North America, and Europe to Latin America. Imagine Florida pompano with ham cheek hash, then eat it.

PASCAL'S ON PONCE

Map pp100–1   French $$$

☎ 305-444-2024; www.pascalmiami.com; 2611 Ponce de León Blvd; mains $26-37; ☽ lunch & dinner Mon-Fri, dinner only Sat

They're fighting the good fight here: sea scallops with beef short rib, crème brulee

and other French fine dining classics set the elegant stage at this neighborhood hangout, a favorite night out among Gables foodies who appreciate time-tested standards.

CAFFE ABBRACCI Map pp100–1   Italian $$

☎ 305-441-0700; 318 Aragon Ave; mains $14-24; ☽ lunch & dinner

Perfect moments in Coral Gables come easy. Here's an especially simple formula: you, a loved one, a muggy Miami evening, a sidewalk table at Abbracci, some northern Italian pasta and a glass of red.

MISS SAIGON BISTRO

Map pp100–1   Vietnamese $$

☎ 305-446-8006; www.missaigonbistro.com; 148 Giralda Ave; mains $11-21; ☽ lunch Mon-Fri, dinner daily

This clean, spare and delicious Vietnamese spot is a good middle-of-the road option for folks seeking a good meal – the caramelized pork and crispy fish spring to mind – without the pomp and circumstance of a huge night out.

MATSURI Map pp100–1   Japanese $$

☎ 305-663-1615; 5759 Bird Rd; mains $5-20; ☽ lunch & dinner Tue-Fri, dinner only Sat & Sun

Note the customers: Matsuri, tucked into a nondescript shopping center, is consistently packed with Japanese. They don't want scene; they want a taste of home – although many are South American Japanese who order *unagi* (eels) in Spanish, a cool dining sight in and of itself. Spicy *toro* (fatty tuna) and scallions, grilled mackerel with natural salt, and an ocean of raw fish are all *oishi* (delicious). The $8 bento lunch makes the rest of the day disappointing compared to your midday meal.

ALLEN'S DRUG STORE

Map pp100–1   American $

☎ 305-665-6964; 4000 Red Rd; dishes $5-8; ☽ breakfast, lunch & dinner

Don't worry: they do diner in the Gables. In Allen's case, they've just plopped one into a pharmacy. Don't let the proximity of Pepto Bismol and retirees put you off the meatloaf, vinyl booths or the little jukeboxes, because this is Florida. You should be eating among a bunch of seniors with walkers. It's called 'cultural immersion.'

GREATER MIAMI

We know this sounds clichéd, but some of Miami's best eats are a bit off the beaten path, especially the exemplars of two South Florida favorites: deli and *parrillada* (Argentine steakouse).

NORTH

GRAZIANO'S Map pp44–5   Argentine $$
☎ 305-225-0008; 9227 SW 40th St; mains $14-34; ☾ lunch & dinner

Anglos love to argue over who does the best South American steak in Miami, but among Argentines the general consensus is this very traditional *parrilla*, located on a strip of gas stations on Bird Rd. Everything is plucked out of Buenos Aires: the quebracho wood on the grill, Argentine customers and, most of all, racks of *lomo* (steak), sweetbreads and blood sausage, gristly bits beloved by *portenos* (Buenos Aires natives), which are tough to find in more Yankee-friendly establishments.

SOUTH

SHORTY'S BBQ Map pp44–5   Barbecue $
☎ 305-670-7732; 9200 S Dixie Hwy; dishes $6-16; ☾ lunch & dinner

If you're gonna make a mess of yourself, best do it by dribbling some smoky barbecue sauce on the long wooden picnic tables at this South Dade institution. It's not the best barbecue in the world, but for Texas-style brisket in South Florida it's as good as life gets.

LOTS OF LOX Map pp44–5   Deli $
☎ 305-252-2010; 14995 S Dixie Hwy; dishes $4-13; ☾ breakfast & lunch

In a city with no shortage of delis, especially in mid-Miami Beach, who would have thought some of the best chopped liver on rye could be found in this unassuming place all the way down in Palmetto Bay? It's bustling, it's friendly and the excellent lunch meats sneer at their cousins on Arthur Godfrey Rd, secure in their dominance of Greater Miami's deli ranks.

DRINKING & NIGHTLIFE

top picks

What's your recommendation? www.lonelyplanet.com/miami

Yes, yes, those are real people going into the club. They just look like they walked out of a magazine.

We probably don't need to tell you Miami's nightlife scene is hot. In point of fact, it's probably hotter than you, unless you happen to be a certain class of celebrity, in which case: we take it back, Ms Portman and Mr Pitt. A Spanish flair for all-night fun, warm weather, big beaches, skimpy clothing, perfect mojitos – yep, this isn't the place for those with Catholic guilt complexes.

On the other hand, it can also feel like it isn't a place for normal human beings. But don't be intimidated. You don't need to be uberwealthy or ultra-attractive to get past the red rope here, just confident. Besides, who cares about the rope? Miami's got kick-ass rock bars, hipsters-gone-wild lounges and the best Latin music scene in America. If you want to bump and grind and look for celebrities who aren't there, you can have it, but Miami will love you just as much if you want to rock out with a Budweiser on a sweaty South Florida evening.

CLUBS & LOUNGES

If you're gonna go out in Miami, ask yourself what you want: Do I want to dance? Hear good tunes? Score? See celebrities? If you answered yes to the first two questions, the Downtown/Wynwood scene might be more to your liking (which isn't to say the beautiful people don't go out there). The scene is just less…well, scene-y). If you answered yes to the last two questions, you may want to stay in South Beach. Also, ask yourself another question: What do I bring? If it's good looks, money or promoter connections, the world is your oyster. If you've got none of the above, you can still party, but be prepared for some ego-crushing. Best overheard conversation in the course of this research:

Guy A: [Looking at model] 'How do you approach a girl like that?'

Guy B: 'In a Mercedes.'

Here's how it breaks down: the South Beach club scene plays on the appeal of celebrity. More famous customers equal more regular customers. Eventually, a strange equilibrium establishes itself where there are enough regular customers to make people assume famous people are there, even if they're not. But those regular customers can't appear *too* regular. So a little social engineering is committed by club-owners and those titans of the cultural scene (ie bouncers) in the form of the red rope. So, how do you get by it?

Be polite Don't be skittish, but don't act like you're J Lo, either. And whatever you do, don't yell at the doorman – or touch him or yank on his clothing – to try to get his attention.

Get guest-listed Ask the concierge at your hotel to help you out, or simply call the club and leave your name; it's often that simple.

Remain confidently aloof Don't stare at the doorman; it's pathetic. Look elsewhere – but look hot doing it.

Be aggressive. Failing that, be rich If there's a clamoring crowd, standing at the back of it and hoping it'll part is about as effective as being meek when you need a seat on the New York subway. Push your way through to the front. Or order bottle service (see right), which usually guarantees you a pass to the front.

Come correct For women, showing a sophisticated amount of skin can be effective, although 'sophisticated' depends on the wearer. We've seen Brazilians in barely-there tops look less trashy than Americans in a standard sorority-girl-miniskirt ensemble. Men, don't wear T-shirts and jeans, unless you are one of those guys who *can* and still look put together. In which case, we're jealous, dude. Also, this is Miami; be a little more daring than a button-up shirt and slacks if you want to stand out from the crowd.

Get there early Do you want to be cool, or do you want to get in? From 10:30pm to 11pm is a golden time for bouncer leniency, but you can't club-hop with this strategy.

If you're a man, bring a woman A man alone is not worth much (unless you're at a gay club, natch); up your value by having a beautiful woman – or two or three – on your arm.

Be a Wilson brother Luke! Owen! Come on in.

Note that there's some overlap between what we call lounges, bars and clubs; a lounge has a bar and dance area, with the emphasis shifting from drinking to dancing throughout the night. Though our listings represent the hottest parties as of press time, we urge you to do some follow-up research when you arrive: talk to friends, your concierge and pick up a copy of the local arts weekly, *Miami New Times,* or a free monthly such as *Miami Living Magazine* or the pint-sized *Ego Miami Magazine.*

BARS

There is a surprising glut of dives in South Beach, the perfect yin to the flash yang of the club scene. And both dives and hot bars abound in Miami proper. But the best place for a simple drink in this city may well be your hotel lobby. For years now, hotel lounges have been the clubs of the season, and on almost any given night, front desks hire DJs for their lobbies and pool areas. Plenty of people use their hotel lobby as a jumping-off point to bigger things, but for many, the lobby is the be-all, end-all destination for the evening out. Restaurant bars have started to build on the same cachet, and the most popular hotels blend all of the genres, keeping a hot eatery on site that happens to have a hotter attached bar (De Soleil, Table 8 and the Table 8 Bar are a good example).

LIVE MUSIC

When most people think about the live-music scene in Miami, they'll start hearing one of two sounds: Latin or hip-hop. And while it's true that these are still the beats that rule this town, there is a lot more going on. Electronica rules at more Design District and Downtown clubs, lovely jazz spots aren't hard to find, and a cozy but strong indie-rock scene centers around Sweat Records (p118) and Churchill's (p150). Still, Miami is the Latin music capital of America; if you want to hear what's emerging in this genre, head on down to La Covacha (p152) and get your dancing shoes on.

WHEN TO GO & HOW MUCH TO SPEND

Unless you're in Coconut Grove, where closing time is now 3am, Miami's one of the most late-night friendly towns in America. Clubs generally stay open from 9pm to 5am; bars open earlier but often shut at the same time.

Ya gotta pay to play in this town. The cover at the big clubs tends to run around $20 to $25. Bars charge anywhere from $3 to $6 for a beer, a little more for mixed drinks. Beers may run you $4 to $10 in a club, but expect to pay as much as $18 for a regular old rum and coke in top-end joints. Don't forget the insidious practice of bottle service, whereby tables are available for sitting if you're willing to shell out about $200 to $2000 for a bottle of booze. This can actually work out well if you're in a large group. At some clubs you'll have to order bottle service or be on the list to enter after a certain hour.

SOUTH BEACH

As you might expect, the party's going on here. Wanna get wild with rappers and Paris Hilton? Check. Suck down an MGD in a dive? Surprisingly, also: check. There's a lot in between as well, and more hotties than any sane person can cope with.

AUTOMATIC SLIMS

Map pp48–9   Bar

☎ 305-675-0795; www.automatic-slims.com; 1216 Washington Ave

Slims sells itself as a seedy rock bar, but it's really a marketing consultant's idea of what a dive bar should be like. The Harley parked out the front, Coyote Ugly ambience and manufactured 'edge' make it the Blink 182 of Miami's nightlife universe: watered-down punk and pretty non-threatening.

ROOM Map pp48–9   Bar

☎ 305-531-6061; www.theotheroom.com/room.html; 100 Collins Ave

The Room is a gem: a crowded, dimly lit boutique beer bar where you can guzzle the best (brew) that Belgium has to offer and gawk at the best (hotties) Miami has to show off. It's hip as hell, but the attitude is as low-key as the sexy mood lighting.

TABLE 8 BAR Map pp48–9   Bar

☎ 305-695-4114; www.table8la.com; 1458 Ocean Dr

Before you settle in for an excellent meal at Table 8 (p127), rock up to the bar and order the best drink in Miami: a Basil 8. It's like a mojito for grown-ups: more mature, with more bite, but still a perfect drink on a hot day.

FELT Map pp48–9   Bar/Billiards

☎ 305-531-2114; 1242 Washington Ave

Having 10 pool tables is one way to stand out from the crowd in these parts, and it seems to be working. Grab a drink and a cue and enjoy this spot's come-one-come-all attitude.

MANGO'S TROPICAL CAFÉ

Map pp48–9   Bar/Cabaret

☎ 305-673-4422; www.mangostropicalcafe.com; 900 Ocean Dr; cover $10-20

Cuba meets Coyote Ugly in this tourist hotspot, where a staff of gorgeous and/or ripped bodies (take your pick) dances, gyrates and puts some serious booty on the floor. Of course, you are here for anthropological reasons: to study the finer nuances of Latin dance. Not to watch the bartender do that thing Shakira does with her butt.

LAUNDRY BAR Map pp52–3   Bar/Lounge

☎ 305-531-7700; www.laundrybar.com; 721 Lincoln Lane N

You can go with coin-operated or cointreau at this dark and groovy hybrid; as they say, 'get sloshed while you wash.' There is a decidedly gay vibe about this place, but Laundry Bar is relaxed and welcomes all, although you may have to step around a few breakdancing poseurs on weekends. By the way, you really can clean your clothes, although every couple in Miami is already making out on the washer units.

SYLVANO SOUTH

Map pp48–9   Bar/Restaurant

☎ 305-673-4344; www.theopiumgroup.com; 124 Collins Ave

This popular Italian eatery converts into a lounge that pulls in models and their hangers-on as the evening sets in. It's a great spot to sit under the humid Miami night and think sultry thoughts about all the gorgeous types smoking (in every sense of the word) on the sidewalk.

CAMEO Map pp48–9   Club

☎ 305-532-2667; www.cameomiami.com; 1445 Washington Ave

This enormous, touristy club, where Gwen Stefani tracks get smooshed into Oakenfold, is where the sexy times are to be had – if by sexy time you mean thumping music, a packed crowd and sweat to slip on. Sunday's gay night (the specific party name frequently changes) is one of the best in town.

MANSION

Map pp48–9 Club

☎ 305-532-1525; www.mansionmiami.com; 1235 Washington Ave

Every night of the week the lines stretch around the block as plebes beg, cajole and strut in a vain attempt to get past that damned red rope. Inside? Well, they don't call it 'Mansion' for nothing. Expect megaclub grandiosity, plenty of attitude, waiting in line for hours and the chance to see Lindsay Lohan do something tabloid worthy.

MYNT Map pp52–3 Club

☎ 786-695-1705; www.myntlounge.com; 1921 Collins Ave

Join the partying stars – Justin Timberlake, Vin Diesel, Britney Spears, etc – by bottle servicing yourself into the VIP section. Otherwise, make friends with the red rope until you can order a drink and then try not to spill it, which is tough in the sweaty scrum of models, Moet and mojitos.

OPIUM GARDEN & PRIVÉ

Map pp48–9 Club

☎ 305-531-5535; www.theopiumgroup.com; 136 Collins Ave

See the boxed text (p147) about trying to break into this most coveted of clubs. Coveted and overrated, as far as we're concerned, but the Opium Group has a vicelike grip on the Miami Beach club scene that's hard to break. Once you're in, flash a wad to either score bottle service or buy your way into several layers of VIP room snobbery.

DEWEY'S TAVERN

Map pp48–9 Dive

☎ 305-532-9980; 852 Alton Rd

Dewey's the deco dive (really; the exterior is a little gem of the genre), and it's as unpretentious as the best sordid watering holes get. Come here to get wasted and menace the crowds seeking serenity on quiet Alton Rd (just kidding – behave yourself!).

top picks

HOTEL BARS

- Circa 39 (p148)
- Chesterfield (p146)
- Level 25 (p149)
- Raleigh Hotel (p146)
- Skybar (p146)

LOST WEEKEND

Map pp48–9 Dive

☎ 305-672-1707; 218 Española Way

The Lost Weekend is a grimy, sweaty, slovenly dive, filled with pool tables, cheap domestics and – hell yeah – a Golden Tee arcade game. God bless it. It's a popular spot with local waiters, kitchen staff and bartenders, so you know that it's a good time.

MAC'S CLUB DEUCE BAR

Map pp48–9 Dive

☎ 305-673-9537; 222 14th St

The oldest bar in Miami Beach (established in 1926), the Deuce is a real neighborhood bar and hype-free zone. It's just straight-up seediness, which, depending on your outlook, can actually be quite refreshing. Plan to see everyone from transgendered ladies to construction workers and hipsters to bikers.

TED'S HIDEAWAY

Map pp48–9 Dive

☎ 305-532-9869; 124 2nd St

Somewhere in the Florida panhandle is a bumpin', fabulous gay club, which clearly switched places with Ted's, a no-nonsense, pool table and sports-showin' 'lounge' smack in the middle of Sofi's elegant chicness.

SCORE Map pp52–3 Gay Club

☎ 305-535-1111; www.scorebar.net; 727 Lincoln Rd

Muscle boys with mustaches, glistening, rippling six-packs gyrating about on stage, and a crowd of men who've decided that shirts really aren't their thing: do we need to spell out the orientation of Score's customer base? This place is still the best dedicated gay bar down on the beach, and the addition of the more mature venue Crème Lounge upstairs will undoubt-edly raise the cachet of this perennial favorite.

TWIST Map pp48–9 — Gay Club
☎ 305-538-9478; 1057 Washington Ave
Never a cover, always a groove, and right across from the police station, this two-story gay hangout has serious staying power and a little bit of something for everyone: six different bars; go-go dancers; drag shows; lounging areas and, oh yeah, a small dance floor.

CHESTERFIELD HOTEL
Map pp48–9 — Hotel Bar
☎ 305-531-5831; 855 Collins Ave
Perch on some prime Collins people-watching real estate and get crunk on the hip-hop-and-zebra-stripe theme they've got going on here. You'd think this would be a pre-funk kinda place, but the setting's so fly, folks end up stationary, sipping on mad martinis 'til they stumble into their rooms.

HOTEL CHELSEA
Map pp48–9 — Hotel Bar
☎ 305-534-4069; 944 Washington Ave
This is a quiet, dark little den with a sleek black bar and one long banquette. Down your martini in one of the sexiest lobbies in South Beach amid mellow locals who like the live DJs and friendly 'tenders.

MARLIN HOTEL
Map pp48–9 — Hotel Bar
☎ 305-604-5000; 1200 Collins Ave
Island Records founder and former Marlin owner Chris Blackwell may have moved on from this favorite hotel, but the beauti-ful bar, bathed heavily in futuristic steel decor, remains as hot as ever. The steady stream of models coming in and out of the bar doesn't make the place any less eyecandescent.

RALEIGH HOTEL
Map pp52–3 — Hotel Bar
☎ 305-534-6300; 1775 Collins Ave
You'd best be orderin' a manhattan if you're gonna sidle up to this cologne-and-leather bar. Like everything else in the Raleigh, this lounge evokes South Beach's good old days, when guys like Al Capone

and Meyer Lanksy cut deals in the corner and jazz set the soundtrack.

SAGAMORE
Map pp52–3 — Hotel Bar
☎ 305-535-8088; 1671 Collins Ave
Should you need a more refined vibe than the madness at the Delano (p176), walk into this cool white lobby, sit across from the plaster death masks (there when we visited anyways), tell 'em hello and have a nice glass of chardonnay.

WAVE HOTEL Map pp48–9 — Hotel Bar
☎ 305-673-0401; 350 Ocean Dr
The Wave's lounge isn't as busy as some of the other hotel bars on the beach, but it's a lot more stylish, with a blend of ultra-modern and classic deco – check out the frosty blue, Tetris-esque stacked squares that make up the main bar, which cast a frozen sexy glow throughout the entire joint.

ROSE BAR AT THE DELANO
Map pp52–3 — Hotel Bar
☎ 305-672-2000; Delano Hotel, 1685 Collins Ave
The ultrachic Rose Bar at this elegant Ian Schrager original is a watering hole for beautiful creatures (or at least those with a healthy ego). Get ready to pay up for the privilege – but also prepare to enjoy it. The tiki bar in the back of the Delano is another winner; wait for staff to set out a wrought-iron table in the shallow end of the pool and you'll start rethinking your definition of opulence.

SKYBAR Map pp52–3 — Hotel Bar/Lounge
☎ 305-695-3900; Shore Club, 1901 Collins Ave
We've never seen so many beautiful people packed into one place, anywhere. Skybar became the bar to beat as soon as it opened, and frankly, it remains so to this day. The three-part venue is fabulous: chill alfresco in a sultan's pleasure garden under enormous, wrought-iron Moroccan lanterns, gaze at the patricians dining in nearby Nobu, or try (and fail, if you're an unlisted travel writer) to get into the all-crimson, all-A-list Red Room.

FLORIDA ROOM AT THE DELANO
Map pp52–3 — Hotel Club
☎ 305-672-2000; Delano Hotel, 1685 Collins Ave

YOU CAN FIND ME AT THE CLUB...

I walked up to the man, nervous, my fingers ready to clench. He was big – real big. Ham hock neck, tree trunk arms. He looked me up and down and opened his mouth.

'Thanks for being patient, man,' he said, before lifting the red rope up.

Meh?

Hold up – this is Miami and the bouncer is acting all polite? Here I am expecting, as a single male, to be totally shut out from South Beach's infamously selective clubbing scene – and the bouncers are accommodating? But in three weeks of essentially contiguous beer-and-whiskies drunk all over Greater Miami, I must admit the evening fun here has defied most of my expectations.

Although it has met a few of them, too. For example: the price to party. To get into Privé (p145), where this story begins, cost $20. That's a pretty standard door charge here, especially for Miami and Miami Beach's 'hottest' megaclubs.

Those quotes around 'hottest' are there because I could not, during my time in Privé, figure out what all the fuss was about. Privé is supposed to be the greatest clubbing experience ever, where Jay-Z serves the Moet and life is basically a hip-hop video, starring you.

Reality: a bunch of girls cordoned off in a 'VIP' area (there is always a VIP area in Miami). A pretty limp, late-90s hip-hop set (Lil' Kim's 'Crush on You' isn't exactly groundbreaking these days). Old, eurotrash-y men in gold chains and tall, Eastern European girls in stiletto boots buy triple-digit bottles of booze for the privilege of being allowed to sit down. This is known as 'bottle service'; you order an overpriced bottle of liquor and get to sit at a table while the other proles knock their knees. I stayed for about an hour and left, wanting my $20 back. There were no celebrities, just tourists looking for them or playing one for the night.

'Wanna buy me an eight-dollar beer?' asks an out-of-towner, gazing awestruck at the sheer mass of model-types packed into this den of iniquity. The Florida Room is as exclusive as they get, plus a popular dancehall/samba piano lounge for local scenesters who eschew the tourist trap megaclubs further down the beach. Show up before 11pm or be on the list (or Lenny Kravitz – who helped design this place) to get in.

BOND STREET LOUNGE
Map pp52–3   Hotel Lounge
☎ 305-398-1806; Townhouse Hotel, 150 20th St
After the sushi eaters head home, a new crowd rolls in – one that prefers litchitinis (lychee martinis) over yellowtail. Throw yourself over a white couch or cylindrical white ottoman, order up, sip and stare at the crowd.

JAZID Map pp48–9   Jazz Club/Lounge
☎ 305-673-9372; 1342 Washington Ave
While the downstairs caters to folks seeking a mellow, candlelit spot to hear live jazz, soul and funk bands, the upstairs lounge has DJs spinning soul, funk and hip-hop to a cool, multiculti crowd. By being cool and not trying to be, this place has remained popular while places all around it have come and gone.

BED Map pp48–9   Lounge
☎ 305-532-9070; www.bedmiami.com;
929 Washington Ave; ☽ Wed-Sun
You probably know this drill: someone sets a bunch of beds around a DJ booth. House music ensues. People go crazy. Except the music is really loud, and you have to order bottle service to lounge, so come with cash if you want to lay down (which seems opposed to the whole, 'Let's go dance' thing, but hey).

BUCK 15 Map pp52–3   Lounge
☎ 305-538-3815; 707 Lincoln Lane
Located in a loft above Miss Yip (p129), B15 manages to blend everything we like about going out – kinda edgy but not scary graffiti chic, cast-off action figures, consistently awesome DJs (Did they just mix 'Your Love' by the Outfield into 'Low' by Flo-Rida? Oh yes they did), free entry, a good mix of the hip and the hot and the drunk and the folks who just don't care but definitely wave their hands in the air – into one shot of nightlife fun.

PURDY LOUNGE
Map pp52–3   Lounge
☎ 305-531-4622; www.purdylounge.com;
1811 Purdy Ave
It's half club, half lounge and all intimate fun at this spot, tucked away from the fray

and open to all, based on the mixed hetero-homo-white-Latino rainbow coalition clientele.

SOFI LOUNGE
Map pp48–9   Lounge
☎ 305-532-4444; www.sofilounge.com; 423 Washington Ave
Not long after its arrival, Sofi Lounge was touted in a *Miami Herald* article as being 'an oasis for skateboarders, surfers, models, club promoters and others disenchanted with the increasingly glutted and pretentious South Beach club scene.' So if you count yourself among them, head here – a dark and narrow space with DJs, live music and special events.

NIKKI BEACH
Map pp48–9   Outdoor Club
☎ 305-538-1111; www.nikkibeach.com; 1 Ocean Dr
Get your groove on outdoors, wandering from immaculate gossamer beach cabana to cabana at Nikki's, which feels like a full moon party gone incredibly upscale. On Sunday *(Sunday!?)* starting around 4pm it's the hottest party in town, as folks clamor to get in and relive whatever it was they did the night before. The attached Pearl Restaurant attracts the dinner club set. It's quite the cool-kid spot too, but who needs food when there are thongs in them thar hills?

ABBEY BREWERY
Map pp52–3   Pub
☎ 305-538-8110; 1115 16th St
The only brewpub in South Beach is on the untouristed end of South Beach (near Alton Rd). It's friendly and packed with folks listening to the Grateful Dead and, of course, slinging back some excellent homebrew: give the Abbey Brown or Oatmeal Stout a shot.

TOUCH
Map pp52–3   Restaurant/Lounge
☎ 305-532-8003; www.touchrestaurant.com; 910 Lincoln Rd
Touch's owners turned Elizabeth Taylor's jewelry box into a lounge: a vintage-y, opulent mess of sensory glitter, gaudy overkill and refined elegance. Drink alongside a slew of Miami's hiperati at this new Lincoln Rd resto-lounge and try not to be overwhelmed.

MIAMI BEACH

BOY BAR Map pp58–9   Bar
☎ 305-864-2697; 1220 Normandy Dr (71st St)
The North Beach boys (and just about everyone else) flock to this neighborhood cruise bar, where everyone plays pool, chills on the back porch and basically avoids indulging in too much South Beach–style madness. Which isn't to say they don't engage in a little bad behavior…

BOTECA Map pp58–9   Bar/Restaurant
☎ 305-757-7735; 916 NE 79th St
If you're missing São Paolo, come to Boteca on Friday evenings to see the biggest Brazilian expat reunion in Miami. *Cariocas* (Rio natives) and their countrymen flock here to listen to samba and bossa nova and chat each other up over (obviously) the best capirinhas in town.

CIRCA 39
Map pp58–9   Hotel Bar
☎ 305-538-3900; 3900 Collins Ave
Tucked off to the back of Circa's moody front lobby, the designer dream bar has a warm, welcoming feel to it. Definitely stop in for a cosmopolitan if you're up this way, before sauntering across the street and checking out the nighttime ocean.

CAFÉ NOSTALGIA
Map pp58–9   Theater
☎ 305-531-8831; 3425 Collins Ave; ⏰ Tue-Sat
Come here to drink sangria and watch old-school crooners get melodramatic on a vintage stage. Sure it's cheesy, but that's the point (look at the name of the place).

DOWNTOWN MIAMI

Tourists don't tend to make it across A1A, sticking to the well-hyped but somewhat overplayed scene in South Beach. That's their loss; to quote 'Bitch I'm From Dade County' (poetic in its prose, visionary in its themes), 'Do not be thinkin' we soft or we sweet/Come on the opposite side of the beach.' The real cutting edge of clubs, pubs and bars is concentrated here, specifically in the edgy transition area between Downtown and Overtown. The lounges here usually feature live music and often double as small clubs.

top picks

LIVE MUSIC

- PS 14 (p150)
- Studio A (right)
- Transit Lounge (below)
- Churchill's (p150)
- La Covacha (p152p152)

TOBACCO ROAD Map pp66–7   Bar
☎ 305-374-1198; 626 S Miami Ave
Miami's oldest bar has been on the scene since the 1920s. These days it's a little touristy, but it's stayed in business for a reason: old wood, blue lights, cigarette smoke and sassy bartenders greet you like a buddy, cold beers are on tap and decent live acts crank out the blues, jazz and rock.

TRANSIT LOUNGE
Map pp66–7   Bar/Live Music
☎ 305-377-4628; 729 SW 1st Ave
Transit exists in some perfect bar conceptual space, possessing the everyone-knows-your-name camaraderie of a dive, the cool-daddio ambience of a good jazz club, the street cred of some of Miami's hottest live acts and a welcoming but ruggedly sexy venue. When you've had enough, run, don't stumble, to nearby La Moon (p134) and soak all that beer up with a hot dog smothered in mayo and potato sticks.

SPACE Map pp66–7   Club
☎ 305-375-0001; www.clubspace.com; 142 NE 11th St
This multilevel warehouse is Miami's main megaclub. With 30,000 sq ft to fill, dancers have room to strut, and an around-the-clock liquor license redefines the concept of after-hours. DJs usually pump each floor with a different sound – hip-hop, Latin, heavy trance – while the infamous rooftop lounge is the place to be for sunrise.

KARU & Y Map pp66–7   Club/Lounge
☎ 305-403-7850; www.karu-y.com; 71 NW 14th St
Karu smacks of an Atlanta hip-hop megaclub in ways good and sundry. Basically a bottle of iced-out Cristal given club form, there's a Dale Chihuly chandelier in the entrance, waterfall out front and restaurant (Karu; Y is the lounge) that serves foie gras lollipops. It's all (literally) smack on the tracks that separate tatty but gentrifying Downtown (bling!) from Overtown's worst projects (bang!). Come here to star in your personal MTV video, and expect to pay for the privilege.

LEVEL 25 Map pp66–7   Hotel Bar
☎ 305-503-6500; Conrad Hotel, 1395 Brickell Ave
When Neo buys Morpheus a drink, they probably meet at this Conrad Hotel spot (guess which floor), where it's all long white lines, low black couches, pin-striped gorgeousity and God's eye views over Biscayne Bay.

M BAR Map pp66–7   Hotel Bar
☎ 305-695-1717; Mandarin Oriental, 500 Brickell Key Dr
The high-class lobby bar here may be tiny, but its martini menu – over 250 strong – isn't. And neither is the bird's-eye view, high up over shimmering Biscayne Bay.

WALLFLOWER GALLERY
Map pp66–7   Live Music
☎ 305-579-0069; www.wallflowergallery.com; 10 NE 3rd St
This gallery hosts an eclectic lineup, from the pop stylings of the Avenging Lawnmowers of Justice to the jazzy Gabe Nixon Band.

STUDIO A Map pp66–7   Live Music/Club
☎ 305-358-7625; www.studioamiami.com; 60 NE 11th St
Next to ginormous Space (left), Studio A is something between an edgy gig venue and mega-mainstage. It's very hit or miss; as a club it can suck, but as a concert hall it pulls in some incredible acts.

PAWN SHOP Map pp66–7   Lounge
☎ 305-373-3511; www.thepawnshoplounge.com; 1222 NE 2nd Ave
This den of hipness still has its original pawn shop facade, with signs announcing 'We buy diamonds' and 'We buy gold.' It's all about true (but glamorous) grit here – and varying DJs who spin funky, edgy electronica.

WHITE ROOM
Map pp66–7   Lounge/Club
☎ 305-995-5050; www.whiteroommiami.com;
1306 N Miami Ave

Miami's hipsters are so, well, Miami – artsy yet glam compared to their London and NYC counterparts. They flock here, where there's the requisite weird movie playing on open-air projectors, Lawrence of Arabia tents curving around an exposed-industrial mainstage and, according to promoters, a shared design-aesthetic-lifestyle-blah blah blah. Hot hipsters get drunk and dance with other hot hipsters. You go, White Room. The very popular Poplife party goes off here on Saturdays.

PS 14 Map pp66–7   Lounge/Live Entertainment
☎ 305-358-3600; 28 NW 14th St

In a city with justice, PS 14 would be packed every night of the week. Live gigs burn up the cute red-lit front room, while the back opens into a lush garden (you could almost forget you're on the edge of Overtown…) where DJs spin and folks chill if they ain't dancing, which you should be.

WYNWOOD, THE DESIGN DISTRICT & LITTLE HAITI

With all the gentrification occurring here, expect this neighborhood's nightlife to blow up in the near future. The monthly Friday Arts Walks (see p84) attract both sophisticated and simplistic club kids from all across the city.

CIRCA 28
Map p82   Lounge
☎ 305-788-1858; www.circa28.com;
2826 N Miami Ave

Miami can work her magic on anyone, even Wynwood's angsty artists. Like Cinderella touched by the Fairy Godmother (or a very good DJ), they transform into glamorous club kids in this two-story hepcat hotspot. Circa 28 is about as sexy and gorgeous as Miami gets, but with its modish library and (semi)literati clientele, it's also intelligent enough to hold a conversation.

GRASS RESTAURANT & LOUNGE
Map p82   Lounge
☎ 305-573-3355; www.grasslounge.com;
28 NE 40th St; 🕙 Tue-Sat

This Design District restaurant-cum-lounge is intimate yet alfresco. Dress your best and head to the velvet-roped entrance; inside, you can either dine on cool Asian-fusion dishes (see Grass Restaurant, p135) or simply posture and dance and watch the door (like everyone else).

CHURCHILL'S Map p82   Pub/Live Music
☎ 305-757-1807; www.churchillspub.com;
5501 NE 2nd Ave, Little Haiti; cover $10-15;
🕙 11am-3am Mon-Sat, noon-3am Sun

Only in Miami: Churchill's is a Brit-owned East End–style pub in the midst of what could be Port-au-Prince. There's a lot of live music here, mainly punk and indie and more punk. Not insipid modern punk either: think the Ramones meet the Sex Pistols. While everyone's getting their ya-ya's off, Haitian hustlers are lurking outside, waiting to park your car or sidle in and enjoy the gig and a beer with you. Brits, this is the place to watch your sports.

LITTLE HAVANA

There's not much in terms of bars and clubs (the best Latin nightlife in town is at La Covacha (p152) here, but who needs bars when you've got kitschy Spanish entertainment?

HOY COMO AYER Map p88   Cuban Club
☎ 305-541-2631; 2212 SW 8th St; cover $8-25

This Cuban hot spot – with authentic music, unstylish wood paneling and a small dance floor – is enhanced by cigar smoke and packed with Havana transplants. Stop in nightly for son (a salsalike dance that originated in Oriente, Cuba), boleros (a Spanish dance in triple meter) and modern Cuban beats.

CASA PANZA
Map p88   Live Entertainment
☎ 305-643-5343; 1620 SW 8th St

It doesn't get cornier than this 'authentic' Spanish taverna (p136), where the live shows, flamenco dancers, Spanish guitarists and audience participation reach new heights of sangria-soaked fun. Drop your cynicism, enter and enjoy.

COCONUT GROVE

Everything here closes at 3am, thanks to stick-in-the-mud city officials.

MIAMI IMPROV

Map p95   Comedy

☎ 305-441-8200; www.miamiimprov.com; 3390 Mary St; tickets $10-70

Part of a national chain, this 3rd-floor club has the usual club-circuit suspects plus monthly Miami Comics, open-mic shows and Urban Nights, which feature some of the stars from Comedy Central's Showtime, HBO's Def Comedy Jam and BET's Comic View.

OXYGEN LOUNGE

Map p95   Lounge

☎ 305-476-0202; www.oxygenlounge.biz; Streets of Mayfair, 2911 Grand Ave; ☽ till 3am

This is the mall underground – literally – of Coconut Grove. It's an elegant, sprawling sushi bar/dance land with space-age decor and packs of Grove beauties, with theme night parties to rock your fine booty every night of the week.

SANDBAR Map p95   Lounge

☎ 305-444-5270; www.sandbargrill.com; 3064 Grand Ave; ☽ till 3am

Sandbar's a little slice of Florida Keys culture – nautical crap on the walls and sport-n-surf-n-fishin' ambience – in the midst of the urban jungle.

CORAL GABLES

There's Gruppie (Gables yuppie) bars all along Miracle Mile, but these two gems will keep you above the silly fray.

BAR Map pp100–1   Bar

☎ 305-442-2730; 172 Giralda Ave

All in a name, right? Probably the best watering hole in the Gables, The Bar is just what the title says (which is ironic in this neighborhood of extravagant embellishment). If you're in the 'hood on Friday come here for happy hour (5pm to 8pm), when all the young Gables professionals take their ties off and basically let loose long into the night.

TITANIC Map pp100–1   Restopub

☎ 305-668-1742; www.titanicbrewery.com; 5813 Ponce de León Blvd

By day, it's an All-American type bar and grill, but at night Titanic turns into a popular University of Miami watering hole. Thursdays tend to be big nights out here.

GREATER MIAMI

IMPROMEDY

Map pp44–5   Comedy

☎ 305-226-0030; Roxy Performing Arts Center; 1645 SW 107th Ave, Greater Miami; tickets $10

This improvisational comedy troupe was formed at Florida International University

---

GAMBLING

Miami's no Vegas, but if you're into blowing wads of money on all-but-rigged games of chance while lots of bells and whistles go off, here are some good places to do so.

Atlantic Casino Miami (Map pp48–9; ☎ 305-532-2111; Miami Beach Marina, Alton Rd at 5th St, South Beach; cruise $20) This gaming cruise offers a plethora of slots, video gambling, poker, roulette and blackjack tables, plus an observation deck and full bars.

Casino Princesa (Map pp66–7; ☎ 305-379-5825; www.casinoprincesa.com; 100 S Biscayne Blvd, Downtown; cruise $9.95) Docked adjacent to the Hard Rock Café in the Bayside Marketplace (p68), the Casino Princesa is a large, upscale yacht that departs on 4½-hour voyages that head 3 miles offshore. The boat has two decks of gaming tables (blackjack and craps are big), slot machines and bars.

Gulfstream Park (off Map pp44–5; ☎ 954-454-7000; www.gulfstreampark.com; 901 S Federal Hwy, Hallandale) Located in Hallandale, which is north of Miami, toward Hollywood, this 60-plus-year-old horse-racing track features almost-daily live racing and nationwide simulcasting. So if you have a hankering for a wager…

Miami Jai Alai (Map pp44–5; ☎ 305-633-6400; www.fla-gaming.com; 3500 NW 37th Ave) The ball game, which came to Miami from Spain via Cuba, combines elements of polo and soccer (but is extremely fast and unique and hard to explain). Everyone bets on games. For more information on jai alai, see p168.

in 1997. You can catch their shows on weekends at the Roxy, west of Coral Gables in Sweetwater.

LAUGHING GAS
Comedy

☎ 305-461-1161; www.laughinggasimprov.com; venues vary; tickets $12

This long-running, wacky improv and comedy-sketch troupe brings its costumed craziness to venues around town, usually in Coral Gables and nearby Miami Lakes. Check the website for more information about upcoming gigs.

LA COVACHA
Map pp44–5 Live Music/Club

☎ 305-594-3717; www.lacovacha.com; 10730 NW 25th St, Doral

Drive out about halfway to the Everglades (just kidding, but only just) and you'll find Covacha, the most hidden, most hip Latin scene in Miami. Actually, it's not hidden; all the young Latinos know about Covacha and love it well, and we do too. It's an excellent spot to see new bands, upcoming DJs (almost all local), an enormous crowd and pretty much no tourists. It throws one of the best parties in the city.

top picks

- Adrienne Arsht Center for the Performing Arts (p154)
- Gusman Center for the Performing Arts (p156)
- Miami International Film Festival (p13)
- Ifé-Ilé Afro Cuban Dance (p157)
- Miami City Ballet (p157)

Miami's artistic merits are obvious, even from a distance. Could there be a better creative base? There's Southern American homegrown talent, migratory snowbirds bringing the funding and attention of northeastern galleries, and the immigrants, of course, from all across the Americas. All these disparate cultures communicate their values via the language of artistic expression. Creole, Spanish and English, after all, are poor languages compared to dance, music and theater.

Yet for years Miami was too pretty to be taken seriously. 'Each place has its own advantages – heaven for the climate, and hell for the society,' Mark Twain once said, a quote that summed up many a snob's opinion of this town. Miami's loyal, vibrant arts community seethed and continued to patronize itself, egged on by yearly arrivals of artsy eccentrics seeking South Florida's anything-goes climes.

And then Art Basel came. The Western Hemisphere's largest contemporary arts festival jogged the world's memory, reminding it that the Magic City earned its nickname by being the kind of town that isn't afraid to challenge conventions, including – actually, especially – aesthetic conventions.

Today art is part of both Miami's character and brand, an integral component of city identity that's used to both attract visitors (Art Basel) and push the revitalization/gentrification of neighborhoods from Downtown to Wynwood. In a city that moves to a Latin/Caribbean beat, it's not surprising there are excellent music and dance troupes here, but 'classical' culture is also evident and has a brand new, beautiful home: the Adrienne Arsht Center for the Performing Arts (p65).

The following are listings of Miami venues. For an in-depth analysis of trends in literature, music, theater, etc in Miami, please see Arts (p28).

PERFORMING ARTS VENUES

ADRIENNE ARSHT CENTER FOR THE PERFORMING ARTS Map pp66–7
☎ 305-949-6722, 786-468-2000; www.arshtcenter.org; 1300 Biscayne Blvd; Metromover Omni
Skeptics, we're sorry, but it's clear this enormous centerpiece of northern Downtown was worth both the wait and the expense. The magnificent venue manages to both humble and enthrall visitors who can't help but marvel at the split-shell design and the way the Arsht seizes upon and utilizes the most common natural resource in Florida: natural, golden sunlight, which comes crashing through huge plate-glass windows. Today the Arsht is where the biggest cultural acts in Miami come to perform; a show here is a must-see on any Miami trip.

COLONY THEATRE Map pp52–3
☎ 305-674-1026; 1040 Lincoln Rd, South Beach
A stunning deco showpiece, this small 1934 performing arts center has 465 seats and great acoustics. It's a treasure that hosts everything from movies and musicals to theatrical dramas, ballet and off-Broadway productions.

CORAL GABLES CONGREGATIONAL CHURCH Map pp100–1
☎ 305-448-7421; www.coralgablescongregational.org; 3010 DeSoto Blvd, Coral Gables
In addition to its impressive choirs, this church hosts various concert series, from jazz to classical, all of which draw regional crowds to its beautiful Mediterranean setting.

FILLMORE MIAMI BEACH AT THE JACKIE GLEASON THEATER Map pp52–3
☎ 305-673-7300; www.gleasontheater.com; 1700 Washington Ave, South Beach
Built in 1951, the Miami Beach's premiere showcase for touring Broadway shows, orchestras and other big musical productions has 2700 seats and excellent acoustics. Jackie Gleason chose to make this theater the home for his long-running 1960s TV show, but now you will find an eclectic lineup of programs – from Elvis

ARTS FESTIVALS

Nary a month goes by without some kind of arts festival going off in one of Miami's neighborhoods. As with all things, events centered on South Beach tend to be well-hyped and can be difficult to attend, although that shouldn't dissuade you from trying to show up. Besides the following list, any of the city's art museums and galleries offer schedules of upcoming events, while the Miami Art Guide (www.miamiartguide.com) is an invaluable insider's peek into the city art scene, and is free and available anywhere around town.

Dance

Annual Tango Fantasy Festival (http://totango.net/ustc) Olé! The largest tango festival in the world outside Argentina takes place in late May and features performances and workshops that span nine days.

Florida Dance Festival (p14; www.floridadanceassociation.org/dance_festival.htm) Choreographers, performers, teachers and students from around the world gather for two weeks in June for learning and performing.

Ifé-Ilé Afro-Cuban Dance & Music Festival (www.ife-ile.org) Anchored by dance, this Afro-Cuban festival also features music, films, art and readings in October via Miami-Dade Community College.

International Ballet Festival of Miami (www.miamihispanicballet.com) Held in September, the week of events showcases America's biggest modern, ballet, jazz and ballroom dance companies.

Music

FIU Music Festival (www.fiu.edu) Featuring everything from chamber music to blues shows, this world-class fest hits every October.

JVC Jazz Festival Miami Beach (www.festivalnetwork.com) Held in various venues in early May, the jazz fest, like other incarnations in places like New York and Newport, attracts top performers in the genre.

Miami Ultra Music Festival (www.ultramusicfestival.us) Ultra sweeps Miami in March with a massive dose of the freshest in electronica. Past artists have included Paul Van Dyk, Tiësto, Carl Cox and Goldie.

International Caribbean Music Festival (☎ 305-891-2944) This mega-concert, generally held in November before Thanksgiving, brings big-name boombastic lineups to Bayfront Park.

Theater

International Hispanic Theater Festival (www.teatroavante.com) A city-wide festival, held in the first two weeks of June, features performances in Spanish, Portuguese and English by companies from all over the world.

Here & Now Festival (www.miamilightproject.com) An annual favorite of the Miami Light Project, this is a March showcase of cutting edge works-in-progress from local dramatists.

City Theatre's Summer Shorts (www.citytheatre.com) This series of one-act plays, held in June, features works from both local and global playwrights.

Film

Miami International Film Festival (p13; www.miamifilmfestival.com) The 23-year-old happening, held in February, has a focus on Ibero-American cinema and documentaries. It's launched the international careers of filmmakers including Pedro Almodóvar and Atom Egoyan.

Miami Latin Film Festival The April event, held in South Beach, includes films from and about the Americas, France, Portugal and Spain.

Miami Gay & Lesbian Film Festival (p14; www.mglff.com) Joining a series of LGBT film fests held in cities across America, this April fest, now in its eighth year, brings queer features, shorts and docs to the big screen.

Brazilian Film Festival of Miami (www.brazilianfilmfestival.com) Held at the Colony Theatre (opposite) in June before it travels to NYC in July, this dynamic cultural fest was founded in 1997.

Costello or Albita one night, to the Dutch Philharmonic or over-the-top musicals the next.

GUSMAN CENTER FOR THE PERFORMING ARTS Map pp66–7
☎ 305-374-2444; www.gusmancenter.org; 174 E Flagler St, Downtown

This ornate venue, within an elegantly renovated 1920s movie palace, services a huge variety of performing arts – film festivals, symphonies, ballet and touring shows. The acoustics are excellent and the fresco ceiling is covered in twinkling stars and clouds.

LIGHT BOX THEATRE & MIAMI LIGHT PROJECT Map p82
☎ 305-576-4350; www.miamilightproject.com; 3000 Biscayne Blvd, Wynwood

The Miami Light Project is a nonprofit cultural foundation that represents innovative shows from theater troupes and performance artists from around the world; recent shows have included Rha Goddess, Global Cuban Fest and Kristina Wong. Shows are performed across the city, but the project is housed at Light Box Studio, which runs an impressive performing-arts program that includes the Mad Cat Theatre original production company, Dolla Jams open-mic series, the D Projects hip-hop theater troupe, and the Miami Hip Hop Exchange performance and education program.

LINCOLN THEATRE Map pp52–3
☎ 305-531-3442; 555 Lincoln Rd, South Beach

Miami Beach's theatrical jewel, an intimate house with great acoustics and a perfect location, hosts a wide variety of performances from local groups to visiting artists. It's also the home of the New World Symphony (opposite).

MIAMI-DADE COUNTY AUDITORIUM Map pp44–5
☎ 305-547-5414; 2901 W Flagler St, Little Havana

On the western edge of Little Havana, this 2500-seat venue with great acoustics has been somewhat eclipsed by the Arsht center, but still holds excellent performances on its lovely stage.

TEATRO DE BELLAS ARTES off Map p88
☎ 305-547-5414; 2901 W Flagler St, Little Havana

The Teatro puts on excellent, often hilarious productions that are beloved by Miami's Latin community, but you'll need to understand Spanish to really enjoy the shows.

CLASSICAL MUSIC & OPERA

The Arsht Center rules the roost when it comes to hosting a solid collection of city chamber orchestras and symphonies. Though formerly the home of three opera companies, Miami has just one now – but it's far from lowly.

CHOPIN FOUNDATION OF THE UNITED STATES Map pp58–9
☎ 305-868-0624; www.chopin.org; 1440 JFK/79th St Causeway, Mid-Beach

This national organization hosts a treasure trove of performances for Chopin fans – the Chopin Festival, a series of free monthly concerts and the less frequent National Chopin Piano Competition, an international contest held in Miami every five years (next scheduled for 2010).

CONCERT ASSOCIATION OF FLORIDA
☎ 877-311-7469; www.concertfla.org; 555 17th St, South Beach

Founded in 1967, this nonprofit association is run by dedicated folks who bring world-class music (and, occasionally, dance) to various venues in Miami, particularly to the Arsht Center (p65). Past events have included the Boston Pops symphony, Itzhak Perlman, a Flamenco Festival, the Deutsche Philharmonie and Luciano Pavarotti on the beach.

FLORIDA GRAND OPERA
☎ 800-741-1010; www.fgo.org

Founded in the 1940s, this highly respected opera company, which stages shows like Madame Butterfly, La Boheme, Tosca and many others, performs throughout the year at the Adrienne Arsht Center for the Performing Arts (p65) and Fort Lauderdale. Ticket offices are in Doral, but it's recommended you purchase online or on the phone.

MIAMI CHAMBER SYMPHONY Map pp100–1
☎ 305-858-3500; Gusman Concert Hall, 1314 Miller Dr, Coral Gables; tickets $15-30; ☯ performances Nov-May

Its yearly series features world-renowned soloists at shows held at the University of Miami's Gusman Concert Hall, which is not to be confused with the downtown Gusman Center for the Performing Arts (opposite).

NEW WORLD SYMPHONY Map pp52–3
NWS; ☎ 305-673-3331; www.nws.org; tickets $20-70; ☷ performances Oct-May

The deservedly heralded NWS serves as a three- to four-year preparatory program for very talented musicians who've already graduated from prestigious music schools. Founded in 1987, the NWS is led by artistic director Michael Tilson Thomas, who still conducts performances for 12 weeks a year despite his national fame and fortune. There is an astonishing number of inspiring and original performances (many of which are free), held at the Lincoln Theatre (opposite).

UNIVERSITY OF MIAMI SCHOOL OF MUSIC
☎ 305-284-6477; www.music.miami.edu; ☷ performances Oct-May

Also held at the Gusman Concert Hall (Map pp100–1; 1314 Miller Dr, Coral Gables), as well as Clark Recital Hall (5501 San Amaro Dr, University of Miami, Coral Gables), these free concerts highlighting university students are a bargain. Seek out the long-running international Festival Miami (☎ 305-284-4940), which features symphonies, chamber music and jazz, and runs from late September to late October.

DANCE
World-class ballet, and modern and international dance scenes can all be found in Miami, where many new companies have formed over the past decade.

BALLET GAMONET
☎ 305-259-9775; www.balletgamonet.org

Founded by former Miami City Ballet dancers in 1997, this contemporary ballet troupe holds unique world premieres, often using hip musical scores written by the likes of Stewart Copeland, U2 and Dave Brubeck. Check the website or call for a performance schedule.

BLACK DOOR DANCE ENSEMBLE
☎ 305-380-6233; www.blackdoordance.org

Established by the Miami-Dade Community College dance department director, Karen Stewart, Miami's premiere African-American dance company performs modern, neo-classical ballet, traditional African pieces and Afro-Caribbean works at various city venues, usually the Colony Theatre (p154) on Lincoln Rd.

BRAZARTE DANCE COMPANY
off Map pp100–1
☎ 305-441-0372; www.brazartedance.com; Coral Gables

The first Brazilian dance company in Florida is based in Coral Gables, and presents lavish, Carmen Mirandaesque shows of Brazilian dance in many styles – folkloric, *capoeira* (an Afro-Brazilian dance that incorporates self-defense moves), lambada and samba. Call for show schedules and venues.

IFÉ-ILÉ AFRO-CUBAN DANCE
☎ 305-476-0388; www.ife-ile.org

A nonprofit organization, Ifé-Ilé promotes cultural understanding through dance, and performs in a range of styles – traditional Afro-Cuban, mambo, rumba, conga, *chancleta* (a Latin dance in which rhythms are amplified by the dancers' wooden shoes), *son*, salsa and ritual pieces. Live musical accompaniment comes courtesy of bongos, piano, timbales and trumpets. Please call or visit the website for the latest performance schedule and associated venues.

LA ROSA FLAMENCO THEATRE
Map pp58–9
☎ 305-899-7730; www.panmiami.org; 13126 NW Dixie Hwy, North Miami

This professional flamenco, salsa and merengue dance company blends flamenco styles with tap, Middle Eastern and Indian movement, and also offers a full range of classes and educational programs.

MIAMI CITY BALLET Map pp52–3
☎ 305-929-7000; www.miamicityballet.org; 2200 Liberty Ave, Miami Beach

Formed in 1985, this troupe is guided by artistic director Edward Villella, who studied under the great George Balanchine at the NYC Ballet. So it's no surprise Balanchine works dominate the repertoire, with shows held at a lovely three-story

THE ARTS DANCE

157

headquarters designed by the famed local architectural firm Arquitectonica. The facade allows passersby to watch the dancers rehearsing through big picture windows, which kinda makes you feel like you're in a scene from *Fame*, except the weather is better and people don't spontaneously break into song. Which is a shame, really.

MIAMI HISPANIC BALLET Map pp66–7
☎ 305-549-7711; www.miamihispanicballet.com; 900 SW 1st St

Directed by Cuban-trained Pedro Pablo Peña, this troupe presents mainly classical ballets based out of the lovely Manuel Artime Theater, the 'largest small venue' in the city.

MOMENTUM DANCE COMPANY
☎ 305-858-7002; www.momentumdance.com

Performing original, modern dance programs at rotating venues for more than 25 years, this small troupe has a focus on education and children's performances.

FILM

In addition to the many standard megaplexes that play Hollywood fare, there are plenty of art-film and indie houses.

ABSINTHE HOUSE CINEMATHEQUE
Map pp100–1

☎ 305-446-7144; 235 Alcazar Ave, Coral Gables

This art-house cinema is a blend of old-fashioned and mod – it has only one screen for independent and foreign films, but a cool lounge serving as an atmospheric snack bar.

BILL COSFORD CINEMA Map pp100–1
☎ 305-284-4861; www.miami.edu/cosford; Memorial Classroom Bldg, off University Dr, Coral Gables

On the University of Miami campus, this renovated art house was launched in memory of the *Miami Herald* film critic. They do him justice, too, with a great lineup of first-run indie and foreign movies, as well as presentations from visiting filmmakers.

IMAX Map pp100–1
☎ 305-663-4629; www.imax.com; Shops at Sunset Place, 5701 Sunset Pl, Coral Gables

This virtual-reality screen, which is way larger than real life, comes with surround sound shows and dramatic, sometimes educational footage that takes advantage of its size; also catch fun stuff best viewed through 3-D glasses.

MIAMI BEACH CINEMATHEQUE
Map pp48–9

☎ 305-673-4567; www.mbcinema.com; 512 Española Way, South Beach

This new addition to the film scene is a great one, as it features a wonderfully curated program of smart documentaries, kitschy classics, holiday-timed screeners, speaking events and film-themed art exhibits. A recent sampling of eclectic programs includes a Russ Meyer tribute, Italian shorts, dance films and Judaica on film.

REGAL SOUTH BEACH CINEMA
Map pp52–3

☎ 305-674-6766; 1100 Lincoln Rd, South Beach

This mod, state-of-the-art, 21-screen theater anchors the western end of Lincoln Rd by being both an architectural delight and a filmgoers' paradise. It shows a good blend of foreign, independent, and critically acclaimed Hollywood stuff.

TOWER THEATER Map p88
☎ 305-644-3307; 1508 Calle Ocho, Little Havana

This 1926 renovated city-owned movie theater, on the National Register of Historic Places, shows Spanish-language films and dubbed English-language films, and hosts music performances and art exhibits in its lobby.

READINGS

Poetry readings abound in Miami, especially among the young hip set that flocks to the multipurpose spaces that have taken over areas like the Design District. They're far from stuffy affairs, usually blending some hip-hop, lounge music and cocktail-swilling into the mix. To hear well-known authors read from new works, stick to renowned bookshops such as Books & Books (below).

BOOKS & BOOKS Map pp52–3
☎ 305-532-3222; www.booksandbooks.com; 933 Lincoln Rd, South Beach

Both the South Beach location of this well-stocked and popular bookseller and its branch in Coral Gables (Map pp100–1; ☎ 305-442-4408; 265 Aragon Ave, Coral Gables) feature frequent solo readings from famous (and not so famous) local authors, as well as group readings on a particular theme (science fiction, Tibetan culture, Brazil) and various book-discussion groups.

WALLFLOWER GALLERY Map pp66–7
☎ 305-579-0069; www.wallflowergallery.com; 10 NE 3rd St, Downtown
In addition to offering a well-rounded lineup of music, dance and film, the gallery features poetry readings, spoken-word artists and open-mic poetry nights.

THEATER
There is ample evidence of a theater-loving community here, who enjoy everything from classical Greek to musicals, Spanish-language to avant-garde. There are options in a variety of neighborhoods, from Coral Gables to South Beach, many housed in lovely, stylish playhouses that evoke a long-ago, more splendorous time.

ACTORS' PLAYHOUSE Map pp100–1
☎ 305-444-9293; www.actorsplayhouse.org; 280 Miracle Mile, Coral Gables
Housed within the 1948 deco Miracle Theater, this three-theater venue stages well-known musicals and comedies, children's theater on its kids stage and more avant-garde productions in its small experimental black-box space. Recent productions have included *Footloose* and *The Wizard of Oz* for the little ones.

COCONUT GROVE PLAYHOUSE
Map p95
☎ 305-442-4000; www.cgplayhouse.com; 3500 Main Hwy
This lovely state-owned theater, anchoring the Grove since 1956, gained fame via the American premiere of Samuel Beckett's

Waiting for Godot (which audiences and critics generally rejected out of hand as opaque and confusing). Although it was closed during research due to debt issues, it is set to reopen by the time you read this, and will hopefully continue to showcase some of Miami's best theater.

EDGE THEATER Map p82
☎ 305-355-0976; 3825 N Miami Ave
The Edge stays true to its name (and Design District locale) by putting on consistently contemporary, artfully imagined productions on a small stage that feels like a makeshift living room filled with props.

GABLESTAGE Map pp100–1
☎ 305-445-1119; www.gablestage.org; 1200 Anastasia Ave, Coral Gables; tickets $15-35
Founded as the Florida Shakespeare Theatre in 1979 and now housed on the property of the Biltmore Hotel after several moves, this company still performs an occasional Shakespeare play, but mostly presents contemporary and classical pieces; recent productions have included *Frozen*, *Bug* and *The Retreat from Moscow*.

JERRY HERMAN RING THEATRE
Map pp100–1
☎ 305-284-3355; www.miami.edu/ring; 1321 Miller Dr, Coral Gables
This University of Miami troupe stages musicals, dramas and comedies, with recent productions including *Falsettos* and *Baby*. Alumni actors include Sylvester Stallone, Steven Bauer, Saundra Santiago and Ray Liotta.

NEW THEATRE Map pp100–1
☎ 305-443-5909; www.new-theatre.org; 4120 Laguna St, Coral Gables
This strong Coral Gables company performs an eclectic mix of contemporary pieces and modern classics that fall squarely between the conventional and alternative. You'll be up close and personal with the actors since there are only 70 seats in the house.

top picks

- Watching the Miami Heat get hot (p167)
- Betting on jai alai (p168)
- Sailing across Biscayne Bay in a chartered boat (p165)
- Bowling a half-century with South Florida Cricket Alliance (p164)
- Ultimate Frisbee on Miami Beach (p166)

SPORTS & ACTIVITIES

There are a few sides to sports in Miami. First: there is the standard American obsession with football, basketball and baseball, and on this front, Miamians can be forgiven for feeling like they have just got off a sports roller-coaster. The Miami Dolphins are the only NFL team to ever pull off a perfect season – but that was waaaay back in 1972. The Miami Heat took the NBA championship in 2006, but got swept out of the play-offs like a bad habit in 2007, which also marked one of the worst seasons ever played by the Miami University Hurricanes – otherwise one of the best college football teams in America. The Florida Marlins won the World Series in 2003, yet by 2006 they were talking about packing up and moving shop to Texas, and *now* they are apparently getting their own stadium. Latin sports are big here too; this is one of the few places in the USA that you can strap on your *cesta* at a standardized jai alai court.

The other side is self-obsession: Miamians like to look good and there are plenty of gyms, yoga classes and such about. If it makes you sweat and look better, rest assured the local trend-obsessed fitness nuts have caught onto it.

HEALTH & FITNESS

Everyone else here has the body of a freakin' Greek god, so why don't you join the club? Besides, working out is one of Miami's favorite forms of people-watching and -meeting, and you, engaged traveler, surely want to do a bit of both. If looking at gorgeous people grunting under iron doesn't do it for you, you might prefer to watch folks clear their pranas and stuff in one of Miami's many yoga studios.

DAY SPAS

On the luxurious side, Brownes Beauty (Map pp52–3; ☎ 305-538-5142; www.brownesbeauty.com; 841 Lincoln Rd, Miami Beach), Agua Spa (Map pp52–3; ☎ 305-673-2900; Delano Hotel, 1685 Collins Ave, South Beach) and Splash Spa (Map pp66–7; ☎ 305-358-3535; Four Seasons, 1435 Brickell Ave, Downtown Miami) will pamper you from head to toe with massages, facials, body wraps and other forms of indulgence. Russian & Turkish Baths (Map pp58–9; ☎ 305-867-8313; Castillo del Mar, 5445 Collins Ave, Mid-Beach) is less glamorous and very popular because of it.

GYMS

CRUNCH Map pp48–9
☎ 305-674-8222; 1259 Washington Ave, South Beach; per day/week $21/88
This offshoot of the New York City fave has great workout equipment, a cool attitude and a slew of unique classes, from Cardio Striptease to Belly Moves. Work those abs, people.

DAVID BARTON GYM Map pp52–3
☎ 305-534-9777; 1510 Bay Rd, Miami Beach; per day/week $20/75, 10-visit pass $150
Another NYC branch, this is the nightclub of health clubs, where striking poses with your already-in-shape bod is the hottest activity of all. It has top-notch equipment, loud club music and dim (and flattering) lighting. Your workout pass gets you into the pool. There's another location in the Delano Hotel (p176).

GOLD'S GYM SOUTH BEACH
Map pp48–9
☎ 305-538-4653; 1400 Alton Rd, South Beach; per day/week $20/90
This outpost of the world's largest gym chain is a 20,000-sq-ft 'super-fitness complex,' featuring cardio machines, free weights, an outdoor patio deck and classes in spinning, boxing, kickboxing, cardio step and lots more. It's South Beach's newest (and biggest) gym.

IDOL'S GYM Map pp52–3
☎ 305-751-7591; 715 Lincoln Lane N, South Beach; per 3 days/week $25/50
Just off Meridian Ave, this small but hip and hottie-filled workout den is best suited for exhibitionists, as the entire space is walled with a glass storefront, giving Lincoln Rd passers-by plenty to gawk at.

SOUTH BEACH IRONWORKS Map pp52–3
☎ 305-531-4743; 1676 Alton Rd, South Beach; per day/3 days/week $15/25/56

Popular with locals, this gym offers lots of yoga and aerobics classes and a super array of workout equipment.

YOGA & PILATES STUDIOS

MIAMI YOGASHALA Map pp52–3
☎ 305-534-0784; www.southbeachyoga.com; 210A 23rd St, South Beach
You'll find classes in guided *ashtanga*, *vinyasa* and power yoga here, plus private sessions, a yoga boutique selling yogic items and frequent workshops.

PILATES MIAMI Map p82
☎ 305-573-4430; 3936 N Miami Ave, Design District; single/5-class $48/230
This Design District loft space offers machine training sessions as well as group classes using mats.

PRANA YOGA CENTER Map pp100–1
☎ 305-567-9812; www.pranayogamiami.com; 247 Malaga Ave, Coral Gables; single/5-class $16/70
Located in Coral Gables, this multifaceted studio offers classes in *ashtanga, prana, vinyasa, hatha, kundalini* and guided meditation.

SYNERGY CENTER FOR YOGA & THE HEALING ARTS Map pp48–9
☎ 305-538-7073; www.synergyyoga.org; 435 Española Way, South Beach; beach/studio $5/16
Check in here for fabulous on-the-beach yoga classes, plus studio sessions in *ashtanga*, basic, gentle, *iyengar, jivamukti* and pilates.

YOGA GROVE Map p95
☎ 305-448-3332; www.yogagrove.com; 3100 S Dixie Hwy, Coconut Grove; single/5-class $15/65
Located in Coconut Grove, this studio is dedicated to the *ashtanga-vinyasa* system made popular in Mysore, India. Other classes include power yoga and the new afroyoga, a blend of yoga and African dance.

ACTIVITIES

Contrary to popular belief, Miami can be experienced from beyond the seat of a convertible car. Skate, windsurf, bike or hike; it all equals sweat and seeing the city from the ground up.

EQUIPMENT RENTAL
Bicycles & Skates

FRITZ'S SKATE SHOP Map pp52–3
☎ 305-532-1954; 730 Lincoln Rd, South Beach; per hr/day $7.50/22; ☼ 10am-10pm
For in-line skate rentals, roll over here. Fritz gives free lessons on Sunday morning at 10:30am – just about the only time there's ever room on the mall anymore.

MANGROVE CYCLES Map p92
☎ 305-361-5555; 260 Crandon Blvd, Key Biscayne; per 2hr/day/week $10/15/45; ☼ 9am-6pm Tue-Sat, 10am-5pm Sun
Key Biscayne is a perfect place to bike; Mangrove has basic, luxury and children's bicycles.

MIAMI BEACH BICYCLE CENTER
Map pp48–9
☎ 305-674-0150; 601 5th St, South Beach; per hr/day/week $8/20/70; ☼ 10am-7pm Mon-Sat, 10am-5pm Sun
Rent Treks, Raleighs and Cannondales at this friendly neighborhood bike shop, right in the southern heart of South Beach.

Water Vessels & Gear

AQUATIC RENTAL CENTER & SAILING SCHOOL Map pp58–9
☎ 305-751-7514 day, 305-279-7424 evenings; 1275 NE 79th St; sailboat rental 2hr/3hr/4hr/day $80/115/135/195, sailing courses $350
If you're a bona fide seaworthy sailor, this place will rent you a vessel. If you're not, they'll teach you how to operate one.

DIVERS PARADISE Map p92
☎ 305-361-3483; Crandon Marina, 4000 Crandon Blvd, Key Biscayne; for certification $250-500
Rent what you need – and learn how to use it if you're a beginner. Just know that the best spot around is in Key Largo (p188), and worth driving to if you're serious about underwater exploration.

FANTASY WATER SPORTS Map pp58–9
☎ 305-940-2628; 100 Sunny Isles Blvd, Sunny Isles; rates vary
Head to Fantasy to rent kayaks and small boats – as well as loud and dreadful jet skis, power boats and wave runners, which, by the way, kill manatees and fish, rip up sea

plants and protected sea grass, scare swimmers, annoy locals and can be dangerous besides. Hint hint.

FLORIDA YACHT CHARTERS Map pp48–9

☎ 305-532-8600, 800-537-0050; 390 Alton Road, South Beach; ☻ 9am-5:30pm

Wanna buzz down to the Keys, or, say, float over to the Bahamas? This place, at the Miami Beach Marina, rents yachts with and without captains (as long as you pass a little practical test).

SAILBOARDS MIAMI Map p92

☎ 305-361-7245; 1 Rickenbacker Causeway, Key Biscayne; single/tandem per hr $15/20

This place also rents out kayaks, and you can also purchase a 10-hour card for $90. To get some exercise for your lower body, you could try renting water bikes, which sit in a kayak-type boat and cost the same as the kayaks. In either case, if you're goal-oriented and need a destination, head for the little offshore sandbar.

URBAN TRAILS KAYAK RENTALS

Map pp58–9

☎ 305-947-0302; 3400 NE 163rd St, Bal Harbour, North Miami Beach

Rent a canoe or kayak for solo exploration, or join one of the company's excellent guided expeditions of the Oleta River or the Everglades.

X-ISLE SURF SHOP Map pp48–9

☎ 305-531-6110; 850 Washington Ave, South Beach; per hr/day $10/30

Rent foam boards and buy used boards for about $120 to $275. New ones start at $400.

BIKING

The Miami-Dade County Parks & Recreation Department (☎ 305-755-7800; www.miamidade.gov/parks) is helpful when it comes to cycling around the city, leading frequent eco bike tours through parklands and along waterfront paths, and offering a list of traffic-free cycling paths on its website. Try the Old Cutler Bike Path, which starts at the end of Sunset Dr in Coral Gables and leads to Matheson Hammock Park and Fairchild Tropical Garden; or the Rickenbacker Causeway, taking you up and over the bridge to Key Biscayne for an excellent workout combined with gorgeous water views. Pedaling to the end of the Key is a lovely way to spend

the afternoon. Oleta River State Park has a challenging dirt trail with hills for off-road adventures. For less strenuous rides, try the side roads of South Beach or the shady streets of Coral Gables and Coconut Grove.

BOWLING

Strike Miami (Map pp44–5; ☎ 305-594-0200), in the Dolphin Mall, is a good example of what happens when Miami's talent for glitz and glamour meets some humble ten-pins.

CRICKET

Really? Yup. Don't forget there's a huge West Indies and Jamaican community in South Florida. The South Florida Cricket Alliance (☎ 305-606-7603; www.southfloridacricket.com) is one of the largest cricket clubs in America, the Cricket Council of the USA (www.cricketcouncilusa.com) is based in Boca Raton, and the first dedicated cricket pitch in the country opened in Lauderhill (where the population is 25% West Indian), west of Fort Lauderdale, in 2008. Contact any of the above if you'd like to watch a test or join a team.

DIVING & SNORKELING

It's better to head down to the Keys for great diving, but between offshore wrecks and the introduction of artificial coral reefs, there's still plenty to look at in Miami if you can part the waters and scratch beneath the surface. Go on a calm day with a group; try Bubbles Dive Center (Map p95; ☎ 305-856-0565; 2671 SW 27th Ave, Coconut Grove), which has divers head out on weekends; or Divers Paradise (p163) of Key Biscayne, which is a good option. South Beach Divers (Map pp48–9; ☎ 305-531-6110; www.southbeachdivers.com; 850 Washington Ave, South Beach) runs regular excursions to Key Largo (again, worth the trip) and around Miami, plus offers three-day classes. Or make the very worthy drive to Biscayne National Park (p227; www.nps.gov/bisc), in the southeastern corner of the county, a huge park that contains the northern tip of the world's third-longest coral reef. Of the park's 173,000 acres, about 95% of them are underwater.

FISHING

Rent a pricey charter (around $800 per day), hop aboard a 'head boat' with 100 or so other fisherfolk (boats are rarely full, and it's only about $30), or cast a line off numerous piers or bridges. You don't need a license if you're fishing from shore or from a bridge or pier (just check for signs, which declare some bridges off-limits). On your own, drop a line at South Pointe Park (Map pp48–9), off the Rickenbacker Causeway or any Key Biscayne beach or from Haulover Beach Park (Map pp58–9). To go for the fishing charter boat, try Crandon Park Marina (Map p92; ☎ 305-361-1281; 4000 Crandon Blvd, Key Biscayne) or Blue Waters Sport Fishing Charters (Map pp66–7; ☎ 305-373-5016; www.fishingmiami.net; Bayside Marketplace, 401 Biscayne Blvd, Downtown Miami). Or catch a group-fishing party boat with the Kelley Fleet (Map pp58–9; ☎ 305-945-3801; Haulover Beach Park, 10,800 Collins Ave, North Beach).

IN-LINE SKATING

Serious crowds have turned promenades into obstacle courses for anyone crazy enough to strap on some blades. Leave the crowded strips to experts and try the ocean side of Ocean Ave, or Lincoln Rd before the shoppers descend.

KAYAKING & CANOEING

Kayaking through mangroves, one of the coolest ecosystems on Earth, is magical: all those spidery trees kiss the water while the ocean breezes cool your flanks. In America, this sort of experience is pretty much uniquely available in places like Haulover Beach Park or Bill Baggs Florida State Park. Equipment rental is cheap, and you won't even need lessons to make the boat go where you want it to. Also, check out Oleta River State Recreation Area (Map pp58–9), with various grove channels on the Intracoastal Waterway that are perfect for a kayak or paddleboat (both of which are available for rental here). If you want a more wilderness-oriented adventure, canoeing around the 10,000 Islands (see the boxed text, p223), or on the Wilderness Waterway (also p223) between Everglades City and Flamingo, is one of the most rewarding nature escapes in South Florida.

ROCK CLIMBING

It's unlikely that you've come to Miami to go rock climbing, but still. If the urge hits, your best bet is to head over to X-Treme Rock Climbing (Map pp44–5; ☎ 305-233-6623; 13972 SW 139th Ct, North Miami; per day $15), where you'll find more than 11,000ft of climbing surfaces, including beginning routes and expert roof overhangs. You can take classes by appointment only.

RUNNING

Running is quite a popular Miami pastime, and the beach is very good for jogging, as it's flat, wide and hard-packed (apparently with amazingly hot joggers). The Promenade (p47) is the stylish place for both, as is the Boardwalk (p57), which shoots north from 21st St and offers great people-watching and scenery as you move along. But more serious runners may appreciate the Flamingo Park running track, located just east of Alton Rd between 11th and 12th Sts; the entrance is on the 12th St side at the east end of the fence. Elsewhere around the city, running is good along S Bayshore Dr in Coconut Grove, around the Riviera Country Club in Coral Gables and anywhere on Key Biscayne. Or try the jogging path that runs along the beach in Bal Harbour, made of hard-packed sand and gravel and stretching from the southern boundary of town to the Haulover Cut passageway. A great resource for races, special events and other locations is the Miami Runners Club (☎ 305-227-1500).

SAILING

Key Biscayne sailing is a pure joy (get outfitted at Aquatic Rental Center & Sailing School, p163), as is gliding along the waters just about anywhere else off Miami. Good starting points include the Miami Beach Marina (Map pp48–9; ☎ 305-673-6000; MacArthur Causeway, 300 Alton Rd, South Beach), which has 400 slips and all sorts of rentals; Haulover Marine Center (Map pp58–9; ☎ 305-945-3934; 15,000 Collins Ave, Haulover), a down-to-earth sort of spot; and Monty's Marina (Map p95; ☎ 305-854-7997; 2550 S Bayshore Dr, Coconut Grove), which is perfect if you have your own boat.

SURFING

We can't say it enough: offshore Miami bears no resemblance to the Banzai Pipeline. So don't get too excited. But on the Beach, the best surfing is just north of South Pointe Park, with 2ft to 5ft waves and a nice, sandy bottom. Unfortunately, there are a few drawbacks: it's usually closer to 2ft than to 5ft (except, of course, before storms); it can get a little mushy (so longboards are the way to go); and it's swamped with weekend swimmers and surfers. It's better further north near Haulover Beach Park (Map pp58–9) or anywhere north of, say, 70th St. Sunny Isles Beach (Map pp58–9), at the Sunny Isles Causeway, is also favored by surfers. Call the recorded surf report (☎ 305-534-7873) for daily conditions or check in with the popular Bird's Surf Shop (Map pp58–9; ☎ 305-940-0929, surf line 305-947-7170; 250 Sunny Isles Blvd, North Miami Beach).

SWIMMING

Some folks in Miami *actually* swim in the gorgeous pools around town, usually just serving as backdrops for the cocktail-swilling set. If a bit of freestyle or breaststroke is your preferred method of body workout, then fear not: there are places for you, even if you're not lucky enough to be staying at a hotel with an excellent swimming hole – among the best of these are the Delano Hotel (p176), Shore Club (p176), Biltmore Hotel (p181), Raleigh Hotel (p177) and Fontainebleau Hilton Hotel & Resort (p179). In Coral Gables, the famous Venetian Pool (p99), known more as a pretty place in which to play and float and gawk, has lap-swimming hours several times a week; call for details, which change regularly . Other options for paddling include the Flamingo Park Swimming Pool (Map pp48–9; ☎ 305-673-7730; 999 11th St, South Beach), which has a swimming pool with some lap lanes.

TENNIS & GOLF

Key Biscayne's Tennis Center at Crandon Park (Map p92; ☎ 305-365-2300; 6702 Crandon Blvd, Key Biscayne) is best known for its annual 10-day Nasdaq 100 Tennis Open, which draws star players each March. But you too can play here; choose from two grass, eight clay and 17 hard courts. The Flamingo Tennis Center (Map pp48–9; ☎ 305-673-7761; 1000 12th St, South Beach) has 19 clay courts that are open to the public; but beware of the zoolike crowds on evenings and weekends. Two other great options are the Salvadore Park Tennis Center (Map pp100–1; ☎ 305-460-5333; 1120 Andalusia Ave, Coral Gables) and the Tropical Park Tennis Center (off Map pp100–1; ☎ 305-873-2230; 7900 SW 40th St, Coral Gables).

Golfers also have many options. Check out the lovely 1925 Biltmore Donald Ross Golf Course (Map pp100–1; ☎ 305-460-5364; 1210 Anastasia Ave, Coral Gables), designed by the Biltmore of that name, which boasts the company of the Biltmore Hotel. Doral Golf Course (Map pp44–5; ☎ 305-592-2000; 4400 NW 87th Ave) is highly rated, which may explain why it's difficult to get in and also why it's the home of the PGA Ford Championship. The wealthy can blow their wad here on golf courses that follow in the path of (literally)

the Masters. For easier access, try the Crandon Golf Course (Map p92; ☎ 305-361-9129; 6700 Crandon Blvd, Key Biscayne), overlooking the bay from its perch on Key Biscayne; or the Haulover Golf Course (Map pp58–9; ☎ 305-940-6719; 10,800 Collins Ave, Haulover), a nine-hole, par-three course that's great for beginners.

ULTIMATE FRISBEE

Ultimate players have a lot of love for each other all over the world, and here they can express that emotion on miles of white sand beach. Check www.miamiultimatefrisbee.org for more details; free-to-join beach games are currently held at 6:30pm and 7:00pm (arrive at 6:15pm) on the beach (right) side of Miami Beach, between 14th and 15th Aves. Bring a white and a dark shirt to play.

SPECTATOR SPORTS

Whenever you visit Miami, you're sure to find something worth watching. Catch football in fall, basketball in winter, baseball in spring and jai alai pretty much anytime in between. The prices listed are estimates; there are plenty of websites (www.coasttocoasttickets.com is a good start) where you can buy everything from $10 nosebleed seats to $10,000 luxury box berths.

FOOTBALL

MIAMI DOLPHINS

☎ 305-620-2578; www.miamidolphins.com; Dolphin Stadium, 2269 NW 199th St, North Dade; admission $29-700; ☻ season Aug-Dec

American football games are a great place to see the national traits of excess and competitiveness on parade. Also, the game rocks. 'Dol-fans' are respectably crazy about their team, even if a Super Bowl showing has evaded them since 1985. Games are wildly popular and the Dolphins are painfully successful, in that they always raise fans' hopes but never quite fulfill them. Superbowl 44 will be held at Dolphin stadium in 2010.

If you're a real football fanatic, you can watch preseason practices near Fort Lauderdale. Take I-95 or Florida's Turnpike to I-595 west to the University Dr exit. Turn left at SW 30th St and make another left. The training facility is half a mile down on the right.

UNIVERSITY OF MIAMI HURRICANES

☎ 800-462-2637; www.hurricanesports.com; admission $25-45

On November 10, 2007, the 'Canes, one of the most successful college football franchises of the past 25 years, were annihilated 48-0 by the University of Virginia, the worst home loss in the team's history. It was their last game in Orange Bowl Stadium, which was perhaps mercifully demolished two months later (they now play in the Dolphin Stadium). For the Hurricanes, once titans of university football, the slow decline began in 2004, culminating in 2007's abysmal losing season. But the team's green-and-orange army isn't going to surrender any time soon, and the insane excitement of game day is still worth experiencing.

BASKETBALL

MIAMI HEAT Map pp66-7

☎ 786-777-4328; www.nba.com/heat; American Airlines Arena, 601 Biscayne Blvd, Downtown; admission $10-375; ☽ season Nov-Apr

The Heat used to be so hot (forgive us). First: Pat Riley took over in 2003. Then they scored the first three draft picks of 2004–05 and, finally, won an NBA championship in 2006. Since then, the team has been trying to recapture that magic momentum by finding the perfect match to round out the driving game of Dwyane Wade and Shaquille O'Neal.

UNIVERSITY OF MIAMI HURRICANES

☎ 800-462-2637; www.hurricanesports.com; BankUnited Center, University of Miami; admission $20

Catch the beloved college Hurricanes shooting hoops at the BankUnited Center at the University of Miami (Map pp100–1).

BASEBALL

MIAMI MARLINS Map pp44-5

☎ 305-626-7400; www.marlins.mlb.com; Dolphin Stadium, 2269 NW 199th St, Opa-Locka; admission $4-55; ☽ season May-Sep

Oh my, the Marlins. In 10 years they won two World Series, but after 2003 things began to fall apart; at one stage Alex Rodriguez was making more scratch than the entire team salary roll. During 2006, when it seemed like their own stadium would never be more than a pipedream, the 'Fish' started thinking of packing their bags for San Antonio, but commissioners have finally approved plans for a new stadium, set to be complete by 2010. In the meantime, games have been held in – where else? – Dolphin Stadium.

UNIVERSITY OF MIAMI HURRICANES

Map pp100–1

☎ 800-462-2637; www.hurricanesports.com; Mark Light Stadium, University of Miami, 6201 San Amaro Dr, Coral Gables; admission $7-15

The Hurricane's un-pro baseball can often please when the Marlins disappoint.

HOCKEY

FLORIDA PANTHERS off Map pp44-5

☎ 954-835-8000; www.floridapanthers.com; Office Depot Center, 1 Panther Pkwy, Sunrise; admission $17-117; ☽ season mid-Oct–mid-Apr

That's right: ice hockey in Miami. The Panthers almost grasped the Stanley Cup in 1996, but since then they've gone steadily downhill, becoming one of the worst teams in the National Hockey League (NHL). Still, watching a game at least gets you out of the heat. And they could always have a comeback, right?

MIAMI MARLIN MADNESS

Ten years. Ten years of backbiting, arguing, begging and cajoling, of almost losing the team to San Antonio and Virginia Beach. Ten years and 70% of an optimistically projected $619-million bill, which will likely be covered (no matter what city officials say) by shuffling public works funds. Put it all together and Miami will get to keep the Florida Marlins (above), rename them the Miami Marlins and house them in Major League Baseball's newest stadium, set to replace the vanquished Orange Bowl in Little Havana. The city of Miami is hoping the new stadium will anchor south Downtown's resurgence, bring baseball fans streaming into the city, and further solidify Miami's position as capital of South Florida. Fans in Broward county, pissed off about the name change, will have to swallow their bitterness. And baseball goes on in South Florida, in a new, air-conditioned, retractable-domed 37,000-seat stadium, which, while small for an MLB venue, may be roomy considering only 375 fans (375!!) came out to a Marlins-Nationals game in September 2007.

Seriously.

MIAMI JAI ALAI

Jai alai (pronounced 'high aligh'), which roughly translates from Spanish as 'merry festival,' is a fascinating and dangerous game. Something of a cross between racquetball and lacrosse, it originated in the Basque region of the Pyrenees in the 17th century, and was introduced to Miami in 1924. The *fronton* (arena) where the games are held is the oldest in the States, having been built just two years after the game was introduced. How is it played? Well, players hurl a *pelota* (a small ball of virgin rubber that's wrapped in goat skin and so powerful it can shatter bullet-proof glass) at more than 170mph to their opponents, who try to catch it with the *cesta* – a woven basket that's custom-made from Spanish chestnut and reeds from the Pyrenees – that's attached to their glove. The game is held in a round robin, and the object is to toss the *pelota* against the front wall of the court with so much speed that the opposition cannot catch it or return it in the fly or first bounce. Audiences wager on the lightning-fast games, said to be the speediest sport on earth.

Catch the action for yourself at Miami Jai Alai (Map pp44–5; ☎ 305-633-6400; 3500 NW 37th Ave; admission $1-5; ☯ matches noon-5pm Wed-Mon, 7pm-midnight Mon, Fri & Sat). It's great fun to watch these guys whack around their *pelota* at lightning speed – and even more exciting to wager bets on who will win.

HORSE RACING

CALDER RACE COURSE off Map pp44–5
☎ 305-625-1311; www.calderracecourse.com; 21,001 NW 27th Ave; admission $2

With live races from May to December, this 1971 track, up toward Hollywood, hosts the Festival of the Sun Derby and always has simulcasts (TV broadcasts) of national races.

GULFSTREAM PARK off Map pp44–5
☎ 954-454-7000; www.gulfstreampark.com; 901 S Federal Hwy, Hallandale; admission $2-4

Catch live races and simulcasts at this classic track/casino.

MOTOR SPORTS

HOMESTEAD MIAMI SPEEDWAY off Map pp44–5
☎ 305-230-7223; www.homesteadmiamispeedway.com; 1 Speedway Blvd, Homestead

If you want to see the sport that truly gets blue collar Miami going, drive out to this $50-million racing center built in 1995, which plays host to National Association for Stock Car Auto Racing (Nascar) and Winston Cup races. The *New York Times* once quipped that it would be hard to imagine anyone in Homestead wanting to see something coming at them at 200mph after Hurricane Andrew, but people do. Go figure.

lonely planet | Hotels & Hostels

Want more Sleeping recommendations than we could ever pack into this little ol' book? Craving more detail – including extended reviews and photographs? Want to read reviews by other travelers and be able to post your own? Just make your way over to **lonelyplanet.com/hotels** and check out our thorough list of independent reviews, then reserve your room simply and securely.

SLEEPING

top picks

- **Cardozo Hotel** (p172)
- **Pelican Hotel** (p172)
- **Circa 39** (p179)
- **Sagamore** (p177)
- **Setai** (p176)
- **Biltmore Hotel** (p181)
- **Shore Club** (p176)
- **Standard** (p182)
- **Hotel St Augustine** (p174)
- **Hotel Shelley** (p174)

SLEEPING

It's in this category, more than any other, where all the hype surrounding South Beach is justified. Lots of places are packed with high quality resorts and boutique sleeping spots. But what sets South Beach apart – what defines it as a travel destination – is the deco district, and the deco district's backbone is hotels. A five-minute jaunt here takes you past many sleeping spots, all with lovingly crafted distinct personalities. And the Beach's glam only grows with every new accommodation option lauded by the travel glossies, which brings the designers, which brings the fashionistas, which brings the models, which brings the tourists, which brings the chefs and…well, you get the idea.

In other words, the architectural elements that make this neighborhood special also house your minibar. And pool. And hot tub. And those aluminum chairs you can't call chairs because you're supposed to refer to them by the name of whoever made them, ie 'Mmm, this Andre De Flipinflap is *so* comfy.' And to be fair, while lots of folks here like to name-drop designers, the fact is guys such as Ian Schrager (Shore Club, p176; Delano, p176) and André Balazs (Raleigh, p177; Standard, p182) really can put together a lovely living space, especially compared to the competition. Elsewhere in Miami, accommodation is more pedestrian – a few private islands, B & Bs and lots of big box corporate resorts (although the latter have upped the bar thanks to the SoBe competition).

You can have attitude if you want it. 'Sexy' and 'intimidating' can go hand in hand, and nothing hits this feeling home (like you're asking out the most popular kid in school) than the towering beach cabanas and sexy backyard lounges of SoBe's megahotels. But there's too much competition around for owners to totally act the snob, and you'll find happy hours in local lounges more about breaking the ice and having fun than seeing and being seen. Mostly.

LONGER-TERM RENTALS

You could consider an apartment rental for longer stays, thriftiness and use of a kitchen. Interhome (☎ 305-940-2299; www.interhome.com), Vacation Home Rentals Worldwide (☎ 800-633-3284) or Craig's List (http://miami.craigslist.org) are a few places to start.

SEASONAL COSTS

Seasons in South Florida refer to tourist density, not the weather. During high season (December to March), expect to pay as much as triple the rate compared to the rest of the year (note that some hotels include shoulder seasons that last from April to June when rates may run 1½ times higher). During major events – Winter Music Conference, Spring Break or South Beach Food & Wine Festival (all in February and March by the way), expect rates to soar through the roof. Also note that many Miami hotels have two- or three-night minimum stays in high season.

ROOM RATES

Generally, a budget hotel will cost roughly $100 a night during low season, while the most expensive places start at $300 (or much more) and rise steeply from there; dorm hostel beds can be had for as low as $22 a night. Hotels fronting the ocean are almost always more expensive, and you may pay more in the form of sleep. 'It's South Beach; if you want to rest, don't stay here,' says one grinning bellboy. No matter where you stay, you'll pay 13% room tax (which is hopefully included in your rate). Some places tack on an obligatory 15% service or 'resort' charges. It's a racket.

And parking is always going to cost you. The best option is often city parking garages, which cost $1 per hour. There's one at 7th St between Washington and Collins (good if you're staying between 5th and 9th Sts), 12th St a half-block west of Washington, 13th St a half-block east of Collins (both good for north of 11th St) and 17th St between Pennsylvania and Meridian Aves (good for accessing Lincoln Rd). Meter lots also cost $1 per hour; you can feed them up to six hours in advance and many accept credit cards. Private garages and lots can run between $8 and $20 a day but don't include in-and-out privileges; hotel valet parking is about $15 to $30 per day but does allow in-and-out.

Hotel cleaning staff should be tipped about $2 a day; tip daily, as they rotate shifts. Hotel porters who carry bags expect $3 to $5, or $1 per bag. Valet parking is worth about $2, to be given when your car is returned to you.

SOUTH BEACH

We're not exaggerating: South Beach may have the best concentration of boutique hotels in the word. At almost all of the following you can expect flat-screen TVs, wi-fi internet (at least in the lobby) and complimentary concierge service that includes getting on the list at local nightclubs. The smaller deco renovations may not have exercise rooms, but most have pools (of course, the ocean is right across the road). The lobbies of many of these hotels turn into swank lounges after the sun goes down, when guests can usually expect free happy hour drinks.

1ST TO 15TH STREETS

HOTEL VICTOR Map pp48–9   Luxury Hotel $$$
☎ 305-428-1234; www.hotelvictorsouthbeach .com; 1144 Ocean Dr; r $489-1595; Ⓟ ▣ ☘
The Victor wins – the hot design stakes, that is. And the fish-tanks-full-of-jellyfish competition (a popular symbol – note the beaded lamps meant to resemble stinging sealife). And the 'damn-that-room-is-fly' pageant too. Designed by L Murray Dixon in 1938, the redone Victor was opened in 2005 to much acclaim; these days, Shaquille O'Neal is famous for throwing parties in the $6000 a night penthouse. Parking costs $32 per day.

TIDES Map pp48–9   Boutique Hotel $$$
☎ 305-604-5070, 800-688-7678; www.thetides hotel.com; 1220 Ocean Dr; r $550-850; Ⓟ ▣ ☘
The 50 ocean-fronting rooms are icy-cool, with their jumbled vintage, ocean organic and indie vibe. The bedding of pure white is overlaid by beige and tan/shell and sealife themes, further offset by cream accents. Rooms come with telescopes for planetary (or Hollywood) stargazing, and the lobby, decked with nautical embellishments, looks like a modern Sea God's palace. Parking costs $35 per day.

DE SOLEIL Map pp48–9   Boutique Hotel $$$
☎ 305-672-4554; www.preferredboutique .com; 1458 Ocean Dr; r $330-750, ste $915-1475; Ⓟ ▣ ☘
There are some hotties working the desk at De Soleil, which has large, grey-black-and-white super suites and the best bathrooms on the beach, plus metal grille balconies overlooking a lovely courtyard and rooftop lounges worthy of Hugh Hefner. Govind Armstrong's deservedly lauded Table 8 (p127) is onsite. Parking costs $32 per day.

MARLIN HOTEL Map pp48–9   Boutique Hotel $$$
☎ 305-604-5000, 800-688-7678; 1200 Collins Ave; r & ste $325-895
Rock star. Live it. Love it. Be it. That's the fantasy you get to play out here, where the deep purple walls are smeared with club sweat, the 12 individualized rooms look like party penthouses, an onsite studio pulls in bands from Aerosmith to U2, and the attached Elite Modeling Agency attracts... well, let's just say hanging in the lobby is a good idea.

BEACON HOTEL Map pp48–9 Hotel $$$
☎ 305-674-8200; www.beacon-hotel.com;
720 Ocean Dr; r low season $150-369, Nov-May
$302-619; Ⓟ 🖥
Overlooking a truly bumpin' slice of
Ocean Dr real estate, the Beacon has a
Grand Dame of a deco lobby and friendly
service, but the rooms are kind of plain.
They're nice, no doubt, with shiny marble
floors and warm wood furnishings, but
the bar is set high here and the Beacon is
still reaching. Parking is available for $20
per day.

HOTEL OCEAN Map pp48–9 Boutique Hotel $$$
☎ 305-672-2579; www.hotelocean.com; 1230
Ocean Dr; r $199-325, ste $290-1500; Ⓟ 🖥
This intimate, Mediterranean-style hotel
isn't pompous or exclusive, but the waterfront suites have every right to be. Most
of the hotel's 27 large rooms have ocean
views and lots of light streaming in;
some have a private terrace, and all have
brightly tiled bathrooms and colorfully
painted walls. Parking will cost you $28
per day.

HOTEL NASH Map pp48–9 Boutique Hotel $$$
☎ 305-674-7800; www.hotelnash.com; 1120
Collins Ave; r $159-300, ste $545-855; Ⓟ 🖥 ☒
The modern interior of the Nash is beige
and white hot. Or is that cool? Whatever.
This quiet, elegant inn has an expansive
marble lobby leading to 54 rooms that are
cozy while chic and suitably sleek. Parking
is $25 per day.

PELICAN HOTEL
Map pp48–9 Boutique Hotel $$$
☎ 305-673-3373, 800-773-5422; www.pelican
hotel.com; 826 Ocean Dr; r low season $165-500,
high season $240-700; 🖥
When the owners of Diesel jeans pur-
chased the Pelican Hotel in 1999, they
started scouring garage sales for just the
right ingredients to fuel a mad experi-
ment: 30 theme rooms that come off like
a fantasy-suite hotel dipped in hip. From
the funky blue ambience of 'Some Like
It Wet' to the warm 'Cubarean Islands'
lovefest and the playfully perverted 'Best
Whorehouse,' all of the rooms here are
completely different, fun and even come
with their own 'suggested soundtrack'
(although all have beautiful recycled-oak
floors).

top picks

LOVELY LOBBIES

- Delano (p176)
- Essex House Hotel (p175)
- Shore Club (p176)
- Hotel Victor (p171)
- Biltmore (p181)

CASA GRANDE HOTEL Map pp48–9 Hotel $$$
☎ 866-420-2272; www.casagrandesuitehotel.com;
834 Ocean Dr; ste & 1-bedrooms low season
$215-475, Oct-May $315-575; Ⓟ 🖥
Autumnal colors and a splash of bright
citrus start the show in the lobby, but the
main event is the snow-white elegance of
the 35 so-chic rooms, each one an ultra-
modern Scandinavian designer's dream –
although we've gotta say the big, marble
Virgin Mary in the room we visited was
waaaaaay out of place. We do like the flowers on the pillow though; nice touch, guys.
Parking is $30 per day.

CENTURY HOTEL Map pp48–9 Hotel $$$
☎ 888-982-3688; www.centurysouthbeach.com;
140 Ocean Dr; r $120-465, ste $145-515; Ⓟ 🖥
The Century, dating back to 1939, is one of
the best-preserved deco spots on the strip.
It quietly gleams at the far-south, sedate
end of Ocean Dr, its wood floors and white
walls combining for a starkly sumptuous
sleeping experience, setting the perfect
balance of sleekness and warmth. Parking
is approximately $27 per day.

CARDOZO HOTEL
Map pp48–9 Boutique Hotel $$$
☎ 305-535-6500, 800-782-6500; www.cardozo
hotel.com; 1300 Ocean Dr; r & ste low season
$227-454, Nov-May $287-487; Ⓟ 🖥
The Cardozo and its neighbor, the Carlyle,
were the first deco hotels saved by the
South Beach preservation group, and in
the case of the Cardozo, we think they
saved the best for first. Owner Gloria
Estefan, whose videos are looped on flat-
screen mini-TVs in the lobby, likely agrees.
It's the combination of the usual contem-
porary sexiness (white walls, hardwood
floors, high-thread-count sheets) and play-
ful embellishments: leopard skin details,

handmade furniture and a general sense that, yes, you are cool if you stay here, but you don't have to flaunt it. Oh – remember the 'hair gel' scene in *Something About Mary*? Filmed here. Parking is available for $27 per day.

HOTEL Map pp48–9 — Boutique Hotel $$$

☎ 305-531-2222; 801 Collins Ave; www.thehotel ofsouthbeach.com; r low season $235-295, Jan-May $250-425; Ⓟ ▢ ▨
This place is stylin' – and why shouldn't it be, when Todd Oldham designed the boldly beautiful rooms? The theme palette of 'sand, sea and sky' adds a dash of eye candy to the furnishings, as do the mosaic doorknobs and brushed-steel sinks. Many say the Hotel boasts the best rooftop pool in South Beach, overshadowed only by a lovely deco spire (which says 'Tiffany,' because that was the name of this place before the blue-box jewelry chain threatened a lawsuit). Parking costs $25 per day.

HOTEL IMPALA Map pp48–9 Boutique Hotel $$$

☎ 305-673-2021, 800-646-7252; www.hotelimpala miamibeach.com; 1228 Collins Ave; low season r $145-225, ste $225-325, high season r $195-245, ste $345-425; Ⓟ ▢
The Italianate courtyard – and Italian food available at onsite Spiga (p127) – plus the marbled, plush, white rooms, will all make you feel like Maximus Luxurious presiding over his realm. The front desk is very helpful, as befits your royal status. Parking costs $25 per day.

CLINTON HOTEL Map pp48–9 Boutique Hotel $$

☎ 305-938-4040; www.clintonsouthbeach.com; 825 Washington Ave; r $140-396; Ⓟ ▨ ▢
Washington Ave is the quietest of the three main drags in SoBe, but the Clinton doesn't mind. This joint knows it would be the hottest girl in the most crowded party, with her blue velveteen banquettes and uber-contemporary metal ceiling fans. The tiny sun porches in the zen rooms are perfect for breakfast or an evening cocktail. Parking is $27 per day.

BENTLEY BEACH HOTEL
Map pp48–9 — Boutique Hotel $$

☎ 305-938-4600; www.bentleybeachhotel.com; 510 Ocean Dr; r $175-349; Ⓟ ▢ ▨
You like the word 'mahogany?' Reeks of dark, old-school sexy ambience, right?

The folks here agree, and their lobby is a tobacco-brown exemplar of mahogany style – not the wood, per se, but its classy connotations. Shell lamps line the walls and a rooftop pool and Jacuzzi shimmers under the stars. The raised bed in the two-bedroom suite is the coolest sleeping nook in this contender. Parking costs $25 per day.

WALDORF TOWERS HOTEL
Map pp48–9 — Boutique Hotel $$

☎ 305-531-7684, 800-933-2322; www.waldorf towers.com; 860 Ocean Dr; r low season $89-220, Nov-Apr $140-350; Ⓟ ▢
An immaculate white lobby and warm rooms comparable to most boutiques on the strip – blonde hardwoods, shellacked floors and platform beds – feature in this place, but the real thing to look for is the rounded roof. Designed by deco godfather L Murray Dixon, it's meant to resemble a lighthouse shining out from its corner on Ocean Dr. Parking is $24 per day.

KENT HOTEL Map pp48–9 Boutique Hotel $$

☎ 305-604-5068; www.thekenthotel.com; 1131 Collins Ave; r low season $79-350; Ⓟ ▢
Young party types will probably get a kick out of this lobby, filled with fuchsia and electric-orange geometric furniture plus bright Lucite toy blocks, which makes for an aggressively playful welcome. The special Lucite Suite is almost entirely constructed of the see-through material, giving it an icy playground feel. Take refuge in a side garden with Indonesian-style tables, bamboo and hammocks. Parking costs $20 per day.

STRAND Map pp48–9 Boutique Hotel $$

☎ 305-538-9830; www.thestrandoceandrive.com; 1052 Ocean Dr; r $170-315; Ⓟ ▢ ▨
Lying in the low-slung, high-thread-count beds feels like swimming in silk, while en suite bucket chairs were just made for your fine booty. Porthole mirrors on the outside path leading into the crisp lobby remind you you're going on a voyage: namely, to getting-spoiled town. Parking is $35 per day.

CHESTERFIELD HOTEL
Map pp48–9 — Boutique Hotel $$

☎ 305-531-5831; www.southbeachgroup.com; 855 Collins Ave; r $130-195, ste $170-330; Ⓟ ▢

Hip-hop gets jiggy with zebra-stripes on the curtains and cushions in the small lobby, which turns into one of the hoppin'-est happy hours on Collins when the sun goes down. Leave a tip for the giant African statue while you're draining that mojito. The Chesterfield is part of the ubiquitous South Beach Group, which tries to be hip, hot and affordable by cutting costs via Ikea-like furniture that can look flimsy if closely inspected, although the big picture is always sleek and beautiful. Parking costs $30 per day.

AVALON HOTEL Map pp48–9   Hotel $$

☎ 305-538-0133, 800-933-3306; www.avalon hotel.com; 700 Ocean Dr; r low season $150-239, late Dec-Mar $169-305; P ⬜ ⬛

In a classic, streamline 1941 building, this hotel is perhaps known more for the white-and-yellow 1955 Lincoln convertible parked out front than for its rooms, which are simple and pleasant, with puffy white duvets and clean-lined Ikea-style furniture. Parking costs $27 per day.

HOTEL ASTOR Map pp48–9   Hotel $$

☎ 305-531-8081, 800-270-4981; www.hotelastor .com; 956 Washington Ave; r $125-290; P ⬜ ⬛ ⬛

They lay the retro-punk on thick in the Astor lobby, glamorizing and exaggerating the Age of Transportation into a hip caricature of itself: a gigantic industrial fan blows over a ceiling studded with psychedelic 'lamp balls', all suspended over a fanciful daydream of an old-school pilot's club. The earth-toned rooms are relaxing, but good luck chilling out: the small swimming pool gets covered at night to make room for club-goers who bop on the back-patio lounge. Parking is available for $25 per day.

WAVE HOTEL Map pp48–9   Boutique Hotel $$

☎ 305-673-0401, 800-501-0401; www.wavehotel .com; 350 Ocean Dr; r $159-259; ⬜

Dark blue, plush molded furniture and curving, cool lines – painted into the floors, arranged along the ceilings and hinted at in the couch arrangement – give the lobby a sense of tidal momentum. There's a space-race-age theme (as in '50s Sputnik-era retro chic) going on in the rooms; you gotta love the lamps, which look like cartoon bubble helmets from *Buck Rogers*. Parking costs $20 per day.

HOTEL ST AUGUSTINE

Map pp48–9   Boutique Hotel $$

☎ 305-532-0570, 800-310-7717; www.hotelst augustine.com; 347 Washington Ave; r $120-280; P ⬜

Wood that's blonder than Barbie and a crisp-and-clean deco theme combine to create one of Sofi's most elegant yet stunningly modern sleeps. The familiar, warm service is the cherry on top for this hip-and-homey standout, although the frame-your-face, soothing lighting and glass showers – that turn into personal steam rooms at the flick of a switch – are pretty appealing too. Parking costs $15 per day.

WINTER HAVEN Map pp48–9   Hotel $$

☎ 305-531-5571, 800-395-2322; www.winter havenhotelsobe.com; 1400 Ocean Dr; r low season $119-199, high season $149-259; P ⬜ ⬛

Al Capone used to stay here; maybe he liked the deco ceiling lamps in the lobby, with their sharp, retro-sci-fi lines and grand-gothic proportions, and the oddly placed oriental mirrors (which have nothing to do with deco whatsoever). A young but laid-back crowd hangs at the Haven, which sits on the pretty people end of Ocean Dr. Parking is $25 per day.

OCEAN FIVE HOTEL

Map pp48–9   Boutique Hotel $$

☎ 305-532-7093; www.oceanfive.com; 436 Ocean Dr; r & ste $150-250; P

This boutique hotel is all pumpkin-bright, deco-dressed-up on the outside, with cozy, quiet rooms on the inside that exude a maritime-meets-vintage theme, with a dash of Old West ambience on top. Think mermaid murals on pale stucco walls. There are no balconies here, but the attached restaurant is a warm, friendly spot to cop a drink and a fine Italian meal before strolling up Ocean Dr. Parking is $25 per day.

HOTEL SHELLEY Map pp48–9   Hotel $$

☎ 305-531-3341; www.hotelshelley.com; 844 Collins Ave; r low season $95-165, high season $105-260; ⬜

Gossamer curtains, a lively lounge and a sublimely relaxing violet-and-blue color-scheme combines with orb-like lamps that look like bunched-up glass spiderwebs. The rooms are as affordably stylish as the rest of the offerings in the South Beach Group.

ESSEX HOUSE HOTEL

Map pp48–9   Boutique Hotel $$

☎ 305-534-2700, 800-553-7739; www.essexhotel
.com; 1001 Collins Ave; r low season $89-325, ste
$129-349; 🖳 🐾

When you gaze at this lobby, one of the
best preserved interiors in the deco district,
you're getting a glimpse of South Beach's
glorious, gangster heyday. Beyond that the
Essex has helpful staff, rooms furnished
with soft, subdued colors and a side ve-
randa filled with rattan furnishings that's
a particularly pleasant people-watching
perch.

HOTEL CHELSEA

Map pp48–9   Boutique Hotel $$

☎ 305-534-4069; www.thehotelchelsea.com; 944
Washington Ave; r $110-205; 🅿 🖳

When you walk into the Chelsea's stylish
lobby, you're greeted by a sultry, black and
yellow floral pattern that feels like it's been
lifted from a lingerie catalogue. The motif
carries on into the dimly lit, yet sumptuous
vintage rooms – which should really be
called boudoirs – where the shaded chandeliers provide just the right glow. Parking
costs $30 per day.

BLUE MOON

Map pp48–9   Hotel $$

☎ 305-673-2262, 800-553-7739; www.bluemoon
hotel.com; 944 Collins Ave; r low season $95-220,
late Dec-Mar $173-279; 🅿 🖳

The service here couldn't be friendlier, and
while the hotel isn't technically deco, it's
not too shabby either. The rooms are crisp
and clean, and a kitschy, unpretentious
atmosphere of tropical twee dominates
throughout. Parking is $25 per day.

WHITELAW HOTEL

Map pp48–9   Boutique Hotel $$

☎ 305-398-7000; www.whitelawhotel.com; 855
Collins Ave; r low season $95-130, Nov-Apr
$125-210; 🅿 🖳

The Whitelaw is the punky middle brother
of its boutique South Beach Group
siblings. Surreal murals wrap around a
graphic designer's dream of a lounge
that's constantly kicking to hot rock (and
hosting hotter guests). After the white
Belgian sheets, white robes, billowy white
curtains and white floors, the sea-blue
bathrooms come as a welcome shock (to
be fair, the blinds are chrome). Parking
costs $30 per day.

PRINCESS ANN HOTEL

Map pp48–9   Hotel $

☎ 305-534-2196; www.princessann.com; 920
Collins Ave; r $70-169, ste $140-295

Pretty building. Pretty prices. Pretty…aver-
age rooms, to be honest. But the Princess
Ann provides friendly service and comfy
beds sans SoBe attitude in a central locale –
as central as it gets, what with the Collins
Ave parade stumbling past the lobby every
two minutes.

OHANA HOSTEL

Map pp48–9   Hostel $

☎ 305-534-2650; 750 Collins Ave; dm $33,
r $156; 🖳

Seriously, does the same brusque French
guy work the counter of every hostel
in America? We're just sayin'. When we
visited, he was definitely in this pleasant,
unsigned hostel, tucked next to a surf shop.
The rooms are kept sparkly clean, an international crowd chills in the lounge, and all
is basically well in this corner of the budget
travel world.

MIAMI BEACH INTERNATIONAL
TRAVELERS HOSTEL

Map pp48–9   Hostel $

☎ 305-534-0268, 800-978-6787; www.hostel
miamibeach.com; 236 9th St; dm $29-44,
r $59-159; 🖳

The rooms here are a tad worn, but security is good, the staff friendly and the
lobby cheerful. Half of the 100 rooms are
private; the others are four-bed dorms.
Strictly speaking, you'll need an out-of-
state university ID, HI card, US or foreign
passport with a recent entry stamp or an
onward ticket to get a room, but these
rules are only enforced when the hostel's
crowded.

SOUTH BEACH HOSTEL

Map pp48–9   Hostel $

☎ 305-534-6669; www.thesouthbeachhostel.com;
235 Washington Ave; dm $20-28, r $60-174; 🖳

On a quiet end of Sofi, this relatively new
hostel has a happening common area and
simple spartan rooms. It's not too flashy,
but staff are friendly and the on-site bar
(open 'til 5am) seems to stay busy. The
property is split between six-bed dorms
and private rooms; regarding the latter,
couples are probably better off in midrange
hotel rooms elsewhere on the Beach, which
are probably twice as nice for the same
price.

MONDRIAN Map pp48–9   Resort

☎ 305-672-2662, 877-809-0007; www.mondrian southbeach.com; 1100 West Ave

'The idea at the Mondrian', says this con-dotel's PR flack, 'is to take the concept of the Delano and the Shore Club to the next level.' The *next* level? Weren't the other two opulent enough? Guess not. Morgan Hotel Group has hired Dutch design star Marcel Wanders (whose name they'll drop 'til it falls through the floor) to basically crank it up to 11. The theme is inspired by *Alice in Wonderland* (if penned by Crockett from *Miami Vice*) – columns carved like giant table legs, chandelier showerheads, im-ported Delft tiles with beach scenes instead of windmills and magic walls with mor-phing celebrity faces (perhaps because the morphing nature of celebrity is what fuels South Beach's glamour?). Oh, and it'll have a private island (natch). It's set to open in late 2008 on South Beach's Bay side, with the Mondrian on one side and the Delano on the other; you can just imagine a Morgan Group pincer of gentrification squeezing out what's left of the normal neighborhood in a few years.

11TH TO 23RD STREET

The satellites of two huge condotel com-plexes, the W (www.wsouthbeachresidences.com; 2201 Collins Ave) and the Gansevoort (www.gansevoortsouth .com; 2399 Collins Ave), should be open when you read this. These guys want to compete with the Delano and its Morgan Group buddies, so expect completely over-the-top opulence and resort-level rates.

SETAI Map pp52–3   Luxury Hotel $$$

☎ 305-520-6000; www.setai.com; 101 20th St; r & ste $900-6000; P ⃞ ⃞

There's a linga in the lobby – nothing says high-end luxury like a Hindu phallus. It's all part of the aesthetic at Miami's most ex-pensive sleep, where a well-realized theme mixes Southeast Asian temple architecture, Chinese furniture, contemporary luxury and conceptual atmosphere. Each floor is staffed by 24-hour teams of butlers, while rooms are decked out in chocolate teak wood, clean lines, and Chinese and Khmer embellishments (although we think the studio is small for four figures). Service is outstanding and surprisingly down to earth. Parking costs $34 per day.

DELANO HOTEL Map pp52–3   Luxury Hotel $$$

☎ 305-672-2000, 800-555-5001; 1685 Collins Ave; r & ste low season $330-815, Jan-Apr $405-1750; P ⃞ ⃞

The Delano opened in the 1990s and im-mediately started ruling the South Beach roost. Today, spoiled teen princesses want their rooms to be converted into Delano-esque, ultra-white fairy-tale sleeping nooks on MTV's *Super Sweet 16*. Is this a reminder of the hotel's pop culture cred, or a sign the coolest cat on the block is getting passé? Decide for yourself. Because if there's a quintessential 'I'm-too-sexy-for-this-song' South Beach moment, it's when you walk into the Delano's lobby, which has all the excess of an over-budgeted theater set. 'Magic mirrors' in the halls disclose weather info, tide charts, even inspirational quotes, while the pool area resembles the courtyard of a Disney prin-cess's palace, with a giant chess set, floor-to-ridiculously-high-ceiling curtains on two-story waterfront rooms and Bedouin tent cabanas outfitted with flat-screen TVs. Parking costs $37 per day.

SHORE CLUB Map pp52–3   Luxury Hotel $$$

☎ 305-695-3100; www.shoreclub.com; 1901 Col-lins Ave; r & ste $295-1550; P ⃞ ⃞

Imagine a zen ink brush painting. What's beautiful isn't what's there, but what gets left out. If you could turn that sort of art into a hotel room, it might look like the stripped-down yet serene digs of the Shore Club. Yeah, yeah: it's got the 400-thread-count Egyptian cotton sheets, Mexican sandstone floors, etc; a lot of hotels in SoBe lay claim to similar luxury lists. What the Shore Club does like no other hotel is arrange these elements into a greater whole that's impressive in its understatement; the aesthetic is compelling because it comes across as

top picks

PARTY HOTELS

- Chesterfield Hotel (p173)
- Delano (above)
- Townhouse Hotel (opposite)
- Whitelaw Hotel (p175)
- South Beach Hostel (p175)

an afterthought. For those who thrive on aristocratic appeal, Miami's Nobu branch is here, as is the impossibly exclusive Moroccan-themed Skybar (p146). Parking costs $42 per day.

LOEWS MIAMI BEACH

Map pp52–3   Luxury Hotel $$$

☎ 305-604-1601, 800-235-6397; www.loewshotels .com; 1601 Collins Ave; r $339-1075; P 🖳 🖳
If for some reason you're missing big, conventioneer-style boxes, come to Loews. There are 800 lovely (if identikit) rooms, a fitness center, pool, private beachfront, *six* restaurants (including the popular Emeril's) and endless meeting rooms. Parking costs $33 per day.

SAGAMORE Map pp52–3   Boutique Hotel $$$

☎ 305-535-8088; www.sagamorehotel.com; 1671 Collins Ave; r & ste $305-1050; P 🖳 🖳
Spencer Tunick got 600 people to pose nude in massively structured photo shoots set all around the Sagamore in 2007. Nude art installation – that's hot, but also expected at this hotel–cum–exhibition space, which likes to blur the boundaries between interior decor, art and conventional hotel aesthetics. For instance, rows of plaster death masks line the area around the bar – TGI Friday's, take note! – and even the rooms double as art galleries, thanks to a talented curator and an impressive roster of contributing artists. Parking costs $35 per day.

RALEIGH HOTEL

Map pp52–3   Boutique Hotel $$$

☎ 305-534-6300, 800-848-1775; www.raleigh hotel.com; 1775 Collins Ave; r $295-395, ste $425-850; P 🖳 🖳
While everyone else was trying to get all modern, the Raleigh painstakingly tried to restore itself to pre-war glory. It succeeded in a big way. Celebrity hotelier André Balazs managed to capture a tobacco-and-dark-wood men's club ambience and old-school elegance while simultaneously sneaking in modern design elements and amenities. Have a swim in the stunning pool; Esther Williams used to. Parking costs $30 per day.

ROYAL PALM HOTEL Map pp52–3   Hotel $$$

☎ 305-604-5700; www.royalpalmmiamibeach .com; 1545 Collins Ave; low season r $169-369, ste $299-559, high season r $189-429, ste $389-689; P 🖳 🖳

Even the luggage trolleys here have a touch of curvy deco flair, to say nothing of the chunky staircase and mezzanine, which are the best Beach examples of the deco theme of the building as cruise liner. Note the porthole windows, wire railings and a general sense of oceanic space; you can almost hear waves slapping the side of the building. There's a glut of Britto art in the lobby (and even a Britto-themed restaurant), and rooms are suitably luxurious. Parking costs $39 per day.

NATIONAL HOTEL

Map pp52–3   Boutique Hotel $$$

☎ 305-532-2311, 800-327-8370; www.national hotel.com; 1677 Collins Ave; r $269-509; P 🖳 🖳
The lobby looks like a 1920s speakeasy married to 21st-century interior design, while outside, the loooooooooooooong pool seems to double as a red (well, teal) carpet for beach royalty that runs right up to this deco landmark and back to a busy tiki bar. Rooms can't match the pool or lobby's preening good looks, but they are extremely ritzy. Parking costs $37 per day.

ALBION Map pp52–3   Boutique Hotel $$$

☎ 305-913-1000; www.rubellhotels.com/albion; 1650 James Ave; low season r $155-220, ste $200-265, high season r $245-265, ste $320-390; P 🖳 🖳
Designer Carlos Zapata bills the Albion as the nexus of cutting-edge design, where the role models are Vincent Gallo and Martha Graham and the minibar's stocked with condoms and Red Bull. They've splashed a bit of color onto the white-and-stainless-steel rooms, although their sleekness still mutes the intended warm impact. Parking costs $25 per day.

TOWNHOUSE HOTEL

Map pp52–3   Boutique Hotel $$

☎ 305-534-3800, 800-688-7678; www.townhouse hotel.com; 150 20th St at Collins Ave; r $105-195, ste $395-450; 🖳 🖳
You'd think the Townhouse was designed by the guy who invented the ipod, but no, it was Jonathan Morr and India Mahdavi, who have fashioned a cool white lobby and igloolike rooms with random scarlet accents and a breezy rooftop lounge. Who needs mints on pillows when the Townhouse provides beach balls? Parking costs $25 per day.

SURFCOMBER Map pp52–3   Boutique Hotel $$

☎ 305-532-7715; www.surfcomber.com; 1717 Collins Ave; r $190-260; P 💻 🐕
Simply one of the best classical deco structures in Miami, the Surfcomber is (shhhh) actually owned by Doubletree. Well, more power to 'em; the chain has renovated this property into an immaculate state. Note the movement-suggestive lines on the exterior and semi-circular, shade-providing 'eyebrows' that jut out of the windows. Also especially note the lobby – the rounded, aeronautic feel of the space suggests you're entering a 1930s airline lounge, but no, you're just going to your room. Parking is $39 per day.

AQUA HOTEL Map pp52–3   Boutique Hotel $$

☎ 305-538-4361; www.aquamiami.com; 1530 Collins Ave; r & ste $142-282; P 💻 🐕
A front desk made of shiny surfboard sets the mellow tone at this former motel, the old family kind where the rooms are set around a pool. That old-school vibe barely survives under the soft glare of aqua (imagine that) spotlights and an alfresco lounging area, popular with the mostly gay clientele. The sleekness of the rooms is offset by quirky furniture, like a sumptuous chair made of spotted cowhide. Parking costs an extra $35 per day.

DORCHESTER HOTEL
Map pp52–3   Boutique Hotel $$

☎ 305-531-5745, 800-327-4739; www.hoteldorchester.com; 1850 Collins Ave; r & ste $119-249; P 💻 🐕
'I put my mother-in-law here,' says the manager of this recently renovated boutique. And it's true: the Dorchester isn't aiming for SoBe sexy. But families on a budget who want to experience classic deco architecture would do well to check this place out; otherwise, keep moving. Parking costs $25 per day.

CAVALIER HOTEL
Map pp48–9   Boutique Hotel $$

☎ 305-531-3555, 800-688-7678; www.cavaliermiami.com; 1320 Ocean Dr; low season r $99-129, ste $199, Oct-May r $129-155, ste $229; P 💻
The Cavalier Hotel's exterior is a rare Ocean Dr example of the Maya/Inca inspiration that graced some deco facades (look for Mesoamerican details such as the step pattern on the sides of the building). Inside?

The Cavalier sacrifices ultra-hip for Old Florida casualness, which is frankly kinda refreshing. We love the earthy touches in the rooms, such as batik fabrics in tones of brown and beige.

GREENVIEW Map pp52–3   Boutique Hotel $$

☎ 305-531-6588, 877-782-3557; www.greenviewhotel.com; 1671 Washington Ave; r low season $95-150, ste low season/175-230, r/ste high season $160/260
Aw, the Greenview is so cozy and sweet – like a hotel run by your grandma. Seriously, the staff will probably bake cookies if you ask nicely. Furnishings are spare, with sisal rugs and bamboo lamps, plus black-and-white photos on the walls – grandma again.

BEACHCOMBER HOTEL
Map pp48–9   Boutique Hotel $

☎ 305-531-3755, 888-305-4683; www.beachcombermiami.com; 1340 Collins Ave; r $89-189; 💻
Green sets the stage at this deco classic, with a green-banana-colored facade, a soothing, mint-green lobby, green-flecked terrazzo floor, seafoam-green couches and a chartreuse bar, all floating beneath sleek aluminum ceiling fans. The rooms, while not quite as seductive as the entrance, are basic, cozy and clean.

HADDON HALL HOTEL
Map pp52–3   Hotel $

☎ 305-531-1251; 1500 Collins Ave; r & ste low season $70-180; P 🐕 💻
Built in 1941, the Haddon Hall is recognizable for its excellent deco exterior, all curving walls and billowy buttresses, and a red-lit, palm-fringed courtyard, like a crimson Collins Ave lighthouse. Unfortunately, the rooms aren't particularly memorable (although they come with kitchenette *and* ugly paintings!), but the price is right. Parking costs $20 per day.

TROPICS HOTEL & HOSTEL
Map pp52–3   Hostel $

☎ 305-531-0361; www.tropicshotel.com; 1550 Collins Ave; dm $27, r $100-135; 🐕
The surprisingly nice Tropics (which looks a bit skeezy from the outside) sports a big swimming pool and patio area that seems consistently packed with chatting travelers. The clean four-bed dorms have an attached bathroom; private rooms are basic and serviceable.

CLAY HOTEL & MIAMI BEACH INTERNATIONAL HOSTEL

Map pp48–9   Hostel $

☎ 305-534-2988, 800-379-2529; www.clayhotel .com; 1438 Washington Ave; dm $25-29, r $60-260; ☐

How many HI hostels are located in a 100-year-old Spanish-style villa? The Clay has clean and comfortable rooms, from single-sex, four- to eight-bed dorms to decent private rooms, many of which are located in a medina-like maze of adjacent buildings. Staff are harassed due to sheer volume, but are friendly and helpful. This is yet another place where Al Capone got some shut-eye.

MIAMI BEACH

FONTAINEBLEAU HILTON HOTEL & RESORT Map pp58–9   Resort $$$

☎ 305-538-2000, 800-548-8886; www.fontaine bleau.hilton.com; 4441 Collins Ave; r low season from $369, late Dec-May $469; ℗ ☐ ☒

Probably Miami Beach's most recognizable landmark, the 1200-room Fontainebleau opened in 1954, when it became a celeb sunning spot and set of many a Hollywood production (including *Goldfinger, The Bellboy* and *Scarface*). A 2003 renovation added every conceivable amenity, including beachside cabanas, seven tennis courts, grand ballroom, shopping mall and an ab-fab swimming pool. Throw in the towering condotels of the Fontainebleau II and III and you've got one of the grandest lodgings in Miami. Parking costs $30 per day.

EDEN ROC RESORT Map pp58–9   Resort $$$

☎ 305-531-0000, 800-327-8337; www.edenroc resort.com; 4525 Collins Ave

The Roc, set to re-open after a renovation in 2008, is the rival grand dame to the next door Fontainebleau. The big overhaul aims to turn this venerated resort into a combination of large-scale convention center and northern colony of SoBe cool, with six pools (including an adult-only one overlooking the ocean), 349 guestrooms and all the bells, whistles and kitchen sinks you'd expect out of a major high-end resort.

COURTYARD HOTEL Map pp58–9   Hotel $$

☎ 305-538-3373; www.miamicourtyard.com; 3952 Collins Ave; r low season $249-454, high season $170-400; ℗ ☐ ☒

Look for the big, beautiful deco facade of the Cadillac building and you've found the Marriott-owned Courtyard, which tries valiantly to be a cut above the corporate chain it is. With its excellent exterior, cushy mattresses and free *Newsweeks*, this is probably the best of the large-scale chains lining Collins Ave. Parking is $24 per day.

PALMS SOUTH BEACH

Map pp58–9   Boutique Hotel $$

☎ 305-534-3119; www.thepalmshotel.com; 3025 Collins Ave; r & ste $140-400; ℗ ☐ ☒

The lobby of the Palms manages to be imposing and comfortable all at once; the soaring ceiling, cooled by slow-spinning giant rattan fans, makes for a colonial villa on convention-center steroids vibe. Upstairs the rooms are perfectly fine if a tad bland.

CLARIDGE HOTEL

Map pp58–9   Boutique Hotel $$

☎ 305-604-8485, 888-422-9111; www.claridgefl .com; 3500 Collins Ave; r $120-280; ☐ ☒

This 1928 Mediterranean-style palace feels like an (admittedly Americanized) Tuscan villa, with a sunny honey-stone courtyard enclosing a sparkling pool, framed by palms, frescoed walls and stone floors. The soothing, old-world rooms are set off by rich earth tones, and staff are eager to please.

CIRCA 39 Map pp58–9   Boutique Hotel $$

☎ 305-538-3900, 877-824-7223; www.circa39 .com; 3900 Collins Ave; r $122-279; ☐ ☒

If you love South Beach style but loathe the attitude, Circa's got your back. The lobby, with its multicolored light board, molded furniture and wacky embellishments, is one of the funkiest in Miami, the hallways are low-lit under sexy red lamps and the icy-blue-and-white rooms are hip enough for the most exclusive scenesters (although Circa frowns on snobs). Be you family, gay or just love laid-back fun, this hotel welcomes all.

BEACH HOUSE BAL HARBOUR

Map pp58–9   Boutique Hotel $$

☎ 305-535-8600, 877-782-3557; 9449 Collins Ave; r $105-267; ☐ ☒

The Beach House is a down-to-earth inn with a Keys-y feel, complete with wainscoting, conch shells and fresh-looking, blue-ticking sheets in every room. But the Bal Harbour Shops across the street will keep you anchored in Miami-glitz reality.

INDIAN CREEK HOTEL

Map pp58–9   Boutique Hotel $$

☎ 305-531-2727, 800-491-2772; www.indiancreek hotel.com; 2727 Indian Creek Dr; r $90-279; 🐾

Get your room key – attached to a plastic alligator – and walk through the old Miami lobby, spruced up with souvenir-stand schlock, to your comfortable, earthy-warm digs. Or wander out to the surprisingly modern pool, where happy, sexy people are ready to have a good time. Mix in a friendly staff and an easy walk to the boardwalk, and you've got a perfect little boutique hotel.

BAY HARBOR INN & SUITES

Map pp58–9   Inn $$

☎ 305-868-4141; www.bayharborinn.com; 9660 E Bay Harbor Dr; r $150-$210; Ⓟ ▯ 🐾

Operated by earnest Johnson & Wales University students as an integral part of their hands-on hospitality training, this upscale small hotel has a warmer, more country feel than the sleek spaces you get used to seeing in Miami.

DOWNTOWN MIAMI

MANDARIN ORIENTAL MIAMI

Map pp66–7   Luxury Hotel $$$

☎ 305-913-8288, 866-888-6780; www.mandarin oriental.com; 500 Brickell Key Dr; r & ste $395-5000; Ⓟ ▯ 🐾

The Mandarin shimmers on Brickell Key, which is actually annoying – you're a little isolated from the city out here. Not that it matters; there's a luxurious world within a world inside this exclusive compound, from swank restaurants to a private beach and skyline views that look back at Miami from the far side of Biscayne Bay. Rooms are good in a luxury-chain kinda way, but nothing sets them apart from other sleeps in this price range. Parking costs an extra $26 per day.

FOUR SEASONS MIAMI

Map pp66–7   Luxury Hotel $$$

☎ 305-358-3535; www.fourseasons.com/miami; 1435 Brickell Ave; r & ste $275-1400; Ⓟ ▯ 🐾

The marble common areas double as an art gallery, a massive spa caters to corporate types and there are sweeping, coulda-been-a-panning-shot from *Miami Vice* views over Biscayne Bay in some rooms. The 7th-floor terrace bar Bahia is pure mojito-

laced, Latin-loved swankiness, especially on Thursdays and Fridays from 6pm to 8pm, when ladies drink free. Parking costs $33 per day.

CONRAD MIAMI

Map pp66–7   Luxury Hotel $$$

☎ 305-503-6500; www.conradhotels.com; 1395 Brickell Ave; r & ste $169-1225; Ⓟ ▯ 🐾

The Conrad is trying to slide bits of South Beach celebrity into its grey-suited facade via hot promotion parties and cool lizard-lounges, but really, this is a 36-story tower of glass, steel and business traveler amenities. Don't be ashamed Conrad: you're a credit to the genre, from the 25th-floor power-broker sky lobby to a location in the heart of Brickell's flash and finance. Parking costs $33 per day.

MIAMI RIVER INN

Map pp66–7   B&B $$

☎ 305-325-0045, 800-468-3589; www.miami riverinn.com; 119 SW South River Dr; r $69-199; Ⓟ ▯ 🐾

Cute mom-and-pop B&Bs stuffed full of antique furniture, pretty-as-lace gardens and a general 'Aw, thanks for breakfast' vibe are comparatively rare in this city. The River Inn, listed on the National Register of Historic Places, bucks this trend, with charming New England–style rooms, friendly service and one of the best libraries of Miami literature in the city. In a place where every hotel can feel like a loud experiment in graphic design, this relaxing watercolor invites you onto the back porch.

KEY BISCAYNE

RITZ-CARLTON KEY BISCAYNE

Map p92   Luxury Hotel $$$

☎ 305-365-4500, 800-241-3333; www.ritzcarlton .com; 455 Grand Bay Dr; r & ste $215-3000; Ⓟ ▯ 🐾

Sure, it's 'just' another Ritz Carlton. But it's also pretty unique. There's the magnificent lobby, vaulted by four giant columns lifted from a Cecil B DeMille set – hell, the whole hotel's lifted from a DeMille set. Tinkling fountains, the view of the bay and marble grandeur provide an un-chain-y sense of early-20th-century style and glamour. Rooms and amenities are predictably excellent. Parking costs $30 per day.

SILVER SANDS BEACH RESORT
Map p92   Resort $$

☎ 305-361-5441; www.key-biscayne/silversands
.com; 301 Ocean Dr; r $129-189, cottages $279-329;
P ♨

Silver Sands: aren't you cute, with your one-
story, stucco tropical tweeness? How this
little, Old Florida–style independent resort
has survived amid the corporate compe-
tition is beyond us, but it's definitely a
warm, homey spot for those seeking some
intimate, individualized attention – to say
nothing of a sunny courtyard, garden area
and outdoor pool.

COCONUT GROVE

GROVE ISLE CLUB & RESORT
off Map p95   Resort Hotel $$$

☎ 305-858-8300, 800-884-7683; www.groveisle
.com; 4 Grove Isle Dr; r $219-529, ste $389-879;
P ♨ ♨

One of those 'I've got my own little island'
type places, Grove Island is just off the
coast of Coconut Grove. This stunning
boutique hotel's got colonial elegance, lush
tropical gardens, sunset views over Biscayne Bay, amenities galore and the cachet
of staying in your own floating temple of
exclusivity.

SONESTA HOTEL & SUITES COCONUT
GROVE Map p95   Hotel $$$

☎ 305-529-2828; 2889 McFarlane Rd; r $165-500;
P ♨ ♨

The Coco Grove outpost of this luxury
chain has decked its rooms out in almost-
all-white with a splash of color South
Beach style. The posh amenities, from
flat-screen TVs to mini-kitchenettes, add
a layer of luxury on this surprisingly hip
big box. Parking is available here for $23
per day.

RITZ-CARLTON COCONUT GROVE
Map p95   Luxury Hotel $$$

☎ 305-644-4680, 800-241-3333; www.ritzcarl-
ton.com; 3300 SW 27th Ave; r & ste $189-399;
P ♨ ♨

The third of a power troika of Ritz-Carltons
in Miami, this one overlooks the bay, has
totally rich rooms and offers butlers for
every need, from shopping and web surf-
ing to dog walking and bathing. The mas-
sive spa is stupendous. Parking is an extra
$30 per day.

GRAND BAY MIAMI
Map p95   Hotel $$

☎ 305-858-9600, 800-433-4555; www.grandbay
miami.com; 2669 S Bayshore Dr; r $109-239, ste
$159-859; P ♨ ♨

Thirteen stories tall and tucked between
Coco Walk and the bay, this waterfront
resort occupies the upscale middle ground
between mall shopping and sea breezes.
Rooms are pretty if predictable. Parking
costs $24 per day.

MUTINY HOTEL
Map p95   Hotel $$

☎ 305-441-2100, 888-868-8469; www.mutiny
hotel.com; 2951 S Bayshore Dr; ste $119-259;
P ♨ ♨

This small luxury bayfront hotel, with 120
one- and two-bedroom suites, featuring
balconies, boasts an indulgent staff, high-
end bedding, gracious appointments,
fine amenities and a small heated pool.
Although it's on a busy street, you won't
hear the traffic once inside. Parking costs
$24 per day.

CORAL GABLES

BILTMORE HOTEL
Map pp100–1   Hotel $$$

☎ 305-445-1926, 800-727-1926; www.biltmore
hotel.com; 1200 Anastasia Ave; r & ste $219-2500;
P ♨ ♨

The Biltmore is such an iconic piece of
architecture it's easy to forget its original
purpose: as a hotel. Though the standard
rooms can be kinda small, a stay here is
a chance to sleep in one of the great laps
of American luxury. Make sure to catch a
ghost tour and a dip in the largest hotel
pool in the continental USA. Parking costs
$25 per day.

WESTIN CORAL GABLES
Map pp100–1   Hotel $$

☎ 305-441-2600; www.starwoodhotels.com; 180
Aragon Ave; r $195-295, ste $235-425; P ♨ ♨
Here's another surprisingly independent
outpost of a luxury chain. From the colon-
naded building, with its 1920s-meets-
Mediterranean revival wonderland of
marble columns and shiny stone floors, to
little touches like towels twisted to look like
kissing swans set on your bed, this Westin
has a warm, idiosyncratic touch of charac-
ter and class. Parking costs $12 per day.

DAVID WILLIAM HOTEL
Map pp100–1　　　　　　　　　　　Hotel $$
☎ 305-445-7821; www.starwoodhotels.com; 180 Aragon Ave; r $109-299; 🖳 🖳
It looks like a big box on the outside, but inside, the lobby is a headrush of chandeliers and pink champagne marble. Staff are very helpful and rooms are big and beautiful (if not particularly interesting); you could probably swim laps across the huge mattresses.

HOTEL PLACE ST MICHEL
Map pp100–1　　　　　　　　　　　Hotel $$
☎ 305-444-1666; www.hotelplacestmichel.com; 162 Alcazar Ave; r $125-245; 🅿
The Michel's more Metropole than Miami, and that's a compliment. The old-world wooden fixtures, refined sense of tweedy style and dinner jacket ambience don't get in the way of friendly service, while a lovely restaurant and cool bar-lounge are as elegant as the hotel they occupy. Parking is $9 per day.

GREATER MIAMI

INN AT THE FISHER ISLAND CLUB
Map pp44–5　　　　　　　　　　　Resort $$$
☎ 305-535-6080, 800-537-3708; www.fisher island.com; r $600-2250; 🖳 🖳
If you're not Jeb Bush, the only way to see Fisher Island is to stay at this luxurious resort. Whether in 'simple' rooms or Vanderbilt-era cottages, your money will be well spent: there's one of the best-rated spas in the country, plus eight restaurants (seems like overkill given the island's size) and enough royal perks to please an Egyptian pharaoh.

TRUMP INTERNATIONAL SONESTA
BEACH RESORT Map pp58–9　　　Resort $$$
☎ 305-692-5600, 800-766-3782; www.trump sonesta.com; 18,001 Collins Ave; r & ste $169-889; 🅿 🖳 🖳

top picks

BEST SLEEPS OFF SOBE

- Standard (below)
- Circa 39 (p179)
- Miami River Inn (p180)
- Indian Creek Hotel (p180)
- Biltmore Hotel (p181)

Located up in Sunny Isles, Trump's take on Miami is just as you would expect: 32 stories of ocean views, a ballroom and luxury rooms, along with a spa and extensive kids' program. The lagoon pool is full of waterfalls and palm trees and there are four onsite restaurants. Parking costs $24 per day.

STANDARD Map pp44–5　　Boutique Hotel $$$
☎ 305-673-1717; 40 Island Ave; r & ste $195-750; 🅿 🖳 🖳
Look for the upside down 'Standard' sign on the old Lido building on Belle Island (between South Beach and Downtown) and you'll find the Standard – which is anything but. This excellent boutique place blends hipster funk with South Beach sex, and the result is a '50s motel gone glam. There are organic, wooden floors, raised white beds and gossamer curtains, which open onto a courtyard of earthly delights, including a heated *hammam* (Turkish bath). Here, the crowd, which feels like the Delano kids with a bit more maturity, gather to flirt and gawk. Shuttles ferry you to the Sagamore every 30 minutes, so you're never too isolated from the scene – unless you want to be, and given the grace of this place, we'd totally understand why. Parking costs $10 per day.

THE FLORIDA KEYS & KEY WEST

Take: one part, rednecks. Add: snowbirds. Sprinkle with a large number of Cuban immigrants and Eastern European guest workers. Include: gay community (may consist of 'sedate partners who just bought an art gallery' and 'screaming drag queens of the night'). Garnish with Bahamans. Set attitudes at 'tolerant' and 'eccentric.'

Turn up the eccentric. Finish with rum. *Lots* of rum.

Bake in searing Florida sun and serve on 45 islands scattershot over a 113-mile-long chain, connected by one long-ass road. Throw in the government of the only Republic to successfully secede from the United States. Yes, those Conch Republic Flags say 'We Seceded Where Others Failed,' and that's the Keys in a conch shell: equal parts tacky, quirky and, damn it, alluring.

Hang out here for awhile and you start turning into a 'Freshwater Conch' – a permanent transplant – real quick. The Keys are *out there*; it's three or four hours at a good clip from Key West, at the end of the chain, back to Miami. Come out this far, and you either contract cabin fever or fall in love.

But don't just rush for Key West, because there's lots of charm and island authenticity on the other islands. After all, it's these little, lovely, crazy communities that have survived hurricanes, gentrification and gouging real estate prices to live the real American Dream – do whatever the hell you want and get away with it, an attitude that truly defines the Keys.

Getting here can be half the fun – or, if you're unlucky, a whopping dose of frustration. Imagine a tropical island hop, from one bar-studded mangrove islet to the next, via one of the most unique roads in the world: the Overseas Highway, also known as US Hwy 1. On a good day, driving down the Overseas, with the windows down, the wind in your face and the twin teal sisters of Florida Bay and the Gulf of Mexico stretching on either side, is the American road trip in tropical perfection. On bad days, it's sitting behind some fat guy with a mid-life crisis and a Harley during periodic bouts of gridlock. The waypoints on this road are the mile markers (MM), which count down from Key Largo (MM 106) all the way to the end of the road (and sobriety): MM 0 in Key West.

Greyhound (☎ 800-229-9424) buses serve all Key destinations along US Hwy 1, departing from Downtown Miami and Key West; you can pick up a bus along the way by standing on the Overseas Hwy and flagging one down, Mexico-style. If you fly into Fort Lauderdale or Miami, the Keys Shuttle (☎ 888-765-9997) provides door-to-door service to most of the Keys ($70/80/90 to the Upper and Middle Keys/Lower Keys/Key West). Reserve at least a day in advance. Or skip the road altogether and take a four-hour sea trip via the Key West Express (☎ 866-593-3779; www .seakeywestexpress.com; adult/child roundtrip $106/70, one-way $53), which departs from the Miami Seaquarium (p93) at 9:30am daily (8:30am Sundays).

One of the best ways to see the Keys is by bicycle. The flat elevation and ocean breezes are perfect for cycling, and the Florida Keys Historic Overland Trail (www.fkoht.org), which will connect all the islands from Key Largo to Key West, is set to be complete by 2012. As of this write-up, 60 miles of this excellent trail were already paved, although it's currently possible to bike through all the Keys by riding the shoulder of roads (it takes three days at a good clip).

You can fly into one of two airports. Key West International Airport (EYW) has frequent flights from major cities – some direct, but most going through Miami – and Marathon Airport (☎ 305-743-2155) has less frequent, more expensive flights.

top picks

FLORIDA KEYS & KEY WEST

- Advancing early liver failure at the Green Parrot (p209) or the Hurricane (p196)
- Spotting Key Deer (p197)
- Watching sunsets in Mallory Square (p203)
- Feeding the fish at Robbie's (p191)
- Munching on pizza at the No Name Pub (p198)

ITINERARIES
The Overseas Pub Crawl

Lots of people come to the Keys for different reasons: to fish, to relax, to escape. But almost all of them get a little trashed. With this in mind, what follows is the ultimate Keys pub crawl – not just down Duval St, but an island to island stumble down the entire Overseas Hwy. Don't drive drunk; the trip is broken up island to island, and you can catch a cab on each Key.

Start slow at Alabama Jack's (p190), quintessential gateway to the Keys: a shack on a mangrove bay filled with guys in sleeveless shirts ready to get their fish on. Now head down the Overseas Hwy to Islamorada and steel your body for its oncoming trials. Watch the sunset and achieve zen with a Red Stripe and an unbeatable view of Florida Bay from the gorgeous private island of trendy Casa Morada (p193), then call a taxi, or find a designated driver. Even Miami's glitterati hang out at Hog Heaven (p193), while the full moon party at Morada Bay (p192) is one of the most popular throw-downs in the islands.

Wake up, sleepyhead! Next stop: Marathon. The Island Fish Company (p196) prides itself on having the largest outdoor tiki bar in the Keys; we just like the service and strong drinks. Ditto for the Hurricane (p196), which is, for our money, the friendliest bar in the Keys. Finish your night (long into the morning) at the Satanically divey, dark and dangerous Brass Monkey (p196).

Have a herbal tea as you continue your way down the Lower Keys. There's only one watering hole today, but it's an atmospheric one: the famous No Name Pub (p198) on the Key of the same no-name. We'll bypass other bars of the Lower Keys so you can sleep in Key West and, like a knight of old, prepare for the battle ahead.

You may be tempted to try a Duval Crawl like every other frat boy in Key West, but we recommend a more nuanced approach. Start with a shot at Captain Tony's Saloon (p209), where Hemingway *really* drank (sorry, Sloppy Joe's), and a beer at the rockin' Hog's Breath (p209) for that slight touch of Duval vomit-on-your-neighbor ambience. Now gather your dignity and have an excellent martini at the classy jazz bar in Virgilio's (p210) and finish the night with a digestif – no, not really, just another beer – at the one, the only, the excellent Green Parrot (p209).

Now fish your liver out of the toilet, dude.

Wild, Wild Keys

The Keys are nothing if not beautiful, and you won't find a comparable mangrove island habitat in North America. Here's how you can get closer to the unique nature of the Conch Republic.

First: get out of your car. If you've got a bike and some endurance, why not try exploring the islands via the Florida Keys Historic Overland Trail. While it was only halfway complete as of this write-up, using a combination of trail and shoulder riding you can cross the islands in three days.

However you get around, stop at John Pennekamp Coral Reef State Park (p188) to enjoy a walk through the mangroves and a glass-bottom tour of local reefs. Donate some money to our injured, fine-feathered friends at the Florida Keys Wild Bird Rehabilitation Center (p189), one of many Keys animal hospitals and research centers. From Robbie's Marina (p191) in Islamorada, kayak over the waters to Indian Key State Historic Site (p191) or bike around the Matecumbe Keys, which offer some of the sweeping-est views of Florida Bay and the Gulf of Mexico. Anne's Beach (p191) is a great spot for stomping over the shallow mud flats, which feel oh-so-squishy between your toes.

Crane Point Museum (p195) in Marathon is a lovely little preserve of Keys habitats and fun for the kids to boot. Just down the road, the Turtle Hospital Research Center (p195) is a convalescent home for injured sea turtles, a good cause, and a fun place to while away an afternoon.

Keep driving south and…ooh! Tiny deer! Key deer (p197) run all over Big Pine and No Name Key, so have a look at these cutesy dollops and visit their buddies, a pair of American alligators, who like to bask at a pond known as Blue Hole (p198).

Key West itself isn't the best nature destination, but do spend an hour at the Eco-Discovery Center (p204), which is lovingly put together, enjoyable, educational, and unlike everything else in Key West, doesn't charge admission and has free parking.

Only in the Keys

What – America's only tropical hardwood habitat, a string of islands inhabited by alcoholic fishermen connected by some of the longest bridges and causeways in the world, isn't weird enough on its own? Fine.

Head down (and we mean down) to the Jules' Underseas Lodge (p190), the only underwater hotel in the world, and dream happy dreams of mermaids and decompression. If you can't afford Jules, the next best thing to sleeping underwater is on it at the awesome Key Largo House Boatel

FLORIDA KEYS

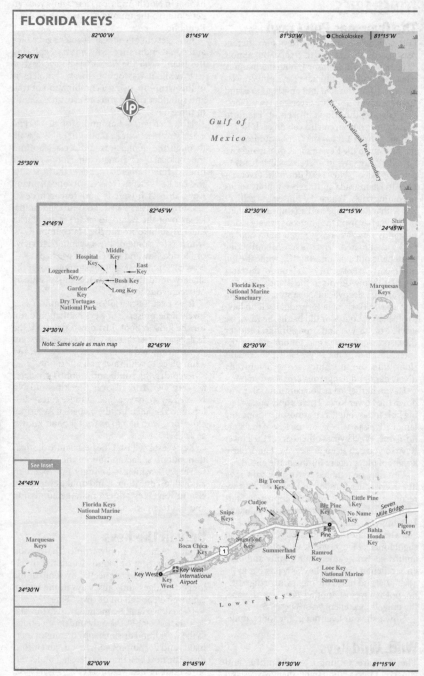

82°00'W   81°45'W   81°30'W ○ Chokoloskee 81°15'W

25°45'N

Gulf of

Mexico

Everglades National Park Boundary

25°30'N

82°45'W   82°30'W   82°15'W

24°45'N   Shark
                                                          24°45'N

Hospital   Middle
Key   Key   East
Loggerhead   → Key
Key   → Bush Key   Florida Keys   Marquesas
Garden   ← Long Key   National Marine   Keys
Key   Sanctuary
Dry Tortugas
National Park

24°30'N

Note: Same scale as main map   82°45'W   82°30'W   82°15'W

See Inset

24°45'N

Florida Keys   Big Torch
National Marine   Key
Sanctuary   Cudjoe   Little Pine
                           Snipe   Key   Big Pine Key   Seven
                           Keys   Key   No Name Mile Bridge
Marquesas   Key
Keys   Big   Bahia   Pigeon
                     Boca Chica   Sugarloaf   Pine   Honda   Key
                     Key   Key   Key
                          1   Summerland
24°30'N   Key West ○ Key West   Key   Ramrod
                        ⊞ International   Summerland Key   Looe Key
                 Key   Airport   Key   National Marine
                 West   Sanctuary
                          L o w e r   K e y s

82°00'W   81°45'W   81°30'W   81°15'W

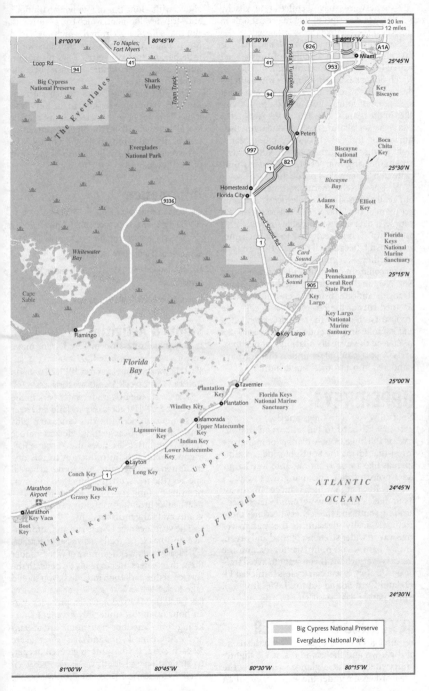

(p190). Afterwards, have a coffee at the kitschy yet classy (a description that may exist only in the Keys) Key Largo Conch House (opposite).

Feed some tarpon at Robbie's Marina (p191), or just enjoy watching a bunch of tourists get scared to death by the enormous fish. Did you watch *Flipper* as a kid? Want to swim with his descendants? Go to the Dolphin Research Center (p194), one of four (count 'em) dolphin swim sites in the islands. The Old Seven Mile Bridge (p195) and Pigeon Key (p195) are the 'world's largest fishing bridge' and a lovely old plantation island, right next to the current Seven Mile Bridge, an engineering marvel of, well, seven-mile (actually, 6.765 miles) proportions.

We know we've mentioned them already, but really: dog-sized widdle deer! You only get them at the National Key Deer Refuge (p197). Of course, if deer are too adorable for you, Perky's Bat Tower (p199) is a great place to see bats…no, wait, it isn't, because all the bats flew away as soon as they were moved in.

You could almost include the entire island of Key West in this itinerary, but there are some strange standouts from the end of the road: six-toed cats at the Hemingway House (p204); the tropical-Goth noir of the Key West Cemetery (p205); and karaoke and drag queens at 801 Bourbon Bar (p210). And the surreally hilarious 'guided tour' of Casa Antigua (p206), all reminders that you have wandered into a tropical sanitarium.

UPPER KEYS

No, really, you're in the islands!

It is a bit hard to tell when you first arrive, as the huge, root-y blanket of mangrove forest that forms the South Florida coastline spreads like a woody morass into Key Largo. As a point of fact, the mangroves actually become Key Largo, which is more famous for its undersea than above-ground views. Keep heading south and the scenery becomes more archipelagically pleasant as the mangroves give way to wider stretches of road and ocean, until – bam – you're in Islamorada and the water is everywhere. If you want to avoid traffic on US Hwy 1, you can try less trafficked FL 997 and Card Sound Rd to FL 905 (toll $1), which passes Alabama Jack's (p190).

KEY LARGO & TAVERNIER

We ain't gonna lie: Key Largo (both the name of the town and the island it's on) is slightly underwhelming at a glance. 'Under' is the key word, as it's under the water, rather than above, with a long line of low-lying hammock and strip development, which truly captivates. But that's Key Largo from the highway. Head down a side road and duck into this warm little bar, or that converted Keys plantation house, and the island idiosyncrasies become more pronounced.

The 33-mile-long Largo, which starts at MM 106, is the longest island in the Keys, and those 33 miles have attracted a lot of marine life, all accessible from the biggest concentration of dive sites in the islands. The town of Tavernier (MM 93) is just south of the town of Key Largo.

Information

Key Largo Chamber of Commerce (☎ 305-451-1414, 800-822-1088; www.keylargo.org; MM 106 bayside; ☺ 9am-6pm) Helpful office; has area-wide information.

Key Largo post office (MM 100 bayside)

Mariner Hospital (☎ 305-434-3000; Tavernier, MM 91.5 bayside)

Tavernier post office (MM 91.5 bayside)

Sights & Activities

If you make one stop in Key Largo, make sure it's John Pennekamp Coral Reef State Park (☎ 305-451-1202; www.pennekamppark.com; MM 102.5 oceanside; 1 person $3.50, 2 people $6, each additional person 50¢; ☺ 8am-sunset), the first underwater park in the USA. There's 170 acres of parkland and over 75 sq miles of ocean in this sanctuary, plus some pleasant beaches and decent nature trails. The latter includes the Mangrove Trail, a good boardwalk introduction to this oft-maligned, ecologically awesome arboreal species (the trees, often submerged in water, breathe via long roots that act as snorkels – neat). Stick around for nightly campfire programs and ranger discussions.

The visitor center is well-run and informative and has a perfectly serviceable aquarium (☺ till 5pm) that gives a glimpse of what's under them thar waters. But to really go beneath the surface of this park (pun intended), you should take a glass-bottom boat (opposite) or snorkel-sailing tour (adult/child $34.95/29.95), which provides over an hour of almost uniformly excellent snorkeling time. The four-hour tours are at 9am and 1:30pm; mask, fins and snorkel rental are $2 each extra. If you want to go even deeper, try straight-up snorkeling trips (adult/child $28.95/23.95) or diving excursions (call ☎ 305-451-6300 for all trips; $50).

DIYers may want to take out a canoe or kayak (canoe or single kayak/double kayak per hr $12/$17) to journey through a three-mile network of canoe trails, or you can rent powerboats, starting at $210 per day. Call ☎ 305-451-6325 for boat rental information.

The most popular glass-bottom-boat tour (☎ 305-451-6300; John Pennekamp Coral Reef State Park, Key Largo, MM 102.5 oceanside; adult/child under 12 yrs $22/15) lasts 2½ hours and leaves at 9:15am, 12:15pm and 3pm. You won't be ferried around in some rinky-dink fishing boat; you're brought out in a safe, modern 38ft catamaran from which you'll ooh and aah at filigreed flaps of soft coral, technicolor schools of fish, dangerous-looking barracudas and massive, yet ballerina-graceful sea turtles. To learn more about the reef in this area, go to www.south eastfloridareefs.net.

The Florida Keys Wild Bird Rehabilitation Center (☎ 305-852-4486; www.fkwbc.org; 93,600 Overseas Hwy, MM 93.6; $5 donation suggested; ⊗ 8am-6:30pm) is the first of many animal hospitals you'll come across built by critter-loving Samaritans throughout the Keys. This one is an alfresco bird hospital that cares for avians that have swallowed fish hooks, had wings clipped in accidents, been shot by BB pellets, etc. A lovely little trail leads back to a nice vista of Florida Bay and a wading bird pond. The center is great – but it does smell like bird doo.

There are dive shops galore in Key Largo, most of which are located within Pennekamp Park. Two other recommended options are Silent World Dive Center (☎ 305-451-3252, 800-966-3483; www.silentworldkeylargo.com; MM 103.2 bayside) and Amoray Dive Resort (☎ 305-451-3595, 800-426-6729; www.amoray.com; MM 104.2 bayside), which also features villa-like accommodations.

OK movie fans, particularly Bogie buffs: here's the skinny. The Caribbean Club Bar (☎ 305-451-9970; MM 104 bayside) is, in fact, the only place in Key Largo where Key Largo, starring Humphrey Bogart and Lauren Bacall, was filmed (the rest of the island was a Hollywood soundstage). If that's not enough, the original African Queen, of the same-titled movie, is docked at the Holiday Inn at MM 100. Just walk around the back. Call ☎ 305-451-4655 for more info. And finally, Rick's Bar from Casablanca is up and running in the middle of Pennekamp State Park…just kidding.

If you approach Key Largo from FL 905 you'll be driving through Crocodile Lake National Wildlife Refuge, one of the last wild sanctuaries for the threatened American crocodile,

indigo snake and Key Largo woodrat, among others – the latter enterprising fellow likes to build 4ft x 6ft (1.2m x 2m) homes out of forest debris, proving even wildlife in Florida want enormous homes. Unfortunately, this really is a refuge; the wildlife areas are closed to the public, and your chances of seeing the species we've mentioned from the road is negligible.

The Greyhound bus stops at MM 99.6 oceanside.

Eating

Key Largo Conch House (☎ 305-453-4844; www.keylargocoffeehouse.com; MM 100.2 oceanside; lunch $8-14, dinner $13-25; ⊗ breakfast, lunch & dinner Mon-Sat, breakfast & lunch Sun) A wi-fi hotspot, coffeehouse and innovative kitchen that likes to sex up local classics (conch in a lime and white wine sauce or in a vinegar sauce with capers), set in a restored old-school Keys mansion wrapped in a *Gone With the Wind* verandah? Yes please, and more of it.

Tugboat Restaurant (☎ 305-453-9010; 2 Seagate Blvd; mains $9-24; ⊗ lunch & dinner daily, breakfast Sat & Sun) Head east from the MM 100 traffic light and you'll be grateful once you pull up to this locals' favorite, where the seafood is simply sumptuous. If the weather's good – and it invariably is – eat out back in the appropriately dubbed Garden of Eatin'.

Num Thai Restaurant & Sushi Bar (☎ 305-451-5955; 103,200 Overseas Hwy; lunch dishes $6-10, dinner mains $7-18; ⊗ lunch Mon-Fri, dinner daily) The whole Japanese-Thai fusion thing comes straight outta Miami and takes a trip south to this strip mall locale, which is bright, bouncy, and the right antidote for you addicts jonesing for your next wasabi fix.

Mrs Mac's Kitchen (☎ 305-451-3722; MM 99.4 bayside; breakfast & lunch $5-7, dinner $9-18; ⊗ breakfast, lunch & dinner Mon-Sat) When Applebee's stuffs its wall full of license plates, it's tacky. When Mrs Mac's does it, it's home-y. Plus, the food here packs in the locals (and the pounds) and the tourists and their dogs and pretty much anyone/thing else on the island.

DJ's Diner (☎ 305-451-2999; 99,411 Overseas Hwy; mains $6-14; ⊗ breakfast, lunch & dinner) You're greeted by a mural of Humphrey Bogart, James Dean *and* Marilyn Monroe – that's a lot of Americana. It's all served with a heapin' helpin' of diner faves, vinyl-boothed ambience and South Florida staples such as *churrasco* and conch.

Drinking & Nightlife

Alabama Jack's (☎ 305-248-8741; www.alabamajacks .com; dishes $10-16; ☼ 11am-7pm) Welcome to your first taste of the Keys: zonked out weirdos on motorcycles getting drunk on a mangrove bay. Wildlife lovers: you may spot the rare mulleted version of *Jacksonvillia Redneckus*! But seriously, everyone raves about the conch fritters, and the fact that the place has to close because of nightly onslaughts of mosquitoes means this place is as authentically Florida as they come.

Big Fish (☎ 305-453-0820; 99,010 Overseas Hwy; dishes $8-17; ☼ 11:30am-4am) All-you-can-eat stone crabs? Karaoke? *And* lesbian nights? Sign us up! Look for the sea-green seafood shack-cum-bar-cum-nightclub waiting for you off the Overseas Hwy.

Fish House Encore (☎ 305-451-0650; www.fishhouse .com; MM 102.3) A funky-yet-upscale addition to the Key Largo eatery the Fish House, this piano lounge offers a nightly, festive karaoke blow-out (as well as the seafood and steaks of the Fish House, served on a lovely outdoor patio).

Sushi Nami (☎ 305-453-9798; MM 99.5 bayside) In addition to sushi dinners served with a flourish on the bay, weekend evenings offer live music.

Tavernier Towne Cinemas (☎ 305-853-7003; www.taver niercinemas.com; MM 92) This multiplex, showing new releases, is a perfect rainy-day option.

Sleeping

Jules' Undersea Lodge (☎ 305-451-2353; www.jul.com; 51 Shoreland Dr, MM 103.2 oceanside; per person $375-647) Sure, you could wait for the much touted, super-luxurious 'Hydropolis' hotel to open in Dubai. But until then, the only place you and your significant other can join the 'five-fathom club' (we're not elaborating) is tiny Jules, the world's only underwater hotel. In addition to two private guest rooms (there's just the *teensiest* nautical theme – everywhere), there are common rooms, a fully stocked kitchen/dining room and wet room with hot showers and gear storage. Telephones and an intercom connect guests with the surface. Guests must be at least 10 years old and you gotta dive to get here – plus, there's no smoking or alcohol. If you just want to visit, sign up for a three-hour mini-adventure ($125), which also gives access to breathing hookahs (120ft-long air hoses for tankless diving). Open-water div-ing certification courses take three days and start at $495.

Kona Kai Resort & Gallery (☎ 305-852-7200, 800-365-7829; www.konakairesort.com; MM 97.8 bayside; r $211-327, ste $296-940; P ⚑ ⚑) This intimate hideaway features 11 airy rooms and suites (with full kitchens), all warmly contemporary. It also happens to house one of the better galleries in this corner of the Keys, so pay attention artheads. There's plenty for you to do – from tennis, kayaking and paddleboating to lounging away the day in one of the hammocks that dot the palm-strewn, white-sand beach.

Largo Lodge (☎ 305-451-0424, 800-468-4378; www .largolodge.com; MM 102 bayside; low season apt $95-115, cottage $125-155, high season apt/cottage $150/195; P) The manager of the property couldn't be friendlier, and his six hidden cottages, tucked into a glimmery secret tropical garden with a private swimming cove, couldn't be cozier. And, as a side note, there couldn't be more squirrels having the run of the joint.

Key Largo House Boatel (☎ 305-766-0871; www .keylargohouseboatel.com; Shoreland Dr, at MM 103.5, oceanside; small houseboat $75; large houseboat $150) If you can't afford to sleep underwater at the Jules' Undersea Lodge (left), why not sleep on it here? There are three houseboats available, and more importantly, they're a steal. The largest one is incredibly spacious and fairly well decorated for the Keys, with a minimum of sea-themed crap and plenty of *National Geographic* issues to pass the time. The boats are right on the docks (and across from a bar), so there's no issue of being isolated from land (or booze). Call ahead for directions, as the 'boatel' is a little off the beaten track.

Stone Ledge Paradise Inn (☎ 305-852-8114; http:// fabulousvacations.com/stoneledgeparadiseinn; 95320 Over-seas Hwy; r low season $78-98, high season $88-118, villas low season $185-250, high season $250-300; P) This is a pink palace (well, squat bunch of motel blocks) of old-school American seaside kitsch. The wooden fish hung on every door are only the tip of the nautical tack iceberg, but the real joy is the sweeping view over Florida Bay at the back of the property.

John Pennekamp Coral Reef State Park (☎ 305-451-1202, 800-326-3521; www.pennekamppark.com; MM 102.5 oceanside; per night $31.49, pavilion $32.25-53.75; P) You don't even have to leave Pennekamp at closing time if you opt for tent or recreational-vehicle (RV) camping, but be sure to make a reserva-tion, as the sites fill up fast.

ISLAMORADA

Islamorada (that's eye-luh-murr-*ah*-da). Also known as 'The Village of Islands.' Doesn't that sound pretty? Well, it really is. This little string of pearls (well, Keys) – Plantation, Upper and Lower Matecumbe, Shell and Lignumvitae – shimmers as one of the prettiest stretches of the islands. This is where the scrubby mangrove is replaced by unbroken horizons of ocean and sky, one perfect shade of blue mirroring the other. Islamorada stretches across some 20 miles, from MM 90 to MM 74.

Information

Islamorada Chamber of Commerce (☎ 305-664-4503, 800-322-5397; www.islamoradachamber.com; MM 83.2 bayside; ⚇ 9am-5pm Mon-Fri, 10am-3pm Sat & Sun) Located in an old caboose.

Post office (MM 82.9 oceanside)

Sights & Activities

You might think a marina makes an odd sightseeing destination, but everyone in Islamorada knows Robbie's Marina (☎ 305-664-9814; www.robbies.com; MM 77.5 bayside; ⚇ 8am-6pm), and it really is the happiest dock on Earth. More than a boat launch, Robbie's is a local flea market, tacky tourist shop (all the shells you ever wanted, trust us), sea pen for tarpons (very big-ass fish) and jump-off for excellent fishing expeditions all wrapped into one driftwood-laced compound. There's a glut of boat rental and tour options here. The party boat (half-day/night/full day trips $35/40/60) is just that: a chance to drink and fish and basically achieve Keys zen. Or, for real zen (ie the tranquil as opposed to drunken kind), go on an ecotour ($39) on an electrically propelled silent boat deep into the mangroves, hammocks and lagoons. If you don't want to get on the water, at least feed the freakish tarpons from the dock ($2.79 per bucket, $1 to watch).

Only accessible by boat, Lignumvitae Key State Botanical site (☎ 305-664-2540), pronounced lignum-*vite*-ee, encompasses a 280-acre island of virgin tropical forest and roughly a zillion jillion mosquitoes. The official attraction is the 1919 Matheson House, with its windmill and cistern; the real draw is a nice sense of shipwrecked isolation. Strangler figs, mastic, gumbo-limbo, poisonwood and lignumvitae trees form a dark canopy that feels more South Pacific than South Florida. Guided walking tours (1¼ hours) are given at 10am and 2pm Thursday to Monday. You'll have to get here via Robbie's (left); boats depart for the 15-minute trip (adult/child $20/12) about 30 minutes prior to each tour and reservations are recommended.

For an even greater sense of tropical timelessness, come to Indian Key Historic Site (☎ 305-664-2540). In 1831 renegade wrecker (ship-wreck salvager) Jacon Housman turned this quiet island into a thriving town, complete with a warehouse, docks, streets, hotel and about 40 to 50 permanent residents. By 1836 Indian Key was the first seat of Dade County, but four years later the inhabitants of the island were killed or scattered by Indian attack during the Second Seminole War.

There's not much here today – just foundation remains, some cisterns, Housman's grave and jungly tangle. But there are trails (which follow the old layout of the town streets) and an observation tower and the pleasure of walking among ruins and paddling around in utter isolation in a canoe or kayak – which, by the way is the only way out here. Robbie's used to bring boats this way, and still does boat rentals (single/double/glass-bottom kayak/canoe $20/27.50/30/30 per hour). You can see the island from the water on an ecotour with Robbie's ($39), but short of kayakers and canoeists, no-one was allowed to dock at the harbor due to storm damage at the time of our visit.

To get his railroad built, Henry Flagler had to quarry out some sizable chunks of Key. The best evidence of those efforts can be found at Windley Key Fossil Reef Geological State Park (☎ 305-664-2540; MM 85.5; per vehicle $3.50). Besides having a mouthful of a name, Windley has leftover quarry machinery scattered along an 8ft former quarry wall; the latter offers a cool (and rare) public peek into the strata of coral that forms the ground in these parts. Ranger tours are offered at 10am and 2pm on Monday to Thursday for $2.50.

One of the best beaches in these parts is Anne's Beach (☎ 305-853-1685; MM 73 oceanside), where the sand opens up on a sky-bright stretch of tidal flats and a green tunnel of hammock and wetland. The mudflats are a joy to get stuck in, and will be much loved by the kids.

At MM 81, note the Hurricane Memorial, perhaps the only memorial in America to depict a wind-blown palm tree, which commemorates the 435 victims of the great hurricane of September 2, 1935.

SWIMMING WITH DOLPHINS – SHOULD YOU?

There are four swim-with-the-dolphin (SWTD) centers in the Keys, and a lot more arguments both for and against the practice.

Arguments For

- While SWTD sites are commercial, they are also research entities devoted to learning more about their charges.
- The dolphins raised on-site are legally obtained and not captured from the wild.
- The dolphins are used to humans and pose a negligible danger to swimmers, especially when overseen by expert trainers.
- Dolphin swim programs increase knowledge of dolphins and conservation among customers.
- At places such as the Dolphin Research Center, the dolphins can actually swim out of their pens into the open water but choose not to.

Arguments Against

- Dolphins are social creatures that require interaction which is almost impossible to provide in captivity.
- SWTD tourism encourages the capture of wild dolphins in other parts of the world.
- Dolphin behavior is never 100% predictable. Dolphins can seriously injure a human, even while playing.
- SWTD encourage customers to think of dolphins as anthropomorphized 'friends,' rather than wild animals.
- Dolphins never appreciate captivity. Those that voluntarily remain in SWTD sites do so to remain close to food.

If you decide to swim or see dolphins in the Keys, here are some options; keep in mind you usually need to speak English to go on a dolphin swim (for the instructors, not the cetaceans).

Theater of the Sea (☎ 305-664-2431; www.theaterofthesea.com; Islamorada, MM 84.5 bayside; swim programs $175; 🕑 9:30am-4pm) has been here since 1946. Structured dolphin swims and sea lion ($135) programs include 30 minutes of instruction and 30 minutes of supervised swim. You can also swim with stingrays ($55).

Dolphins Plus (☎ 305-451-1993, 866-860-7946; www.dolphinsplus.com, off MM 99.5 bayside; swim programs $165-250), a Key Largo center, specializes in recreational and educational unstructured swims. They expect you know a good deal before embarking upon the swim, even though a classroom session is included.

See Grassy Key (p194) for information on the Dolphin Research Center and Hawk's Cay resort (p194).

Area dive shops include Holiday Isle Dive Shop (☎ 305-664-3483, 800-327-7070; www.diveholidayisle.com; MM 84.5 oceanside) and Ocean Quest (☎ 305-664-4401, 800-356-8798; MM 88.5), a training facility located at the Smugglers Cove Resort.

The Greyhound bus stops at the Burger King at MM 82.5 oceanside.

Eating

Pierre's (☎ 305-664-3225; www.pierres-restaurant.com; MM 81.6 bayside; mains $24-40; 🕑 dinner) Why hello two-story waterfront plantation – what are you serving? Toro sashimi…good, quality start. Oysters Rockefeller with black truffles. Mmmm – old school with a decadent modern twist. Pan-seared duck with baby apples? Splurge, traveler, on possibly the best food between Miami and Key West.

Mile Marker 88 (☎ 305-852-9315; www.marker88.info; MM 88 bayside; mains $9-30; 🕑 5-9pm Tue-Sun, brunch Sun) It's chef-owned, has a good view of Florida Bay and an even better menu of surf-and-turf-y faves, plus 25¢ clams and oysters dur-

ing happy hour. Try the $140 beluga caviar for a splurge.

Whale Harbor Buffet (☎ 305-664-0604; www.morada bay-restaurant.com; MM 81.6 bayside; adult/child $28.95/14.95; 🕑 lunch & dinner) Take every ugly stereotype of the American obesity crisis and have them all realized in this appropriately named 80-course buffet. It's located right below Wahoo's, so you can always get a beer after you wipe out some small species of gulf shrimp.

Morada Bay (☎ 305-664-9888; www.moradabay -restaurant.com; MM 83.5 oceanside; lunch $10-15, dinner mains $21-27; 🕑 breakfast, lunch & dinner) If you can ignore the overwhelmed service and awful bands that occasionally 'headline' the lunch rush, this is a lovely, laid-back Caribbean experience, complete with imported powder-white sandy beach, nighttime torches, tapas and fresh seafood.

Manny & Isa's Kitchen (☎ 305-664-4757; MM 81.9 oceanside; lunch $5-8, dinner $12-22; 🕑 lunch & dinner Wed-Mon) Recently moved into some precious new digs, this Spanish-American joint has great daily specials, lobster enchiladas, *ropa vieja* (shredded beef) and ginormous paella platters.

Spanish Gardens Cafe (☎ 305-664-3999; MM 80.9 oceanside; dishes $9.50-15; ☽ breakfast & lunch) A great option for those sick of fried everything, this pink, Barcelona-esque café serves sandwiches and salads dripping with manchego cheese, chorizo, piquillo peppers and all the other Iberian stuff that get foodies in heat.

Bob's Bunz (☎ 305-664-8363; www.bobsbunz.com; MM 81.6 bayside; dishes $6-12; ☽ breakfast & lunch) The service at this cute café is energetic and friendly in an only-in-America kinda way, and the food is fine, filling and cheap. Key Lime anything at this bakery is highly regarded, so buy that souvenir pie here. A sister restaurant that stays open for dinner (Bob's Bunz Too) is just across the road.

Drinking & Nightlife

Loreli Restaurant & Cabana Bar (☎ 305-664-4656; www.lorelifloridakeys.com; MM 82 bayside) Look for the big mermaid and join the crowds for watered-down cocktails, live music and sunset raucousness fuelled by happy-hour specials from 4pm to 6pm.

Hog Heaven (☎ 305-664-9669; www.hogheavensportsbar.com; MM 85 oceanside) We're tempted to place this joint in the eating section, as the seafood nachos are so good. But it deserves pride of place in 'drinking' thanks to the huge crowds that trip all the way down from Fort Lauderdale for some backporch, alfresco imbibing.

Wahoo's (☎ 305-664-9888; MM 83.5 oceanside) Deep inside every man beats the heart of a Florida redneck. Get in touch with this inner truth here, where guys who look like ZZ Top members clean fish on the docks during happy hour. Trust us: fish guts make beer better.

Morada Bay (☎ 305-664-0604; MM 81.6 bayside) In addition to its excellent food (opposite), the Bay holds monthly full-moon parties that attract the entire party people population of the Keys.

Woody's (☎ 305-664-4335; MM 82 bayside) Sometimes you just gotta say it: this place is a strip club. And yet it's so much more: pizza parlor, live venue for local rockers Big Dick & the Extenders, host of weekly James Joyce discussion circles and…no, wait, scratch the last one. You gotta be 21 (and shorn of thy dignity) to get in.

Sleeping

Cheeca Lodge & Spa (☎ 305-664-4651, 800-327-2888; www.cheeca.com; MM 82 oceanside; r $309-810; P ☖ ☙) This plush conference-style resort, recently converted into a partial condotel property, is for those who like to be pampered. There are steel drums on the terrace, monkeys carved onto the hallway lamps and bamboo on the wallpaper, in case you couldn't figure out the aesthetic theme. Rooms are plush and the spoiling never stops.

Casa Morada (☎ 305-664-0044, 888-881-3030; www.casamorada.com; 136 Madeira Rd, off MM 82.2; ste low season $239-499, Nov-May $329-659; P ☖ ☙) Contemporary chic comes to Islamorada, but it's not gentrifying away the village vibe. Rather, the Casa adds a welcome dab of sophistication to conch chill: a Keystone standing circle, freshwater pool, manmade lagoon, plus a *Wallpaper* magazine–worthy bar that overlooks Florida Bay, all make this boutique hotel well worth a reservation. It's a bit of South Beach style over the Jimmy Buffet blah.

La Siesta Resort & Marina (☎ 305-664-2132; www.lasiestaresort.com; MM 80.5 oceanside; ste $160-420; P ☙) OK: the decor is a bit dated and more than a bit obsessed with the whole nautical-tropical theme (how they achieved that special shade of sea green in the carpet we cannot say). But the suites and apartments are as spacious as they get down here, service is friendly, the pool is busy and the ocean views are lovely.

Ragged Edge Resort (☎ 305-852-5389; www.ragged-edge.com; 243 Treasure Harbor Rd; units $69-249; P ☙) This low-key and popular efficiency and apartment complex, far from the maddening traffic jams, has 10 quiet units and friendly hosts. The larger studios have screened-in porches. There's no beach, but you can swim off the dock and at the pool.

LONG KEY

The 965-acre **Long Key State Recreation Area** (☎ 305-664-4815; MM 67.5 oceanside; admission per car $3.50, plus per person 50c) takes up much of Long Key. It's about 30 minutes south of Islamorada, a tropical clump of gumbo-limbo, crabwood and poisonwood trees, a picnic area fronting a long, lovely sweep of teal water and lots of wading birds in the mangroves. Two short nature trails head through distinct plant communities. The park also has a 1½-mile canoe trail through a saltwater tidal lagoon and rents out canoes (hour/day $5/10) and ocean-going kayaks (two/four hours $17.20/32.25).

If you want to stay here, make reservations this minute: it's tough to get one of the 60 sites at the Long Key State Recreation Area (☎ 305-664-4815, reservations 800-326-3521; www.reserveamerica.com; MM 67.5 oceanside; sites $31.49; P). They're all waterfront, making this the cheapest (and probably most unspoiled) ocean view (short of squatting on a resort) you're likely to find in Florida.

MIDDLE KEYS

As you truck down the Keys, the bodies of water get wider until you reach the big boy: Seven Mile Bridge, one of the world's longest causeways and a natural divider between the Middle and Lower Keys. In this stretch of islands you'll cross specks such as Conch Key and Duck Key, green, quiet Grassy Key, and finally Key Vaca (MM 54 to MM 47), where Marathon, the 2nd-largest town and most Key-sy community in the islands, is located.

GRASSY KEY

At first blush Grassy Key seems pretty sedate. Well spotted; Grassy is very much an island of few attractions and lots of RV lots and trailer parks. These little villages were once the heart of the Keys, where retirees, escapists, fishermen and the wait staff who served them lived and drank and dreamt (of a drink). Some of these communities remain, but development is relentless, and so, it seems, is the migration of the old conch trailer towns.

Sights & Activities

By far the most popular activity on this island is swimming with the descendants of Flipper (the TV dolphin) at the Dolphin Research Center (☎ 305-289-1121; www.dolphins.org; MM 59 bayside; adult/child under 4yrs/child 4-12 yrs/senior $19.50/free/13.50/16.50, swim programs $180-650; ☼ 9am-4pm). Of all the dolphin swimming spots in the Keys we tend to prefer this one; the dolphins are free to leave the grounds and a lot of marine biology research goes on behind the (still pretty commercial) tourist activities, such as getting a dolphin to paint your T-shirt or playing 'trainer for a day' (for $650, you better love your dolphins).

Curry Hammock State Park (☎ 305-289-2690; MM 56.2 bayside; $3.50 per vehicle; ☼ 8am-sunset) is small but it's sweet and the rangers are just lovely. Like most parks in the Keys, it's a good spot for preserved tropical hardwood and mangrove habitat – a 1.5-mile hike takes you through both environments. Local waters are blissfully free of power boats, which is a blessing down here. Rent a kayak (single/double for two hours $17.20/21.50) or, when the wind is up, join the crowds of windsurfers and kiteboarders.

New and increasingly popular is the non-profit Marathon Aqua Ranch (☎ 305-743-6135; www.marathonaquaranch.com; MM 59 oceanside; ☼ 9am-5pm), an alfresco…well, fish ranch. At the time of our visit the facility was pretty much a small lake stuffed with all sorts of finned friends, but as it gets off the ground the ranch is set to develop into a hands-on introduction to aquaculture and sustainable fishing. Activities include feeding snapper ($2) and cobia ($5) and the fun 'snorkel during a fish-feeding frenzy' option ($45).

Sleeping & Eating

Hawk's Cay Resort (☎ 305-743-9000, 800-432-2242; www.hawkscay.com; 61 Hawk's Cay Blvd, Duck Key, off MM 61 oceanside; r & ste low season $225-1105, high season $345-1545; P ☐ ☒) Now, if after one dolphin swim center and fish ranch you're thinking, 'Man, I *still* want to play with some sealife…', don't worry: Hawk's Cay Resort is there for you. The Cay is an enormous luxury compound that could well have its own zip code, and besides a series of silky-plush rooms and nicely appointed townhouses, it has more activities than you can shake a…flipper at. Which is to say, the Cay has its own dolphin pool – plus a sailing school, snorkeling, tennis and boat rentals.

Rainbow Bend (☎ 305-289-1505; www.rainbowbend.com; MM 58 oceanside; r low season $165-280, high season $313-339; P ☒) More budget and Keys-kitsch are these big pink cabanas, where the efficiencies and suites are bright, the tiki huts are shady, the bedsheets are ghastly, the beach swing is…um, swing-y and the ocean is (splash)…right there. Half-day use of the Bend's Boston whalers (motorboats), kayaks and canoes is complimentary.

Wreck Galley & Grill (☎ 305-743-8282; MM 59 bayside; $13-20; ☼ lunch & dinner) The Wreck doesn't offer too many surprises – fisherman types knocking back brew and feasting on wings – but it's definitely a local haunt, where island politicos like to tongue wag about the issues (fishing).

MARATHON

Marathon, the second-biggest Keys' community, is trying to sell herself as Key West for families these days, but still has an edge. There are just too many pirates, fishermen, bar workers and fun-loving hotel staff here to make Marathon totally G-rated. It's an easy place to fall in love with, or fall in love on. Marathon sits right on the halfway point between Key Largo and Key West, and is a good place to stop on a lazy road trip across the islands.

Information

Fisherman's Hospital (☎ 305-743-5533; MM 48.7 oceanside) Has a major emergency room.

Food for Thought (☎ 305-743-3297; Gulfside Village Shopping Center, MM 51 bayside) A combination bookstore and health-food shop.

Marathon Visitors Center Chamber of Commerce (☎ 305-743-5417, 800-262-7284; www.floridakeys marathon.com; MM 53.5 bayside; ⏰ 9am-5pm) Sells Greyhound tickets.

Sights & Activities

We hope that you're not nature-trailed out, because Crane Point Museum (☎ 305-743-9100; www .cranepoint.net; MM 50.5 bayside; adult/student or child over 6 yrs/senior $7.50/4/6; ⏰ 9am-5pm Mon-Sat, noon-5pm Sun) is one of the nicest spots on the island to stop and smell the roses. And the pinelands. And the palm hammock, a sort of palm jungle (imagine walking under giant, organic Japanese fans), which only grows between MM 47 and 60. There's also Adderly House, a preserved example of a Bahamanian immigrant cabin (which must have *baked* in summer) and 63 acres of green goodness to stomp through. The grounds were donated by Mary and Francis Crane, the odd Florida landowners who didn't decide to pave over their backyard. This is a great spot for the kids, who will love the pirate exhibits in an on-site museum and yet another bird hospital.

Speaking about animal safe havens, who doesn't love the Turtle Hospital (☎ 305-743-6509; www.theturtlehospital.org; 2396 Overseas Hwy; adult/child $15/7.50)? We know, we shouldn't anthropomorphize animals, but sea turtles just seem so sweet, so it's sad and heartening to see the injured and sick ones well looked after in this motel-cum-sanctuary. The whole set-up is a labor of love by Richard Moretti, who's quite the Keys character himself. Tours are educational and fun and offered at 10am, 1pm and 4pm.

Tucked away down Sombrero Beach Rd, Sombrero Beach (Sombrero Beach Rd, off MM 50 oceanside) is one of the few white-sand, mangrove-free beaches in the Keys. It's a good spot to lay out or swim, and it's free.

If the kids are still restless (or if you are), stop in at the Marathon Community Park & Marina (12,222 Overseas Hwy), which has athletic fields and a skatepark for disaffected adolescents. The marina, better known as Boot Key Harbor (www .bootkeyharbor.com), is one of the best-maintained working waterfronts in the Keys, and is an excellent spot to book charter fishing and diving trips. Ask around (as players in this game change fairly frequently), and expect to burn a hole in your wallet – just fueling a boat for a day's fishing costs hundreds of dollars.

Five-acre Pigeon Key (☎ 305-289-0025; MM 47; www.pigeonkey.net; adult/child $11/8.50; ⏰ tours 10am, 11:30am, 1pm & 2:30pm), about 2 miles west of Marathon and basically below the Old Seven Mile Bridge, is a National Historic District. For years the island housed rail workers and maintenance men; today you can tour the Key's historic structures or just relax on the beach and get in some snorkeling. Ferries leave from Knight's Key (to the left of the Seven Mile Bridge if you're traveling south) to Pigeon; the last one returns at 4pm. The Old Seven Mile Bridge, meanwhile, serves as 'the World's Longest Fishing Bridge;' park at the northeastern foot of the bridge and have a wander.

Good excursion options include Sombrero Reef Explorers (☎ 305-743-0536; www.sombreroreef.com; 19 Sombrero Rd, off MM 50 oceanside) and Tilden's Scuba Center (☎ 305-743-7255; www.tildensscubacenter.com; 4650 Overseas Hwy), both offering snorkeling and diving expeditions through nearby sections of the coral reef.

Marathon Kayak (☎ 305-743-0561; www.marathon kayak.com; 6363 Overseas Hwy) does three-hour guided mangrove ecotours (per person $45), full-day mangrove ecotours ($85), three-hour sunset tours ($45), instruction (included) and rentals (half-day/full-day $35/50).

The Marathon Cinema & Community Theater (☎ 305-743-0994; www.marathontheater.org; 5101 Overseas Hwy) is a good, old-school, single-stage theater that shows movies and plays in big reclining seats (with even bigger cupholders).

You can fly into Marathon Airport (☎ 305-743-2155, MM 50.5 bayside) or go Greyhound, which stops at the airport.

Eating

Porky's (☎ 305-289-2065; 1400 Overseas Hwy; lunch $7.75-15, dinner $15-23; ✆ lunch & dinner) The barbecue is smoky and good, and only accentuated by the salt winds coming in off the docks – which are right below your feet.

Keys Fisheries (☎ 305-743-4353; www.keysfisheries .com; 3502 Gulf View Ave; mains $7-14; ✆ lunch & dinner) The lobster Reuben is the stuff of legend, but you can't go wrong with any of the excellent seafood sandwiches, which are served with sass (to order you have to identify your favorite car, color, etc, depending on the mood of the guy behind the counter). Expect pleasant levels of seagull harassment as you dine on a working waterfront.

Villa Blanco (☎ 305-289-7900; 2211 Overseas Hwy; dishes $7-12; ✆ breakfast, lunch & dinner Mon-Sat) We're not making this statement lightly; this is South Florida after all. But the roast pork here may be the best Cuban dish we've had in Miami and outside of it. It's pillow-y, soft, luscious, citrus tangy – yet comforting. It's also freakishly huge, as you will be if you eat in this friendly if barebones cafeteria too often.

Wooden Spoon (☎ 305-743-8383; MM 51 oceanside; dishes $3-9; ✆ breakfast & lunch) It's the best breakfast around, served by sweet Southern women who know their way around a diner. The biscuits are fluffy, but they drown so well in that thick, delicious sausage gravy, and the grits are the most buttery soft starch that you'll have the pleasure to see besides your eggs.

Dion's (☎ 305-743-4481; MM 51 bayside; fried chicken dinner $4-6; ✆ 24hr) Hold on – it's a gas station. Well, gas stations treated you right in Miami, didn't they (see El Carajo, p138)? Dion's does the best fried chicken in the Keys: crisp but juicy but plump but rich, and with gooey, melty mac and cheese and sweet fried-but-just-firm-enough plantains on the side…oh man, we'll be right back.

Drinking

Island Fish Company (☎ 305-743-4191; www.islandfishco .com; MM 54 bayside; ✆ lunch & dinner) The Island's got friendly staff pouring strong cocktails on a sea breeze–kissed tiki island overlooking Florida Bay. Chat with your friendly Czech or Georgian bartender, tip well, and they'll top up your drinks without you realizing it. The laid-back by-the-water atmosphere is quintessentially Keys.

Hurricane (☎ 305-743-2200; www.thehurricanegrille .com; MM 49.5 bayside; mains $8-19) The food is fantastic (the mini-hamburger sliders in particular). The staff is sassy, sarcastic and warm. The drinks will kick your ass out the door and have you back begging for more. The ambience: locals, tourists, mad fishermen, rednecks and the odd journalist saddling up for endless Jaeger bombs before dancing the night away to any number of consistently good live acts. It's the best bar before Key West, and it deserves a visit from you.

Brass Monkey (☎ 305-743-4028; Marathon, MM 52) When Col Kurtz whispers, 'The horror, the horror,' in *Apocalypse Now* he was probably thinking about the night he got trashed in this scuzziest of dives, the preferred watering hole for off-the-clock bar and wait staff in Marathon.

Sleeping

Tranquility Bay (☎ 305-289-0888; www.tranquilitybay.com; MM 48.5 bayside; r $300-650; Ⓟ ▯ ▦) If you're serious about going upscale, you should be going here. Tranquility Bay is a massive condotel resort of plush townhouses, high-thread-count sheets and all-in-white chic, which houses and sleeps the endless waves of gentrifying glitterati from up north. The grounds are enormous and activity-filled; they really don't want you to leave.

Seascape Ocean Resort (☎ 305-743-6455; 1075 75th St, off MM 50.5 oceanside; r $165-255; Ⓟ ▦) The classy, understated luxury in this B&B manifests in the nine rooms, which all have a different feel, from old-fashioned cottage to sleek boutique. Seascape also has a waterfront pool, kayaks for guests to use and a lovely lobby-lounge where you'll find breakfast and afternoon wine and snack (all included).

Anchor Inn (☎ 305-743-2213; 7931 Overseas Hwy; r $79-150; Ⓟ) Family-owned and operated, the Inn consists of seven rooms sporting a vaguely nautical theme. Loud green dolphin hat racks aren't the classiest touch in home furnishing, but that's kind of the point: the vibe here is island casual.

Siesta Motel (☎ 305-743-5671; www.siestamotel.net; MM 51 oceanside; r year-round average $77; Ⓟ ▯) Head here for one of the cheapest, cleanest flops in the Keys – and it's got great service, to boot.

Knights Key Campground (☎ 305-743-4343, 800-348-2267; MM 47 oceanside; sites $35-85; Ⓟ) On the northern end of the Seven Mile Bridge, this 200-site campground – overdeveloped and full of family campground bells and whistles – has many on-water sites and some sites specifically for tenters.

LOWER KEYS

The Lower Keys are fierce bastions of conch culture (although the loose zoning laws locals favor are ironically putting them square in the path of big development). Some families have been Keys castaways for generations, and there are bits of Big Pine that feel more Florida Panhandle than Overseas Hwy. Whether or not this is a good thing is a matter of perspective, but rest assured the islands get pretty rural and redneck-y before opening into tiki-tastic Key West.

BIG PINE, BAHIA HONDA & LOOE KEY

Big Pine is home to endless stretches of quiet roads (once you leave the overdeveloped highway), Key West employees who found a way around astronomical real-estate rates and packs of wandering key deer. Bahia Honda's got everyone's favorite sandy beach, while Looe offers amazing reef-diving opportunities.

Information

All of the following are on Big Pine:

Big Pine Key public library (☎ 305-872-0992; Big Pine Shopping Center, Key Deer Blvd)

Lower Keys Chamber of Commerce (☎ 305-872-2411; www.lowerkeyschamber.com; MM 31 oceanside; ☺ 9am-5pm Mon-Fri, 9am-3pm Sat)

Post office (MM 30 bayside)

Sights & Activities

Bahia Honda State Park (☎ 305-872-2353; www.bahia hondapark.com; MM 36.8 oceanside; per car $3.50, plus per person 50c; ☺ 8am-sunset), with its long, white-sand (and seaweed strewn) beach is the big attraction in these parts. While the beach is popular with Keys types it's a bit over-rated (although it was voted 'Best Beach in Continental America' by Conde Nast…in 1992). As a tourist, the more novel experi-ence is walking a stretch of the old Bahia Honda Rail Bridge, which offers nice views of the surrounding islands. Or check out the nature trails (ooh, butterflies!) and sci-ence center, where helpful park employees help you identify stone crabs, fireworms, horseshoe crabs and comb jellies. Ladies: no matter how far away from the crowds you hike for privacy, rangers can eject women who sunbathe topless.

Big Pine's other big attraction is the famed Big Pine Flea Market (MM 30.5 oceanside; ☺ 8am-sunset Sat & Sun), which probably rivals local churches for weekly attendance. You know how we keep harping on about how weird Keys residents are? Well, imagine rummaging through their closets and seeing their deepest, darkest se-crets – on sale for 50¢!

Pronounced 'Loo,' Looe Key National Marine Sanctuary is located off Big Pine on a 'groove and spur reef' (we're not sure what that means, but we're gonna try it next time we're at the club). It can only be visited through a specially arranged charter-boat trip (☎ 305-292-0311). The National Marine Sanctuary is named for an English frigate that sank here in 1744, and the Looe Key reef contains the 210ft *Adolphus Busch* – used in the 1957 film *Fire Down Below* – which was sunk in 110ft of water in 1998.

Now, what would make Bambi cuter? Mini-Bambi. Introducing: the Key deer, an endangered subspecies of white-tailed deer which prance about primarily on Big Pine and No Name Keys. The folks at the National Key Deer Refuge Headquarters (☎ 305-872-0774; http://nationalkeydeer.fws.gov; Big Pine Shopping Center, MM 30.5 bayside; ☺ 8am-5pm Mon-Fri) are an incredibly help-ful source of information on the deer and all things Keys. The refuge sprawls over several islands, but the sections open to the public are on Big Pine and No Name.

Once mainland-dwellers, the deer were stranded during the formation of the Keys, where they shrank and had single births (as opposed to large litters) to deal with reduced resources. While you won't see thundering herds of dwarf-ish does, the little cuteballs are pretty easy to spot if you're persistent and patient. In fact, they're so relatively common you really need to pay attention to the reduced speed limits (note: speed limits drop further at night), because cars are still the biggest killer of Key deer.

To visit the refuge, take Key Deer Blvd (it's a right at the lights off the Overseas Hwy at the southern end of Big Pine) north for 3½ miles from MM 30.5. Your first stop is Blue Hole, a little pond (and former quarry) that's now the largest freshwater body in the Keys. This small park is home to turtles, fish, wading birds and two alligators, including a hefty sucker named 'Bacardi.' Apparently lots of idiots have taken to (illegally) feeding the wildlife; please don't follow in their stupid footsteps.

Less than a mile long, Watson's Nature Trail and Watson's Hammock are a quarter mile further along the same road. No Name Key gets few visitors (it's basically a residential island), but it's a reliable spot for deer watching. Go on to Watson Blvd, turn right, then left onto Wilder Blvd. Cross Bogie Bridge and you'll be on No Name.

Looe Key Reef Resort & Dive Center (☎ 305-872-2215, 800-942-5397; MM 27.5 oceanside) and Paradise Divers (☎ 305-872-1114; MM 38.5 bayside) rent out equipment and lead local reef dives. Strike Zone Charters (☎ 305-872-9863, 800-654-9560; MM 29.5 bayside) has four-hour snorkeling and diving trips aboard glass-bottom boats that explore the thousands of varieties of colorful tropical fish, coral and sea life in the Looe Key sanctuary. And the Bahia Honda park concession (☎ 305-872-3210) offers daily snorkeling trips at 9:30am and 1:30pm. Reservations are a good idea in high season. With all that said, you can easily paddle around any of the islands in your own kayak or canoe, or snorkel at spots that catch your fancy. Some of the local inter-Keys channels are so shallow you can walk from island to island, although we don't recommend doing so unless you're confident in your tide chart knowledge.

Eating

No Name Pub (☎ 305-872-9115; www.nonamepub.com; N Watson Blvd, off MM 30.5 bayside; dishes $7-18; ☽ 11am-11pm) The No Name's one of those off-the-track places that everyone seems to know about. It feels isolated, it looks isolated, yet somehow, the tourists are all here. Which doesn't detract in the slightest from the kooky ambience, friendly service, excellent locally brewed beer and primo pizzas served up at this colorful semi-dive.

Good Food Conspiracy (☎ 305-872-3945; MM 30 oceanside; dishes $6.75-9; ☽ 9:30am-7pm Mon-Sat, 9:30am-5pm Sun) This place serves pork fat and baby seal tacos. Just kidding! Rejoice, hippies: all the greens, sprouts, herbs and tofu you've been dreaming about during that long, fried food–studded drive down the Overseas are for sale in this friendly little health food shop. Note the big pink shrimp out front, and the attractive women who love to pose beneath it.

Coco's Kitchen (☎ 305-872-4495; Big Pine Key Shopping Center, MM 30.5 bayside; breakfast dishes $2-5, sandwiches & mains $2.25-6; ☽ 7am-7:30pm Tue-Sat) Enter through the oddly mirrored storefront into this tiny luncheonette, where local fishers join shoppers from the next door Winn Dixie for diner fare and local gossip.

Sleeping

Little Palm Island Resort & Spa (☎ 305-872-2524, 800-343-8567; www.littlepalmisland.com; ste $1091-2072; ☐ ☚) How do you get here? By boat or by plane, accompanied by a big wad of money. If you can afford to get here you can afford to spoil yourself, and this exclusive island, with its zen gardens, blue lagoons and general Persian Empire air of decadent luxury, is very good at spoiling you.

Deer Run Bed & Breakfast (☎ 305-872-2015; 1997 Long Beach Dr off MM 33 oceanside; r $175-300; ☐ ☚) This state-certified green lodge and vegetarian B&B is isolated on a lonely, lovely stretch of Long Beach Dr. It's a garden of quirky delights, complemented by assorted love-the-earth paraphernalia, street signs and four simple but cozily scrumptious rooms with names such as Eden, Heaven and Utopia. The helpful owners will get you out on a boat or into the heated pool for some chillaxation, while they whip up organic, vegetarian meals, yet somehow, in the midst of all this, the vibe isn't self-righteous hippie. More like: wow, what a friendly place.

Parmer's Place Guesthouse (☎ 305-872-2157; www.parmersresort.com; 565 Barry Ave, Big Pine Key, off MM 28.5 bayside; r, efficiencies & units $99-304; ☐ ☚) Appearing deceptively small from the outside, this five-acre property takes up a nice chunk of Little Torch Key and fills it with inviting rooms that overlook local cuts and channels. The rooms are spacey, although you'd be mad not to step outside them and enjoy a view of the islands from your balcony.

Looe Key Reef Resort (☎ 305-872-2215, 800-942-5397; www.divekeys.com; MM 27.5 oceanside; r $80-175; ☐ ☚) The focus of this Ramrod Key motel is diving, so, predictably, the 20 motel rooms are basic. The thatched-roof tiki bar is a big drinking hole for Ramrod Key residents.

Big Pine Key Fishing Lodge (☎ 305-872-2351; MM 33 oceanside; sites without/with electricity $35/40, motel efficiencies $80-100; P ⬤) This tidy canal-side spot has a loyal clientele of snowbirds who wouldn't call anywhere else their Keys home. Key deer wander the clean grounds, staff are friendly and there are plenty of activities for the kids. The lodge, geared towards fishing and diving types, does boat rentals.

Bahia Honda State Park Campground (☎ 305-872-2353; www.reserveamerica.com; MM 37; sites $31.49, cabins $136.30; P) The excellent park has six cabins, each sleeping six, and 200 almost bayside and oceanside sites. Reserve well in advance.

SUGARLOAF & BOCA CHICA KEYS

This is the final stretch before the holy grail of Key West. There's not much going on – just a few good eats and one thoroughly batty roadside attraction.

This lowest section of the Lower Keys goes from about MM 20 to the start of Key West.

Sights & Activities

It resembles an Aztec-inspired fire lookout, but the wooden Perky's Bat Tower (Sugarloaf Key; MM 17) is actually one real-estate developer's vision gone utterly awry. In the 1920s Richter C Perky had the bright idea to transform this area into a vacation resort. There was just one problem: mosquitoes. His solution? Build a 35ft tower and move in a colony of bats (he'd heard they eat mosquitoes). He imported the flying mammals, but they promptly took off and Perky never built anything else near here.

Eating

Mangrove Mama's (☎ 305-745-3030; MM 20 oceanside; lunch $10-15, dinner mains $19-25; ✆ 11:30am-3:30pm & 5:30-10pm) This groovy roadside eatery serves up Caribbean-inspired seafood – coconut shrimp, spicy Conch stew, lobster – best enjoyed on the backyard patio accompanied by live reggae.

Sugarloaf Food Company (☎ 305-744-0631; MM 24 bayside; breakfast $2.25-4.25, lunch $5-9; ✆ breakfast & lunch Mon-Sat) A cozy, airy alternative to fried dullness, the Food Company specializes in excellent sandwiches and salads and hand-crafted postcards with fairies on them. Um, have a sandwich.

Baby's Coffee (☎ 800-523-2326; MM 15 oceanside; ✆ 7am-6pm Mon-Fri, 7am-5pm Sat & Sun) This very cool coffeehouse has an on-site bean-roasting plant and sells bags of the aromatic stuff along with excellent hot and cold java brews (as well as essentials from yummy baked goods to Dr Brommer's liquid soap).

Sleeping

Sugarloaf Lodge (☎ 305-743-3211; Sugarloaf Key, MM 17; r $95-150; P ⬤) The 55 motel-like rooms are nothing special, though every single one has a killer bay view. There is also an on-site restaurant, a tiki bar, a marina and an airstrip, from which you can charter a seaplane tour or go skydiving.

Sugarloaf Key Resort KOA (☎ 305-745-3549, 800-562-7731; 251 County Rd, off MM 20 oceanside; tent sites $42-70, RV sites $62-105) This highly developed KOA (Kampground of America) has about 200 tent sites and 200 RV sites, with amenities including beachfront volleyball, swimming pool, minigolf and new sunset cruises.

KEY WEST

If you're too weird for mainland Florida – and yes, that is a valid description for a crazy few – they ship you out to Key West, the most beautifully strange (or is it strangely beautiful?) island in America. This place is seriously screwy, in a (mostly) good way. There's no middle separating the High and Low Brow, that's for sure. On one side of the road: literary festivals, Caribbean villas, tropical noir and expensive art galleries. On the other: an S & M fetishist parade, frat boys vomiting on their sorority girlfriends and 'I Love to Fart' T-shirts (seriously).

Like all good things, Key West is threatened by gentrification. Pity especially the wait- and bar-staff on Duval St, who simply cannot afford to live on the island they've helped make into everyone's party. But the whole funky insanity thing is stronger here than the rest of the Keys, probably because weirdness is still integral to the Key West brand (whereas developers are happy to flatten the other islands into identikit resorts). This town is still defined by its motto, which we love: One Human Family, an ideal that equals a tolerant, accepting ethos where anything goes and life is always a party (or at least a hungover day after). The color scheme: watercolor pastels cooled by breezes

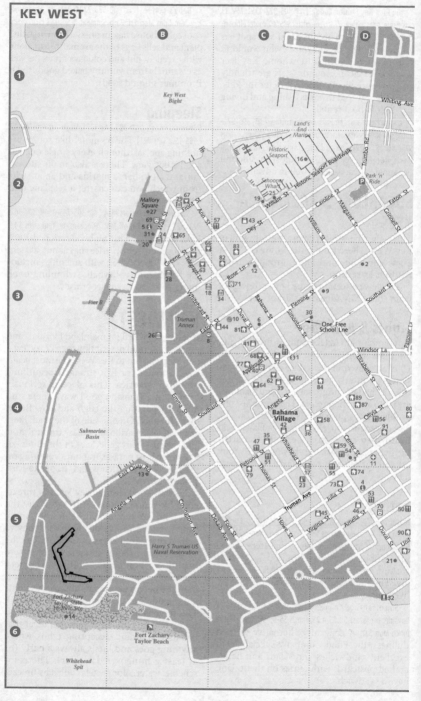

KEY WEST

Key West Bight

Whiting Ave

Land's End Marina

Historic Seaport

16

Historic Seaport Boardwalk

Park 'n' Ride

Turnbo Rd

Schooner Wharf

19   25   William St

Caroline St

Eaton St

Margaret St

Crannel St

Mallory Square
27
67
29   Front St
5   69
31   24   Ann St
20   65
61   Greene St   66
Telegraph Ln   63   82
28
18   71
34

57   Dey St   43
83
Rose Ln   12
Bahama St   Fleming St   9   Southard St
Simonton St   2
30   One Free School Ln

Whitehead St   Eaton St   10   6
26   44   81
8   41
68   48   77   Applerouth Ln   37   1   Windsor La   Elizabeth St
40   62   84   Olivia St
64   39   60

Pier B

Truman Annex

Submarine Basin

Emma St   Southard St   Angela St   Bahama Village   42   58   36   Center St   89   87   56   80   91

Margaret St   William St

East Quay Rd
13
Angela St

Covington Ave

Decab Ave

Fort St

Harry S Truman US Naval Reservation

47   35
Petronia St   51
Thomas St   79
23   17
Truman Ave
Howe St   Virginia St   Amelia St   Julia St   Duval St   United
45   46   53   73   74   4   55   11   3   59   54
70   50   90   21   32
Fort Zachary Taylor State Historic Site
14
Fort Zachary Taylor Beach

Whitehead Spit

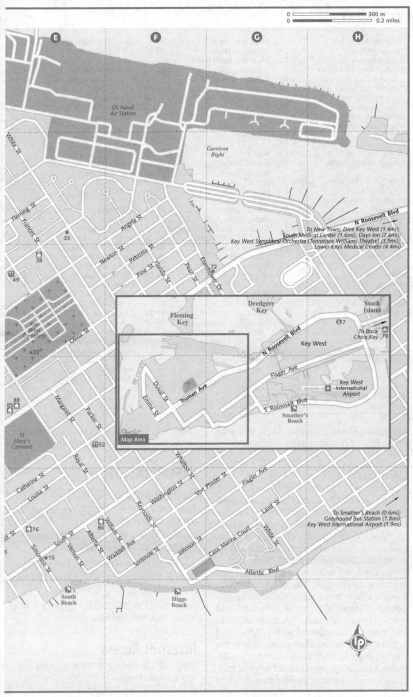

0   300 m
0   0.2 miles

White St

Fleming St

Frances St

33

38

49

Angela St

Newton St

Petronia St

Pine St

Florida St

Pearl St

Key West Cemetery

22

Olivia St

88
85

Margaret St

Packer St

52

St Mary's Convent

Catherine St

Louisa St

Royal St

76

Whalton St

Washington St

Reynolds St

Von Phister St

Flagler Ave

Laird St

White St

Simonton St

South St

Vernon St

William St

Alberta St

Waddell Ave

Seminole St

Johnson St

Casa Marina Court

86

15

Atlantic Blvd

South Beach

Higgs Beach

US Naval Air Station

Garrison Bight

N Roosevelt Blvd

To New Town; Dive Key West (1.4mi);
South Medical Center (1.6mi); Days Inn (2.6mi);
Key West Symphony Orchestra (Tennessee Williams Theatre) (3.9mi);
Lower Keys Medical Center (4.4mi)

72

Eisenhower Dr

Fleming Key

Dredgers Key

Stock Island

7

To Boca Chica Key

78

N Roosevelt Blvd

Key West

Flagler Ave

Key West International Airport

S Roosevelt Blvd

Smather's Beach

Duval St

Emma St

Truman Ave

Map Area

To Smather's Beach (0.6mi);
Greyhound Bus Station (1.8mi);
Key West International Airport (1.9mi)

KEY WEST

on a sunset-kissed Bahaman porch. Welcome to the End of America. Have a drink.

ORIENTATION

The island of Key West is roughly oval-shaped, divided into Old Town and New Town. New Town is where working folks live – families with kids and hotel employees who have been priced out of other neighborhoods. Old Town, a seriously pleasant collection of colonial architecture, shady palms and tropical light, is where the inns, eateries and museums are, centering on Duval St. The north end of Old Town is a 'high street' slush of alcohol, aggression and cheap T-shirt stands. The south end caters to the gay population; restaurants, clubs and bars are interspersed with galleries and high-end boutiques. Downtown streets are laid out in a grid, with street numbers (usually painted on lamp posts) in a hundred-per-block format, counting upward from Front St

(100) to Truman Ave/US Hwy 1 (900) and so on. Mallory Sq is at the far northwest tip.

INFORMATION
Bookstores

For books in this very literary town, check out the following:

Flaming Maggie's (☎ 305-294-3931; 830 Fleming St) Specializes in gay books and periodicals.

Key West Island Books (☎ 305-294-2904; 513 Fleming St) Has an excellent selection of works by Key West writers, past and present.

Public Library (☎ 305-292-3535; 700 Fleming St) South Florida's first library. Founded in 1892.

Internet Access

Sippin' (☎ 305-293-0555; 424 Eaton St; per min 20¢) Near the center of town.

Media

Keeping up with local goings-on is easy, as this well-read town has nearly 10 newspapers (though some are entertainment-only rags):

Citizen (www.keysnews.com) A well-written, oft-amusing daily.

Key West Keynoter (www.keynoter.com) A *Miami Herald*–owned weekly.

National Public Radio (NPR) Tune into 91.3 FM.

Solares Hill (www.solareshill.com) Slightly activist take on community interests.

Medical Services

The following provide Key West's most accessible medical services:

Lower Keys Medical Center (☎ 305-294-5531, 800-233-3119; 5900 College Rd, Stock Island, MM 5) Has a 24-hour emergency room.

South Med (☎ 305-295-3838; 3138 Northside Dr) Dr Scott Hall caters especially to the gay community, but also serves visitors.

Truman Medical Center (☎ 305-296-4399; 540 Truman Ave; ⏰ 9am-4:45pm Mon-Fri, 9:30am-noon Sat) Come here for less-critical problems.

Money

Bank of America (☎ 305-296-1204; 510 Southard St, Key West)

Post

Post office (400 Whitehead St; ⏰ main lobby 8:30am-9pm Mon-Fri, 9:30am-noon Sat)

Tourist Information

Key West Chamber of Commerce (☎ 305-294-2587; www.keywestchamber.org; 402 Wall St, Mallory Sq; ⏰ 8:30am-6:30pm Mon-Sat, until 6pm Sun) An excellent source of information.

Key West Welcome Center (☎ 305-296-4444, 800-284-4482; 3840 N Roosevelt Blvd; ⏰ 8am-7:30pm Mon-Sat, 9am-6pm Sun) Sells discounted attraction tickets and helps with accommodations.

SIGHTS
Mallory Square

Take all those energies, subcultures and oddities of Keys life – the hippies, the rednecks, the foreign types and the tourists – and focus them

---

KEY WEST HISTORY

The area's first European settlers were the Spanish, who, upon finding Indian burial sites, named the place Cayo Hueso (pronounced kah-ya way-so, meaning Bone Island), a name that was later anglicized into Key West. Purchased from a Spaniard by John Simonton in 1821, Key West was developed as a naval base in 1822, and for a long while, Key West's times of boom and bust were closely tied to the military.

The construction of forts at Key West and on the Dry Tortugas brought men and money. As well, the island's proximity to busy and treacherous shipping lanes (which attracted pirates) created the wrecking industry – salvaging goods from downed ships. Wrecking was profitable, so much so that by the mid-19th century, Key West was the biggest town in Florida.

In the late 1800s, the area became the focus of mass immigration and political activity for Cubans fleeing oppressive conditions under Spanish rule and trying to form a revolutionary army. Along with them came cigar manufacturers, who turned Key West into the USA's cigar manufacturing center. That would end when workers' demands convinced several large manufacturers, notably Vicente Martínez Ybor and Ignacio Haya, to relocate to Tampa in southwest Florida.

During the Spanish-American War, Key West was an important staging point for US troops, and the military build-up lasted through WWI. All of the Keys began to boom when Henry Flagler constructed his Overseas Hwy, running a series of causeways from the mainland to Key West. In the late 1910s, with Prohibition on the horizon, Key West became a bootlegging center, as people stocked up on booze (we'd note they've never really stopped).

After the city went bankrupt during the Great Depression a 1935 hurricane depleted what little enthusiasm remained. Then WWII breathed new life into Key West when the naval base once again became an important staging area. And everyone in Washington was certainly happy about those warships when the Bay of Pigs crisis unfolded in 1961.

Key West has always been a place where people bucked trends. A large society of artists and craftspeople congregated here at the end of the Great Depression because of cheap real estate, and that community continues to grow (despite today's pricey real estate). While gay men have long been welcomed, the gay community really picked up in earnest in the 1970s. Today it's one of the most renowned and best organized in the country.

THE CONCH REPUBLIC – ONE HUMAN FAMILY

Conchs (pronounced 'conk' as in 'bonk,' not 'contsh' as in 'bunch') are people who were born and raised in the Keys. It's a rare title to achieve. Even transplants can only rise to the rank of 'Freshwater Conch.' You will hear reference to, and see the flag of, the Conch Republic everywhere in the islands, and therein lays an interesting tale.

In 1982 US border patrol and customs agents erected a roadblock at Key Largo to catch drug smugglers and illegal aliens. As traffic jams and anger mounted, many tourists disappeared. They decided they'd rather take the Shark Valley Tram in the Everglades, thank you very much. To voice their outrage, a bunch of fiery Conchs decided to secede from the USA. After forming the Conch Republic, they made three declarations (in this order): Secede from the USA; declare war on the USA and surrender; and request $1 million in foreign aid. The roadblock was eventually lifted, and every February, Conchs celebrate the anniversary of those heady days with nonstop parties, and the slogan 'We Seceded Where Others Failed.'

Today the whole Conch Republic thing is largely a marketing gimmick, but that doesn't detract from its official motto: 'One Human Family.' This emphasis on tolerance and mutual respect has kept the Keys' head and heart in the right place, accepting gays, straights, and peoples of all colors and religions, which is sometimes more than can be said for its parent republic to the north.

into one torchlit, family-friendly (but playfully edgy), sunset-enriched street party. The child of these raucous forces is Mallory Sq, one of the greatest shows on Earth. It all begins as the sun starts to set, a sign for the madness that it's OK to break out. Watch a dog walk a tightrope, a man swallow fire, British acrobats tumble and sass each other. Have a beer. And a conch fritter. And wait for the sun to dip behind the ocean and the carnival to really get going.

Hemingway House

Key West's biggest darling, Ernest Hemingway, lived in this gorgeous Spanish-colonial **house** (☎ 305-294-1575; www.hemingwayhome.com; 907 Whitehead St; adult/child 6-12 yrs $11/6; 🕑 9am-5pm) from 1931 to 1940. Poppa moved here in his early 30s with wife No 2, a *Vogue* fashion editor and (former) friend of wife No 1. *The Short Happy Life of Francis Macomber* and *The Green Hills of Africa* were produced here, but Hemingway didn't just work; like all writers he wasted a lot of time, specifically by installing Key West's first saltwater swimming pool. The construction project set him back so badly he pressed his 'last penny' into the cement on the pool's deck. It's still there today, along with the evil descendants of his famous six-toed cat, who basically rule the house and grounds. The author's old studio is preserved as he left it – when he ran off in 1940 with wife No 3.

Florida Keys Eco-Discovery Center

So: you've been making your way down the Keys, visiting all these lovely state parks and nature reserves, thinking, 'Gosh, could there be a place that ties all the knowledge of this unique ecological phenomenon into one fun, well-put-together educational exhibit?' OK, maybe those weren't your exact thoughts, but this is exactly what you get at this excellent **center** (☎ 305-809-4750; 35 East Quay Rd in Truman Annex; admission free; 🕑 9am-4pm Tue-Sat), which does a marvelous job of filling in all the wild details of the natural Keys. The kids love it here, and by the way, it's free *and* has free parking, an abnormality around here.

Fort Zachary Taylor Historic State Park

'America's Southernmost State Park' (we get it, Keys Chamber of Commerce – Key West is southern), this **park** (☎ 305-292-6713; Truman Annex; $3.50 per vehicle; 🕑 8am-sunset) is oft-neglected by authorities and visitors, which is a shame as it's a nice place to while away a quiet afternoon. The actual fort's walls are still standing, and within the compound those most-blessed of nerds – historical re-enactors – put on costumes and act out scenes from Civil War and pirate days. Butterflies flit over the grounds, and the beach is quiet and quite pretty to boot.

Key West Butterfly & Nature Conservancy

Bring the kids, now. This vast domed **conservatory** (☎ 305-296-2988; www.keywestbutterfly.com; 1316 Duval St; adult/child $10/7.50; 🕑 9am-5pm) lets you stroll through a magic garden of flowering plants, colorful birds and up to 1800 fluttering butterflies, all live imports from around the globe.

Nancy Forrester's Secret Garden

Choose this gem of a garden (☎ 305-294-0015; www.nfsgarden.com; One Free School Lane; admission $6; ⏱ 10am-5pm) over the more touted gardens, as it truly feels secret and far-removed from the more raucous goings-on in town. Nancy, who lives on the property, invites you to bring lunch (but no cell phones!) into her oasis of lush palms, orchids and chatty caged parrots and macaws.

Museum of Art & History at the Customs House

There is art at the end of the road, and you'll find the best at this museum (☎ 305-295-6616; www .kwahs.com; 281 Front St; adult/child $7/5; ⏱ 9am-5pm), which is worth a look-see if only for its gorgeous home – the grand Customs House, long abandoned until its impressive renovation in the '90s. Actually, this place is worth a look-see for any number of reasons, including a permanent display of massive portraits, *Who Is Key West?* by painter Paul Collins, and some of the best showcases of international (particularly Caribbean) art in the region.

Key West Cemetery

A darkly alluring gothic labyrinth beckons (rather incongruously) at the center of this pastel town. Built in 1847, the cemetery crowns Solares Hill, the highest point on the island (with an elevation of all of 16ft/4.9m). Some of the oldest families in the Keys rest in peace – and proximity – here. With body space at a premium, the mausoleums stand practically shoulder to shoulder, but island quirkiness penetrates the gloom: seashells and green macramé adorn headstones with inscriptions such as, 'I told you I was sick.' Get chaperoned by George Born, of the Historic Florida Keys Foundation (☎ 305-292-6718), who gives guided tours for $10 per person at 9:30am on Tuesday and Thursday from the main gate at Margaret and Angela Sts.

Wreckers' Museums

The old Key West economy was built on wrecking – salvaging sunken ships and their treasures. The modern tourism industry is at least partly built on wrecking museums: three, to be exact. The home of Confederate blockade-runner Francis B Watlington, the

Wreckers' Museum/Oldest House (☎ 305-294-9502; 322 Duval St; adult/child $5/1; ⏱ 10am-4pm), is filled with period antiques and has enjoyable, volunteer-led tours. The Key West Shipwreck Historeum Museum (☎ 305-292-8990; www.shipwreckhistoreum.com; 1 Whitehead St; adult/child 4-12 yrs $9/4.50; ⏱ 9:45am-4:45pm) is a bit more lively, with a cast of actors taking you back to 1856, when the *Isaac Allerton* was destroyed by a hurricane in the Saddlebunch Keys. Finally, the Mel Fisher Maritime Heritage Museum (☎ 305-294-2633; 200 Greene St; adult/ child $10/6; ⏱ 9:30am-5:30pm) presents an impressive amount of artifacts salvaged by Fisher in 1985, along with a world map showing shipping routes taken by the Spanish ships he discovered.

Southernmost Point

There's no way we're going to dissuade you from having your picture taken at this red-and-black buoy at the corner of South and Whitehead Sts, which isn't even the southernmost point (that's in the off-limits naval base around the corner). But we'll say it anyways: this is the most overrated attraction in Key West.

Key West Lighthouse

You can climb up 88 steps to the top of this lighthouse (☎ 305-294-0012; www.kwahs.com; 938 Whitehead St; adult/student over 7 yrs/senior $8/4/6; ⏱ 9:30am-4:30pm), built in 1846, for a decent view. But honestly, it's just as enjoyable to gaze up at the tower from the leafy street below.

Little White House

President Harry S Truman (The one who came after Franklin Roosevelt? Marshall Plan? Helped start the Cold War? Never mind.) used to vacation at this house (☎ 305-294-9911; 111 Front St; adult/child 5-12 yrs $11/6; ⏱ 9am-4:30pm), which is as lushly luxurious as you'd expect, and open only for guided tours (though the two rooms of the Harry S Truman Annex, with displays on political and presidential trivia, are free). Plenty of Truman's possessions are scattered about, but the real draw is the guides, who are intensely intelligent, quirky and helpful.

Heritage House

Of all the many historic Key West homes open to visitors, this Caribbean-Colonial house (☎ 305-296-3573; www.heritagehousemuseum.org; 410 Caroline St;

admission $5; ☺ 10am-4pm Mon-Sat) is among the most wonderful to walk through. That's because it's rarely crowded, has passionate guides, and contains original furnishings and antiques, from a piano from the court of Marie Antoinette to a set of dining chairs from the 1600s. All have been collected and preserved by seven generations of a local family. The Robert Frost Cottage, where the poet stayed for 16 winters, is out back, along with another wonderful garden.

Bahama Village

Bahama Village was the old Bahamanian district of the island, and in days past it had a colorful Caribbean feel about it – which is resurrected a bit during the Goombay Festival (opposite). But today the village is pretty gentrified, and those areas that haven't been swallowed into a sort of pseudo-Duval periphery zone are, if not rough, not exactly great for a tourist stroll either. At 405 Petronia St is the 'Office of the Secretary General of the Conch Republic,' where you can see all manner of CR crap.

Casa Antigua

This was technically Hemingway's first house in Key West and the spot where he wrote *A Farewell to Arms*, but it isn't all that notable except for a lush garden in the back and one of the kitschiest 'guided tours' in America. Here's how it breaks down: go to the Pelican Poop Gift Shoppe (☎ 305-296-3887; www.pelicanpoop.com; 314 Simonton St), which now occupies the Casa, and pay the $2 garden entrance fee (and let the kitsch begin!). Go into the peaceful green area out the back. And then a recorded tape plays at the volume God uses whenever he says anything that begins with 'Let there be...' At this ear-splitting volume, a man with a voice that can only be described as Big Gay Al raised in Dixie lays down the history of the Casa for you. It's gloriously hilarious.

The Studios of Key West

This new nonprofit showcases about a dozen artists' studios in a gallery space (☎ 305-296-0458; www.tskw.org; 600 White St; ☺ 10am-6pm) located in the old Armory building that includes a lovely sculpture garden. Besides its public visual arts displays, TSKW hosts readings by local authors such as Robert Stone, literary and visual workshops, concerts, lectures and community discussion groups. Essentially, it's become the accessible heart of this city's

top picks

KEYS FOR KIDS

- Key West Aquarium (☎ 305-296-2051; www.keywestaquarium.com; 1 Whitehead St at Mallory Sq; adult/child $9/4.50; ☺ 10am-6pm)
- Florida Keys Eco Discovery Center (p204)
- Glass-bottom boat tours at John Pennekamp State Park (p188)
- Key West Butterfly & Nature Conservancy (p204)
- Turtle Hospital (p195)
- Conch Tour Train (opposite)
- Ghost tours (opposite)
- Key Deer spotting (p197)
- Key West Cemetery (p205)
- Robbie's Marina (p191)

enormous arts movement, and offers a good point-of-entry for visitors who want to engage Key West's creative scene but don't have a clue where to start.

ACTIVITIES
Beaches

Key West is *not* about beach-going. In fact, for true sun 'n' surf, locals go to Bahia Honda (p197) whenever possible. Still, the three city beaches on the southern side of the island are lovely and narrow, with calm and clear water. South Beach is at the end of Simonton St. Higgs Beach, at the end of Reynolds St and Casa Marina Ct, has barbecue grills, picnic tables and a big crowd of gay sunbathers and Key West's Eastern European seasonal workforce. Smathers Beach, further east off S Roosevelt Blvd, is more popular with jet skiers, parasailers, teens and college students. The best local beach, though, is at Fort Zachary Taylor (p204); it's worth the admission to enjoy the white sand and relative calm.

Diving & Snorkeling

Because of pollution and activity, there's no snorkeling to speak of on Key West beaches, so most dive companies take you off-island. At some dive sites, nondivers can go along and snorkel. Dive companies set up at kiosks around Mallory Sq and other places in town, notably the corner of Truman and Duval Sts. Check these well-established places: Subtropic

Dive Center (☎ 305-296-9914, 800-853-3483; www.sub tropic.com; 1605 N Roosevelt Blvd) and Dive Key West (☎ 305-296-3823, 800-426-0707; www.divekeywest.com; 3128 N Roosevelt Blvd).

Boating

You'll also find plenty of folks hawking sail and other boat rides. The Jolly II Rover (☎ 305-304-2235; www.schoonerjollyrover.com; Schooner Wharf, cnr Greene & Elizabeth Sts; cruise $35) is a gorgeous tan-bark (reddish-brown) 80ft schooner that embarks on daily sunset cruises under sail. It looks like a pirate ship (aarrr!) and even has the cannons to back the image up. Liberty Clipper (☎ 305-292-0332; www.libertyfleet.com; William St, at Schooner Wharf) is a 125-footer modeled after the biggest sailing craft of the 19th century. Dinner cruises (adult/child $79/55) and sunset sails (adult/child $65/45) are both magical ways of getting the salt and sea in your face.

TOURS

Old Town Trolley Tours (☎ 305-296-6688; www.trolleytours .com/key-west; adult/child $27/13) are a great introduction to the city. The 90-minute, hop-on, hop-off narrated tram tour starts at Mallory Sq and makes a large, lazy loop around the whole city, with nine stops along the way. Trolleys depart every 15 to 30 minutes from 9am to 4:30pm daily. The narration is hokey, but you'll get a good overview of Key West, its history and gossipy dirt about local issues and people in the news.

Conch Tour Train (☎ 305-294-5161; www.conchtourtrain .com; adult/child $27/13) is run by the same company as the trolley tours, though this one seats you in breezier linked train cars with no on/off option. It runs from 9am to 4:30pm.

Glass Bottom Boat Discovery Tours (☎ 305-293-0099; foot of Margaret St, Historic Seaport; www.discoveryunder seatours.com; adult/child 5 yrs & under/child 6-11 yrs $40/free/16) depart daily in summer at 11:30am, 2:30pm and sunset, and in winter at 10:30am, 1:30pm and sunset. In Key West style, the sunset cruise includes a complimentary glass of bubbly.

The Orchid Lady (☎ 877-747-2718; www.eorchidlady .com/tours.php) provides a thoroughly unique Key West experience, with guided walk-throughs of three lush, orchid-filled gardens with Orchid Lady Bobbi Mazer. Tours are 9:30am, 11am and in the afternoon by appointment (per person $25).

Also worth noting is Sharon Wells' Walking & Biking Guide to Historic Key West (www.seekeywest.com), a booklet of self-guided walks available for free at inns and businesses around town, written by a local.

There are a couple of ghost tours in town, which you'll either find frightening or corny; either way they're fun. Original Ghost Tours (☎ 305-294-9255; from Crowne Plaza La Concha Hotel; adult/child $15/10; ⏰ 8pm & 9pm) features stories about souls who inhabit locations including the Hard Rock Café, of all places; and Ghosts & Legends of Key West (☎ 305-294-1713; adult/child $18/10; ⏰ 7pm & 9pm) promises to take you 'off the beaten track' to places 'only a Conch could show you,' including the old city morgue and a small cemetery. Reservations are recommended for both.

FESTIVALS & EVENTS

You gotta see Fantasy Fest, held throughout the week leading up to Halloween in late October. It's when all the inns get competitive about decorating their properties, and when everyone gets decked out in the most outrageous costumes they can cobble together (or decked down in daring body paint). The Goombay Festival (www.goombay-keywest.org), held during the same out-of-control week, is a Bahamian celebration of food, crafts and culture. The Annual Key West Literary Seminar (http://keywestliteraryseminar.org/lit), now in its 23rd year, draws top writers from around the country each January (although it costs hundreds of dollars to attend); while the Hemingway Days festival, held in late July, brings parties, a 5km run and an Ernest look-alike contest. WomenFest (www.womenfest.com), in early September, attracts thousands of lesbians who just want to party; while November's Parrot Heads in Paradise Convention (www.phip.com/motm.asp) is for, you guessed it, Jimmy Buffet fans (rabid ones only, natch). Contact the Key West Art & Historical Society (☎ 305-295-6616; www.kwahs.com) to get the skinny on upcoming studio shows, literary readings, film festivals and the like, such as the annual Robert Frost Poetry Festival (www .robertfrostpoetryfestival.com), held in April.

SHOPPING

Bright and breezy art galleries, excellent cigars, leather fetish gear and offensive T-shirts – Key West, what don't you sell?

Bésame Mucho (☎ 305-294-1928; 315 Petronia St) This place is stocked with high-end beauty products, eclectic jewelry, clothing and housewares.

Dogs on Duval (☎ 305-296-8008; 800 Duval St) Pet accoutrement, like university doggie sports jerseys, is on the rack behind – puppies! Heart-wrenchingly cute puppies. What, you don't like puppies? Don't talk to us.

Garcia Cigars (☎ 305-293-0214; 629 Duval St) There are plenty of cigar shops in Key West, but our favorite is this shackfront, where a sweet Cuban woman sells hand-rolled goods while she quotes and constantly reads the *Bible*, all in the face of the drunken screams of a hundred horny frat boys.

Leather Master (☎ 305-292-5051; 415 Applerouth Lane) Besides the gladiator outfits, studded jock-straps and S & M masks, they do very nice bags and shoes here. Which is what you came for, right?

Island Style (☎ 305-292-7800; 620 Duval St) You'll either love or loathe these pastel-and-tropical bright knick-knacks, furniture sets and home-wares, but do visit, because the island's aesthetic is heavily influenced by this sort of place.

Montage (☎ 305-295-9101; 512 Duval St) Had a great meal or wild night at some bar or res-taurant in the Keys? Well, this store probably sells the sign of the place (along with lots of Conch Republic tat), which makes for some nice souvenirs.

Peppers of Key West (☎ 305-295-9333; 602 Greene St) For a downright shopping party, bring your favorite six-pack with you right into this store and settle in at the tasting bar, where the en-tertaining owners use double entendres to hawk mouth-burning hot sauces such as their own Right Wing Sauce (Use Liberally).

Project Lighthouse (☎ 305-292-0999; 418 Eaton St) Lighthouse is a community organization that runs programs for street kids (Key West is a popular runaway destination); it partly sup-ports itself by selling arts and crafts made by its charges.

Whitehead Street Pottery (☎ 305-294-5067; 322 Julia St) and the **Haitian Art Co** (☎ 305-296-8932; 600 Frances St) are excellent art-gallery shops.

Wishbliss Boutique (☎ 305-294-6336; 1102 Duval St) Tasteful, vintage-y, hip-to-almost-hippie clothes on Duval's south end.

EATING

There's a great concentration of good restau-rants, from greasy diners to high-end fusion-concept cuisine, in this relatively small town. When it comes to eating, sticking to Duval St isn't a bad idea, although there are some real gems down the side streets as well.

Blue Heaven (☎ 305-296-8666; http://blueheavenkw .homestead.com; 729 Thomas St; dinner mains $19-38; ☽ din-ner daily, breakfast & lunch Mon-Sat, brunch Sun) Proof that location is *nearly* everything, this is one of the quirkiest venues on an island of oddities. Cus-tomers and a local chicken flock dine in the spacious courtyard where Hemingway once officiated boxing matches; restrooms are in the adjacent former brothel. But Blue Heaven may have become a victim of its own success. It's sometimes uncomfortably crowded, and the food is hit or miss, even on basics as sim-ple as cornbread.

Nine One Five (☎ 305-296-0669; www.915duval.com; 915 Duval St; mains $16-34; ☽ 6pm-midnight) There is a war being raged for Duval St's identity. On the one side: an army of alcoholic aggres-sion and tribal band tattoos. On the other: this immaculate, modern and elegant eating experience, with its creative, New American-dips-into-Asia menu. Korean ribs over pad thai show Eastern promise, but scallops siz-zling in black truffle butter are deliriously French. The excellent interior artwork is a nice touch.

Café Sole (☎ 305-294-0230; www.cafesole.com; 1029 Southard St; lunch $5-11, dinner $25-32; ☽ lunch & din-ner) Conch carpaccio with capers? Yellowtail fillet and foie gras? Oh yes. This locally and critically acclaimed venue is known for its cozy back porch ambience and innovative menus, cobbled together by a chef trained in southern French techniques who works with island ingredients. The memory of the anchovies on crostini makes us smile as we type. It's simple – fish on toast! – but it's the sort of simple yet delicious that makes you feel like mom's whipped up something special for Sunday dinner.

Seven Fish (☎ 305-296-2777; www.7fish.com; 632 Olivia St; mains $15-26; ☽ dinner) This simple yet elegant tucked-away storefront is the per-fect place for a romantic feast of homemade gnocchi or sublime banana chicken. The

KEY LIME PIE

Many places claim to serve the original Key lime pie, but no-one knows who discovered the tart treat. Types of crust vary, and whether or not the pie should be topped with meringue is debated. However, the color of Key lime pie is not open to question. Beware of places serving green Key lime pie: Key limes are yel-low, not green. Restaurants that add green food color-ing say that tourists expect it to be green. Steer clear.

dining room might be the zen-est interior in the islands.

Camille's (☎ 305-296-4811; www.camilleskeywest.com; 1202 Simonton St; breakfast $3-13, lunch $4-13, dinner $14-25; ☺ breakfast, lunch & dinner) This healthy-and-tasty neighborhood joint is the kind of place where players on the Key West High School softball team are served by friends from their science class, and the hostess is the pitcher's mom. But it's also the kind of place where the homey facade conceals a sharp kitchen that makes a mean chicken salad sandwich.

Thai Cuisine (☎ 305-294-9424; www.keywestthaicuisine .com; 513 Greene St; lunch $10-12, dinner $15-24; ☺ lunch Mon-Fri, dinner daily) There's surprisingly good Thai to be had here near the top of Duval. It's not Bangkok, but the weather's just as nice and there are no túk-túk drivers or ladyboys interrupting your meal.

Salsa Loca (☎ 305-292-1865; http://salsalocakeywest .com; 918 Duval St; mains $11-16; ☺ 11am-10pm Tue-Thu, 11am-11pm Fri-Sat, noon-10pm Sun) Across the Keys, everyone from bartenders to developers to fishermen are swearing by the Mexican food at this colorful spot, with its tropical-night-and-tequila scented backyard patio. Of course, the bucket-deep margaritas probably improve everyone's impression of the place.

El Siboney (☎ 305-296-4184; www.elsiboneyrestaurant .com; 900 Catherine St; dishes $9.50-16; ☺ 11am-9:30pm) This is a rough and ready Cuban joint where the portions are big and there's no screwing around with either high-end embellishment or a lesser theme restaurant's bells and whistles. It's rice, it's beans, it's cooked with a craftman's pride, and it's good.

Café (☎ 305-296-5515; 509 Southard St; mains $7-13; ☺ 11am-10pm Mon-Sat) The Café is the only place in Key West that exclusively caters to herbivores. By day, it's a cute, sunny, earthy-crunchy luncheonette; by night, with flickering votive candles and a classy main dish (grilled, blackened tofu and polenta cakes), it's a sultry-but-healthy dining destination.

Conch Town Cafe (☎ 305-294-6545; 801 Thomas St; dishes $5-14; ☺ 11:30am-7:30pm) Too many people ignore this walk-up/carry-out, with its plastic patio furniture and scruffy island vibe. It's a shame, as it serves conch – good for more than listening to the ocean – deliciously 'cracked' (deep-fried) with a lip-puckeringly sour lime marinade. You'll be tempted to wash it down with the house-made smoothies, but be warned: they're more milky than refreshing.

Flamingo Crossing Ice Cream (☎ 305-296-6124; 1107 Duval St; ice cream $3.50-6; ☺ till 11pm) It's fresh, it's homemade, it's the best damn 'scream on the island. The butter pecan and mint chocolate chip (Together. Trust us) are almost as nice as the impeccable service.

DRINKING & NIGHTLIFE

Basically, Key West is a floating bar. 'No, no, it's a nuanced, multi-layered island with a proud nautical and multicultural histo–' bzzzt! Floating bar. Make your memories (or lack thereof) at one of the following. Bars close at 3am; for gay venues, see p210.

Captain Tony's Saloon (☎ 305-294-1838; 428 Greene St) The propagandists would have you believe Sloppy Joe's was Hemingway's original bar, and that's technically true, but the physical place where the old man drank was right here (Sloppy Joe's was eventually moved around the corner and into frat boy hell). Hemingway's third wife (a journalist sent to profile Poppa) seduced him in this very bar, wallpapered with business cards from around the world (including this travel writer's).

Cowboy Bills (☎ 305-295-6226; 618 Duval St) Do your best bow-legged saunter here for some (very) over-the-top country-n-western vibe, live honky tonk and weekly 'sexy bull-riding' competitions. If you just spilled your Miller High Life in excitement, turn off Blue Collar Comedy Tour and git on down here.

Garden of Eden Bar (☎ 305-296-4565; 224 Duval St) Go to the top of this building and discover Key West's own clothing-optional drinking patio. Lest you get too excited, cameras aren't allowed, most people come clothed, and those who do elect to flaunt their birthday suits are often…erm…older.

Green Parrot (☎ 305-294-6133; 601 Whitehead St) The oldest bar on an island of bars, this rogue's cantina opened in the late 19th century and hasn't closed yet. The owner tells you the parachute on the ceiling is 'weighed down with termite turds,' while a blues band howls through clouds of smoke. Defunct business signs and local artwork litter the walls and, yes, that's the city attorney showing off her new tattoo at the pool table. Men: check out the Hieronymus Bosch–like painting Proverbidioms in the restroom, surely the most entertaining urinal talk piece on the island.

Hog's Breath (☎ 305-292-2032; 400 Front St) A good place to start the infamous Duval Pub Crawl, the Hog's Breath is a rockin' outdoor bar with good live bands and better cold Coronas.

Island Dogs Bar (☎ 305-295-0501; 505 Front St) 'Come as you are,' reads the sign, and as it's written,

GAY & LESBIAN KEY WEST

Though less true than in the past, visiting Key West is still a rite of passage for many LGBT (lesbian, gay, bisexual and transgender) Americans, as gays and lesbians have always had a major impact on the local culture. Just as there is a straight trolley tour, you can hop aboard the Gay & Lesbian Trolley Tour of Key West (☎ 305-294-4603; $20), departing from the corner of South and Simonton Sts at 11am on Saturdays and providing commentary on local gay lore and businesses (you'll also see the sites of the infamous Monster club). It's organized by the Key West Business Guild, which represents many gay-owned businesses; the guild is housed at the Gay & Lesbian Community Center (☎ 305-292-3223; www.glcckeywest.org; 513 Truman Ave), where you can even access the internet – for free! – on one of the few computers, plus pick up loads of information about local gay life. For details on gay parties and events, be sure to grab a copy of the free weekly *Celebrate* (www.celebratekeywest.com).

Gay nightlife, in many cases, blends into mainstream nightlife, with everybody kind of going everywhere these days. But the backbone of the gay bar scene can be found in a pair of cruisey-type watering holes that sit across the street from one another, Bourbon St Pub (724 Duval St) and 801 Bourbon Bar (801 Duval St), which can be summed up in five words: drag queen–led karaoke night. For a peppier scene that includes dancing and occasional drag shows, men and women should head to Aqua (☎ 305-294-0555; 711 Duval St), while women will enjoy the backyard pool bar at the women's inn Pearl's Rainbow (☎ 305-292-1450; 525 United St).

so it goes in this hip (for Key West) joint, which seems to attract a younger crowd.

Irish Kevin's (☎ 305-292-1262; 211 Duval St) One of the most popular megabars on Duval, Kevin's has a pretty good entertainment formula pinned down: nightly live acts that are a cross between a folk singer, radio shock jock and pep rally cheerleader. The crowd consistently goes ape-poo for acoustic covers of '80s favorites. Basically, this is a good place to see 50 women from New Jersey do tequila shots, scream 'Livin' On a Prayer' at the top of their lungs and then inexplicably sob into their Michelob. It's more fun than it sounds.

La Te Da (☎ 305-296-6706; www.lateda.com; 1125 Duval St) While the outside bar is where locals gather for mellow chats over beer, you can catch high-quality drag acts – big names come here from around the country – upstairs at the fabulous Crystal Room on weekends. More low-key cabaret acts grace the downstairs lounge.

Virgilio's (☎ 305-296-1075; 524 Duval St, entrance on Applerouth Lane) This bar/stage is as un-Keys as they come, and frankly, Thank God for a little variety. This town needs a dark, candle-lit martini lounge where you can chill to jazz and get down with some salsa, and Virgilio's handsomely provides.

THE ARTS

Key West Players (☎ 305-294-5105; www.waterfrontplay house.com; Waterfront Playhouse, Mallory Sq) Catch high-quality musicals and dramas from the oldest running theater troupe in Florida, which has a November through April season.

Key West Symphony Orchestra (☎ 305-292-1774; www .keywestsymphony.com; Tennessee Williams Theatre) Key West's critically acclaimed orchestra performs classics from Debussy, Beethoven and Mendelssohn from December through April.

Red Barn Theatre (☎ 305-296-9911; www.redbarn theatre.org; 319 Duval St) An occasionally edgy and always fun, cozy, little local playhouse.

SLEEPING

There's a glut of boutique hotels, cozy B&Bs and four-star resorts on this island at the end of America, so sleepers won't be wanting for accommodation. Although we've labeled some options as more 'central' than others, the fact is any hotel in Old Town puts you within walking distance of all the action. Budget in Key West means $100 and under, while a midrange stay runs between $150 and $200; top-end options rise from there. High season generally refers to the time between mid-December and April. Historic Key West Inns (☎ 800-549-4430; www.historickeywestinns.com) is an excellent grouping of six boutique properties, most of which are listed here.

Chain hotels include Best Western Hibiscus (☎ 305-294-3763; 1313 Simonton St); Days Inn (☎ 305-294-3742; 3852 N Roosevelt Blvd), one of the cheapest places in town; and Crowne Plaza La Concha (☎ 305-296-2991; 430 Duval St), which has a top-floor bar and observatory open to nonguests (though you'll mainly gaze at unexciting rooftops).

Though all people, gay and straight, will be welcome just about anywhere, there are some exclusively gay inns, noted here. All of the following properties have air-conditioning except campgrounds. Lodgings have higher rates during the 'season' (mid-December to April). In addition, many properties add a 'shoulder' or mid-season that runs from late spring to early fall; rates may fall between low and high during these periods. Many hotels (especially smaller properties) enforce two-night minimum stays. Expect rates to be extremely high during events such as New Year's and Fantasy Fest, when some places enforce as many as seven (!) night minimum stays.

Top End

Gardens Hotel (☎ 305-294-2661, 800-526-2664; www .gardenshotel.com; 526 Angela St; r & ste low season $200-435, high season $325-645; P 🖳 🖳) Would we be stating the obvious if we mentioned this place has really nice gardens? In fact, the 17 rooms are located in the Peggy Mills Botanical Gardens, which is a longish way of saying 'tropical paradise.' Inside, Caribbean accents mesh with the fine landscaping to create a sense of green-and-white-and-wood space that never stops massaging your eyes.

Paradise Inn (☎ 305-293-8007, 800-888-9648; http:// theparadiseinn.com; 819 Simonton St; r & ste low season $169-369, high season $269-599; P 🖳 🖳) Another winner from Historic Inns of Key West, this friendly compound houses some simple-but-elegant rooms, suites and cottages. The suites are highly recommended: classy but not stodgy, breezy enough for a tropical idyll but not so laid-back that they're tacky. Although the cottages, with their Jacuzzi jet bathtubs, aren't so bad either...

Big Ruby's Guesthouse (☎ 305-296-2323, 800-477-7829; www.bigrubys.com; 409 Appelrouth Lane; r low season $119-191, mid-Dec–Mar $315 599; P 🖳 🖳) This gay-only place looks like a refined conch mansion on the outside, but once you get to your room you'll see it's all contemporary, white and sleeker than a designer's decadent dreams. The clothing-optional lagoon pool is capped by a treetop walkway, elegant decking and tropical palms; plus there are fine linens and lots of privacy.

Curry Mansion Inn (☎ 800-253-3466, 305-294-5349; http://currymansion.com; 511 Caroline St; r low season $195-$285, high season $240-$365; P 🖳 🖳) In a city full of stately 19th-century homes, the Curry Mansion is especially handsome. All the geographic elements of an aristocratic American home come together here, from plantation-era Southern colonnades to a New England–style widow's walk and, of course, bright Floridian

rooms with canopied beds, and bougainvillea and breezes on the verandah.

Cypress House (☎ 800-525-2488, 305-294-6969; www .cypresshousekw.com; 601 Caroline St; r & ste low season $135-$330, high season $159-$380; P 🖳 🖳) This plantation-like getaway has wraparound porches, leafy grounds, a secluded swimming pool and spacious, individually designed bedrooms with four-poster beds. It's lazy, lovely luxury in the heart of Old Town, although we'd recommend rooms in the Main House and Simonton House over the blander guest studios. Parking costs $10 per day.

Budget & Midrange

Truman Hotel (☎ 305-296-6700; www.trumanhotel.com; 611 Truman Ave; r low season $195-285, high season $240-365; P 🖳 🖳) Close to the main downtown drag, these teal-and-teak rooms have huge flat screen TVs, kitchenettes and bouncy fluff-erific beds that'll serve you well after the inevitable Duval Crawl (which is only steps from your door).

Pearl's Rainbow (☎ 305-292-1450, 800-749-6696; www.pearlsrainbow.com; 525 United St; r & ste low season $120-199, high season $209-399; P 🖳 🖳) Key West's sole women-only place is one of the best low-key lesbian resorts in the country, an intimate garden of tropical relaxation and enticing rooms scattered across a few cottages. A clothing-optional backyard pool bar is the perfect spot for al-fresco happy hour, or to enjoy your free brekkie.

Almond Tree Inn (☎ 800-311-4292, 305-296-5415; www.almondtreeinn.com; 512 Truman Ave; r $159-399; P 🖳 🖳) Palm-lined pool. Palm tree lamps. Palm-engraved headboard. Plus wicker dressers and sea green walls. Sure, the tropical theme is laid on thick, but hey, it's the Keys, and besides, there's a 5pm to 7pm happy hour by the pool.

Merlin Inn (☎ 305-296-3336, 800-642-4753; 811 Simonton St; low season $89-225, high season $135-300; P 🖳 🖳) Set in a secluded garden with a pool and elevated walkways, everything here is made from bamboo, rattan and wood. Throw in the high ceilings and exposed rafters in the rooms and this hotel oozes colonial-tropical atmosphere. Unfortunately, the sheets on some of the beds might remind you of granny's house.

Mermaid & Alligator (☎ 305-294-1894, 800-773-1894; www.kwmermaid.com; 729 Truman Ave; r low season $148-198, high season $218-298; P 🖳 🖳) It takes a real gem to stand out amid the jewelry store of

DETOUR: DRY TORTUGAS NATIONAL PARK

After all those Keys, connected by all that convenient road, the nicest islands in the archipelago require a little extra effort. Ponce de León named them Las Tortugas – 'The Turtles' – for the sea turtles that roamed here. A lack of fresh water led sailors to add a 'dry.' Today the 'Dry Tortugas' are a national park under the control of the Everglades National Park office (☎ 305-242-7700; www.nps.gov/drto), only accessible by boat or plane.

Originally the Tortugas were the US's naval perch into the Gulf of Mexico. But by the Civil War, Fort Jefferson, the main structure on the islands, had become a prison for Union deserters and at least four people, among them Dr Samuel Mudd, who had been arrested for complicity in the assassination of Abraham Lincoln. Hence, a new nickname: Devil's Island. The name was prophetic; in 1867 a yellow fever outbreak killed 38 people, and after an 1873 hurricane the fort was abandoned. It reopened in 1886 as a quarantine station for smallpox and cholera victims, was declared a national monument in 1935 by President Franklin D Roosevelt, and was upped into national park status in 1992 by George Bush Sr.

The park is open for day trips and overnight camping, which provides a rare phenomenon: a quiet Florida beach. Garden Key has 13 campsites ($3 per person, per night), which are given out on a first-come, first-served basis. Reserve early by calling the Everglades National Park office. There are toilets, but no fresh-water showers or drinking water; bring everything you'll need. The sparkling waters offer excellent snorkeling and diving opportunities. A visitor center is located within fascinating Fort Jefferson.

If you're hungry, watch for Cuban-American fishing boats trolling the waters. They'll happily trade for lobster, crab and shrimp; you'll have the most leverage trading beverages. Just paddle up to and bargain for your supper. In March and April, there is stupendous bird-watching, including aerial fighting. Star-gazing is mind-blowing any time of the year.

Getting There

If you have your own boat, the Dry Tortugas are covered under National Ocean Survey chart No 11438. Otherwise, the Yankee Freedom II (☎ 305-294-7009, 800-634-0939; www.yankeefreedom.com; Key West Seaport) operates a fast ferry between Garden Key and the Key West Seaport (at the northern end of Margaret St). Round-trip fares cost $124/109 per adult/child. Reservations are recommended. Continental breakfast, a picnic lunch, snorkeling gear and a 45-minute tour of the fort are all included.

Seaplanes of Key West (☎ 305-294-0709; www.seaplanesofkeywest.com) can take up to 10 passengers (flight time 40 minutes each way). A four-hour trip costs $229/free/149/179 per adult/child under 2 yrs/child 2-6 yrs/child under 12 yrs; an eight-hour trip costs $405/free/270/325. Again, reserve at least a week in advance.

Keys hotels, but this place, located in a 1904 mansion, more than pulls off the job. Each of the nine rooms is individually designed and a great mix of modern comfort, Keys colonial ambience and playful laughs. The treetop suite, with its exposed beams and al-coved bed and bathroom, is our pick of this idiosyncratic litter.

Chelsea House (☎ 305-296-2211; www.chelseahousekw .com; 707 Truman Ave; r low season $120-180, high season $200-290; P 🖳 🐾) This perfect pair of Victorian mansions beckons with large vaulted rooms and big comfy beds, with the whole shebang done out in floral, but not dated, chic. The old-school villa ambience clashes – in a nice way – with the happy vibe of the guests and the folks at reception.

Key Lime Inn (☎ 800-559-4430; 725 Truman Ave; r $99-289, ste $109-329; P 🖳 🐾) These cozy cottages are all scattered around a tropical hardwood backdrop. Inside, the blissfully cool rooms are greener than a jade mine, with wicker

furniture and tiny flat-screens on hand to keep you from ever leaving.

Avalon Bed & Breakfast (☎ 305-294-8233; www .avalonbnb.com; 1317 Duval Ave; r low season $89-169, high season $169-289; 🖳 🐾) A cute, restored Victorian house on the quiet end of Duval blends attentive service with club deck ceiling fans, tropical lounge room rugs, and black and white photos of olde-timey Key West. Music the cat likes to greet guests at reception.

Abaco Inn (☎ 305-292-4040; http://abaco-inn.com; 415 Julia St; r $119-189; 🖳) This intimate gem, tucked away on a quiet and diverse residential block, has three simple, airy and stylish rooms, all with wood floors and ceiling fans. There's no breakfast, but there is a small, shaded garden and a couple of warm and knowledgeable hosts. An excellent find.

Caribbean House (☎ 305-296-0999; www.caribbean housekeywest.com; 226 Petronia St; r low season $55, high season $75; P 🖳) This is a cute, canary-yellow Caribbean cottage in the heart of Bahama

Village. The 10 small brightly colored guest rooms aren't too fancy, but it's a happy, cozy bargain – with free breakfast, no less.

Key West Youth Hostel & Seashell Motel (☎ 305-296-5719; www.keywesthostel.com; 718 South St; dm members/nonmembers $25/28, motel r low season $75, high season $110-150; P) They've improved this place over the past few years – it's not quite as mildew-y and the common area feels more youth hostel-y and less skeezy. The dorms are still the cheapest sleeping option in town (although you get what you pay for). Single rooms aren't worth the cost, given what you can get at a similar rate around the way.

Boyd's Key West Campground (☎ 305-293-9301, www.boydscampground.com; 6401 Maloney Ave; tent sites low season non-waterfront/waterfront $50/60, mid-Nov–mid-Apr $60/70, water & electricity $75-110; P) Just outside town on Stock Island (turn south at MM 5), Boyd's has upwards of 300 sites. There's a bus stop for downtown practically at their front door.

GETTING THERE & AROUND

Key West International Airport (EYW) is off S Roosevelt Blvd on the west side of the island. Expect to spend $150 to $180 for a round-trip flight between Miami and Key West. With a little luck and good timing, you can get a direct, round-trip flight between New York City and Key West for as low as $300. Flights from Los Angeles ($350 in summer, $575 in winter) and San Francisco ($400 year-round) usually have to stop in Tampa, Orlando or Miami first. American Airlines (☎ 800-433-7300) and US Airways (☎ 800-428-4322) have several flights a day. Cape Air (☎ 305-352-0714, 800-352-0714; www.flycapeair.com) flies between Key West and Naples, with round-trip fares ranging from $105 to $250. From the Key West airport, a quick and easy taxi ride into Old Town will cost about $10.

Greyhound (☎ 305-296-9072; www.greyhound.com; 3535 S Roosevelt Blvd) has two buses daily between Key West and Downtown Miami. Buses leave Miami for the four-hour, 25-minute journey at 12:35pm and 6:50pm ($38.50 to $44 one-way), and Key West at 8:55am and 5:45pm going the other way.

Once you're in Key West, the best way to get around is by bicycle (rentals are about $10 a day). Other options include the City Transit System (☎ 305-292-8160; tickets 75¢), with color-coded buses running about every 15 minutes; the convenient Bone Island Shuttle (☎ 305-293-8710; 3-day pass $7, kids free), which makes frequent loops around both New and Old Town; moped rentals (for about $20 a day); mopeds, which generally rent for $30 for four hours ($35 for a six-hour day); or the ridiculous electric tourist cars, or 'Conch cruisers,' which travel at 35mph and rent for about $30 an hour or $170 for an entire day. As far as regular rental cars go, don't even bother in Key West.

THE EVERGLADES

THE EVERGLADES

South Florida is known for beauty. The model in her tight jeans; that renovated deco hotel; the glitter and sweep of the sun on Biscayne Bay and the city skyline.

But none of the above compares to an alligator's back breaking the blackwater. An anhinga flexing its wings before breaking into a corkscrew dive. The slow, dinosaur-flap of a great blue heron gliding over its domain. Or the sun kissing miles of unbroken sawgrass as it sets behind humps of skeletal cypress domes.

No words can really seize the soft curves of this geography, the way the light attaches to water running under the grass, or the mud-and-wood smell of an eroded limestone hole sunk into a pine hammock. In a nation where natural beauty is measured by its capacity for drama, the Everglades subtly, contentedly flows on.

Forget what you've heard about airboats and swamp buggies. The Glades should be approached with the same silence and gentle persuasion she shows her inhabitants. Come by car and canoe, bike, kayak or walk around the park. To understand the way a nutrient-rich patch of water produces a mosquito that feeds a frog, who becomes lunch for a gator, who snaps up a fish that gets speared by an anhinga under these long, low marsh winds, you need to be still. In the quiet spaces, you realize the Everglades, so often dismissed as a swamp, are more beautiful than all the sin and flash Miami can produce. South Beach changes by the day. The Glades have beautifully endured forever, and if we're very lucky, they'll last that much longer.

top picks

THE EVERGLADES

- Sunset over the ingress road to Pa-hay-okee Overlook (p226)
- Hell's Bay paddling trail (p226)
- Big Cypress Gallery (p222)
- Gator nuggets and frog legs at Seafood Depot (p223), Everglades City
- Spotting alligators at night, Royal Palm Visitor Center (p225)

GETTING THERE

The largest subtropical wilderness in the continental USA is easily accessible from Miami. The Glades, which comprise the 80 southernmost miles of Florida, are bound by the Atlantic Ocean to the east and the Gulf of Mexico to the west. The Tamiami Trail (US Hwy 41) goes east–west, parallel to the more northern (and less interesting) Alligator Alley (I-75).

INFORMATION

Ernest Coe Visitor Center (☎ 305-242-7700; www.nps.gov/ever; Hwy 9336; 9am-5pm) The principal visitor center is packed with excellent information and there are also rangers who can answer any of your questions.

Everglades Area Chamber of Commerce (☎ 239-695-3941; cnr US Hwy 41 & Hwy 29, Everglades City; 9am-5pm) Provides general information about businesses and attractions in the region.

Everglades National Park visitor centers (☎ 305-242-7700; www.nps.gov/ever; 40,001 State Rd 9336, Homestead) The main park entry points have visitor centers, where you can get maps, camping permits and ranger information. Pay the entrance fee ($10 for seven days) only once to access at all points. Fishers need a license; call ahead at ☎ 888-347-4356.

Flamingo Visitor Center (☎ 239-695-2945; 9am-4:30pm) On the park's southern coast.

Gulf Coast Visitor Center (☎ 239-695-3311; Hwy 29, Everglades City; 9am-4:30pm) This northwesternmost ranger station provides access to the 10,000 Islands area.

Royal Palm Visitor Center (☎ 305-242-7700; Hwy 9336; 8am-4:15pm) Adjacent to Ernest Coe Visitor Centre.

Shark Valley Visitor Center (☎ 305-221-8776; Tamiami Trail; 9:15am-5:15pm) Sells tickets for the tram tour.

HOW DOES IT ALL WORK?

It's tempting to think of the Everglades as a swamp, but 'prairie' may be a more apt description. The Glades, at the end of the day, are grasslands that happen to be flooded for most of the year, but visit during the dry season (winter) and you'd be forgiven for thinking the Everglades was the Everfields.

So where's all the water coming from? Look north, all the way to Lake Okeechobee and the small lakes and rivers that band together around Kissimmee. Florida dips into the Gulf of Mexico at its below-sea-level tip, which happens to be the lowest part of the state geographically *and* topographically. Run-off water from central Florida flows down the peninsula via a series of streams and rivers, *over* and *through* the Glades, and into Florida Bay. The glacial pace of the flood means that this seemingly stillest of landscapes is actually in constant motion. Small wonder that the Calusa Indians called the area Pa-hay-okee (grassy water). Much beloved conservationist Marjory Stoneman Douglas (1890–1998) called it the *River of Grass*; in her so-named book she reveals that Gerard de Brahm named the region the River Glades, which became Ever Glades on later English maps.

So what happens when nutrient-rich water creeps over a limestone shelf? The ecological equivalent of *bow-chika-bow-wow*. Beginning at the cellular level, organic material blooms in surprising ways, clumping and forming into algal beds, nutrient blooms and the ubiquitous periphyton, which are basically clusters of algae, bacteria and detritus (ie stuff). Periphyton ain't pretty: in the water it resembles puke streaks and the dried version looks like hippo turds. But you should kiss it when you see it (well, maybe not), because in the great chain of the Everglades, this slop forms the base of a very tall organic totem pole. The smallest tilt in elevation alters the flow of water and hence the content of this nutrient soup, and thus the landscape itself: all those patches of cypress and hardwood hammock are areas where a few inches of altitude create a world of difference between biosystems.

THE FIGHT FOR THE GRASSY WATERS

For years the River of Grass flowed on, concealing wading birds, fish, otters, frogs, skunk, deer, panthers, alligators, etc. And that sound, just out of earshot? Oh, just Florida being settled by thousands of homesteaders…

Enter business, stage right. Cattle ranchers and sugar growers, attracted by mucky waters and Florida's subtropical climate (paradise for sugarcane), successfully pressured the government to make land available to them. In 1905 Florida governor Napoleon Bonaparte Broward personally dug the first shovelful of what was to become one of the most destructive diversions of water in the world. The Caloosahatchee River was diverted and connected to Lake Okeechobee. Hundreds of canals were cut through the Everglades to the coastline to 'reclaim' the land, and the flow of lake water was restricted by a series of dikes. Farmland began to claim areas of land previously uninhabited by humans.

Unfortunately, the whole River of Grass needs, y'know, the river to survive. And besides being a pretty place to watch the birds, the Everglades act as a hurricane barrier and kidney. Kidney? Yup: all those wetlands leeched out pollutants from the Florida Aquifer (the state's freshwater supply). But when farmland wasn't diverting the sheet flow, it was adding fertilizer-rich wastewater to it. Result? *Bow-chika-wow-chika-wow wow-wow*. Bacteria, and eventually plant-life bloomed at a ridiculous rate (they call it fertilizer for a reason), upsetting the fragile balance of resources vital to the Glades' survival.

Enter Marjory Stoneman Douglas, stage left. Ms Douglas gets the credit for almost single-handedly pushing the now age-old Florida issue of Everglades conservation; for more on this titan of the American environmental movement, see the boxed text (p221).

Despite the tireless efforts of Douglas and other environmentalists, today the Florida Aquifer is in serious danger of being contaminated and drying up. On July 2, 2007, the water level in Okeechobee reached an all-time low of 8.82in. Mercury levels are so

---

EVERGLADES READS

The Everglades: River of Grass (1947, Rinehart & Company), by Marjory Stoneman Douglas (p221). The classic, by that classiest of crusaders.

Crackers in the Glade (2000, University of Georgia Press), by Rob Storter. A lovely sketchbook/journal by a Glades native, fisherman, hunter, conservationist and self-taught artist.

Liquid Land (2003, University of Georgia Press), by naturalist Ted Levin. An extremely informative book on both the environment of the Glades and the fight to save it.

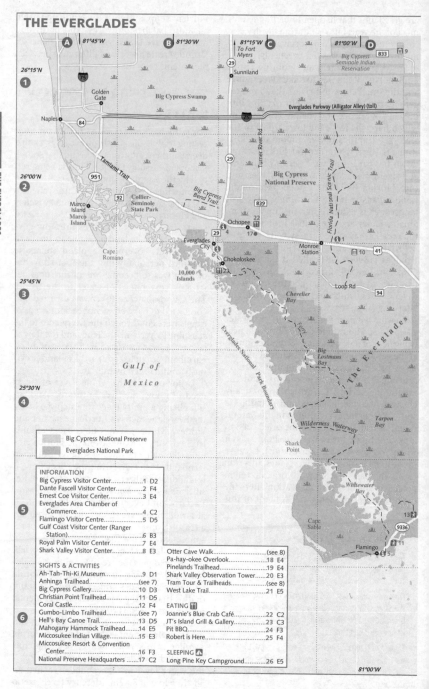

THE EVERGLADES

Big Cypress National Preserve

Everglades National Park

INFORMATION

Big Cypress Visitor Center	1	D2
Dante Fascell Visitor Center	2	F4
Ernest Coe Visitor Center	3	E4
Everglades Area Chamber of Commerce	4	C2
Flamingo Visitor Centre	5	D5
Gulf Coast Visitor Center (Ranger Station)	6	B3
Royal Palm Visitor Center	7	E4
Shark Valley Visitor Center	8	E3

SIGHTS & ACTIVITIES

Ah-Tah-Thi-Ki Museum	9	D1
Anhinga Trailhead	(see 7)	
Big Cypress Gallery	10	D3
Christian Point Trailhead	11	D5
Coral Castle	12	F4
Gumbo-Limbo Trailhead	(see 7)	
Hell's Bay Canoe Trail	13	D5
Mahogany Hammock Trailhead	14	E5
Miccosukee Indian Village	15	E3
Miccosukee Resort & Convention Center	16	F3
National Preserve Headquarters	17	C2

Otter Cave Walk	(see 8)	
Pa-hay-okee Overlook	18	E4
Pinelands Trailhead	19	E4
Shark Valley Observation Tower	20	E3
Tram Tour & Trailheads	(see 8)	
West Lake Trail	21	E5

EATING

Joannie's Blue Crab Café	22	C2
JT's Island Grill & Gallery	23	C3
Pit BBQ	24	F3
Robert is Here	25	F4

SLEEPING

Long Pine Key Campground	26	E5

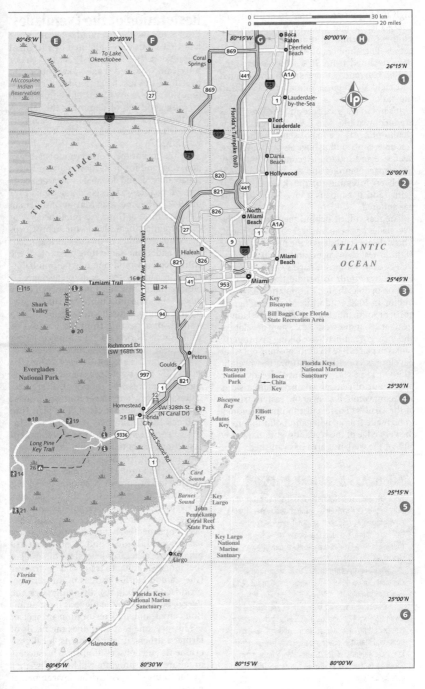

high fishermen are warned to eat only one Everglades-caught bass per week; pregnant mothers and children should avoid bass altogether. The numbers of wading birds nesting have declined from 90% to 95% since the 1930s. Currently, there are 15 endangered and eight threatened animal species within the park.

It's not that agriculture and the Everglades are incompatible. The EAA (Everglades Agricultural Area) is a major state and national resource, contributing huge amounts of sugar, beef, rice and sod to the economy. But every time smart planning and wise water disposal has been foregone for quick development gains (and it happens a lot), South Florida has suffered.

The real culprit behind the demise of the Everglades has been unchecked development. This delicate ecosystem is the neighbor of one of the fastest growing urban areas in America. The current water drainage system in South Florida was built to handle the needs of 2 million people; the local population topped 6 million in 2000. And while Miami can't grow north or south into Fort Lauderdale or Homestead, it can move west. Real estate developers and local governments are hiking up property values in places like Hialeah, pushing out what developers consider economic deadweight (the working class who have already been priced out of central Miami). McMansions are being vomited all over the eastern fringes of the Glades. There's just too much money to be made from paving and polluting up to the very edge of the wetlands, and that's why 50% of the wetlands area has vanished.

AIR BOATS & SWAMP BUGGIES

Air boats are flat-bottomed skiffs that use powerful fans to propel themselves through the water. Their environmental impact has not been determined, but one thing is clear: air boats can't be doing much good, which is why they're not allowed in the park.

Swamp buggies are enormous balloon-tired vehicles that can go through wetlands, creating ruts and damaging wildlife.

Air boat and swamp buggy rides are offered all along US Hwy 41 (Tamiami Trail). Please think twice before getting on a 'nature' tour. Loud whirring fanboats and marsh jeeps are a crappy way to experience the quiet serenity of the Glades. More importantly, you may be helping to disturb the Everglades' delicate balance.

Restoration of the Everglades

Efforts to save the Everglades began in the late 1920s, but were sidelined by the Great Depression. In 1926 and 1928, two major hurricanes caused Lake Okeechobee to overflow; the resulting floods killed hundreds. So the Army Corps of Engineers did a *really* good job of damming the lake. A bit too good: the Glades were essentially cut off from their source, the Kissimmee watershed.

In the meantime, conservationists began donating land for protection, starting with a square mile of land donated by a garden club. The Everglades was declared a national park in 1947, the same year Marjory Stoneman Douglas' *River of Grass* was published.

By draining the wetlands, the Army Corps made huge swathes of inland Florida inhabitable, and at the same time guaranteed the entire region would one day be uninhabitable. The canal system sends, on average, 1.7 billion gallons of water into the ocean every *day*. At the same time, untreated runoff flows unfiltered into natural water supplies. Clean water is disappearing from the water cycle while South Florida's population gets bigger by the day.

Enter the Comprehensive Everglades Restoration Project (CERP; www.evergladesplan.org). CERP is designed to address the root of all Everglades issues: water, where to get it, how to divert it and ways to keep it clean. The plan is to unblock the Kissimmee, restoring remaining Everglades lands to pre-development conditions while maintaining flood protection, providing freshwater for South Florida's populace and protecting earmarked regions against urban sprawl. It sounds great, but lawsuits and mistrust between developers, environmentalists and state government have delayed the entire process. Today CERP has been implemented, but the cost of the project has bloomed from around $8 billion to $19 billion, and, as regards federal funding, 'all of that money is going to Iraq,' said one ranger (the state of Florida had, as of this writing, promised $4.5 billion). Bringing back the Everglades remains the biggest, most ambitious environmental restoration project in US history, one that combines the needs of farmers, fishers, urban residents, local governments and conservationists. The success or failure of the program will be a bellwether for the future of the American environmental movement.

GLADES GUARDIAN

In a state known for eccentrics, no-one can hold a candle to Marjory Stoneman Douglas. Not just for her quirks, but for her drive, a persistent, unbreakable force that fueled one of the longest conservation battles in American history.

Born in 1890, Douglas moved to Florida after her failed first marriage and worked for the *Miami Herald* and eventually as a freelance writer, producing short stories that are notable for both the quality of the writing and progressive themes: *Plumes* (1930) and *Wings* (1931), published in the *Saturday Evening Post*, addressed the issue of Glades bird poaching when the business was still immensely popular (the feathers were used to decorate ladies' hats).

In the 1940s, Douglas was asked to write about the Miami River for the Rivers of America Series and promptly chucked the idea in favor of capturing the Everglades in her classic, *The Everglades: River of Grass*. Like all of Douglas' work the book is remarkable for both its exhaustive research and lyrical, rich language.

River of Grass immediately sold out of its first printing, and public perception of the Everglades shifted from 'nasty swamp' to 'national treasure.' Douglas went on to be an advocate for environmental causes ('It is a woman's business to be interested in the environment. It's an extended form of housekeeping'), women's' rights and racial equality, fighting, for example, for basic infrastructure in black Overtown.

Still, today she's remembered as Florida's favorite environmentalist. Always immaculately turned out in gloves, dress, pearls and floppy straw hat, she'd bring down engineers, developers, politicians, and her most hated opponents, sugar farmers ('They should go at any time, now, as far as I'm concerned. Pick up and go. Any minute. We won't miss them a bit.'), by force of her oratory alone. She kept up the fight, speaking and lecturing without fail, until she died – in 1998 at the age of 108.

Today it seems every environmental institution in Florida is named for Douglas, but were she around, we doubt she'd care for those honors. She'd be too busy planting herself in the CERP office, making sure everything was moving along on schedule, and scolding like a heroic schoolmarm if it wasn't.

ROAD TRIPPING

Although the grassy waters extend outside Everglades National Park (the third-largest in the continental USA), you really need to enter the park to experience it. There are three main entrances: one along the southeast edge near Homestead and Florida City (Ernest Coe); at the central-north side on the Tamiami Trail (Shark Valley); and a third at the northwest shore (Gulf Coast), past Everglades City.

These entrances allow for two good road trips (easy day trips, or more leisurely two-day trips) from Miami. You can head west along the Tamiami Trail, past the Miccosukee reservation, all the way to Everglades City and the crystal waters of the 10,000 islands.

The other day-trip option is to enter at Coe and take Hwy 9336 to Flamingo through the most 'Glades-y' landscape in the park, with unbroken vistas of wet prairie, big sky and long silences.

TRIP 1: ALONG THE TAMIAMI TRAIL

Calle Ocho (p87) happens to be the eastern end of the Tamiami Trail, which cuts through the Everglades to the Gulf of Mexico. So go west, young traveler, along US Hwy 41, a few dozen miles and several different worlds away from the city where the heat is on.

Past Hialeah, Miami fades like a trail of diminishing Starbucks until…*whoosh*…it's all huddled forest and open fields and a big canal off to the side (evidence of US 41's diversion of the Glades' all-important sheet flow). The surest sign the city is gone and the Glades have begun is the Confederate flag decals on Pit BBQ (p223). The empty road runs past the Miccosukee Resort & Convention Center (☎ 305-925-2555, 877-242-6464; www.miccosukee.com; 500 SW 177th Ave; r Nov-Apr $150), where the long storied legacy of the nation's indigenous peoples has culminated in…slots. Lots of slots, and comatose gamblers pouring quarters into them. If the Miccosukee and Seminole are cashing in on this stuff, more power to them, but it's still depressing to watch.

The tackiness gets worse as you head west into unending swamp-tour territory. Airboat operators in these parts require three things: intimate knowledge of the backcountry, a moustache and killer tats. Rockin' out to Sky-nyrd doesn't hurt, either.

Shark Valley & Loop Rd

After endless variations of 'Zeke's Swamp Boat Alligatorama!', Shark Valley's friendly, knowledgeable rangers feel like a gift.

The most popular and painless way to immerse yourself in the Everglades is via the two-hour tram tour (☎ 305-221-8455; adult/child under 12 yrs/senior $13.25/8/12.25) here that runs along the

AH-TAH-THI-KI MUSEUM

If you want to learn about Florida's indigenous Americans, come to this Seminole museum (☎ 863-902-1113; www.seminoletribe.com/museum; Big Cypress Seminole Indian Reservation, Clewiston; adult/senior & child $6/4; ⏱ 9am-5pm Tue-Sun), 17 miles north of I-75. All of the excellent educational exhibits on Seminole life, history and the tribe today were founded on gaming proceeds, which provide most of the tribe's multimillion-dollar operating budget.

The museum is good for tribal business, but the folks here really are dedicated to giving visitors a closer understanding of the Seminole and Miccosukee people. It's not the wild Glades, and there are aspects of this 60-acre cypress forest – such as alligator wrestling – that leave something to be desired, but it's a breakthrough for the tribe. Until recently, the tribe had kept to itself where tourism was concerned. Seminole Safari excursions (☎ 941-949-6101, 800-617-7516; www.seminoletours.com) offer day (adult/child $49/34) and overnight (adult/child $114/90) very touristy packages. The overnight packages include sleeping in a screened-in chickee, listening to campfire storytelling, taking an airboat or swamp buggy ride and having Indian meals (catfish, fry bread, gator nuggets).

15-mile asphalt trail. If you only have time for one Everglades activity, this should be it, as guides are informative and witty, and you'll likely see gators sunning themselves on the road. Halfway along the trail is the 50ft-high Shark Valley Observation Tower, an ugly concrete structure that offers dramatically beautiful views of the park.

At the park entrance, the easy Otter Cave walk makes a boardwalk-ed loop through a thick copse of tropical hardwoods before emptying you out, disoriented, right back into the Shark Valley parking lot.

A little further up you can detour down Loop Rd, which offers four interesting sites. One: gambling-enriched Miccosukee (this is still their reservation), whose houses all seem to have shiny new pick-up trucks parked out front. Two: great pull-offs for viewing flooded forests, where egrets that look like pterodactyls perch in the trees. Three: scary, isolated Florida types who make it very clear trespassers will be sorry. And four: the short, pleasantly jungly Tree Snail Hammock Nature Trail. Be warned that the Loop is a rough, unpaved road.

Big Cypress & Ochopee

Stay west on 41 to see Clyde Butcher's Big Cypress Gallery (☎ 941-695-2428; www.clydebutcher.com; Tamiami Trail; ⏱ 10am-5pm Wed-Mon), a highlight of any Everglades trip. In the great tradition of Ansel Adams, Clyde's large-format black-and-white images elevate the swamps to a higher level; he's found a quiet spirituality in the brackish waters and you might, too, with the help of his eyes. Every Labor Day (first weekend in September) Clyde holds a gala event, which includes a fun, $20 swamp walk onto his 30-acre property.

The 1139-sq-mile Big Cypress National Preserve (named for the size of the park, not its trees) is the result of a compromise between environmentalists, cattle ranchers and oil-and-gas explorers. The area is integral to the Everglades' ecosystem: rains that flood the preserve's prairies and wetlands slowly filter down through the Glades.

About 45% of the cypress swamp (actually a group of mangrove islands, hardwood hammocks, slash pine, prairie and marshes) is protected. Great bald cypress trees are nearly gone, thanks to pre-preserve lumbering, but dwarf pond cypress trees fill the area with their own understated beauty.

The Big Cypress Visitor Center (☎ 941-695-4111; ⏱ 8:30am-4:30pm), about 20 miles west of Shark Valley, has great exhibits for the kids and an outdoor, water-filled ditch popular with alligators; or there's the National Preserve Headquarters (☎ 941-695-2000; ⏱ 8am-4:30pm Mon-Fri), just east of Ochopee, which also has information and hosts cultural programs such as artist-in-residence exhibits.

There are 31 miles of the Florida National Scenic Trail (FNST) within Big Cypress National Preserve. From the southern terminus, which can be accessed via Loop Rd, the trail runs 8.3 miles north to the Tamiami Trail. There are two primitive campsites with water wells situated along the trail; pick up a map at the visitor center. Most campsites are free, and you needn't register. Monument Lake (low season free, site Dec 15–Apr $16) campsite has water and toilets.

Drive to the hamlet of Ochopee (population about four)...no...wait...turn around, you missed it! Then pull over and break out the cameras: Ochopee's claim to fame is the country's smallest post office. It's housed in a former toolshed and set against big park skies; a friendly postal worker patiently poses for snapshots.

EATING

Joannie's Blue Crab Café (☎ 941-695-2682; Tamiami Trail, east of Ochopee; dishes $10-13; ⊗ 9am-5pm) This quintessential shack, with open rafters, shellacked picnic tables and alligator kitsch serves OK food on paper plates.

Pit BBQ (☎ 305-226-2272; 16,400 SW 8th St, between Miami & Shark Valley; dishes $4-9; ⊗ 11am-11:30pm) The barbecue's decent and served on picnic tables with a side of country music and Confederate flag accoutrement. You gotta love it (otherwise, don't stop).

Everglades City

The end of the track is an old Florida fishing village of raised houses, turquoise water and scattershot emerald-green mangrove islands. Hwy 29 runs south through town into the peaceful, residential island of Chokoloskee, past a great, psychedelic mural of a gator on a shed.

'What's there to do around here?' we ask our waitress.

'Eat.' Pause. 'Or go on an Everglades tour.'

North American Canoe Tours (NACT; ☎ 941-695-3299/4666; www.evergladesadventures.com; Ivey House Bed & Breakfast, 107 Camellia St; ⊗ Nov–mid-Apr) rents out camping equipment and canoes for full/half days ($35/$25) and touring kayaks ($45 to $65). You get 20% off most of these services and rentals if you're staying at the Ivey House Bed & Breakfast (p224), which runs the tours. Tours shuttle you to places such as Chokoloskee Island, Collier Seminole State Park, Rabbit Key or Tiger Key for afternoon or overnight excursions ($25 to $450).

INFORMATION

Everglades Area Chamber of Commerce (☎ 941-695-3941; cnr US Hwy 41 & Hwy 29; ⊗ 9am-5pm)

Gulf Coast Visitor Center (☎ 941-695-3311; Hwy 29; ⊗ 8:30am-5pm) Has loads of information on the 10,000 Islands.

EATING

Seafood Depot (☎ 239-695-0075; 102 Collier Ave; dishes $12-28; ⊗ lunch & dinner) Don't totally sublimate your desire for fried food, because the gator tail and frog legs here offers an excellent way to honor the inhabitants of the Everglades: douse them in Tabasco and devour them.

JT's Island Grill & Gallery (☎ 239-695-3633; 238 Mamie St, Chokoloskee; dishes $4-12; ⊗ 11am-3pm late Oct–May) Just a mile or so past the edge of town, this awesome café-cum–art gallery sits in a restored 1890 general store. It's outfitted with bright, retro furniture and piles of kitschy books, pottery, clothing and maps (all for sale). But the best part is the food (lunch only) – fresh crab cakes, salads, fish platters and veggie wraps, made with locally grown organic vegetables.

SLEEPING

Rod & Gun Club Lodge (☎ 941-695-2101; 200 Riverside Dr; r low season $85, mid-Oct–Jun $139; Ⓟ) Built in the 1920s as a hunting lodge by Barron Collier (who needed a place to chill after watching workers dig his Tamiami Trail), this masculine place, fronted by a lovely porch, has a restaurant that serves anything that moves in them thar waters.

Parkway Motel & Marina (☎ 239-695-3261; 1180 Chokoloskee Dr; r $99-120; Ⓟ) An extremely friendly

---

CANOE CAMPING ON 10,000 ISLANDS

One of the best ways to experience the serenity of the Everglades – somehow desolate yet lush, tropical and foreboding – is by paddling the network of waterways that skirt the northwest portion of the park. The 10,000 Islands consist of many (but not really 10,000) tiny islands and a mangrove swamp that hugs the southwestern-most border of Florida. The Wilderness Waterway, a 99-mile trail between Everglades City and Flamingo, is the longest canoe trail in the area, but there are shorter trails near Flamingo.

Most islands are fringed by narrow beaches with sugar-white sand, but note that the water is brackish, and very shallow most of the time. It's not Tahiti, but it's fascinating. You can camp on your own island for up to a week.

Getting around the 10,000 Islands is pretty straightforward if you religiously adhere to National Oceanic & Atmospheric Administration (NOAA) tide and nautical charts. Going against the tides is the fastest way to make a miserable trip. The Gulf Coast Visitor Center sells nautical charts and gives out free tidal charts. You can also purchase charts prior to your visit – call ☎ 305-247-1216 and ask for chart Nos 11430, 11432 and 11433.

owner (and even friendlier dog) run this veritable testament to the old-school Floridian lodge: cute small rooms and one cozy efficiency in a one-story motel building.

Ivey House Bed & Breakfast (☎ 941-695-3299; www .iveyhouse.com; 107 Camellia St; lodge $60-85, inn $85-140; P ▣) This family-run place, with its lovely tropical inn (and somewhat less impressive lodge) serves good breakfasts in its small Ghost Orchid Grill. Plus it operates some of the best nature trips around (p223).

TRIP 2: HOMESTEAD TO FLAMINGO POINT

Head south of Miami to drive into the heart of the park and the best horizons of the Everglades. Plus, there are plenty of side trails and canoe creeks to detour onto.

Homestead & Florida City

Homestead is one of the fastest growing cities in America, and while it isn't exactly scenic (although the 'main street' area is cute enough), it's a fair improvement from the crime-ridden strip mall it used to be. Still, there are plenty of strip clubs on the way down here (including the excellently named 'Booby Trap'). Florida City is pretty much Homestead South.

Krome Ave (Hwy 997) and Rte 1 cut through both towns, and the latter houses one of the great attractions of roadside America.

'You will be seeing unusual accomplishment', reads the inscription on the rough-hewn quarried wall. Oh hell yes. There is no greater temple to all that is weird and wacky about South Florida than the Coral Castle (☎ 305-248-6345; www.coralcastle.com; 28,655 S Dixie Hwy; adult/youth 7-18 yrs/senior & student $9.75/5/6.50; ☯ 7am-8pm). The legend: a Latvian gets snubbed at the altar. Comes to America. Moves to Florida (of course; he's crazy). Hand carves, unseen, in the dead of night, a monument to unrequited love: a rock compound that includes a 'throne room,' sun dial, stone stockade (his intended's 'timeout area') and revolving boulder gate that engineers around the world, to this day, cannot explain. Oh, and there are audio stations situated around the place that explain the site in a replicated Latvian accent, so it feels like you're getting a narrated tour by Borat.

Ah, Florida.

INFORMATION

Chamber of Commerce (☎ 305-247-2332; 43 N Krome Ave, Homestead; ☯ 9am-noon & 1-5pm Mon-Fri) Stop here for Everglades information.

SHOPPING

ArtSouth (☎ 305-247-9406; 240 N Krome Ave, Homestead; ☯ 10am-6pm Tue-Fri, from noon Sat & Sun) This colony of artists' studios is a good place to see local talent, and pick up Glades-inspired artwork.

EATING

Farmer's Market Restaurant (☎ 305-242-0008; 300 N Krome Ave, Florida City; lunch dishes $8-10, dinner dishes $12-14; ☯ 5:30am-9pm) This restaurant's as fresh and hardy as the produce in the next-door farmer's market and its rural worker clientele.

Casita Tejas (☎ 305-248-8224; 27 N Krome Ave, Homestead; dishes $6.50-11; ☯ lunch & dinner) This popular storefront eatery on the main drag has affordable, delicious Mexican lunches and dinners.

Rosita's (☎ 305-246-3114; 199 W Palm Dr, Florida City; mains under $10; ☯ 8:30am-9pm) There's a more working-class Mexican crowd here, testament to the sheer awesome-ness of the tacos and burritos.

SLEEPING

Best Western Florida City/Homestead Gateway to the Keys (☎ 305-246-5100, 800-937-8376; www.bestwestern .com; 411 S Krome Ave, Florida City; r $115-158; P ▣ ☲ ☙) A standard, comfy motel that is well positioned for Glades exploring.

Redland Hotel (☎ 305-246-1904; 5 S Flagler Ave, Homestead; r $75-150; P ▣) This historic inn has clean, individualized rooms with a distinct doily vibe. The building served as the town's first hotel, mercantile store, post office, library and boarding house (for real!) and is now favored by folks who want more of a personal touch than you can get from the chains.

Everglades International Hostel (☎ 305-248-1122, 800-372-3874; www.evergladeshostel.com; 20 SW 2nd Ave, Florida City; dm $22, d $50-65; P ▣) Located in a cluttered, comfy 1930s boarding house, this friendly hostel has six-bed dorms and private doubles (and a 'semi-private' with a window onto the dorm room) with shared bathroom. This is a good base to meet other Glades travelers, rent gear or book park tours. A garden and high-speed internet round out the deal.

PYTHONS, GATORS & CROCS, OH MY!

Gators

Alligators are common in the park, although not so much in the 10,000 Islands, as they tend to avoid saltwater. If you do see an alligator, it probably won't bother you, unless you do something overtly threatening or angle your boat between it and its young. If you hear an alligator making a loud hissing sound, get the hell out of Dodge. That's a call to other alligators when a young gator is in danger. Finally, never, ever, ever feed an alligator – it's stupid and illegal.

Crocs

Crocodiles are less common in the park, as they prefer coastal and saltwater habitats. They are more aggressive than alligators, however, so the same rules apply. With perhaps only a few hundred remaining in the USA, they are also an endangered species.

Weather

Thunderstorms and lightning are more common in summer than winter. But in summer the insects are so bad you won't want to be outside anyway. In emergency weather, rangers will search for registered campers, but under ordinary conditions, they won't unless they receive information that someone's missing. If camping, have a friend or family member ready to contact rangers if you do not report back by a certain day.

Insects

You can't overestimate the problem of mosquito and no-see-ums (tiny biting flies) in the Everglades; they are, by far, the park's worst feature. While in most national parks there are warning signs showing the forest-fire risk, here the charts show the mosquito level (☎ 305-242-7700 for a report). In summer and fall, the sign almost always says 'extremely high.' You'll be set upon the second you open your car door. The only protections are 100% DEET or, even better, a pricey net suit.

Snakes

There are four types of poisonous snake in the Everglades: diamondback rattlesnake (*Crotalus adamanteus*); pigmy rattlesnake (*Sistrurus miliarius*); cottonmouth or water moccasin (*Agkistrodon piscivorus conanti*), which swim along the surface of water; and the coral snake (*Micrurus fulvius*). Wear long, thick socks and lace-up boots – and keep the hell away from them. Oh, and now there are Burmese pythons prowling the water too. Pet owners who couldn't handle the python have dumped the animals into the swamp, where they've adapted like…well, a tropical snake to a subtropical forest. There's already evidence of alligators and pythons getting into rumbles, and while this is admittedly cool in a Nature's Ultimate Fighting Championship kinda way, in all seriousness the python is an invasive species that is badly mucking up the natural order of things.

Ernest Coe & Royal Palm to Flamingo

Drive past Florida City, through miles of paper-flat farmland and past an enormous, razor-wired jail (it seems like an escapee heads for the swamp at least once a year) and turn left when you see the signs for Robert Is Here (p226) – or stop by so the kids can pet a donkey. Keep down this road as the farmland loses its uniformity and the flat land becomes more tangled, wild and studded with pine and cypress. After a few more miles you'll enter the park at Ernest Coe Visitor Center (☎ 305-242-7700; www .nps.gov/ever; Hwy 9336; ☼ 8am-5pm). Have a look at the excellent exhibits, including a diorama of 'typical' Floridians (the fisherman looks like he should join ZZ Top).

Just past here is the Royal Palm Visitor Center (☎ 305-242-7700; Hwy 9336; ☼ 8am-4:15pm), which offers the easiest access to the Glades in these parts. Two trails, the Anhinga and Gumbo Limbo (the latter named for the Gumbo Limbo tree, also known as the 'tourist tree' because its bark peels like a sunburned Brit), take all of an hour to walk and put you face to face with a panoply of Everglades wildlife. Gators sun on the shoreline, anhinga spear their prey and wading birds stalk haughtily through the reeds. Come at night for a ranger walk onto the boardwalk and shine a flashlight into the water to see one of the coolest sights of your life: the glittering eyes of dozens of alligators prowling the waterways.

Rte 9336 cuts through the soft heart of the park, past long fields of marsh prairie, white, skeletal forests of bald cypress and dark clumps of mahogany hammock. There are plenty of trails to detour down; all of the following are half a mile (800m) long. Mahogany Hammock leads into an 'island' of hardwood forest floating on the water-logged prairie, while the Pinelands takes you through a copse of rare, spindly swamp pine and palmetto forest. Further on, Pa-hay-okee Overlook is a raised platform that peeks over one of the prettiest bends in the river of grass. The West Lake Trail runs through the largest protected mangrove forest in the Northern Hemisphere.

The real joy here is canoeing into the bracken heart of the swamp. There are plenty of push-off points, all with names that sound like they were read off Frodo's map to Mordor, including Hell's Bay, The Nightmare, Snake Bight and Graveyard Creek. Our favorite is Hell's Bay. 'Hell to get into and hell to get out of,' was how this sheltered launch was described by old Gladesmen, but damn if it isn't heaven inside: a capillary network of mangrove creeks, sawgrass islands and shifting mudflats, where the brambles form a green tunnel and all you can smell is sea salt and the dark, organic breath of the swamp. Three chickee sites (wooden platforms built above the waterline) are spaced along the trail.

Further down you can take a good two-hour, 1.8-mile (2.9km) hike to Christian Point. This dramatic walk takes you through several Glades environments: under tropical forest, past columns of white cypress and over a se-ries of mudflats (particularly attractive on grey, cloudy days), and ends with a dramatic view of the windswept shores of Florida Bay.

The area around Flamingo Visitor Center was damaged by Hurricane Wilma, and its restaurants and lodges were closed when we visited, but you can still rent boats or go on a backcountry boat tour with the Pelican (☎ 239-696-3101; adult/child $18/9; boats leave 10am, 1pm & 3pm); a 1½-hour sailing schooner tour (adult/child/sunset $22/14/33) is also available. Or rent a canoe (per hr/day/half-day $8/22/32) or sea kayak (half-day/day $35/45) and explore the channels and islands of Florida Bay on your own.

EATING & SLEEPING

Robert Is Here (☎ 305-246-1592; 19,200 SW 344th St, Homestead; ⏰ 8am-7pm Nov-Aug) More than a farmer's stand, Robert's is an institution. This is redneck Florida at its kitschy best, in love with the Glades and the agriculture that surrounds it. There's a petting zoo for the kids, live music at night, plenty of homemade preserves and sauces, and while everyone goes crazy for the milkshakes – as they should – do not leave without having the fresh orange juice. It's the best in the world.

National Park Service (NPS; ☎ 800-365-2267; www .nps.gov/ever/visit/backcoun.htm; sites low season free, Nov-Apr $14) The campgrounds here are run by the NPS. None of these primitive, barely shaded sites have hookups. Depending on the time of year, cold-water showers are either bracing or a welcome relief.

Long Pine Key Campground (☎ 800-365-2267; free low season, Nov-Apr $14) This is the best bet for car campers, just west of Royal Palm Visitor Center.

WILDERNESS CAMPING

Three types of backcountry campsites are available: beach sites, on coastal shell beaches and in the 10,000 Islands; ground sites, which are basically mounds of dirt built up above the mangroves; and 'chickees,' wooden platforms built above the water line where you can pitch a free-standing (no spikes) tent. Chickees, which have toilets, are the most civilized; there's a serenity found in sleeping on what feels like a raft levitating above the water. Ground sites tend to be the most bug-infested.

Warning: if you're just paddling around and see an island that looks pleasant for camping but isn't a designated campsite, beware – you may end up submerged when the tides change.

From November to April, camping permits cost $10 plus $2 per person per night; in the low season sites are free, but you must still self-register at Flamingo and Gulf Coast Visitor Centers.

Some back country tips:
- Store food in a hand-sized, raccoon proof container (available at gear stores).
- Bury your waste at least 10in below ground, but keep in mind some ground sites have hard turf.
- Use a back-country stove to cook. Ground fires are only permitted at beach sites, and you can only burn dead or drowned wood.

BISCAYNE NATIONAL PARK

Just to the east of the Everglades is Biscayne National Park, or the 5% of it that isn't underwater. Huh? Well, a portion of the world's third-largest reef happens to sit here off the coast of Florida. Fortunately, this unique 300-sq-mile park is easy to explore independently with a canoe or via a glass-bottom-boat tour. Its offshore keys, accessible only by boat, offer pristine opportunities for camping. Generally, summer and fall are the best times to visit the park; you'll want to snorkel when the water is calm. This is some of the best reef-viewing and snorkeling you'll find in America, outside Hawaii (and nearby Key Largo).

Biscayne National Underwater Park (☎ 305-230-1100) offers glass-bottom-boat viewing of the exceptional reefs, canoe rentals, transportation to the keys, and snorkeling and scuba-diving trips. All tours require a minimum of six people, so call to make reservations. Three-hour glass-bottom-boat trips depart at 10am (adult/child $24.45/16.45). Canoe rentals cost $12 per hour and kayaks $16; they're rented from 9am to 3pm. Three-hour snorkeling trips (adult/child $35/30) depart at 1:15pm daily; you'll have about 1½ hours in the water. Scuba trips depart at 8:30am Friday to Sunday ($54).

Long Elliott Key has picnicking, camping and hiking among mangrove forests; tiny Adams Key has only picnicking and equally tiny Boca Chita Key has an ornamental lighthouse, picnicking and camping. No-see-ums are invasive, and their bites are devastating. Make sure your tent is devoid of miniscule entry points.

Information

Dante Fascell Visitor Center (☎ 305-230-7275; www.nps.gov/bisc; 9700 SW 328th St; ⊗ 8:30am-5pm) Shows a great introductory film for a good overview of the park and has maps, information and excellent ranger activities.

Sleeping

Primitive camping costs $10 per night; you pay on a trust system with exact change on the harbor (rangers cruise the Keys to check your receipt). Bring in all supplies, including water, and carry everything out. There is no water on Boca Chita, only saltwater toilets, and since it has a deeper port, it tends to attract bigger (and louder) boaters. There are cold-water showers and potable water on Elliott, but it's always good to bring your own since the generator might go out.

FORT LAUDERDALE

Pity the Fort. It's dismissed as a family-friendly Miami, a more sedate South Beach, less culturally advanced and more yuppie-oriented, blah blah blah. And there's a grain – a *grain* – of truth to this. But hey: we're comparing it with Miami. *Any* town's gonna look sedate set next to the Magic City. Put Fort Lauderdale anywhere else in the country – say, in Pennsylvania – and folks would be calling it party town USA.

Actually, they did, back in the heady 1980s, when Fort Lauderdale was Spring Break central. But being the frat-boy Riviera never stuck too well in this town's craw, and Lauderdale worked hard to overcome its public perception as host of the world's biggest wet T-shirt contest.

Well, it succeeded. Today Fort Lauderdale has an excellent arts scene (thank you very much), a pretty riverwalk, a beach that's arguably better than anything in Miami, a layout interlaced with beautiful canals (hence the nickname Venice of America) and, yes, great nightlife. Come 40 minutes north of Miami, knock some sea stories out of the yachties (see the boxed text, p235) who congregate here, and recognize that Fort folks are justified for feeling a little resentful of their southern sister's long shadow.

Fort Lauderdale has three distinct sections: the beach, east of the Intracoastal Waterway; downtown; and Port Everglades, the cruise port south of the city. US Hwy 1 (also called Federal Hwy) cuts through downtown, while Hwy A1A runs by the ocean; it's also called Atlantic Blvd and Ocean Blvd, depending if you're north or south of Sunrise Blvd. The main arteries between downtown and the beach are Sunrise Blvd to the north, Las Olas Blvd in the center and 17th St to the south.

INFORMATION

Broward General Medical Center (☎ 954-355-4400; 1600 S Andrews Ave, Port Everglades)

Broward Main Library & Cultural Information Center (☎ 954-356-7444; 100 South Andrews Ave; ☺ 9am-9pm Mon-Thu, till 5pm Fri-Sat, 12-5:30pm Sun) Visit for info on upcoming shows and art exhibitions, or just to read and pick up wi-fi.

Clark's Out of Town News (☎ 954-467-1543; 303 S Andrews Ave) Gather both local and foreign newspapers at Clark's.

Greater Fort Lauderdale Convention & Visitors Bureau (☎ 954-765-4466; www.sunny.org; 1850 Eller Dr, Port Everglades; ☺ 8:30am-5pm Mon-Fri) Has an excellent array of visitor information.

Lauderdale-by-the-Sea Chamber of Commerce (☎ 954-776-1000; 4201 Ocean Dr)

Main post office (☎ 800-275-8777; 1900 W Oakland Park Blvd)

New Millennium Internet Café (☎ 954-566-2111; 3337 NE 33rd St)

SIGHTS & ACTIVITIES
Museum of Art

This museum (☎ 954-525-5500; www.moafl.org; 1 E Las Olas Blvd; adult/student & child over 12 yrs $10/7; ☺ 11am-7pm Fri-Wed) is simply one of Florida's best. The permanent collection includes works by Picasso, Matisse, Dalí and Warhol, while rotating galleries showcase local talent and regional artwork. Make sure to check out the 'Indigo Room,' an amazing installation by a Haitian-American artist that captures, in soft, wine-dark sea shades, the pain and hope of both immigrant movement and Haitian history.

Museum of Discovery & Science

If you don't take the kids here, you're a mean parent. From the 52ft Great Gravity Clock,

Florida's largest kinetic energy sculpture, to exhibits on the Everglades, funky inventions and musical kaleidoscopes, the museum (☎ 954-467-6637; www.mods.org; 401 SW 2nd St; adult/child/senior $15/12/14; 🕑 10am-5pm Mon-Sat, noon-6pm Sun) is a major treat for kids, and frankly fun for parents too. Admission also includes an IMAX 3D show.

Fort Lauderdale Historical Society

Discover a Florida of colonial villas and bougainvillea, rather than Mickey Mouse and Miami, at this organization (☎ 954-463-4431; www.old fortlauderdale.org; 231 SW 2nd Ave; admission $5; 🕑 11am-5pm Tue-Sun), which maintains the Hoch Heritage Center, a historic research facility; the century-old New River Inn, Philemon Bryan House and King-Cromartie House, open for tours; and the 1899 Replica Schoolhouse. The museum mounts exhibits on Fort Lauderdale and Broward County history and Seminole folk art and also offers guided walking tours of historic downtown. Call for details.

Riverwalk/Las Olas Riverfront

The thing to do here is amble along this pleasant meandering pathway (☎ 954-468-1541; www .goriverwalk.com) between a number of city sights, restaurants and shops. Las Olas Riverfront (☎ 954-522-6556; SW 1st Ave at Las Olas Blvd) is a giant shopping mall with stores, restaurants, a movie theater and live entertainment nightly; it's also the place to catch many river cruises (see Tours, p234).

Stranahan House

One of Florida's oldest residences, the landmarked Stranahan House (☎ 954-524-4736; www.strana hanhouse.com; 335 SE 6th Ave; adult/child $12/7; 🕑 1-3pm Wed-Sun) is a fine example of Florida frontier design. Constructed from Dade County pine, the house has wide porches, tall windows, a Victorian parlor, original furnishings and fine tropical gardens. It was built as the home and store for Ohio transplant Frank Stranahan, who built a small empire trading with the Seminole but killed himself by jumping into the New River after real estate and stock market losses in the late 1920s.

Bonnet House

Lovely Bonnet House (☎ 954-563-5393; www.bonnet house.org; 900 N Birch Rd; adult/student & child 6-18 yrs/senior $20/16/18, grounds only $10; 🕑 10am-4pm Tue-Sat, noon-4pm Sun) has 35 subtropical acres filled with native and imported tropical plants, including a vast orchid collection. Tours of the house are guided (1¼ hours), but you are free to walk the grounds and nature trails on your own.

Fort Lauderdale Beach Promenade

This lovely promenade runs along Fort Lauderdale Beach, which is a finer stretch of sugary sand than anything you'll find in Miami. It may not have the models (although there are plenty of hotties) and fashion shoots, but frankly it's a far better place for some sun, sand and swimming.

International Swimming Hall of Fame

Basically, if you love swimming, you should already be at this museum (☎ 954-462-6536; www.ishof .org; 1 Hall of Fame Dr/SE 5th St; adult/child under 12yrs/student $8/free/4; 🕑 9am-5pm), where the exhibits include thousands of photographs and Olympic mementos, from Johnny Weissmuller's Olympic medals to Mark Spitz's starting block.

Hugh Taylor Birch State Recreation Area

This state park (☎ 954-564-4521; 3109 E Sunrise Blvd; per vehicle of 2-8 people $4, per pedestrian or bicyclist $1; 🕑 8am-sunset), which has recently undergone a major renovation of trails and landscaping, contains one of the last significant maritime hammocks left in Broward County, as well as mangroves, a freshwater lagoon system and several endangered plant and animal species (including the gopher tortoise and golden leather fern).

Wannado City

It's worth a short day trip to the nearby City of Sunrise for this kids' theme park (☎ 954-838-7100; www.wannadocity.com; Purple Parrot Way, Sawgrass Mills Mall; admission over/under 14 yrs $27.95/15.95), which asks children, 'Whatchya wanna do?' Get it? Never mind. Kids get to experience our crushing day-to-day as something fun and exciting in a series of little villages, costumes and games that lets them act as circus ringmaster, perform surgery, investigate a crime scene and, of course, have mom and dad buy plenty of souvenirs. Daily hours vary by season; call for more info.

FORT LAUDERDALE

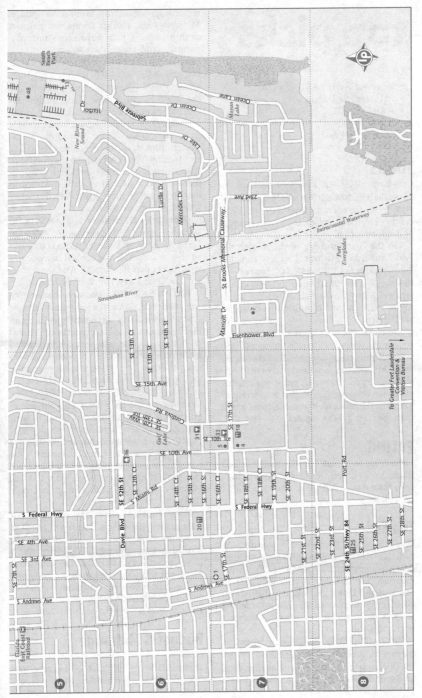

233

top picks

FOR KIDS

- Museum of Discovery & Science (p230)
- Fort Lauderdale Beach (p231)
- Water Taxi (p238)
- Mai Kai (right)
- Wannado City (p231)

TOURS

Carrie B (☎ 954-768-9920; www.carriebcruises.com; from Las Olas Blvd at SE 5th Ave near Cheesecake Factory; adult/child $16/9; ☽ Nov-Apr) is a waterfront tour on a 19th-century riverboat replica. It's a fun 1½ hours of deadpan kitsch.

On the first Saturday of the month the Fort Lauderdale Historical Society runs the Historic Walking Tour (☎ 954-463-4431; from New River Inn lobby; $5), a one-hour stroll focusing on the area's rich historic district; there's also a full-moon evening tour monthly. Reservations are required.

Jungle Queen Riverboat (☎ 954-462-5596; www.jungle queen.com; from Bahia Mar Yacht Center; tour/tour with dinner $13.50/30) runs three-hour tours of the waterfront, Millionaires' Row and part of the Everglades on a paddlewheeler; four-hour evening excursions include all-you-can-eat shrimp or barbecue dinners and, if possible, more kitsch than the *Carrie B* can muster.

EATING

Lauderdale fully matches Miami in the food stakes. From grubby (but tasty) dives to high end, four-star luxury, this town's got it all on a platter.

Top End

Riley McDermott's (☎ 954-767-6555; www.rileymcder motts.com; 401 E Las Olas Blvd; mains $28-65) In Lauderdale's culinary equivalent of a $2000-a-night escort, a cold blue bar abuts an icy rack of raw seafood. Down that oyster – hell, down six of 'em – then saw into a mouth-melting steak as your wallet burns into ash. Oh, but it burns so good…

Mark's Las Olas (☎ 954-463-1000; www.chefmark.com /markslasolas; 1032 E Las Olas Blvd; mains $26-50; ☽ lunch Mon-Fri, dinner daily) The excellent menu here takes on a state-by-state theme, sampling high-end regional specialties from around the country: Minnesota elk, Florida pompano, that sort of thing, served in a surprisingly unstuffy, pumpkin-and-chocolate interior.

Johnny V's (☎ 954-761-7920; www.johnnyvlasolas .com; 625 E Las Olas; lunch $10-16, dinner $25-42; ☽ lunch & dinner) Chef Johnny Vinczenz is a darling of the South Florida foodie scene, as this restaurant unceasingly lets you know, but the marketing tack doesn't detract from excellent American cuisine united by a subtle Southwestern thread; corn sauce, blue corn chips, etc. Johnny V's also plain spoils you, with specials such as a triple-duck extravaganza that ends with duck liver stuffed with wild mushrooms. The shee-shee fish tacos are our favorite lunch on Las Olas.

Chima (☎ 954-712-0580; www.chima.cc; 2400 E Las Olas Blvd; all-you-can-eat $35; ☽ dinner Mon-Sat, 2-9:30pm Sun) Yerba mate, several roasted, fatted cows and an all-you-can eat buffet cooked *churrascaria* style (over open-flame pits)? And the servers are cowboys? Sorry, gauchos? Sign us up.

Trina (☎ 954-567-8020; www.trinarestaurantandlounge .com; Atlantic Hotel, 601 N Fort Lauderdale Beach Blvd; mains $21-39) This modish restaurant specializes in Mediterranean-kissed takes on Florida's natural bounty, such as pan-seared grouper and an Atlantic paella of local seafood tossed with spicy chorizo. The atmosphere is pleasantly loud and chaotic for such an upscale joint.

Mai Kai (☎ 954-563-3272; www.maikai.com; 3599 N Federal Hwy; mains $16-35; ☽ dinner) This old-school Polynesian joint is pure tiki kitsch – with strong drinks served in funny wooden-idol cups thrown in for good measure. Vegas-style shows ($9.95 extra) can accompany your weekend-evening meals, which range from Hawaiian chicken to seafood with noodles. Whatever else you do, don't forget the froofy cocktails.

Himmarshee Bar & Grille (☎ 954-524-1818; 210 SW 2nd St; mains $16-25; ☽ 11am-2:30pm Mon-Fri, 6-10:30pm) The Himmarshee modestly claims to be 'the most dynamic restaurant in the city.' We'll leave the verdict on that claim to your judgment, but this joint does make a strong bid, with excellent creative American cuisine including monkfish in a beet ginger emulsion and chestnut honey-glazed duckling.

Budget & Midrange

Casablanca Cafe (☎ 954-764-3500; 3049 Alhambra St; mains $13-30; ☽ 4-10pm Tue-Sat) Located in a two-story Med-revival house that overlooks

SWABBING THE DECKS, CHASING DOWN TIPS – LIVING THE YACHT CREWING LIFE *Rick Starey*

Among its other nicknames – Venice of America (for its waterways) and Liquordale (for obvious reasons) – Fort Lauderdale is known among the nautical set as the yachting capital of the world. It's home to thousands of luxury motoryachts and sailboats, and somebody's gotta make them run. Enter a water-loving workforce with varying experience, many of whom divide their time between Fort Lauderdale (winter) and places up north such as New England (summer).

For those who join this workforce, it means great coin, idyllic destinations, divine cuisine, incredible cultures and the mystic beauty of the ocean. Combine that with scrubbing decks, polishing stainless steel, detailing acute and minute features and then scrubbing a few more decks. Reveling in a portion of the former and getting down and dirty in a lot of the latter is the life of a deckhand aboard a luxury yacht. Here is an industry where money is flaunted for fun, excess is paramount and bottom lines are ignored at all costs.

Life onboard requires a certain type of individual, as close quarters, communal living and a stacked dictatorship come together to provide a unique atmosphere. Always present is a heavily regimented pecking order that is essential in any offshore activity. Another aspect is that you can't leave the office, meaning you are at the ship's beck and call 24/7. Even when you're nursing a nasty hangover.

The job of a 'decky' could best be described as a jack-of-all-trades. You become a world-class cleaner, meaning your chamois is not only your best mate but your greatest tool. You'll learn a bit about engines, fiddle with radars, paint anchors, throw heaving lines, study weather patterns and may even learn to read a chart or two. But, above all, the quality of a deckhand is best judged in two simple departments: work ethic and an eye for detail.

Fort Lauderdale is the place to be for aspiring crewmen as it's justifiably regarded as the luxury yachting capital of the world with thousands of captains looking for their next crew. The megayacht industry can be a postcard lifestyle: sailing off into another perfect sunset with tax-free cash, lifelong friends and crystal-clear memories. The yachting game at its best is almost unbeatable; at its worst, well, did I mention the decks?

Joining a Crew

According to sailors on the docks, as of 2008 crew could expect to earn around $2000 to $3000 per month; captains can pull in as much as $15,000 per month. These days, it is essential to obtain the STCW95 certificate. Although it costs $1100, it displays an investment of sorts from the applicant and makes finding a job a whole lot easier.

Agencies

Placing agencies include Crew Finders (☎ 954-522-2739; www.crewfinders.com; 408 SE 17th St), Crew4Crew (www .crew4crew.net), and the Crew Network (☎ 954-467-9777; 1800 SE 10th St). Triton Magazine and www.findacrew .net have also been recommended to us.

When to Go

A great time to make your presence felt is the month or so leading up to any boat show (October to November), as there is plenty of work in preparing the boats, and if you make the right impression, there is a solid chance you may be taken on. If not, you will build up your contacts list so you, as a product, will get more airtime.

What to Bring

For international arrivals, along with the STCW95, getting hold of a B1B2 visa sets you on sail for the job of your choice. Pack half as many clothes as you'd planned, and twice as much money.

Women Crew Members

The role of women within the industry is developing. However, women seeking crew work should only get on a boat that they're happy with.

Networking

Two great places to network are Waxy O'Connor's Irish Pub (☎ 954-525-WAXY; 1095 17th St Causeway) and Quarterdeck (☎ 954-423-4197; 1541 Cordova Rd).

Rick Starey is a Lonely Planet author as well as a deckhand onboard a luxury yacht.

some prime beach-front real estate, this is the perfect spot to down some parmesan-crusted catfish while gazing out past the stucco and palm trees at the perfect, pregnant full moon.

Sublime: World Vegetarian Cuisine (☎ 954-615-1431; 1431 N Federal Hwy; mains $8-18; 🕑 5:30-9pm Sun-Thu, 5:30-10pm Fri-Sat) Frustrated vegans will rejoice over Sublime's massive menu, take-out café and a shopping boutique brimming with cruelty-free products. The menu here changes daily, but always reflects global cuisines, with options such as ancho-orange glazed soy steak, pueblo corn enchiladas and red lentil-quinoa loaf and mushroom burgers.

Floridian (☎ 954-463-4041; 1410 E Las Olas Blvd; dishes $7-15; 🕑 24hr) The diner is a northeast invention, but Florida makes it her own in this kitschy-decorated, tropi-colorful greasy spoon at the quiet end of Las Olas.

Carlos & Pepe (☎ 954-467-7192; 1302 SE 17th St; dishes $7-15; 🕑 11:30am-11pm Mon-Sat, 2-10pm Sun) Like all good, cheap Mexican places, C & P's is located in an unassuming strip mall that camouflages the excellent grub within.

Lester's Diner (☎ 954-525-5641; 250 Hwy 84; dishes $7-12; 🕑 24hr) The late-night crowd at this excellent diner is as colorful a mix of humanity as you'd want, including ancient retirees having a 3am dinner, Cuban club kids decked out to the nines, rednecks chatting over mugs of coffee and one silly travel writer who was so drunk he almost passed out on his Reuben. Woops.

Charlie's Bar-b-q (☎ 954-522-7659; 1571 S Federal Hwy; dishes $6-12; 🕑 10:30am-7pm Mon-Sat) Get your ribs and chicken fix handled at Charlie's. It's bare bones on the inside, but you can smell that sweet, smoky barbecue from across the parking lot.

Zona Fresca (☎ 954-566-1777; 1635 N Federal Hwy; mains $3-7) The food may come quickly at this jumpin' highway stop, but Zona is no fast-food joint. Follow the local hipsters inside for cheap, fresh and delicious Mexican eats, such as grilled-veggie or shrimp burritos, taco combo plates and tostada salads, washed down with Mexican beer.

Brew Urban Cafe (☎ 954-523-7191; 209 SW 2nd Ave; $2-5; 🕑 'til late) Ah. You're one of those types who needs a coffee shop filled with shaggy artsy-fartsies and whiny indie music wherever you go, but you think Starbucks is too corporate, right? Brew's as good as you're gonna get here, hipster.

DRINKING & NIGHTLIFE

Fort Lauderdale bars stay open until around 4am on weekends and 2am during the week. The area now dubbed 'Old Town' could conceivably be renamed 'Party-all-the-time Town.'

Dicey Riley's (☎ 954-522-2202; 217 SW 2nd St) In the beating heart of Old Town's fearsome bacchanal, Dicey's is filled with beautiful people. Drunk, drunk, wasted beautiful people.

Elbo Room (☎ 954-563-7889; 3339 N Federal Hwy) This dive bar achieved immortality thanks to the 1960s classic *Where the Boys Are*. It hit its stride during the Spring Break years and, based on the huge crowds that flock here every night, hasn't lost it since.

Golden Lyon Bar (☎ 954-467-0671; Riverside Hotel, 620 E Las Olas Blvd) This mellow alternative has a cabaret-piano bar scene and swank cocktails.

O'Hara's Jazz Café (☎ 954-524-1764; 722 E Las Olas Blvd) O'Hara's is a nice escape from both screaming madness and too-mellow snooty-ness, coming down somewhere in the dark, sexy but casual jazz bar area of the scale.

Poor House (☎ 954-522-5145; 110 SW 3rd Ave) Enjoy great microbrews, diverse live music and a multigenerational crowd.

Tarpon Bend (☎ 954-523-3233; 200 SW 2nd St) A popular after-work spot that gets rowdier and more fun as the night wears on.

Waxy O'Connor's Irish Pub (☎ 954-525-9299; 1095 17th St) Besides being an Irish pub that actually employs Irish people (novel), you're almost guaranteed to meet some yachtie pirate types here, especially on Fridays.

SLEEPING

The splashiest hotel experiences – offering spa services, restaurants, pools, etc – can be found on the beach (they're also usually the priciest). Meander inland, and you'll discover some wonderful inns with old-Florida charm, many of which exclusively cater to gay guests (see the boxed text, p238). Expect to pay an average of $200 a night for top-end hotels and less for budget and midrange stays.

Top End

Atlantic (☎ 954-567-8020; www.theatlantichotelfort lauderdale.com; 601 N Fort Lauderdale Beach Blvd; r $269-859; 🅿 🖳 🐾) The Atlantic might as well be called 'The South Beach Lauderdale,' because that's the showy over-the-top style this luxurious beauty brings to the local accommodation

GAY & LESBIAN FORT LAUDERDALE

Fort Lauderdale is as cool as it is thanks in no small part to the successful integration of Miami's gay scene – an integration that worked, perhaps, a little too well (regarding nightlife anyways). Gay Miami became indiscernible from Greater Miami, and in an effort to reclaim a sense of community, the boys started moving north. Fort Lauderdale had an influx of both artsy intelligentsia and cutting edge club kids (who were a bit more sophisticated, if just as hedonistic as the Spring Breakers).

Thus, what Cherry Grove is to its neighbor, the Fire Island Pines, Fort Lauderdale is to South Beach – a little more rainbow-flag-oriented and a little less exclusive. And for the hordes of gay boys who flock here, either to party or settle down, therein lies the charm. You don't need to be A-list to feel at home, and you won't have any trouble finding 'the scene.' Fort Lauderdale is home to more than 25 gay bars and clubs; about a dozen gay guest houses; and a couple of way-gay residential hubs, including Victoria Park and Wilton Manors, more recently gay-gentrified and boasting endless nightlife options, including the very popular Rosie's Bar & Grill (☎ 954-567-1320; 2449 Wilton Dr) and Georgie's Alibi (☎ 954-565-2626; 2266 Wilton Dr). Even the Miami boys make the trip here for the dance parties held at Coliseum (☎ 954-832-0100; 2520 Miami Rd), especially on Saturdays, when circuit DJs such as Monty Q and Brett Henrichsen blow in for gigs.

Ladies: check out New Moon (☎ 954-563-7660; 2400 Wilton Dr) for lots of drinks, lots of girls and lots of fun. For information on everything queer, stop by the helpful Gay & Lesbian Community Center (☎ 954-463-9005; www .glccftl.org; 1717 N Andrews Ave), which provides information, meeting space and events such as bingo parties. To shop for hot duds (from hot dudes), try the exclusive T-shirts, jeans, belts and accessories at the Ruff Riders (☎ 954-828-1401; 918 N Federal Hwy) boutique, which has a cultish following at its Provincetown location up north. Gay guest houses are plentiful; see Sleeping (p238) for some suggestions, or visit www.gayftlauderdale.com. And consult the glossy, weekly listings rag Hot Spots to keep updated on the best gay nightlife; it's available at local gay bars, inns and eateries.

game. The design is bathed in rich hues of orange and brown, while spacious rooms are lighter in tone; each has balconies with sliding glass doors and gorgeous sea views. We'd just like to add that the staff, male and female, are hot enough to have their own saucy calendar.

Pillars (☎ 954-467-9639, 800-800-7666; www.pillarsho tel.com; 111 N Birch Rd; r $200-550; P ⬚ ⬚) The folks running Pillars are incredibly friendly, which is the icing on this lovely old mansion's cake. Other ingredients include a caramel-and-coffee colored lounge and library, stunning back courtyard view of the Lauderdale canals (water taxi stops here) and immaculate, ornate rooms.

Riverside Hotel (☎ 954-467-0671, 800-325-3280; www .riversidehotel.com; 620 E Las Olas Blvd; r 189-439; P ⬚ ⬚) This elegant 1936 hotel, sitting right in the center of downtown and fronted by stately columns, has an old-fashioned Main Street feel to it. It's never been one of the most stylish sleeps in Fort Lauderdale, and the rooms, while lovely, don't stand out for any reason, but the Las Olas location is a big plus.

St Regis Resort & Spa (☎ 954-465-2300; 1 N Fort Lauderdale Beach Blvd; r from $250; P ⬚ ⬚) Gatsby would be right at home in the royal atrium lobby of this grandiose, marble beach resort. There are 24 stories and endless amenities available, as you'd expect from such a powerful beachfront player.

Budget & Midrange

Tropi Rock (☎ 954-564-0523, 800-987-9385; www.tropirock .com; 2900 Belmar St; r $76-120; P ⬚) Family-run and very friendly, the Rock is a joyous bundle of green awnings, brightly tiled walkways, jungly walkways and a sparkling pool. Along with the Martindale, it's a perfect midrange solo-traveler or family-holiday option. Best of all: no Spring Breakers allowed.

Martindale Hotel (☎ 954-467-1841; www.martindaleat thebeach.com; 3016 Bayshore Dr; r $70-110; P ⬚) The wonderful Martindale and next door Shell Hotel are lovely little examples of the American mom & pop motel, surviving (literally) under the shadow of the enormous ultramodern W resort construction site. The Martindale has a sweet little mustard-colored deco facade, and both hotels have clean, comfy rooms and a shady, relaxing pool where you can imagine Lauderdale days gone by.

Joanne's Crew House (☎ 954-527-1636; 916 SE 12th St; per week $135; P ⬚ ⬚) Fort Lauderdale's most established crew house, Joanne's is set in a residential area in a sprawling, ranch-style house. Fifteen people can await employment in five bedrooms (four bathrooms) in style. There's a big screened-in backyard, a pool and a barbecue area on the 1-acre property. Joanne calls boat owners to tell them who's staying at the house.

GAY STAYS

Pineapple Point (☎ 888-844-7295; www.pineapplepoint.com; 315 NE 16th Tce; r $159-195, ste $235-449; 🖳)
A supremely stylish gay guest house set in intimate, verdant surroundings, the Point boasts tasteful rooms with four-poster beds, sumptuous duvets, hardwood floors and sun porches. There's a clothing-optional pool, of course.

Royal Palms Resort (☎ 954-564-6444, 800-237-7256; www.royalpalms.com; 2901 Terramar St; r $169-319) One of the best gay stays in America has 1000 blooming orchids in its gorgeous garden. They put orchids on your pillow. They even put one in your toilet after they clean it. Thai Airways would be jealous. Did we mention the Egyptian cotton sheets? Management is excellent, as is the ambience, which goes from tropical serene to tropical sultry with a change in the wind.

Schubert Resort (☎ 866-763-7435, 954-763-7434; www.schubertresort.com; 855 NE 20th Ave; r $99-199; 🅿 🖳 🖳) Why should Miami be the only place with deco style? The Schubert is a retro inn with newly renovated rooms housed in the shell of a 1953 motel. Behind the neon sign out front you'll find sleek rooms with marble baths and boldly striped bedspreads; many of them surround a lovely pool. Note the inn's frisky, clothing-optional policy.

La Casa Del Mar (☎ 954-467-2037; www.lacasadelmar.com; 3003 Granada St; r $80-119, kitchenette $89-149, large units $179-240) This family-owned, homey B&B has cute 'n' cozy rooms, studios and one-bedroom units. They're crisp, bright, white and comfortable, and nestled around a tropical garden. A full breakfast is included.

Worthington Guest House (☎ 954-563-6185, 800-445-7036; www.worthingtonguesthouse.com; 543 N Birch Rd; r $99-200) Hmmm. Looks like a fun, clothing-optional resort (sound of loud laughter and shrieks emerge from behind rainbow flag–bedecked gate). Sounds like a fun clothing-optional resort. Why, it *is* a popular, garden-enclosed clothing-optional resort!

Beach Plaza Hotel House (☎ 954-566-7631; 625 N Fort Lauderdale Beach Blvd; r $109; 🅿 🖳 🖳) It's tough to get closer to the beach for such a good price. Despite basically being a budget doss, this hotel is well-run and good value, with typically Floridian polished tile floors, a sky's-wide-open courtyard, shimmery pool and free parking.

Beach Hostel (☎ 954-567-7275; www.fortlauderdalehostel.com; 2115 N Ocean Blvd; dm $20, r for 2 $45 or $55; 🖳) This hot-pink, 61-bed backpacker home is just one block from the beach and about a mile north of the main beach area. Help yourself to breakfast foods (scramble the eggs yourself), log onto the internet and borrow snorkeling gear. Just know that you'll need a passport to bunk.

GETTING THERE & AROUND

The Fort Lauderdale-Hollywood International Airport (FLL; ☎ 954-359-1200; www.fll.net) is served by more than 35 airlines, including some with nonstop flights from Europe. Jet Blue (www.jetblue.com) has great fares from New York's Kennedy and LaGuardia airports. From the airport, it's a 20-minute drive to downtown, or a $16 cab ride.

By boat, the Port Everglades Authority (☎ 954-523-3404) runs the enormous Port Everglades cruise port (the second busiest in the world after Miami). From the port, walk to SE 17th St and take bus No 40 to the beach or to Broward Central Terminal. If you're coming here in

your own boat (not unlikely here), head for the Radisson Bahia Mar Yacht Center (☎ 954-764-2233).

By bus, the Greyhound station (☎ 954-764-6551; www.greyhound.com; 515 NE 3rd St at Federal Hwy) is about four blocks from Broward Central Terminal, the central transfer point for buses in the Fort Lauderdale area. Buses to Miami leave throughout the day ($5 one-way, 30 to 60 minutes). By train, Tri-Rail (☎ 800-874-7245; www.tri-rail.com) runs between Miami and Fort Lauderdale ($6.75 round-trip, 45 minutes). Amtrak (☎ 800-872-7245; www.amtrak.com) passenger trains also run on Tri-Rail tracks. The Fort Lauderdale station (200 SW 21st Tce) is just south of Broward Blvd and just west of I-95.

Once you're in town, driving provides the best way to access every part of spread-out Fort Lauderdale. But the flatness here makes it easy to get around by bike. Check with your hotel – many have bikes to loan or rent. TMAX (☎ 954-761-3543), a free shuttle with service every 15 minutes or so, runs between downtown sights; between the beach and E Las Olas Blvd and the Riverfront; and between Tri-Rail and E Las Olas Blvd and the beaches.

Finally, the fun Water Taxi (☎ 954-467-6677; www.watertaxi.com; 651 Seabreeze Blvd) plies the canals and waterways between 17th St to the south, Atlantic Blvd/Pompano Beach to the north, the New River to the west and the Atlantic Ocean to the east. A $12 daily pass entitles you to unlimited rides.

TRANSPORTATION

Miami is a major international airline hub, particularly for American Airlines, and it's the first port of call for many flights from Latin America. Most flights come into Miami International Airport (MIA), although many are also directed to Fort Lauderdale–Hollywood International Airport (FLL). Seeing as it is located at the tip of the USA, Greater Miami is more of a termination of highways and rail lines, rather than a major land-transit interchange area. Fort Lauderdale attracts pleasure boaters from around the world, while the Port of Miami is the largest cruise port in the world; Carnival, Royal Caribbean, Norwegian, Discovery and Oceania, among others, all set out from here. Flights, tours and rail tickets can be booked online at www.lonelyplanet.com /travel_services.

AIR
Airport
Miami is served by all major carriers via two main airports: Miami International Airport (MIA) and the Fort Lauderdale–Hollywood International Airport (FLL), half an hour north. MIA (Map pp44–5; ☎ 305-876-7000; www.miami -mia.com) is the third busiest airport (after JFK and LaGuardia in New York City) in the country. Just 6 miles west of Downtown, the airport is open 24 hours and is laid out in a horseshoe design. There are left-luggage facilities on two concourses at MIA, between B and C and on G; prices vary according to bag size.

The Fort Lauderdale-Hollywood International Airport (off Map pp44–5; ☎ 954-359-1200; www.broward .org/airport; 320 Terminal Dr), about 30 miles north of Miami just off I-95, often serves as a lower-

AIRPORT SECURITY
It's tighter than ever. X-ray machines scan all carry-on baggage; more bags than ever are hand-searched. Sharp objects such as nail files, forks and Swiss Army knives will be confiscated from your carry-on baggage; pack everything sharp in your checked baggage. If you are carrying high-speed film (1600 ASA and above), take the film out of the canisters and pack them in a clear plastic bag or container. Ask the X-ray inspector to visually check your film.

cost alternative to MIA, especially because it's serviced by popular, cut-rate flyers including Southwest Airlines and JetBlue.

BICYCLE
Miami may be flat as a pancake, but it's also plagued by traffic backups and speedy thoroughfares, so judge the bike-ability of your desired route carefully. It's a perfectly sensible option in South Beach, though, as well as through most Miami Beach 'hoods and, of course, on Key Biscayne. Use a sturdy U-type bike lock, as mere chains and padlocks do not deter people in these parts.

Bicycles are allowed only on specific Metrorail and Tri-Rail routes; you can also bike across the causeways.

Rental
There are several places in South Beach and on Key Biscayne to rent bicycles for a fee of about $20 a day.

BOAT
Though it's doubtful you'll be catching a steamer to make a trans-Atlantic journey, it is quite possible that you'll arrive in Miami via a cruise ship, as the Port of Miami (Map pp44–5; ☎ 305-371-7678; www.miamidade.gov/portofmiami), which received nearly four million passengers in 2003, is known as the 'cruise capital of the world.' Arriving in the port will put you on the edge of Downtown Miami; taxis and public buses to other local points are available from nearby Biscayne Blvd.

GETTING INTO TOWN

Miami International Airport

It's a quick cinch to get there from just about anyplace in Miami, especially from Mid-Beach. If you're driving, just follow the Julia Tuttle Causeway, or I-195, west until you hit Rte 112, which goes directly to the airport. Other options include the free shuttles offered by most hotels, a taxi ($26.50 flat rate to South Beach; metered, from South Beach, is only about $10), the Airport Owl night-only public bus, or the SuperShuttle (☎ 800-874-8885; www.supershuttle.com) shared-van service, which will cost about $14 to South Beach. Be sure to reserve a seat the day before.

Fort Lauderdale–Hollywood International Airport

Put the money you save toward getting to Miami once you land; either rent a car at one of the many Fort Lauderdale agencies (p242), or take the free shuttle from terminals 1 and 3 to the airport's Tri-Rail (☎ 800-874-7245; www.tri-rail.com) station; you can ride this commuter train into Miami. The schedule is infrequent, though, so you may want to opt for the Bahama Link (☎ 800-854-2182; 1-2 people $45-60) shared-van service or the cheaper SuperShuttle (☎ 954-764-1700; www.supershuttle.com), which will cost about $25 to South Beach.

BUS

Greyhound (☎ 800-231-2222; www.greyhound.com) is the major carrier in and out of town. There are four major terminals: Airport terminal (☎ 305-871-1810; 4111 NW 27th St); Main Downtown terminal (Map pp66–7; ☎ 305-374-6160; 1012 NW 1st Ave); North Miami terminal (Map pp58–9; ☎ 305-945-0801; 16560 NE 6th Ave); and the Southern Miami terminal (Map pp44–5; ☎ 305-296-9072; Cutler Ridge Mall, 20,505 S Dixie Hwy). There are several buses daily to New York City ($115 one-way, 27 to 30 hours) and Washington, DC ($109, 23 to 25 hours); five to New Orleans ($95, 20 to 22 hours); and 10 daily to Atlanta ($95, 16 to 18 hours).

The local bus system is called Metrobus (☎ 305-770-3131; www.miamidade.gov/transit) and, though it has an extensive route system, know that you may very well spend more time waiting for a bus than you will riding on one. Each bus route has a different schedule and routes generally run from about 5:30am to about 11pm, though some are 24 hours. Rides cost $1.25 and must be paid in exact change with a token, coins or a combination of a dollar bill and coins (most locals use the monthly Metropass). An easy-to-read route map is available online.

In South Beach, an excellent option is the South Beach Local Circulator (☎ 305-770-3131), a looping shuttle bus with disabled-rider access that operates along Washington between South Pointe Dr and 17th St and loops back around on Alton Rd on the west side of the beach. Rides cost only 25¢ and come along every 10 to 15 minutes between 7:45am and 1am Monday to Saturday and 10am to 1am Sunday and holidays. Look for official bus stops,

every couple of blocks, marked by posts with colorful Electrowave signs.

Coral Gables has its own new shuttle in the form of a hybrid-electric bus disguised as a Trolley. It's free, but good for getting around Gables only (also, you often have to put up with some cutesy barbershop quartet). Its north–south route runs along Ponce de León Blvd from the Douglas Metrorail Station to SW 8th St (between 6:30am and 8pm Monday to Thursday, and 6:30am and 11pm Friday), while the east–west twilight route runs along Miracle Mile from Anderson Rd to Douglas Rd (between 3pm and 7pm Monday to Thursday, and 3pm and 10pm Friday). Trolleys run about every 10 to 15 minutes.

CAR & MOTORCYCLE

Finding your way here from other points in the USA is not hard; follow any other major Interstate to I-95 south, which will eventually take you directly into Downtown Miami. Be aware that gasoline prices are not so cheap these days: in early 2008 they averaged $3.20 a gallon (a bit less than 4L) in Miami. From New York, expect a 19-hour trip without stops. And remember that speed limits change from state to state.

The urban sprawl of metro Miami means most visitors, unless staying in one neighborhood, will end up driving. Though getting around is quite easy to figure out, expect serious rush hour traffic from 7am to 9am and 4pm to 6pm weekdays, as well as constant snarls along Collins Ave and Ocean Dr during high season, especially on weekends. Dixie

Hwy (US Hwy 1) often gets backed up and clogged, and this holds particularly true for those heading south into the Florida Keys, where it's the only road around. The Downtown area near Brickell was a nightmare during this research, but this was partly because of construction projects. It's a safe bet that anywhere where construction is occurring will equal serious driving headaches.

On the bright side, traffic is *really* light in the Everglades.

Driving

Miami Beach is linked to the mainland by four causeways built over Biscayne Bay. They are, from south to north: the MacArthur (also the extension of US Hwy 41 and Hwy A1A), Venetian ($1.50 toll), Julia Tuttle and John F Kennedy. The most important north–south highway is I-95, which ends at US Hwy 1 south of Downtown. US Hwy 1, which runs from Key West all the way north to Maine, hugs the coastline. It's called Dixie Hwy south of Downtown and Biscayne Blvd north of Downtown. The Palmetto Expressway (Hwy 826) makes a rough loop around the city and spurs off below SW 40th St to the Don Shula Expressway (Hwy 874, a toll road). Florida's Turnpike Extension makes the most western outer loop around the city. Hwy A1A becomes Collins Ave in Miami Beach.

Miami has an annoying convention of giving major roads multiple names. So for example, Bird Rd is both SW 40th St and Hwy 976. Hwy 826 is the Palmetto Expressway. US Hwy 1 is the Dixie Hwy – except in Downtown, when it becomes Biscayne Blvd. Hwy 836 is the Dolphin Expressway, while in Miami Beach 5th St becomes A1A. Calle Ocho is SW 8th St, as well as the Tamiami Trail, *and* US 41 (phew), and Hwy 959 is Red Rd, except when it's SW 57th St. Somehow, this all isn't as confusing as it reads on paper – most road signage indicates every name a route may have – but it can be frustrating to first time Miami drivers.

Besides the causeways to Miami Beach, the major east–west roads are SW 8th St; Hwy 112 (also called Airport Expressway); and Hwy 836 (also called Dolphin Expressway), which slices through Downtown and connects with I-395 and the MacArthur Causeway, and which runs west to the Palmetto Expressway and Florida's Turnpike Extension.

Miami drivers are…how can we put this delicately…aggressive, tailgating jerks who'd cut off their grandmother if they could figure out how to properly change lanes. OK, now that *that's* off our chests, we are, of course, kidding. Only some Miami drivers fit the above description, but there are enough of these maniacs about to make driving here a nightmare. We blame the nouveau riche and their SUVs and Hummers, although there's a fair number of retirees plodding along and, here and there, a travel writer who read their map wrong.

CLIMATE CHANGE & TRAVEL

Climate change is a serious threat to the ecosystems that humans rely upon, and air travel is the fastest-growing contributor to the problem. Lonely Planet regards travel, overall, as a global benefit, but believes we all have a responsibility to limit our personal impact on global warming.

Flying & Climate Change

Pretty much every form of motor transport generates CO_2 (the main cause of human-induced climate change) but planes are far and away the worst offenders, not just because of the sheer distances they allow us to travel, but because they release greenhouse gases high into the atmosphere. The statistics are frightening: two people taking a return flight between Europe and the US will contribute as much to climate change as an average household's gas and electricity consumption over a whole year.

Carbon Offset Schemes

Climatecare.org and other websites use 'carbon calculators' that allow travellers to offset the greenhouse gases they are responsible for with contributions to energy-saving projects and other climate-friendly initiatives in the developing world – including projects in India, Honduras, Kazakhstan and Uganda.

Lonely Planet, together with Rough Guides and other concerned partners in the travel industry, supports the carbon offset scheme run by climatecare.org. Lonely Planet offsets all of its staff and author travel.

For more information check out our website: www.lonelyplanet.com.

Parking

Though it can get annoying (especially when you have to feed quarters into meters), parking around town is pretty straightforward. Regulations are well-signed and meters are plentiful (except perhaps on holiday-weekend evenings in South Beach). Downtown, near the Bayside Marketplace, parking is cheap but a bit confusing: you must find a place in the head-on parking lots, buy a ticket from a central machine, and display it in your windshield. Generally, finding street parking in South Beach is a nightmare, but in other parts of town it tends to be fairly hassle free. See p170 for a detailed list of garages and suggestions on where to park in relation to which hotels. Always lock your car and keep valuables out of sight.

On Miami Beach there's metered street parking on Washington and Collins Aves and Ocean Dr – and on most other streets (except Lincoln Rd and residential areas). Meters are enforced from 9am to midnight. Most allow you to pay for up to three hours, although some have increased that range to six hours. Many meter machines include a credit card option (thank God); failing that, you may want to purchase a Meter Card, available from the **Miami Beach City Hall** (Map pp52–3; 1st fl, 1700 Convention Center Dr); the **Miami Beach Chamber of Commerce** (Map pp52–3; 1920 Meridian Ave); any municipal parking lot or any Publix grocery store. Denominations come in $10, $20 and $25 (and meters cost $1 per hour).

There are many municipal parking garages, which are usually the easiest and cheapest option; look for giant blue 'P' signs. Find them at Collins Ave at 7th St, Collins Ave at 14th St, Washington Ave at 12th St, Washington Ave at 16th St, and 17th St across from the Jackie Gleason Theater of the Performing Arts (perfect if you're headed to Lincoln Rd). If you park illegally or if the meter runs out, parking fines are about $20, but a tow could cost $75.

Rental

All the big operators, and a host of smaller or local ones, have bases in the Miami/Fort Lauderdale area, and advance reservations are advisable, especially in high season. Car rental companies in the area include the following:

Alamo (☎ 800-327-9633; www.alamo.com)

Avis (☎ 800-831-2847; www.avis.com)

Budget (☎ 800-527-0700; www.budget.com)

Continental (☎ 305-871-4663; www.continentalcar.com)

Thrifty (☎ 800-367-2277; www.thrifty.com)

top picks

GREEN TRAVEL

- Biking, especially along the Florida Keys Overland Heritage Trail (p184)
- Metromover
- Tri-rail
- Gables Trolley
- Walking! Especially in South Beach, which is barely 2 miles (2.8km) long.

Rental rates in Florida tend to be lower than in other big American cities, though they do fluctuate, depending on the company, day of the week and season. Expect to pay about $200 a week for a typical economy car at most times; around the Christmas-holiday time, however, you could pay upwards of $900 a week for the same vehicle. Phone around to compare prices, and know that booking ahead usually ensures the best rates. Most companies include unlimited mileage at no extra cost, but taxes and a host of surcharges increase the final bill, as could insurance. While many credit cards cover a loss/damage waiver, or LDW (sometimes called a collision/damage waiver, or CDW), meaning that you don't pay if you damage the car, as well as liability insurance, you should make *absolutely* certain before driving in the litigious USA.

Bring your driver's license if you intend to rent a car; visitors from some countries may find it wise to back up their national license with an International Driving Permit, available from many local auto clubs (including the Automobile Association of America; www.aaa.com). Most operators require that you be at least 25 years of age and have a major credit card in your own name.

TAXI

Outside MIA and the Port of Miami, where taxis buzz around like bees at a hive, you will use a phone to hail a cab. A consortium of drivers has banded together and formed a Dispatch Service (☎ 305-888-4444). If the dispatch service is busy, try Metro (☎ 305-888-8888), Sunshine (☎ 305-445-3333) or Yellow (☎ 305-444-4444) for a ride.

Taxis in Miami have flat and metered rates. The metered fare is $3.90 for the first mile, and $2.20 each additional mile, but given the cost of fuel in America, this could well change by the time you read this. You will not have to pay extra for luggage or extra people in the cab, though you are expected to tip an additional 10% to 15%. Add about 10% to normal taxi fares (or a dollar, whichever is greater). If you have a bad experience, get the driver's chauffeur license number, name and license plate number and contact the Taxi Complaints Line (☎ 305-375-2460).

TRAIN

The main Miami terminal of Amtrak (Map pp44–5; ☎ 305-835-1222, 800-872-7245; www.amtrak.com; 8303 NW 37th Ave) connects the city with the rest of continental USA and Canada. Travel time between New York and Miami is a severe 27 to 30 hours and costs $99 to $246 one-way. The Miami Amtrak station has a left-luggage station, which costs $2 per bag.

Around Miami the Metromover (www.miami dade.gov/transit), equal parts bus, monorail and train, is helpful for getting around the Downtown area. It offers visitors a great perspective on the city and a cheap – it's free! – orientation tour of the area (see p71). The one- and two-car, rubber-wheeled, computer-controlled (and therefore driver-less) vehicles operate on three lines on two elevated-track 'loops,' covering Downtown as far south as the Financial District Station of Brickell Ave and as far north as the School Board Station up on NW 15th St and NE 1st Ave. You can transfer to the Metrorail at Government Center.

Metrorail (www.miamidade.gov/transit), meanwhile, is a 21-mile-long heavy rail system that has one elevated line running from Hialeah through Downtown Miami and south to Kendall/Dadeland. Trains run every five to 15 minutes from 6am to midnight. The fare is $1.50, or 75¢ with a Metromover transfer. The regional Tri-Rail (☎ 800-874-7245; www.tri-rail .com) double-decker commuter trains run the 71 miles between Dade, Broward and Palm Beach counties. For longer trips (to Palm Beach, for instance), Tri-Rail is very inefficient. Fares are calculated on a zone basis, and the route spans six zones. The shortest distance traveled costs $4 round-trip. The most you'll ever pay is for the ride between MIA and West Palm Beach ($11 round-trip). No tickets are sold on the train, so allow time to make your purchase before boarding. All trains and stations are accessible to riders with disabilities. For a list of stations, go to the Tri-Rail website.

DIRECTORY

BUSINESS HOURS

Office hours in Miami operate on the usual 9am to 5pm Monday to Friday schedule, with some larger branches having Saturday morning hours as well. Shops usually stay open for business till later, depending on the neighborhood, with 9pm being the typical closing time in malls or other shopping districts. Some restaurants close on Mondays, while many of the nightclubs only operate from Wednesday or Thursday through the weekend.

CHILDREN

Miami is very kid-friendly. All those public parks and recreation areas help, along with the attractions that star animals, from Seaquarium (p93) to Jungle Island (p105). Rainy-day activities abound, and include the Miami Children's Museum (p106). Be sure to check with your hotel – especially if it's in South Beach – to make sure it's kid-friendly and not too full of loud partiers.

For more information, advice and anecdotes, read *South Florida Parenting Magazine,* available at major booksellers, and Lonely Planet's *Travel with Children* by Cathy Lanigan.

Babysitting

When it's time to head out for some adult time, check with your hotel, as many offer child-care services – especially big resorts such as the Four Seasons, Loews and the Fontainebleau Hilton. Or call Nanny Poppinz (☎ 305-607-1170; www.nannypoppinz.com).

CLIMATE

Ideal conditions exist between December and May, when temperatures average between 60°F and 85°F (16°C and 30°C), and average rainfall is a scant 2.14in per month. Summer is very hot and humid, with thunderstorms rolling in at 3pm or 4pm – not to mention the constant threat of hurricanes. August is both the rainiest and hottest month – and there's always the chance of hurricanes. Call ☎ 305-229-4522 for a weather report. See the climate charts following.

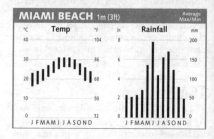

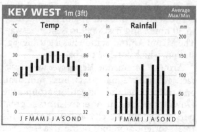

COURSES

It never hurts to learn a thing or two while you're on vacation – especially if it's a skill that could come in particularly handy while you're here.

Salsa Dancing

Going out to a Latin club and being a wallflower feels awful. Drop into a class or two at Salsa Mia (☎ 305-987-3033; www.salsamia.com; 1-/2-/5-night pass $40/50/100) or Latin Heat Salsa Studio (☎ 305-868-9418; www.latin-heat.com; Miami Beach locations vary; per class $10).

Spanish

Take a crash course at South Beach Languages Center (Map pp48–9; ☎ 305-531-5331; www.miamispanishclasses .com; 227 13th St; monthly classes) or the University of Miami (Map pp100–1; ☎ 305-284-4727; www.miami.edu/fast spanish; 7-day intensives). Unfortunately, there were no tourist-oriented Creole classes available at the time of research.

Cooking

You can learn how to fix up some fusion and Floribbean from local celeb chefs at restaurants such as Wish (☎ 305-674-9474; $175; see p126) and Azul (☎ 305-913-8358; $175; see p133).

CUSTOMS REGULATIONS

United States customs allows each person over the age of 21 to bring in 1L of liquor and 200 cigarettes or 50 cigars, duty-free, into the country. US citizens are allowed to import, duty-free, $400 worth of gifts, while non-US citizens are allowed to bring in $100 worth. United States law permits you to bring in or take out as much as US$10,000 in American or foreign currency, traveler's checks or letters of credit without formality. Larger amounts of any or all of the above – there are no limits – must be declared to customs. It's forbidden to bring in chocolate liqueurs, pornography, lottery tickets and items with fake brand names, among other sundries. For a complete and ever-changing list, visit www.customs.ustreas.gov.

Due to Miami's infamous popularity as a drug-smuggling gateway, local customs officers are known to be quite thorough in their examination of backpackers and other travelers who may fit a particular profile. They may not be very polite – but you should be. Dress neatly and carry lots of traveler's checks and credit cards, or show other signs of prosperity lest they think you're here to work illegally.

DISCOUNT CARDS

If you qualify, you can sometimes use an International Student Identity Card (ISIC) for discounts to museums, tourist attractions and on some airfares. And parents, take note: the new South Florida Parenting Kids Fun Pass, a promotional tool of *South Florida Parenting* magazine, is now available at all Publix supermarkets and the information booths at the Dadeland Mall. Each pass is $11.95 and grants free entry for kids 12 and under (when accompanied by a full-paying adult) to a slew of family attractions including Miami Metrozoo (p106), Miami Children's Museum (p106), Miami Seaquarium (p93) and many more.

ELECTRICITY

Electric current in the USA is 110V to 115V, 60Hz. Outlets may be suited for flat two- or three-prong plugs. If your appliance is made for another electrical system, you will need a transformer or adapter; if you didn't bring one along, check any major drugstore, hardware or electronics store.

EMBASSIES & CONSULATES

Most consulates are in Miami, but a few are in Coral Gables. Citizens of Australia and New Zealand may contact the British consulate or the Canadian consulate for emergency assistance, as neither country maintains consular offices in Miami.

Canada (Map pp66–7; ☎ 305-579-1600; http://geo .international.gc.ca/can-am/miami/menu-en.asp; Suite 1600, 200 South Biscayne Blvd, Miami, FL 33131)

France (☎ 305-372-9799; www.consulfrance-miami.org; No 1050, 1395 Brickell Ave, Miami, FL 33131)

Germany (☎ 305-358-0290; www.germany.info/miami; No 22, 100 Biscayne Blvd Miami, FL 33132)

Japan (☎ 305-536-0147; www.miami.us.emb-japan .go.jp; No 3200, 80 SW 8th St, Miami, FL 33130)

Mexico (☎ 786-268-4900; www.sre.gob.mx/miami; 5975 SW 72th St, Miami, FL 33143)

Spain (☎ 305-446-5511; www.conspainmiami.org; No 203, 2655 S Le Jeune Rd, Coral Gables, FL 33134) (305) 446-5511

UK (Map pp66–7; ☎ 305-374-3500; www.britainusa .com/miami; Miami Brickell Bay Dr, Miami, FL 33131)

EMERGENCY

Dial ☎ 911 for police, fire and medical emergencies, which is a free call from any phone. The inside front cover of the Miami *White Pages* lists a slew of emergency numbers. The following are some useful ones:

Beach Patrol (☎ 305-673-7711)

Coast Guard Search (☎ 305-535-4314)

Hurricane Hotline (☎ 305-229-4483)

Poison Information Center (☎ 800-282-3171)

Rape Hotline (☎ 305-585-7273)

Suicide Intervention (☎ 305-358-4357)

GAY & LESBIAN TRAVELERS

LGBT visitors account for nearly $100 million in annual revenues to the Miami area. Expect to feel comfortable being open with your same-sex partner – displays of affection won't raise an eyebrow in most places or with most hotel clerks, especially in South Beach. For information on gay businesses, get the *Miami Gay & Lesbian Yellow Pages,* widely available at South Beach shops, or visit their website at www.glyp.com and click on 'Miami.' Or give a call to the South Beach Business Guild (☎ 305-534-3336), a sort of LGBT chamber of commerce.

Local gay publications include the *Weekly News, Express Gay News, Hot Spots, Scoop* and *Wire*. Find them all, and much more, at gay bookstore Lambda Passage (Map pp58–9; ☎ 305-754-6900; 7545 Biscayne Blvd, North Miami).

HOLIDAYS
Public Holidays
Below are national or public holidays – days on which you can expect government offices (and some restaurants and shops) to be closed.

New Year's Day January 1

Martin Luther King Jr Day Third Monday in January

Presidents Day Third Monday in February

Easter A Sunday in March or April

Memorial Day Last Monday in May

Independence Day July 4

Labor Day First Monday in September

Columbus Day Second Monday in October

Veterans Day November 11

Thanksgiving Fourth Thursday in November

Christmas December 25

INTERNET ACCESS
Finding access to email is a cinch. The majority of hotels and hostels these days have computers for you to log onto or wireless service that's free or cheap to laptop-toting guests. You can also find plenty of strong connections at places including public libraries (☎ 305-535-4219; www.mdpls.org) and internet cafés. For a list of hotspots, visit www.wi-fihotspotlist.com and click on Miami.

LEGAL MATTERS
Florida law tends to be tougher than most states to the north when it comes to drug possession. If you are approached by police officers, just use common sense: be polite and do what they ask – up to a point. You are presumed innocent until proven guilty in a court of law, and you cannot be searched without good reason. If you are arrested, you must be read your rights under the Miranda Law. Don't try to bribe any officer – that's a crime.

To purchase alcohol or cigarettes you must be at least 21; to drive or give sexual consent you must be 17. It's illegal to walk around on the street with an open alcoholic drink – beer, liquor, frozen cocktail, whatever – even though you'll see tipsy tourists doing it. If you're driving, all liquor has to be unopened (not just sealed, but new and untouched) and stored in the trunk. Florida's drunk-driving laws are among the toughest in the country. Driving under the influence of alcohol (technically a 0.08 blood-alcohol content) or drugs in Florida carries a $5000 fine in addition to suspension of your license and possible imprisonment.

MAPS
All car rental companies are required by law to hand out decent city and area maps when they rent a car. But you can purchase ones that are even better: Rand McNally, AAA and Dolph Map Company all make maps of the Miami area, and Lonely Planet produces a laminated foldout map of the Miami area that includes Key West and Fort Lauderdale. The best free map is from the Greater Miami & the Beaches Convention & Visitors Bureau (p249).

MEDICAL SERVICES
Clinics
For physician referrals 24 hours daily, contact the Visitor's Medical Line (☎ 305-674-2222) of the Mount Sinai Medical Center. The Miami Beach Community Health Center (Map pp48–9; ☎ 305-538-8835; 710 Alton Rd; ☽ 7am-3:30pm Mon-Fri) charges fees based on your income. Arrive early since walk-in clinic lines are usually very long. Bring ID. If you're foreign born, bring your passport and I-94 card, the arrival/departure document for nonimmigrant visitors that's issued by the Immigration & Naturalization Service (INS). United States citizens should bring proof of residence and income. For more information, contact the INS (☎ 305-536-574; 7880 Biscayne Blvd). If you need dental attention, try ☎ 800-DENTIST (☎ 800-336-8478).

Emergency Rooms
In a serious emergency, call ☎ 911 for an ambulance to take you to the nearest hospital's emergency room (ER). Mount Sinai Medical Center (Map pp58–9; ☎ 305-674-2121; 4300 Alton Rd) is the area's best. Whatever your deal – visitor, no insurance, etc – the hospital must treat you. But, in return, you must eventually pay. And the ER fees are stellar. Then there are additional charges for X rays, casting, medicines, analysis…*everything*, so the cost of a visit can easily top $1000.

Pharmacies

The most ubiquitous drugstores are blue-signed Eckerd (☎ 305-538-1571) and the red-signed Walgreens (☎ 305-261-2213), both of which have some 24-hour branches. Call for the nearest location.

MONEY

The US dollar is the wimpy pushover of the currency world these days, so come on over and take advantage of our economic woes. The dollar is divided into 100 cents (100¢) with coins of one cent (penny), five cents (nickel), 10 cents (dime), 25 cents (quarter) and relatively rare 50 cents (half dollar).

Bank notes are called bills. Be sure to check the corners for amounts, as they're all the same size and color. Circulated bills come in denominations of $1, $5, $10, $20, $50 and $100. The US has two designs of bills in circulation, but you'd have to study them closely to notice.

There are three straightforward ways to handle payments: cash, US-dollar traveler's checks (just as good as cash, but replaceable if lost or stolen) and credit/debit cards.

Changing Money

If you prefer cash, try to change a good chunk in your own country before you arrive in Miami, as exchange rates here are notoriously skimpy. If you must change money, do it at banks. Try Bank of America (☎ 305-350-6350), which offers foreign-exchange services in its branches – or money-changing operations such as Thomas Cook (☎ 305-285-2348, 800-287-7362). Exchange rates change constantly, but to get an idea, see the exchange-rate chart inside this book's front cover.

NEWSPAPERS & MAGAZINES

The best is the much-lauded *Miami Herald,* which covers local, national and international news and began achieving fame back in the late '80s and early '90s when the murder rate was at its peak. Writers from the *Herald* – Edna Buchanan, Carl Hiassen and columnist Dave Barry – have achieved national fame, and coverage is go-getter. The *Sun-Sentinel* covers South Florida, and the *Sun Post* provides in-depth, weekly analysis (and it's free). Miami's Spanish-speaking population is serviced by dailies such as *El Nuevo Herald* and *Diario Las Americas.* The hip, alternative

take on goings-on include the weeklies the *Street* and the *Miami New Times,* both free, politically progressive and heavy on arts and entertainment coverage.

There are several good local magazines, including the excellent *ML: Miami Living Magazine,* a glossy filled with quirky feature articles and food and nightlife listings; *Home Miami,* about real estate and home design; and *Loft,* about the visual arts and design scene.

ORGANIZED TOURS

More so than many American cities, Miami's outer layer can be tough to penetrate, particularly because its fascinating pockets are so spread out and different from one another, and because their shiny surfaces can be intimidating. But that's where a good tour guide – whether on foot, boat or bus – comes in handy.

Air/Boat/Bike/Bus Tours

Action Helicopter Tours (Map p82; ☎ 305-358-4723; Watson Island; tours $69-149) runs 12- to 35-minute jaunts above South Beach, Fisher Island, the Port of Miami, Bayside Marketplace, Coconut Grove and the houses of the rich and famous.

Bayside Marketplace (Map pp66–7; ☎ 305-379-5119; 401 Biscayne Blvd; adult/child $14/7; ☯ 11am-7pm) runs boat tours. For harbor tours, head downtown and hop aboard the *Island Queen,* Captain Jimmy's Fiesta Cruises or the smaller speedboat *Bayside Blaster.* Boats depart hourly. Tours include commentary about the famous folk who live on Star Island and a bit of history, but generally they're alluring because of the skyline views of the dramatic nighttime neon (though you can't see the celebrities' houses at dusk).

The Dade County parks system leads frequent bike tours through peaceful areas of Miami and Miami Beach, including along beaches and on Key Biscayne. Times vary; call Eco-adventure Bike Tours (☎ 305-365-3018; www.miamidade.gov/parks; tours $25) for details.

Is it a bus, or is it a boat? No, you won't look too cool gliding through South Beach on this bus/boat hybrid, but the wacky vehicle run by Miami Duck Tours (Map pp52–3; ☎ 877-DUCK-TIX, 786-276-8300; 1665 Washington Ave; adult/child/senior $32/18/26; ☯ 10am-6pm) does provide a nice, high perspective (and amusing commentary) of South Beach and Downtown sites, and, when it enters the water, the moneyed homes of Biscayne Bay shores. Tours depart hourly and last 90 minutes.

The well-established Miami Nice Tours (☎ 305-949-9180; www.miaminicetours.com; tours $36-70) has a wide range of guided bus excursions to the Everglades, the Keys and Fort Lauderdale, as well as trips around Miami, some including stops at the Miami Seaquarium (p93), Bayside Marketplace (p68) and Jungle Island (p105).

Walking Tours

Art Deco Welcome Center (Map pp48–9; ☎ 305-531-3484; 1001 Ocean Dr; guided tours per adult/child/senior $20/free/$15, self-guided tours per adult/senior $15/10; ❂ 10:30am Wed, Fri & Sat, 6:30pm Thu) tells the fascinating stories and history behind the art-deco hotels in the South Beach historic district, either with a lively guide from the Miami Design Preservation League, or with a well-presented recording and map for self-guided walks (try to go with the guides). Tours last 90 minutes. The league also leads architectural walks of North Beach, and 'Deco Underworld' tours about the Prohibition era in Miami Beach.

For a great perspective on many different aspects of the city, call the lively Dr Paul George (☎ 305-375-1621; tours $25-42; ❂ 10am Sat, 11am Sun), historian for the Historical Museum of Southern Florida (p69). He leads several popular tours – including those that focus on Stiltsville, Miami crime, Little Havana and Coral Gables at twilight – between September and late June. Dr George also offers private tours by appointment.

Downtown Miami Welcome Center (Map pp66–7; ☎ 305-379-7070; Olympia Theater, 174 E Flagler St; tours $10; ❂ 10:30am Sat) can help you to see beyond the construction sites and crumbling facades of Downtown for an explanation of historic sites from the original Burdines (p116) to the Gesu Church, dating from 1925. The tours are by group only, and run by the Welcome Center, housed in the historic Olympia Theater (p69).

Urban Tour Host (☎ 305-416-6868; www.miamicultural tours.com; Suite 1048, 25 SE 2nd Ave; tours from $20) has a rich program of custom tours that provides face-to-face interaction in all of Miami's neighborhoods. A deluxe city tour includes Coral Gables, South Beach, Downtown and Coconut Grove, and there's also a new Downtown Miami interactive walking tour, on Wednesday and Saturday from 10am to noon.

POST

Currently, rates for 1st-class mail within the USA are 41¢ for letters up to 1 ounce (28g) and 26¢ for postcards. International airmail rates differ from country to country, but in general run about 90¢ for a half-ounce letter (69¢ to Mexico and Canada). International postcard rates are 69¢. You can check online at www.usps.gov. Convenient post offices include the Miami Beach Post Office (Map pp48–9; 1300 Washington Ave; ❂ 8am-5pm Mon-Fri, 8:30am-2pm Sat) and the branch in Ocean View (Map pp58–9; 445 W 40th St; ❂ 8am-5pm Mon-Fri, 8:30am-2pm Sat).

RADIO

91.3-FM WLRN is the public NPR affiliate, with intelligent discussion shows, Creole news and jazz music; 90.5-FM WVUM is the University of Miami's alternative-everything station; and 88.9-FM WDNA is the community public radio station. Also tune into 1320-AM WLQY for French and Creole news and 95.7-FM for Latin music.

SAFETY

Miami has about double the national murder rate and three times the national aggravated assault rate. Although criminals don't tend to target strangers, it's best to keep your wits about you, especially in Overtown, Liberty City and Little Haiti. Dangers run from aggressive vagrants to calculating muggers. Try not to walk around alone at night in these neighborhoods.

In Downtown Miami, use particular caution near Overtown, the Greyhound station and around causeways, bridges and overpasses where homeless people and some refugees have set up shantytowns. The main danger in Miami Beach is drunk tourists.

Natural dangers include strong sun (have high SPF sunscreen), mosquitoes (use a spray-on repellent) and hurricanes (between June and November). There's a hurricane hot line (☎ 305-229-4483), which gives information on all the things you need to make a decision about if and when you leave.

TELEPHONE

All phone numbers within the USA consist of a three-digit area code followed by a seven-digit local number. If you are calling locally in Miami, you must dial the area code plus the seven-digit number. (Leave off the preceding

1 before local calls – just start with ☎ 305 or ☎ 786.) If you are calling locally in the Keys or Key West, you only have to dial the seven-digit number. The area codes for the Keys are ☎ 305 and ☎ 786, for the Everglades it's ☎ 305 and Everglades City is ☎ 239. Fort Lauderdale has the area codes ☎ 954 and ☎ 754. If you are calling long distance, dial 1 plus the three-digit area code and then the seven-digit number. If you're calling from abroad, the international country code for the USA is '1.'

The ☎ 800, ☎ 888, ☎ 877 and ☎ 866 area codes are toll-free numbers within the USA and sometimes for Canada as well.

Directory assistance is reached locally by dialing ☎ 411. This is free from most pay phones, but costs as much as $1.25 from a private phone. For directory assistance outside your area code, dial ☎ 1 plus the three-digit area code followed by 555-1212.

To place an international call direct, dial ☎ 011 plus the country code and area code (dropping the leading 0) and then the number. From a pay phone, dial all those numbers before inserting coins; a voice will come on telling you how much to put in the phone after you dial the number. For international operator assistance and rates, dial ☎ 00. Canada is treated like a domestic call. In general, it's cheaper to make international calls at night.

Local calls from public phones cost 35¢, and don't give change. They're cheaper than using the phone in your hotel room, as almost all hotels add a service charge of 50¢ to $1 for each local – and sometimes toll-free – call made from a room phone. They also add hefty surcharges for long-distance calls, 50% or even 100% on top of their carrier's rates.

Cell Phones

Anyone who's anyone in Miami has a cell phone, and you can rent one almost as easily as you can buy soda from a machine. You can bring your own, but since the USA doesn't have a standardized system, check with your service provider to see if your phone will work in Miami. (Most of the world works on the GSM network at 900 or 1800 MHz, though Miami offers GSM access at 1900 MHz; Europeans should be OK with a tri-band phone.)

Phonecards

Phone debit cards in denominations of $5, $10, $20 and $50 allow purchasers to pay in advance, with access through a toll-free number. Look for these ubiquitous cards in convenience stores and drugstores. You shouldn't have to pay more than 25¢ per minute on domestic long-distance calls, but some are as high as 45¢ per minute. When using phone debit or calling cards, you will have to punch in an access code rather than be able to stick the card into the phone like you can in places outside the US. Be cautious of people watching you dial in the numbers – thieves will memorize numbers and use your card to make calls to all corners of the earth.

TIME

Miami is in the US Eastern standard time zone, three hours ahead of San Francisco and Los Angeles, and five hours behind GMT/UTC (so when it's noon in Miami, it's 5pm in London). Daylight saving time takes place from the first Sunday in April through the last Sunday in October. The clocks 'spring forward' one hour in April and 'fall back' one hour in October, both at 1am.

TOILETS

There are public toilets at several spots on South Beach (such as the Art Deco Welcome Center), but generally speaking, the area doesn't offer much in the way of public facilities. Bars, fast food places and Starbucks are also a good bet.

TOURIST INFORMATION

There are several tourist offices located in the Greater Miami area, all of which offer advice of varying usefulness and hand out visitors' guides, pamphlets and flyers, as well as discount tickets to many of the area's attractions.

In South Beach, there's the Art Deco Welcome Center (Map pp48–9; ☎ 305-672-2014; www.mdpl.org; 1001 Ocean Dr; ☼ 10am-10pm), with tons of Deco District information, and the Miami Beach Chamber of Commerce (Map pp52–3; ☎ 305-672-1270; www.miamibeachchamber.com; 1920 Meridian Ave; ☼ 9am-5pm Mon-Fri). On the mainland, the Greater Miami & the Beaches Convention & Visitors Bureau (Map pp66–7; ☎ 305-539-3000; www.gmcvb.com; 27th fl, 701 Brickell Ave; ☼ 8:30am-5pm Mon-Fri) is helpful, but housed in a confusing high-rise with an attached mazelike parking-garage.

TRAVELERS WITH DISABILITIES

Miami is mainly wheelchair-friendly, although many Deco District doorways may be tight. Many buses, all Tri-Rail trains and stations, and Metromovers are wheelchair accessible. Special-needs travelers can contact the Metro-Dade Transit Agency Special Transportation Service (STS; ☎ 305-263-5406), which provides door-to-door transportation for disabled people; contact them a few weeks before your visit.

The Deaf Services Bureau (☎ 305-668-4407, 800-955-8770; Suite 760, 1320 S Dixie Hwy) has interpreters and an information and referral service. The Florida Relay Service (☎ 305-579-8644, TDD 800-955-8771, voice 800-955-8770, customer service 800-955-8013) connects TDD (Telecommunication Device for the Deaf) users to people without TDDs, 24 hours a day. For information for the blind, contact Lighthouse for the Blind (☎ 305-856-2288; 601 SW 8th Ave).

A number of organizations and tour operators specialize in serving disabled travelers. Among them are Access-Able Travel Source (☎ 303-232-2979; www.access-able.com); Society for Accessible Travel & Hospitality (SATH; ☎ 212-447-7284; www.sath.org); and Travelin' Talk Network (☎ 615-552-6670; www.travelintalk.net).

VISAS

A reciprocal visa-waiver program applies to citizens of certain countries – the UK, Japan, Australia, New Zealand and all Western European countries (except Greece). Citizens of these countries may enter the USA for stays of 90 days or less without having to obtain a visa, but make sure you have a machine-readable passport issued after October 26, 2006; otherwise, you'll need a stamped visa. Contact your nation's passport issuing agency center for more information.

Other travelers (except Canadians) will need to obtain a visa from a US consulate or embassy. All foreign travelers require valid passports to enter the USA.

WOMEN TRAVELERS

Women travelers, especially solo travelers, should develop the habit of traveling with extra awareness of their surroundings. Men may interpret a woman drinking alone in a bar as a bid for male company. If you don't want company, most men will respect a firm but polite 'no thank you.' Use common sense and you'll be fine in Miami.

WORK

Foreigners cannot work legally in the USA without the appropriate work visa, and recent legislative changes specifically target illegal immigrants, which is what you will be if you try to work on a tourist visa.

Miami is ground zero for large numbers of refugees from the Caribbean, notably Haiti and Cuba, so INS checks are frequent. Local businesses are probably more concerned here than anywhere outside Southern California and Texas when it comes to verifying your legal status.

One viable option is to find work on the cruise liners or yachts in the region, which can employ anyone since they operate in international waters. For more information on crew work, see the boxed text (p235).

LANGUAGE

Although visitors to Miami can get away with using only English, to do so is essentially to write off experiencing a huge chunk of the city's culture and life. Spanish may be more widely spoken in the metropolitan area than English, and you will certainly run into people who do not speak any English at all.

If you plan to spend a lot of time in Spanish-speaking neighborhoods, take along Lonely Planet's comprehensive and compact *Latin American Spanish Phrasebook*. If you're planning on romancing some Latin types, the finest resources are *Hot Spanish for Guys and Girls* and *Hot Spanish for Guys and Guys*, both of which contain an amazing number of useful phrases.

A Social Life

Hi!	¡Hola!
Good morning/day.	Buenos días.
Good evening/night.	Buenas noches.
Pleased to meet you.	Mucho gusto.
Goodbye!	¡Adiós!
See you later.	Hasta luego.
Please.	Por favor.
Thank you (very much).	(Muchas) Gracias.
You're welcome/Don't mention it.	De nada.
Yes/No.	Sí/No.
Excuse me. (to get past)	Permiso.
Excuse me. (eg before asking directions)	Perdóneme.
Sorry!	¡Perdón!
Pardon? (as in 'what did you say?')	¿Cómo?
I understand.	Entiendo.
I don't understand.	No entiendo.
Please speak slowly.	Por favor hable despacio.

What's on ...?	
¿Qué pasa ...?	
around here	para acá
this weekend	este fin de semana
today	hoy
tonight	esta noche

Where are the ...?	
¿Dónde hay ...?	
places to eat	lugares para comer
clubs/pubs	boliches/pubs
gay venues	lugares para gays

Is there a local entertainment guide?
¿Hay una guía de entretenimiento de la zona?

A Practical Life

to the left	a la izquierda
to the right	a la derecha
straight ahead	adelante
bus	gua gua or autobús
taxi	taxi
toilet	sanitario
train	tren

Where is ... ?	Donde está ... ?
the bus station	el terminal de gua gua/autobús
the train station	la estación del tren

How much is it?	¿Cuanto cuesta?
Can I look at it?	¿Puedo mirarlo?
I want ...	Quiero ...
good/OK	bueno/a (m/f)
bad	malo/a (m/f)
best	mejor
more	más
less	menos

0	cero	14	catorce
1	uno	15	quince
2	dos	16	dieciséis
3	tres	17	diecisiete
4	cuatro	18	dieciocho
5	cinco	19	diecinueve
6	seis	20	veinte
7	siete	21	veintiuno
8	ocho	30	treinta
9	nueve	40	cuarenta
10	diez	50	cincuenta
11	once	100	cien
12	doce	500	quinientos
13	trece	1000	mil

BEHIND THE SCENES

THIS BOOK

This 5th edition of *Miami & the Keys* was written by Adam Karlin. The 4th edition was written by Beth Greenfield. Earlier editions of this guidebook were written by Kim Grant, Nick Selby and Corinna Selby. This guidebook was commissioned in Lonely Planet's Oakland office, and produced by the following:

Commissioning Editors Jay Cooke, Jennye Garibaldi

Coordinating Editors Susie Ashworth, Rosie Nicholson, Amy Thomas

Coordinating Cartographer Peter Shields

Coordinating Layout Designer Paul Iacono

Managing Editors Bruce Evans, Jennifer Garrett

Managing Cartographers David Connolly, Alison Lyall

Managing Layout Designer Adam McCrow

Senior Editor Katie Lynch

Assisting Editors Laura Gibb, Evan Jones, Kate Whitfield

Assisting Cartographers Joanne Luke, Erin McManus

Cover Designer James Hardy

Project Manager Eoin Dunlevy

Thanks to Suki Gear, Lisa Knights, Raphael Richards, Celia Wood

Cover photographs Closeup of macaw feathers, Miami, George D Lepp/CORBIS (top); art-deco hotels along Ocean Drive, Miami, Richard Cummins/Lonely Planet Images (bottom).

Internal photographs p7 (#2) Danita Delimont/Alamy, p5 (#1) Digital Vision/Alamy, p8 (#3) Stephen Frink, p4 (#3) Getty Images, p4 (#2, #4), p6 (#1, #4), p7 (#4) Jeff Greenberg/Alamy, p2 ImageState/Alamy, p73 Ellen Isaacs/Alamy, p8 (#1) Mark Lewis/Alamy, p5 (#4) PCL/Alamy, p6 (#3) Mark Peterson/Corbis. All other photographs by Lonely Planet Images: p77 Eddie Brady, p6 (#3), p7 (#1), p76 Richard Cummins, p8 (#2), p5 (#3), p75, p79 Lee Foster, p5 (#2), p74, p78 Richard I'Anson, p8 (#4) Greg Johnston, p4 (#1), p6 (#2) John Neubauerk, p3 Witold Skrypczak, p80 Michael Taylor.

All images are copyright of the photographer unless otherwise indicated. Many of the images in this guide are available for licensing from Lonely Planet Images: www .lonelyplanetimages.com.

THANKS
ADAM KARLIN

First and foremost, thank you Basil, Sandra and Anna Paquet for your incredible hospitality during the course of this research. Also, big thanks to Jen Metasavage and Aaron Wrathall in the Keys. Jen, your cornbread's the best. Aaron – next time me, you, the kayak and some beer cozies. Thanks Paula Nino and friends for your insider insights. Thanks Mom, Dad and especially Fliss for your patience. And thanks, and my everlasting respect, to the wonderful rangers of the NPS and Florida's wait and bar

THE LONELY PLANET STORY

Fresh from an epic journey across Europe, Asia and Australia in 1972, Tony and Maureen Wheeler sat at their kitchen table stapling together notes. The first Lonely Planet guidebook, *Across Asia on the Cheap*, was born.

Travelers snapped up the guides. Inspired by their success, the Wheelers began publishing books to Southeast Asia, India and beyond. Demand was prodigious, and the Wheelers expanded the business rapidly to keep up. Over the years, Lonely Planet extended its coverage to every country and into the virtual world via lonelyplanet.com and the Thorn Tree message board.

As Lonely Planet became a globally loved brand, Tony and Maureen received several offers for the company. But it wasn't until 2007 that they found a partner whom they trusted to remain true to the company's principles of traveling widely, treading lightly and giving sustainably. In October of that year, BBC Worldwide acquired a 75% share in the company, pledging to uphold Lonely Planet's commitment to independent travel, trustworthy advice and editorial independence.

Today, Lonely Planet has offices in Melbourne, London and Oakland, with over 500 staff members and 300 authors. Tony and Maureen are still actively involved with Lonely Planet. They're traveling more often than ever, and they're devoting their spare time to charitable projects. And the company is still driven by the philosophy of *Across Asia on the Cheap*: 'All you've got to do is decide to go and the hardest part is over. So go!'

BEHIND THE SCENES

SEND US YOUR FEEDBACK

We love to hear from travelers – your comments keep us on our toes and help make our books better. Our well-traveled team reads every word on what you loved or loathed about this book. Although we cannot reply individually to postal submissions, we always guarantee that your feedback goes straight to the appropriate authors, in time for the next edition. Each person who sends us information is thanked in the next edition – and the most useful submissions are rewarded with a free book.

To send us your updates – and find out about Lonely Planet events, newsletters and travel news – visit our award-winning website: www.lonelyplanet.com/contact.

Note: We may edit, reproduce and incorporate your comments in Lonely Planet products such as guidebooks, websites and digital products, so let us know if you don't want your comments reproduced or your name acknowledged. For a copy of our privacy policy visit www.lonelyplanet.com/privacy.

staff, especially the ones getting priced out of the neighborhoods they make so fun.

OUR READERS

Many thanks to the travelers who used the last edition and wrote to us with helpful hints, useful advice and interesting anecdotes:

Amy Butler, Jill Dauner, Tracey Iliffe, Caroline Mills, Dimphy van Rossum, Alison Woodhouse

ACKNOWLEDGMENTS

Many thanks to the following for the use of their content: Metromover Map © 2005 Miami-Dade County Transit.

Notes

Notes

Notes

INDEX

INDEX

000 map pages
000 photographs

INDEX

INDEX

000 map pages
000 photographs

INDEX

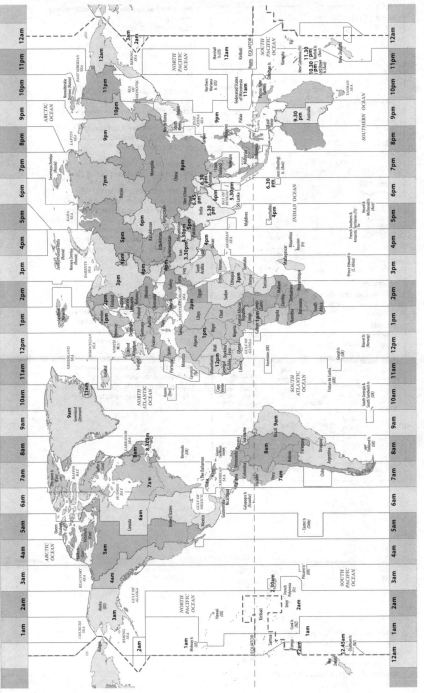

271

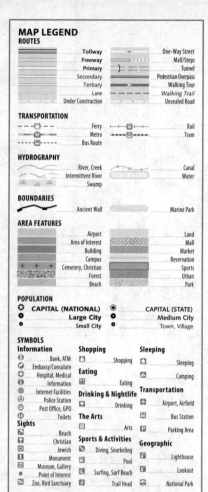

MAP LEGEND

ROUTES

- Tollway
- Freeway
- Primary
- Secondary
- Tertiary
- Lane
- Under Construction
- One-Way Street
- Mall/Steps
- Tunnel
- Pedestrian Overpass
- Walking Tour
- Walking Trail
- Unsealed Road

TRANSPORTATION

- Ferry
- Metro
- Bus Route
- Rail
- Tram

HYDROGRAPHY

- River, Creek
- Intermittent River
- Swamp
- Canal
- Water

BOUNDARIES

- Ancient Wall
- Marine Park

AREA FEATURES

- Airport
- Area of Interest
- Building
- Campus
- Cemetery, Christian
- Forest
- Beach
- Land
- Mall
- Market
- Reservation
- Sports
- Urban
- Park

POPULATION

- ✪ CAPITAL (NATIONAL)
- ◉ CAPITAL (STATE)
- ● Large City
- ● Medium City
- ● Small City
- ○ Town, Village

SYMBOLS

Information
- Bank, ATM
- Embassy/Consulate
- Hospital, Medical
- Information
- Internet Facilities
- Police Station
- Post Office, GPO
- Toilets

Sights
- Beach
- Christian
- Jewish
- Monument
- Museum, Gallery
- Point of Interest
- Zoo, Bird Sanctuary

Shopping
- Shopping

Eating
- Eating

Drinking & Nightlife
- Drinking

The Arts
- Arts

Sports & Activities
- Diving, Snorkeling
- Pool
- Surfing, Surf Beach
- Trail Head

Sleeping
- Sleeping
- Camping

Transportation
- Airport, Airfield
- Bus Station
- Parking Area

Geographic
- Lighthouse
- Lookout
- National Park

Published by Lonely Planet Publications Pty Ltd
ABN 36 005 607 983

Australia Head Office, Locked Bag 1, Footscray, Victoria 3011,
☎ 03 8379 8000, fax 03 8379 8111,
talk2us@lonelyplanet.com.au

USA 150 Linden St, Oakland, CA 94607,
☎ 510 250 6400, toll free 800 275 8555,
fax 510 893 8572, info@lonelyplanet.com

UK 2nd fl, 186 City Rd, London, EC1V 2NT,
☎ 020 7106 2100, fax 020 7106 2101,
go@lonelyplanet.co.uk

© Lonely Planet 2008
Photographs © As listed (p252) 2008

Printed through Colorcraft Ltd, Hong Kong.
Printed in China.